T0213949

Lecture Notes in Computer Science 12045

More information about this series at http://www.springer.com/series/7408

Nazim Madhavji · Liliana Pasquale ·
Alessio Ferrari · Stefania Gnesi (Eds.)

Requirements Engineering: Foundation for Software Quality

26th International Working Conference, REFSQ 2020
Pisa, Italy, March 24–27, 2020
Proceedings

 Springer

Editors
Nazim Madhavji
Computer Science, Middlesex College
Western University
London, ON, Canada

Liliana Pasquale
School of Computer Science
University College Dublin
Dublin, Ireland

Alessio Ferrari ⓘ
Area della Ricerca CNR di Pisa
Istituto di Scienza e Tecnologie
dell'Informazione "Alessandro Faedo"
Pisa, Italy

Stefania Gnesi ⓘ
Area della Ricerca CNR di Pisa
Istituto di Scienza e Tecnologie
dell'Informazione "Alessandro Faedo"
Pisa, Italy

ISSN 0302-9743   ISSN 1611-3349   (electronic)
Lecture Notes in Computer Science
ISBN 978-3-030-44428-0   ISBN 978-3-030-44429-7   (eBook)
https://doi.org/10.1007/978-3-030-44429-7

LNCS Sublibrary: SL2 – Programming and Software Engineering

This Springer imprint is published by the registered company Springer Nature Switzerland AG
The registered company address is: Gewerbestrasse 11, 6330 Cham, Switzerland

Preface

With great pleasure, we welcome the participants and readers to the proceedings of the 26th International Working Conference on Requirements Engineering: Foundation for Software Quality (REFSQ). The REFSQ working conference is the leading European conference series on Requirements Engineering (RE). It is the goal of REFSQ to foster the creation of a strong European RE community across industry and academia. Since the dawn of the field of RE in the 80s, it has influenced the quality of software, systems, and services that we all enjoy on a daily basis.

Academics and practitioners gathered at REFSQ 2020[1] to report on novel ideas, concepts, methods, techniques, tools, processes, product representations, and empirical findings; to reflect upon current research and industrial RE practices; and provide new views on RE. A strong relationship between industry and academia is critical for an applied research field, such as RE, as to incubate high-impact results, both through research on practically relevant problems and rapid technology transfer to industry.

As computer systems are increasingly evolving to be cyber-physical, it is becoming important to explore the role that RE can play in the development of "smart" cyber-physical systems. These are the systems that need to guarantee satisfaction of their requirements, while also dealing with complexity arising from the systems' scale, connectivity, and uncertainty inherent in their operating environment.

To support the development and evolution of these next generation systems, it is thus important to:

- Seek new RE concepts, methods, techniques, tools, and processes
- Create new domain models and specifications that integrate cyber and physical elements including human aspects
- Ensure scalability of analysis techniques (for handling large sets of requirements) and requirements prioritization techniques
- Create techniques for estimating project risks and cost
- Be able to integrate function and data paradigms into the RE process
- Address uncertainty in the operating environment, e.g., by continuously monitoring requirements satisfaction
- Support adaptation of requirements to suit changing conditions.

Through the REFSQ 2020 conference theme "RE & Cyber-Physical Systems," we bring this emerging topic to the attention of the REFSQ community. We would like to thank the keynote speakers for accepting our invitation to present and the interaction this generated among participants.

---

[1] Although we were prepared to have a great REFSQ conference in Pisa, we were concerned about the health of our attendees and about the many concerns we received regarding the coronavirus outbreak in Italy. Therefore, we decided to postpone the REFSQ conference to a later point in time.

REFSQ has a strong history of being a working conference; that is, an event where accepted contributions from research and practice are extensively discussed and elaborated upon in various presentation and discussion formats. Presentations of established research as well as research previews and visions that report on new developments and emerging results were critiqued by a dedicated discussion leader and the participating audience. An important feature of REFSQ is a distinct day that focuses on results and challenges from industrial practice, facilitating a rich exchange between practitioners and researchers.

This main program was complemented by a set of workshops, a doctoral symposium, a session with live studies, and posters and tools. The REFSQ 2020 conference was organized as a three-day symposium. The sessions contributed to the topic of the conference in various ways. Thus, we take pride in that REFSQ is a key event series that promotes the scientific and practical dimensions of the field of RE in a significant way. This would clearly not have been possible without worldwide teams of creative authors conducting RE research and submitting their work to REFSQ for peer review, as well as practitioners sharing their experiences from the trenches.

We are thus honored to be entrusted with the compilation of this volume comprising the REFSQ 2020 proceedings. It features 21 accepted papers (14 full and 7 short papers) on different topics in RE research and practice. The Program Committee (PC) carefully reviewed 84 submissions and selected 5 technical design papers, 9 scientific evaluation papers, 6 research previews, and 1 vision paper. Also, despite the conference being operationally rooted in Europe, REFSQ is an international conference: we have authors, PC members, additional reviewers, and organizers from four continents.

We would like to express our sincere gratitude to all these dedicated individuals who put so much effort in creating, reviewing, and preparing outstanding contributions to the RE field. REFSQ 2020 would certainly not have been possible without them. The various committees are listed below. As editors of these proceedings, we would like to thank the REFSQ Steering Committee members for regular meetings and feedback; we mention Prof. Kurt Schneider, for his availability and for his excellent ongoing guidance. Our special appreciation is afforded to Prof. Klaus Pohl for his long-term support to the REFSQ conferences. We are also indebted to the REFSQ 2019 co-chairs, Dr. Eric Knauss and Dr. Michael Goedicke, for their helpful advice on diverse matters often at inconvenient times. We are grateful to all the members of the PC for their timely and thorough reviews of the submissions and for their time and expertise generously given both online and face to face during the PC meeting. In addition, we thank the PC members who volunteered to serve in the role of shepherd or gatekeeper to authors of conditionally accepted papers. We would like to thank the members of the local organization at the ISTI-CNR in Pisa, Italy, in particular, Dr. Alessio Ferrari and Prof. Stefania Gnesi, for their unfailing support, determination, and availability at all times. We are also indebted to the organizers of other satellite events included in REFSQ 2020: the Workshops Co-chairs: Dr. Mehrdad Sabetzadeh and Dr. Andreas Vogelsang; the Posters and Tools Co-chairs: Dr. Markus Borg and Eduard C. Groen; the Doctoral Symposium Co-chairs: Dr. Vincenzo Gervasi and Dr. Maya Daneva; the Industry Track Co-chairs: Dr. Sarah Gregory and Dr. Angelo Susi; the Live Study Co-chairs: Dr. Nelly C. Fernández and Dr. Luisa Mich; the Social Media and Publicity

Co-chairs: Dr. Muneera Bano and Dr. Davide Fucci; the Student Volunteers Chair: Dr. Davide Basile; the Website Chair: Dr. Giorgio O. Spagnolo; and the Local Financial Chair: Dr. Maurice ter Beek.

We would like to thank the various student volunteers, without whom the conduct of the conference would be arduous. Finally, we would like to thank Vanessa Stricker for her excellent work in coordinating the background organization processes, and Faeq Alrimawi for his support in preparing this volume.

These proceedings consist of articles of original research. We hope that the reader will find it stimulating, interesting, and inspirational to follow up and build upon these works or pursue his/her own research in RE – to ride and enjoy the crest of fast moving technologies and systems that we observe in our society.

February 2020   Nazim Madhavji
                                                              Liliana Pasquale

---

The original version of the book was revised: Two volume editors were added. The correction to the book is available at https://doi.org/10.1007/978-3-030-44429-7_22

Organization

Program Committee Chairs

Nazim Madhavji	Western University, Canada
Liliana Pasquale	University College Dublin, Lero, Ireland

Steering Committee

Kurt Schneider (Chair)	Leibniz Universität Hannover, Germany
Anna Perini (Vice-chair)	Fondazione Bruno Kessler, Italy
Klaus Pohl	Universität Heidelberg, Germany
Fabiano Dalpiaz	Utrecht University, The Netherlands
Paola Spoletini	Kennesaw State University, USA
Nazim Madhavji	Western University, Canada
Liliana Pasquale	University College Dublin, Lero, Ireland
Michael Goedicke	University of Duisburg-Essen, Germany
Eric Knauss	Chalmers University of Gothenburg, Sweden
Erik Kamsties	University of Applied Sciences and Arts Dortmund, Germany
Jennifer Horkoff	Chalmers University of Gothenburg, Sweden
Paul Grünbacher	Johannes Kepler University Linz, Austria
Maya Daneva	University of Twente, The Netherlands
Oscar Pastor Lopez	Universitat Politècnica de València, Spain

Program Committee

Raian Ali	Hamad Bin Khalifa University, Qatar
Joao Araujo	Universidade NOVA de Lisboa, Portugal
Vanessa Ayala-Rivera	University College Dublin, Ireland
Fatma Başak Aydemir	Utrecht University, The Netherlands
Muneera Bano	Swinburne University of Technology, Australia
Nelly Bencomo	Aston University, UK
Dan Berry	University of Waterloo, Canada
Sjaak Brinkkemper	Utrecht University, The Netherlands
Jaelson Castro	Universidade Federal de Pernambuco, Brazil
Nelly Condori-Fernández	Universidade da Coruña, Spain
Luiz Marcio Cysneiros	York University, Canada
Fabiano Dalpiaz	Utrecht University, The Netherlands
Maya Daneva	University of Twente, The Netherlands
Oscar Dieste	Universidad Politécnica de Madrid, Spain
Joerg Doerr	Fraunhofer, Germany
Xavier Franch	Universitat Politécnica de Catalunya, Spain

Eric Yu	University of Toronto, Canada
Yijun Yu	The Open University, UK
Tao Yue	Simula Research Laboratory and Nanjing University of Aeronautics and Astronautics, China
Didar Zowghi	University of Technology Sydney, Australia

Additional Reviewers

Dilrukshi Abeyrathne
Fatma Başak Aydemir
Paul Hübner
Anja Kleebaum
Eriks Klotins
Jordi Marco
Sabine Molenaar
Cristina Palomares

Vik Pant
Tarcísio Pereira
João Pimentel
Astrid Rohmann
Carla Silva
Tjerk Spijkman
Jéssyka Vilela

Organizers

  National Research Council of Italy

THE IRISH SOFTWARE
RESEARCH CENTRE

Sponsors

Gold

 International® Requirements Engineering Board

Contents

Stakeholders Feedback and Training

Agile Methods and Requirements Comprehension

Requirements Modelling

Requirements Visualization

Requirements Specification

How Do Quantifiers Affect the Quality of Requirements?

Katharina Winter[1]($^{(\boxtimes)}$), Henning Femmer[2] (iD), and Andreas Vogelsang[3]($^{(\boxtimes)}$) (iD)

[1] Technische Universität München, Munich, Germany
kathi.winter@tum.de
[2] Qualicen GmbH, Garching, Germany
henning.femmer@qualicen.de
[3] Technische Universität Berlin, Berlin, Germany
andreas.vogelsang@tu-berlin.de

Abstract. [**Context**] Requirements quality can have a substantial impact on the effectiveness and efficiency of using requirements artifacts in a development process. Quantifiers such as "at least", "all", or "exactly" are common language constructs used to express requirements. Quantifiers can be formulated by affirmative phrases ("At least") or negative phrases ("Not less than"). [**Problem**] It is long assumed that negation in quantification negatively affects the readability of requirements, however, empirical research on these topics remains sparse. [**Principal Idea**] In a web-based experiment with 51 participants, we compare the impact of negations and quantifiers on readability in terms of reading effort, reading error rate and perceived reading difficulty of requirements. [**Results**] For 5 out of 9 quantifiers, our participants performed better on the affirmative phrase compared to the negative phrase. Only for one quantifier, the negative phrase was more effective. [**Contribution**] This research focuses on creating an empirical understanding of the effect of language in Requirements Engineering. It furthermore provides concrete advice on how to phrase requirements.

Keywords: Requirements syntax · Natural language · Reqs. quality

1 Introduction

Requirements are a crucial part of the software development process. However, in contrast to the code making up the software, requirements themselves do not have much direct value for a customer. Femmer and Vogelsang define requirements as "means for a software engineering project" [7]. Thus, bad quality in requirements may result in issues that possibly arise in later stages of the development process leading to a rework of process steps, potentially impacting software code or tests, for example. Indicators of these potential quality issues are named "Requirements Smells" [8], including, for instance, ambiguous words or passive voice. In this paper, we examine the use of specific quantifiers as one

© Springer Nature Switzerland AG 2020
N. Madhavji et al. (Eds.): REFSQ 2020, LNCS 12045, pp. 3–18, 2020.
https://doi.org/10.1007/978-3-030-44429-7_1

particular type of requirements smells. Although the use of quantifiers, such as "at least", "all", or "exactly", is substantial in requirements specifications [2], they have not received much attention in literature so far. Questions on how different use and phrasing of quantifiers affect the quality of requirement artifacts remain unacknowledged. To shed light on this topic, we categorize the quantifiers into different scopes and use this categorization as a theoretical foundation to compare them. Each quantifier scope has one semantic interpretation but can be expressed in different syntactic ways. For example, "At least" and "Not less than", belong to the same semantic scope but one is expressed in an affirmative syntax, while the other is expressed in negative syntax.

In this paper, we examine 9 different quantifier scopes and compare the impact on requirements readability. We conducted an experiment with 51 participants and compare reading times, error rates, and perceived difficulty of quantifiers in affirmative and negative syntax. The goal of our research is to provide empirical evidence for justifying requirements writing guidelines and offer best practices on quantifier usage in requirements specifications.

Our results show that the use and phrasing of specific quantifiers has a significant effect on reading times, errors, and perceived difficulty. Based on our results, we formulate concrete advice for writing better requirements.

2   Background

2.1   Quantifiers in the English Language

Determiners are frequent parts of speech in the English language. While determiners in general describe what a noun refers to, for instance, "the", "some", or "their", quantifiers represent a subcategory of determiners referring to a certain quantity of the noun. Keenan and Stavi offer an extensive list of natural language determiners, which includes a substantial number of quantifiers [11]. Many quantifiers have similar meaning. As an example, "at least n" or "n or more" include the same set of items with regard to "n". We categorized the quantifiers according to their semantic scope, i.e. quantifiers of the same category hold true for equal sets. Based on this categorization, we defined 11 scopes, of which two defined as Some and Many are ambiguous and thus irrelevant to this paper, which deals with explicit quantifiers. The 9 exact scopes are: None, All, Exactly n, At least, At most, Less than, More than, One and All but, as depicted in Fig. 1. Exact quantifiers are either numbers, like "one", "two", or "exactly a hundred", which is contained in the scope Exactly n. When speaking of All, every element of a set is included, while None as its counterpart excludes all elements. Some quantifiers are graded: The scope At least is upward entailing, i.e. it includes all elements in the subset $[n, max)$, while the scope At most is its downward entailing counterpart. The scopes More than and Less than are similar, however, they have open intervals, thus exclude the value "n". The scope One refers to a certain instance, rather than any set with a certain property. Quantifiers included in this scope are, for example, "the", or "a", as in "the object", or "a group of objects". The scope All but is the counterpart to this scope, excluding this instance of a set.

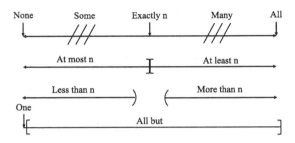

Fig. 1. Quantifier scopes

The quantifiers listed by Keenan and Stavi [11] can be classified into these semantic scope categories. From the original set of determiners, indefinite quantifiers, such as "nearly all" are excluded and duplicates or similar quantifiers, such "five or more" and "a hundred or more" are aggregated into one scope.

Hence, natural language possesses a variety of determiners [9] that can be utilized to express the different scopes of quantification. This presents us the question, whether some determiners are more readable and comprehensible than others with an equivalent semantic scope.

2.2 Affirmative and Negative Sentences

Christensen [4] examined the neurobiological implications of affirmative and negative sentences in the brain. The findings suggest that different brain areas are activated when processing affirmative and negative sentences, i.e. sentences containing a negative operator. Moreover, the brain requires more processing time for negation than for affirmation, thus response time is also longer. Performance, however, is suggested to be equal for both types of sentences. According to Christensen, affirmative sentences involve a simpler semantic and syntactic structure than negative sentences [4]. According to their work, negative sentences entail a more complex syntactical structure, which requires "additional syntactic computation" in the brain [4]. Christensen denotes affirmative polarity as "default", to which negative operators add additional structure. More precisely, when reading negative sentences, the human brain interprets all sentences as affirmative at first and in the second step, adds negative polarity to negative sentences [4].

In the dataset of requirements specifications used as a source for this paper, quantifiers are formulated in both, affirmative and negative form. To express the same semantic scope, one can employ positive and negative structures. For example, one could say "at least ten", or equivalently "no fewer than ten". Which of these two possibilities is more advisable to use in requirements specifications? Although Christensen has given an indication on the answer to this question, it could also be assumable that negative quantifiers yield longer response time, but better reading comprehension.

2.3   Requirements Readability

Requirements artifact quality can be understood as the extent to which properties of the artifact impact activities that are executed based on the artifact. In particular, quality factors affect the effectiveness and efficiency of use [7]. One relevant activity on requirements specifications is reading [1]. Consequently, good quality in practice includes efficient and effective readability of the requirements specifications. We therefore examine the implications of the quality factor quantifiers on effectiveness and efficiency of reading. We understand readability as an indicator for the "ease of understanding or comprehension due to the style of writing" [12]. Readability thus describes reading efficiency and good quality in readability minimizes the reading effort to gain comprehension of the requirements. Reading comprehension indicates effectiveness of reading. When considering readability, the reading performance must not be neglected. Although ease of understanding and sentence comprehension are closely related, good readability that yields a wrong understanding of the phrase is an indicator of bad quality. It is thus required to achieve both, efficiency and effectiveness in requirements specifications.

Objective indicators are one aspect of the assessment of quality in readability. Klare [12] makes a point with the statement: "The reader must be the judge". Hence, subjective perception should also be considered in regard to readability of requirements specifications. Therefore, we examine the readability, comprehension, and subjective perception of syntactically affirmative and negative quantifiers for a limited set of quantifier scopes.

3   Study Design

In this study, we analyze the impact of affirmative and negative quantifier phrases on readability, comprehension, and perceived difficulty.

Research Question 1: How does affirmative and negative syntax of quantifiers impact reading efficiency?

Research Question 2: How does affirmative and negative syntax of quantifiers impact reading effectiveness?

Research Question 3: How does affirmative and negative syntax of quantifiers impact the subjective perception of reading difficulty?

3.1   Data Collection

We conducted an experiment to gather data on the research questions following the guideline by Wohlin et al. [14]. To assess the differences between affirmative and negative quantifiers, we examine the relationship between quantifier syntax and readability, comprehension, and perceived difficulty. We implemented a web-based experiment, which yields a controllable testing environment and allows for a general evaluation of our hypotheses since the experiment questions are not bound to a certain context and thus do not require prior knowledge on a particular topic. Instead, the web application contains an artificial problem to easily gain first results on the research questions.

3.2 Study Objects and Treatments

Based on the research questions, the independent variable that is controlled in this experiment is the syntactical structure of the quantifying sentences. The two treatments are *affirmative* and *negative* syntactical structure. The dependent variables that will be measured in the experiment are the readability, under-standability, and subjective perception of difficulty for each treatment.

Wohlin et al. [14] offer a standard design type for such experiments with one factor and two treatments. Leaning on this design type, we aim "to compare the two treatments against each other". Furthermore, we choose a paired comparison study design, where "each subject uses both treatments on the same object" [14]. We compare the two treatments, affirmative and negative syntactical sentence structure, on sentences addressing the same quantifier scope.

Table 1 lists all samples of quantifiers that are given in the experiment. These samples were made up by us and did not have any specific background or focus. For each quantifier scope, an affirmative quantifier and a negative equivalent is displayed. Note that the scope None is a special case, as it is naturally negative and thus its counterpart is positive. Words in bold are characteristic for the respective syntactic structure.

The task of the experiment was to compare the given sentence with three given situations and decide which of the three situations (one, two, or all three) match the given sentence. The situations are presented as images. Figure 2 depicts one of the 18 answers in the experiment and belongs to the sentence "A highly defective machine has no less than 5 defects". The images are nearly identical, except for quantification, represented in red crosses in this image. The quantifier scope At least, which is stated here in negative syntax, entails the amounts of {five, six, seven, . . . } crosses. Thus, the correct answers to select are Image 1 and Image 2, as they are entailed, whereas Image 3 does not accurately describe the sentence.

As recommended by Wohlin et al. [14], the order of the sentences is ran-domized to prevent the effect of order and have a balanced design, such that the subjects' paths through the experiment are diverse. To further avert information gain from past questions, we not only randomized each sentence pair, but mix all sentences. Moreover, we created sentence pairs with identical quantifying scopes and similar but not equal semantic meaning (see Table 1).

Table 1. Affirmative and negative syntax samples for each quantifier scope.

Scope	Affirmative syntax sample	Negative syntax sample
All	**All** registered machines must be provided in the database	**No** deficit of a machine is **not** provided in the database
None	**All** access is blocked **without** a valid login	**None** of the service workers may have access to 'Budget'
More than	At **more than** 5 deficits the signal token turns red	**Not only** defective machines are displayed in the system
At least	The number of new parts per order must be **at least** 3	A highly defective machine has **no less than** 5 defects
At most	Per machine, **at most** 4 photos can be uploaded to the database	An approved machine has **no more than** 2 minor defects
Less than	**Less than** 3 supervisors may be assigned to each service worker	**Not as many** supervisors **as** 3 may be assigned to each machine
Exactly n	**Exactly** 2 emergency contacts must be displayed at all times	**No more or less than** 2 supervisors must be online at all times
All but	**All** machines **but** the current one must be on the list 'new jobs'	**No** location **but** the location of the current machine is on the map
One	**Only** the location of the current machine is on the map	The current job is the **only** job that is **not** listed in 'last jobs'

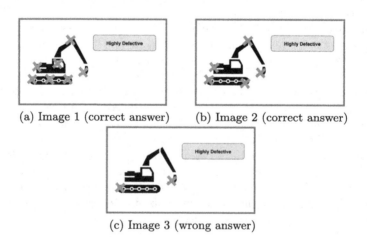

(a) Image 1 (correct answer)   (b) Image 2 (correct answer)

(c) Image 3 (wrong answer)

Fig. 2. Example question from the experiment: which of the images match the sentence "A highly defective machine has no less than 5 defects"?

3.3   Subject Selection

We selected the subjects for the experiment by convenience sampling [14] via mailing lists, or personal and second-degree contacts of the authors. The experiment was conducted online with anonymous participants. Thus, we had no control over the situation and context in which the experiment was executed by each participant. Our web-based experiment was started by 76 participants of which 51 completed the experiment. All figures in this paper refer to the 51 participants that completed the experiment. Prior to the experiment, we ask the participants whether they have a background in computer science (*yes*: 94.1%, *no*: 5.9%), whether they are native English speakers (*yes*: 5.9%, *no*: 94.1%), and what their profession is (*academic*: 23.5%, *professional*: 49.0%, *student*: 27.5%).

3.4   Data Analysis

To answer the proposed research questions, we selected the following metrics.

Readability: To evaluate readability in terms of efficient reading, the effort of reading needs to be measured. Many studies and experiments measure *reading time* as an indicator for the level of difficulty it requires to process a sentence [5,10,13]. Therefore, we also use reading time as an indicator of reading difficulty to examine the effort for a person to understand a sentence. In the experiment, we measured the time that a participant required to read and comprehend the sentence. The counter was started when the sentence appeared on the screen and stopped again when the participant clicked on the button to submit the answer. To examine the differences in reading time between the affirmative and the negative syntax sample for each scope, we applied a Wilcoxon signed-rank test, which is suitable for comparing two paired samples with data that is not normally distributed. As we will see later, the assumption of the Wilcoxon signed-rank test holds, since the reading times in our experiment are not normally distributed. The test returns a *p-value* to assess the significance of the effect and an *effects size* to assess the magnitude of the effect.

Understandability: To measure correctness, we test whether the understanding reflects the true meaning of the sentence or represents a false belief. As discussed in Sect. 2.1, some quantifiers entail a range of correct solutions. For instance, the quantifier `five items or more` entails all numbers of items of five and above (i.e. five, six, seven, ...). For other quantifiers, like `exactly five items`, one number, namely five, is the correct quantification, while all other numbers, like four or six items, do not reflect the true meaning of the quantifier. Hence, the three situations presented as answers in the online experiment are independent and include correct as well is incorrect quantifications of the given statement. We consider a sentence as "understood" if all included and excluded options are correctly identified. To examine the differences in correctly understood sentences, we build a 2×2 contingency table containing the number of participants with correct and incorrect answers in affirmative and negative sentences (see Table 2). Since our samples are matched, we focus on the discordant cells in the contingency table (b and c) and apply an exact binomial test to compare the discordant cell b to a binomial distribution with size parameter $n = b+c$ and probability $p = 0.5$. This test is suggested for 2×2 contingency tables with matched samples and few samples in the discordant cells ($b + c < 25$). As a measure for the effect size, we report the *odds ratio*: $OR = b/c$.

Table 2. 2×2 contingency table of correct and incorrect answers for one scope.

Negative syntax	Affirmative syntax	
	Incorrect	Correct
Incorrect	a	b
Correct	c	d

Perceived Difficulty: For the determination of perceived difficulty, we asked the participants to rate the reading difficulty on a scale with the values "easy", "medium", and "difficult". We use this ordinal scale as it allows for the assessment of less to greater, where intervals are not equal. The perceived difficulty is subjective and intervals between the options "easy" and "medium", as well as between "medium" and "difficult" are not necessarily equal. Furthermore, levels of difficulty may differ in between the category itself. To examine the differences in the perceived difficulty, we applied a Wilcoxon signed-rank test, which is suitable for comparing two paired samples with ordinal data.

3.5　Experiment Validity

Prior to starting the experiment and collecting the data, we launched a test run with three participants to receive feedback on the correctness of language, the comprehensibility of the overall experiment, and remaining technical bugs. Although the affirmative and negative syntax sample for each quantifier describe different situations (see Sect. 3.1), the generated sentences are similar by choosing a narrow vocabulary throughout the experiment. The difference between sentences averages about 1.77 words, where in five cases the affirmative sentence contains more words and in four cases the negative sentences is longer. The sentences have a simple structure, such that other syntactical phenomena, like sentence complexity, do not invalidate the results. On average, the sentences have 11 words. For each sentence, the study subjects have three answer options. To avoid complexity of the answers through e.g. answer sentences that are difficult to understand, the answer options are displayed as images (see Fig. 2). Like the sentences, the images have a similar image vocabulary containing equal symbols and language of form. For each sentence in the experiment, the images have minimal, but distinguishable differences. One or more of these images represent the correct meaning of the sentence given. By providing more than one correct answer, the effect of exclusion by comparison between different images should be avoided and the subject is forced to deal with each answer option separately.

To assure transparency and improve reproducibility, we have published the raw results of the experiment and the R-script that we used for processing the data.[1]

4 Study Results

4.1 Effects on Readability (RQ1)

When examining the collected reading times, we saw that all values were below 77 s, except for two data points where the reading time were 665 s and 12,281 s (both measured for sentences with negative syntax). Since we had no control over the situation in which the experiment was conducted, we consider both data points as outliers, possibly due to a disturbance of the participant, and removed the data points as well as their corresponding affirmative sentences from the dataset. Figure 3 displays boxplots of the remaining reading times for each scope. As shown in the figure, for six of the nine pairs, it took more time on average to read the negative quantifier compared with the positive quantifier of the same scope.

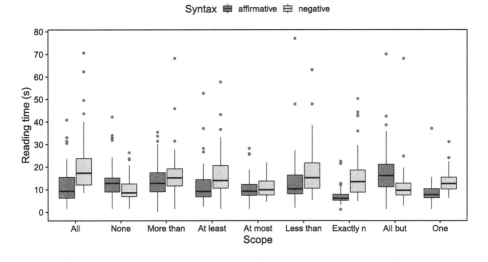

Fig. 3. Distribution of reading times per scope

Table 3 lists the results of the Wilcoxon signed-rank test for each scope in terms of the p-value and effect size for significance level $\alpha = 0.05$.

According to the significance test, the following quantifier scopes exhibit a significant difference in reading time: All, None, At least, Less than, Exactly n, All but, and One. Only for quantifiers At most, and More than, we were not

---

[1] https://doi.org/10.6084/m9.figshare.10248311.

Table 3. Wilcoxon signed-rank test for differences in reading times between affirmative and negative syntax in each scope.

Scope	All	None	More than	At least	At most	Less than	Exactly n	All but	One
p-value	**.000**	**.019**	.077	**.000**	.409	**.001**	**.000**	**.000**	**.000**
Effect size	.46	.23	.18	.37	.08	.32	.58	.52	.52

able to reject the null hypothesis of equal reading times. Among the quantifier scopes, `All but` and `None` yield significantly longer reading times for the affirmative quantifier than for the negative, as depicted in Fig. 3. In all other cases, affirmative quantifiers perform better than their negative equivalences regarding the average reading time. The effect size values indicate small (0.2) to moderate effects (0.5) [6]. An effect size of 0 means that exactly 50% of participants spent less reading time for the affirmative sentence than the mean reading time for the negative case (i.e., there is no difference). A moderate effect size of 0.5 indicates that 69% of participants spent less reading time for the affirmative sentence than the mean reading time for the negative case, while for large effect size (0.8) this is already true for 79% of participants.

4.2   Effects on Comprehension (RQ2)

Figure 4 shows the ratio of incorrect answers per scope. For 6 of the 9 quantifiers, our participants made more errors in the sentence with negative syntax. Only for the quantifier scopes `More than`, `At most`, and `All but`, the participants made more errors in the sentence with affirmative syntax.

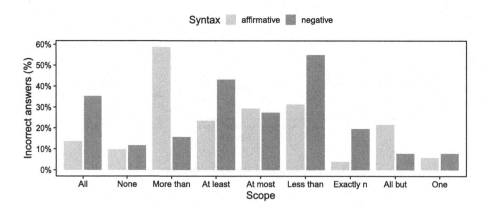

Fig. 4. Distribution of incorrect answers per scope

Table 4 lists the results of the exact binomial test for each scope in terms of the p-value and the odds ratio as a measure for effect size for significance level $\alpha = 0.05$.

Table 4. Binomial test for differences in error ratio between affirmative and negative syntax in each scope

Scope	All	None	More than	At least	At most	Less than	Exactly n	All but	One
p-value	**.007**	1.0	**.000**	**.013**	1.0	**.017**	**.008**	**.016**	1.0
Odds ratio	6.50	1.50	12.50	6.00	1.33	3.40	Inf	Inf	2.00

For 5 of the 9 quantifier scopes, our participants made significantly more errors in the negative sentence. For the scopes All but and More than, our participants made significantly more errors in the affirmative sentences. The odds ratios as a measure for effect size varied between small effects ($or < 2.57$), moderate effects ($2.75 \leq or < 5.09$) and large effects ($or \geq 5.09$) [3]. An odds ration of 6.5 for the scope All, for example, means that the chances of incorrectly answering the negative sentence was 6.5 times higher than the chances of answering the affirmative sentence incorrectly.

4.3 Effects on Perceived Difficulty (RQ3)

After each question in the experiment, the participants were confronted with a self-assessment scale on how difficult they perceived the sentences. Answer options were easy, medium, and difficult. Figure 5 depicts the assessments over the participants.

Table 5 lists the results of the Wilcoxon signed-rank test for each scope in terms of the p-value and effect size for significance level $\alpha = 0.05$.

Table 5. Wilcoxon signed-rank test for differences in perceived difficulty between affirmative and negative syntax in each scope

Scope	All	None	More than	At least	At most	Less than	Exactly n	All but	One
p-value	**.000**	.510	**.000**	**.000**	.141	**.000**	**.000**	.164	**.001**
Effect size	.55	.07	.36	.51	.15	.49	.52	.14	.37

Six of the nine quantifier scopes show significant differences in the perceived difficulty. For all of these scopes, the participants perceived the affirmative phrase as easier. The effect size measures for the scopes with significant differences all indicate moderate effects ($0.35 \leq effect < 0.65$) [6]. For the remaining three scopes, the difference in perceived difficulty is not significant.

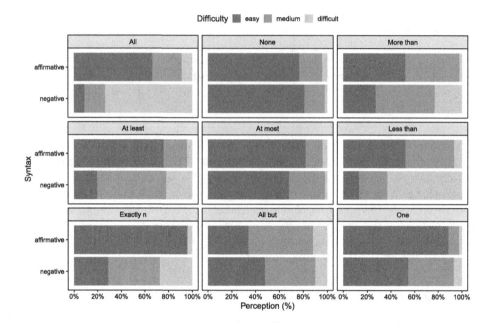

Fig. 5. Subjective perception of sentence difficulty per scope

4.4   Summary of the Results

Figure 6 summarizes the results of the three research questions. The figure shows the scopes and the measured differences with a qualitative evaluation of the effect sizes according to Cohen [6].

Overall, negative quantifiers perform worse in more cases than positive quantifiers, which is clear for the quantifiers All, At least and Exactly n and also apparent for the quantifier Less than. For other quantifiers, results are neutral, like the quantifier None, which is in a special position, as it naturally is formulated in negative syntax, or At most and One, which exhibit neutral objective measurements, but show tendencies in self-assessment towards differences in subjective difficulty. The quantifier More than was the outlier in the measurements regarding the number of mistakes in the positive sentence. Thus, this result should be treated with care. Especially, since self-assessment showed clear tendencies that the negative sentence is more difficult. Last but not least, the extra quantifier All but performed worse in two measurements, namely reading time and self-assessment, and only neutral when it came to the number of wrong answers. Hence, it is the only quantifier that yields a worse overall performance of the positive quantifier.

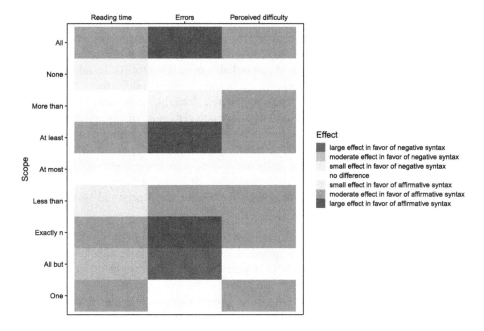

Fig. 6. Summary of results

5   Discussion

5.1   Threats to Validity

For the interpretation of the results, several threats to validity need to be considered.

Construct Validity: Only one specific representative quantifier was stated for each scope in the experiment. Thus, results are inferred from these exact representatives, not the quantifier scopes in general. Using other quantifiers to express a scope may possibly yield different results. In addition, results may depend on the setup of the experiment. As subject area of all sample requirements, we used a software product for machine maintenance. Each quantifier was then embedded in a sentence that was equal for all test subjects and had specific answer options encoded as images. A different use of sentences, images, or other factors, such as the professional background and English proficiency of the subjects, could lead to different results.

Conclusion and Internal Validity: Prior to starting the experiment and collecting the data, we launched a test run with three participants to receive feedback on the correctness of language, the comprehensibility of the overall experiment, and remaining technical bugs. Since we used an experimental design where all participants were faced with all treatments in a random order, we do not expect effects due to a confounding variable. The sample size of 51 subjects is reasonable to draw statistical conclusions. We only asked the participants whether they have a background in computer science, whether they are native English speakers, and what their profession is. We did not analyze the effect of these demographic factors due to the small size of single groups. In addition, we are not able to analyze effects related to further contextual factors of subjects such as experience, closeness to the application domain, or others. We selected the applied statistical tests based on the characteristics of the experiment (e.g., paired samples) and checked the test's assumptions (e.g., normal distribution). All elicited measures (reading times, number of errors, and perceived difficulty) are independent from any kind of judgement by the authors. To make the results transparent, we report p-value and effect size. Still, we used an arbitrary, yet common, significance level threshold of $\alpha = 0.05$ for the statistical tests.

External Validity: Since we used convenience sampling, we cannot claim that our participant group is representative for the group of all people working with requirements. Particularly, participants with a different language background may have more or less difficulties with negative or affirmative syntax. In addition, we used artificial requirements for the treatments. We cannot claim that these are representative for real requirements in the context of each participant.

5.2 Interpretation and Writing Guidelines

Taking the threats to validity into account, we can cautiously interpret these results. We conclude that some quantifiers exhibit better readability and better comprehension when phrased in affirmative syntax. Furthermore, self-perception mostly coincides with readability and comprehension, which might be owed to the fact that longer reading time and the guessing of answers impact the perceived difficulty of the sentences. Nevertheless, even for the quantifier scopes where participants made significantly more errors and spent more reading time with the affirmative syntax, the participants did not perceive the negative phrasing as easier to read (see Fig. 6).

An observation that was surprising to us was the high error rate for the scopes More than (affirmative case) and Less than (negative case). As shown in Fig. 4, almost 60% of our participants answered the question incorrectly. A deeper analysis of the results showed that, for the sentence "more than x...", a large number of participants incorrectly selected the answer that showed exactly x instances. This results is mirrored in the negative case of the Less than scope. Apparently, our participants had difficulties with sentences that represent open intervals. Given that the error ratio for scopes At least, and At most is lower, we may conclude that it is better to use formulations that represent closed intervals.

In summary, we draw the following conclusions that can be used as advice for writing requirements that are faster to read, have lower chances of misinterpretation, and are perceived as easier to read:

1. Use **affirmative** syntax for scopes `All`, `At least`, `Less than`, `Exactly n`, and `One`:
   – Write `All...` instead of `No...not`
   – Write `At least...` instead of `No less than...`
   – Write `Less than...` instead of `Not as many as...`
   – Write `Exactly n...` instead of `No more or less than n...`
   – Write `Only ...` instead of `Only...not`
2. Use **negative** syntax for the scope `None`:
   – Write `None of...` instead of `All...without`
3. Use **closed-interval** formulation instead of open-interval formulation:
   – Write `At least...` instead of `More than...`
   – Write `At most...` instead of `Less than...`
4. In doubt, use **affirmative** syntax since it is perceived as easier.

5.3   Relation to Existing Evidence

Berry and Kamsties [2] noticed that some quantifiers may be dangerous to use in requirements because they create ambiguity. They specifically recommend avoiding indefinite quantifiers, such as "nearly all", and the quantifier *all* with a plural noun because it is not clear whether the corresponding statement applies to each instance separately or to all instances as a whole. In our experiment, the affirmative sentence for the scope `All` contained the quantifier *all* with a plural noun. Although 10% of our participants gave an incorrect answer for this sentence, this number was not particularly higher than in other scopes.

Christensen [4] performed an empirical study on the effect of negative and affirmative statements on response time (i.e., how fast did subjects answer questions about the presented statements) and reading performance (i.e., how often were the answers correct). They found significantly shorter response times for affirmative sentences and lower error rates (differences were not significant). Our results corroborate the results of Christensen in general although there were some scopes with effects in favor of the negative syntax (e.g., `All but`).

6   Conclusion

In the course of this study, we raised questions on the readability, comprehension, and subjective difficulty of affirmative and negative quantifier formulations in natural language requirements. We designed and conducted a web-based experiment, from which we evaluated the results using the time for readability, correctness for comprehension, and self-assessment for subjective difficulty. The results were interpreted and yielded a tendency towards better overall performance of affirmative quantifiers compared to their negative equivalences. This extends and confirms related studies from psycholinguistics. Moreover, our results suggest using quantifiers representing closed intervals instead of open intervals.

Our results depict first empirical impressions on quantifiers in requirements specifications. However, much about this topic remains to examine. First of all, it remains to review, whether the categorization of quantifiers in this study is sensible or whether other categorizations are also possible. Since we only examined one concrete quantifier formulation for each scope, the results may not be generalized to other syntactic representations of the same scope. Future research could thus involve repeating the experiment with a different set of quantifiers in a different context to validate the results and give additional information to eventually generalize the results. Last but not least, certain quantifiers could be proposed as new requirements smells and tools may be used to detect these smells to improve the quality of natural language requirements.

References

1. Atoum, I.: A novel framework for measuring software quality-in-use based on semantic similarity and sentiment analysis of software reviews. J. King Saud Univ. Comput. Inf. Sci. **32**(1), 113–125 (2020)
2. Berry, D.M., Kamsties, E.: The syntactically dangerous all and plural in specifications. IEEE Softw. **22**(1), 55–57 (2005)
3. Chen, H., Cohen, P., Chen, S.: How big is a big odds ratio? Interpreting the magnitudes of odds ratios in epidemiological studies. Commun. Stat. Simul. Comput. **39**(4), 860–864 (2010)
4. Christensen, K.R.: Negative and affirmative sentences increase activation in different areas in the brain. J. Neurolinguist. **22**(1), 1–17 (2009)
5. Cirilo, R.K., Foss, D.J.: Text structure and reading time for sentences. J. Verbal Learn. Verbal Behav. **19**(1), 96–109 (1980)
6. Cohen, J.: Statistical Power Analysis for the Behavioral Sciences. Routledge, New York (2013)
7. Femmer, H., Vogelsang, A.: Requirements quality is quality in use. IEEE Softw. **36**(3), 83–91 (2019)
8. Femmer, H., Mèndez Fernàndez, D., Wagner, S., Eder, S.: Rapid quality assurance with requirements smells. J. Syst. Softw. **123**, 190–213 (2017)
9. Glanzberg, M.: Quantifiers, pp. 794–821. Oxford University Press, Oxford (2006)
10. Graesser, A.C., Hoffman, N.L., Clark, L.F.: Structural components of reading time. J. Verbal Learn. Verbal Behav. **19**(2), 135–151 (1980)
11. Keenan, E.L., Stavi, J.: A semantic characterization of natural language determiners. Linguist. Philos. **9**(3), 253–326 (1986)
12. Klare, G.R.: The measurement of readability: useful information for communicators. ACM J. Comput. Doc. **24**(3), 107–121 (2000)
13. MacKay, D.G.: To end ambiguous sentences. Percept. Psychophys. **1**(5), 426–436 (1966)
14. Wohlin, C., Runeson, P., Höst, M., Ohlsson, M.C., Regnell, B., Wesslén, A.: Experimentation in Software Engineering: An Introduction. Kluwer Academic Publishers, Norwell (2000)

Generation of Formal Requirements from Structured Natural Language

Dimitra Giannakopoulou[1]([⊠]), Thomas Pressburger[1], Anastasia Mavridou[2], and Johann Schumann[2]

[1] NASA Ames Research Center, Moffett Field, CA, USA
{dimitra.giannakopoulou,tom.pressburger}@nasa.gov
[2] SGT, NASA Ames Research Center, Moffett Field, CA, USA
{anastasia.mavridou,johann.m.schumann}@nasa.gov

Abstract. [**Motivation**] The use of structured natural languages to capture requirements provides a reasonable trade-off between ambiguous natural language and unintuitive formal notations. [**Problem**] There are two major challenges in making structured natural language amenable to formal analysis: (1) associating requirements with formulas that can be processed by analysis tools and (2) ensuring that the formulas conform to the language semantics. [**Results**] FRETISH is a structured natural language that incorporates features from existing research and from NASA applications. Even though FRETISH is quite expressive, its underlying semantics is determined by the types of four fields: *scope*, *condition*, *timing*, and *response*. Each combination of field types defines a template with Real-Time Graphical Interval Logic (RTGIL) semantics. We present an approach that constructs future and past-time metric temporal logic formulas for each template compositionally, from its fields. To establish correctness of our approach we have developed a framework which, for each template: (1) extensively tests the generated formulas against the template semantics and (2) proves equivalence between its past-time and future-time formulas. Our approach has been used to capture and analyze requirements for a Lockheed Martin Cyber-Physical System challenge. [**Contribution**] To the best of our knowledge, this is the first approach to generate pure past-time and pure future-time formalizations to accommodate a variety of analysis tools. The compositional nature of our algorithms facilitates maintenance and extensibility, and our extensive verification framework establishes trust in the produced formalizations. Our approach is available through the open-source tool FRET.

Keywords: Structured natural languages · Requirements elicitation · Compositional formalization · Temporal logics · Verification

1 Introduction

Requirements engineering is a central step in the development of safety-critical systems. Requirements are typically written in natural language, which is

N. Madhavji et al. (Eds.): REFSQ 2020, LNCS 12045, pp. 19–35, 2020.
https://doi.org/10.1007/978-3-030-44429-7_2

ambiguous and consequently not amenable to formal analysis. On the other hand, a variety of analysis techniques have been developed for requirements written in formal, mathematical notations [4,7,10,11,17], e.g. completeness, consistency, realizability, model checking, or vacuity checking. Despite the ambiguity of unrestricted natural language, it is unrealistic to expect developers to write high-level requirements in mathematical notations.

FRETISH is a restricted natural language for writing unambiguous requirements, supported by our open source tool FRET[1] (see Fig. 1). FRETISH incorporates features from existing approaches (e.g., property patterns [8] and EARS [19]), and from NASA applications. Even though the FRETISH grammar is quite expressive, its underlying semantics is determined by the types of four fields: *scope, condition, timing*, and *response*. Each combination of field types defines a template with Real-Time Graphical Interval Logic (RTGIL) [21] semantics. There are two challenges in making FRETISH amenable to formal analysis: (1) associating FRETISH requirements with formulas that can be processed by analysis tools, and (2) ensuring that the formulas conform to the FRETISH semantics.

We propose an approach that constructs two metric temporal logic formulas for each FRETISH template: a pure past-time (denoted pmLTL), and a pure future-time (denoted fmLTL) formula, interpreted over finite traces.[2] We support both fmLTL and pmLTL so as to interface with a variety of analysis tools. Formula generation is performed compositionally, based on the types of the template fields. We establish correctness of the produced formalizations through a fully automated framework which, for each template: (1) extensively tests the generated formulas against the template semantics, and (2) proves equivalence between its past-time and future-time formulas. The FRETISH grammar, its RTGIL semantics, the formula generation approach and its verification framework are available through the FRET repository. We report on the application of our approach to the Lockheed Martin Cyber-Physical Systems (LMCPS) challenge [20].

Related Work. Work on gleaning patterns from a body of property specifications resulted in the Specification Pattern System [8], with later extensions for real-time properties [16], composite properties [12], and semantic subtleties [6]. Tools such as Prospec [12], SPIDER [15] and SpeAR [10] were developed to support users in writing requirements according to supported patterns. SALT (Structured Assertion Language for Temporal logic) [3] is a general purpose specification and assertion language designed for readability, which incorporates property pattern features like scope. We use SALT as an intermediate language. The Easy Approach to Requirements Syntax (EARS, [19]) proposed five informal templates that were found to be sufficient to express most high-level requirements; recent work has attempted to formalize the templates in LTL [18]. STIMULUS [14] enables the user to build up a formal requirement by dragging and dropping phrases, and then simulate the system specified by the requirements. ASSERT[TM] [7] uses the constrained natural language SADL for formalizing

---

[1] Formal Requirements Elicitation Tool: https://github.com/NASA-SW-VnV/fret.

[2] fmLTL with infinite-trace semantics can be produced with a very simple modification to our generation algorithms.

domain ontologies, and a requirements language SRL that can express conditions, including temporal conditions, on monitored variables, and constraints on controlled variables. Tools such as VARED [2] and ARSENAL [13] attempt to formalize more general natural language.

Contributions. Our approach is related to all these works by pursuing similar goals and incorporating experience represented by existing requirement templates and patterns. The main driver for our work is to enable intuitive writing of requirements during early phases of the software lifecycle. We do not require users to define the variables used in requirement sentences; variables can be defined later for analysis, or can be connected to models or code as needed for verification [20]. We are not aware of other work that supports the generation of pure past-time, together with finite- and infinite-trace future-time metric temporal logic formulas. We are thus able to connect to analysis tools that may not support the combination of future and past time operators (e.g., CoCoSim [20]). Our developed algorithms are open source, and their compositional nature facilitates maintenance and extensibility. We currently support 112 templates, which may increase in the future to accommodate the needs of FRET users. Finally, unlike previous work, we provide an extensive, open source, automated verification framework for the correctness of the generated formulas. This is crucial for using FRET in safety-critical contexts.

2   Background

Intermediate Language. SALT [3] serves as an intermediate language in our formula generation approach. In particular, several SALT features facilitate our formalization algorithms: operator qualifiers `inclusive`/`exclusive` or `required`/`optional`; scope operators such as `before`, `after`, or `between`; formula simplifications and generation in nuXmv format. Note that we are only able to use scope operators with fmLTL formulas; unfortunately, scope operators in the context of past-time SALT expressions result in formulas with mixed future and past-time operators. Our framework targets pure future-time or pure past-time formulas, i.e., formulas that utilize exclusively future-time or past-time operators, respectively.

We use SALT's propositional operators: `not`, `and`, `or`, `implies`, and the temporal operators: `until`, `always`, `eventually`, `next` for future time, and `since`, `historically`, `once`, `previous` for past-time. A timed modifier: `timed[∼]` where $\sim$ is one of $<$ or $\leq$ turns temporal operators into timed ones (e.g., `once` `timed[≤ 3]`ϕ). Modifier `timed[=]` is also allowed with `previous` and `next`. It is mandatory to specify whether delimiting events are included (`inclusive`) or not (`exclusive`), and whether their occurrence is strictly `required` or `optional`. For example, ϕ `until inclusive required` ψ means that ϕ needs to hold until and including the point where ψ occurs, and moreover ψ must occur in the execution.

Temporal Logics. fmLTL formulas use exclusively future-time temporal operators (X, F, G, U, corresponding to `next`, `eventually`, `always`, `until` in SALT), and look at the portion of an execution that follows the state at which they are interpreted. pmLTL formulas use exclusively past-time temporal operators (Y, O, H, S, corresponding to previous, once, historically, since in SALT); they look at the portion of the execution that has occurred up to the state where they are interpreted. We interpret formulas over discrete time points. An fmLTL/pmLTL formula is satisfied by an execution if the formula holds at the initial/final state of the execution, respectively.

We review the main future and past time operators for LTL by exploring their dualities. The X (resp. Y) operator refers to the next (resp. previous) time point, i.e., $X\phi$ (resp. $Y\phi$) is true iff ϕ holds at the next (resp. previous) time point.[3] The F (resp. O) operator refers to at least one future (resp. past) time point, i.e., $F\phi$ (resp. $O\phi$) is true iff ϕ is true at some future (resp. past) time point including the present time. $G\phi$ (resp. $H\phi$) is true iff ϕ is always true in the future (resp. past). Finally, $\phi U\psi$ is true iff ψ holds at some point t in the future and for all time points t' (such that $t' < t$) ϕ is true. $\phi S\psi$ is true iff ψ holds at some point t in the past and for all time points t' (such that $t' > t$) ϕ is true. Our formalizations often use since inclusive so, in order to reduce formula complexity, we extend LTL with an operator SI where $\phi\,SI\,\psi \equiv \phi\,S\,(\psi\,\&\,\phi)$. This feature is only used when the targeted analysis tools support operator SI. Timed modifiers restrict the scope of temporal operators to specific intervals. For example, $O[\leq 3]$ restricts the scope of operator O to the interval including the point where a formula is interpreted and 3 points in the past.

3   Requirements Language

The FRETISH language aims at providing a vocabulary natural to the user. As such, the FRETISH grammar offers a variety of ways for expressing semantically equivalent notions; for example, conditions can be introduced using the synonyms while, when, where, and if. While certain aspects of FRETISH requirements are in natural language, Boolean expressions, familiar to most developers, are used to concisely capture conditions on state. Internally, each requirement is mapped to a semantic template, used to construct the requirement's formalization. To illustrate the FRETISH language, we use requirement [**AP-003b**] from the LMCPS challenge (see Sect. 6):

> "In roll_hold mode RollAP shall immediately satisfy
> abs(roll_angle) < 6 ⇒ roll_hold_reference = 0."

A FRETISH requirement is automatically parsed into six sequential fields, with the FRET editor dynamically coloring the text corresponding to the fields as the requirement is entered (Fig. 1). The fields are *scope, condition, component, shall, timing,* and *response,* three of which are optional: *scope, condition,* and *timing.* The mandatory *component* field specifies the component that the requirement applies to (e.g., RollAP, the roll autopilot). The *shall* keyword states

---

[3] Yp is false at the first time point, for all p.

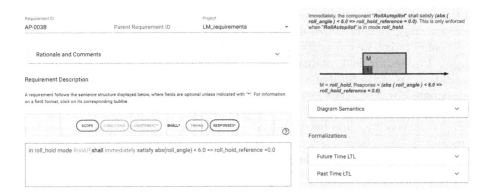

Fig. 1. FRET screenshot: editor (left) and semantics (right) for requirement [**AP-003b**]. Semantics is provided in intuitive textual and diagrammatic forms. The LTL accordions are not expanded to save space but the formulas are displayed in Table 5.

that the component behavior must conform to the requirement. The *response* field currently is of the form *satisfy R*, where *R* is a non-temporal Boolean-valued expression. The three optional fields above specify when the response is, or is not, to occur, which we now describe.

Component behavior is often mode-dependent. Field *scope* specifies the interval(s), relative to when a mode holds, within which the requirement must hold (e.g., "in roll_hold mode"). If scope is omitted, the requirement is enforced on the entire execution, known as *global* scope. For a mode M, FRET provides seven relationships: *before M* (the requirement is enforced strictly before the first point M holds); *after M* (the requirement is enforced strictly after the last point M holds[4]); *in M* (or the synonym *during M*; the requirement is enforced while the component is in mode M); and *not in M*. It is sometimes necessary to specify that a requirement is enforced *only* in some time frame, meaning that it should *not* be satisfied outside of that frame. For this, the scopes *only after*, *only before*, and *only in* are provided.

Field *condition* is a Boolean expression that triggers the need for a response within the specified scope. For example, requirement [**AP-004a**] (Sect. 6) contains the condition *"when steady_state & calm_air"*. Lastly, field *timing* specifies when the response is expected (e.g., immediately) relative to each trigger (or relative to the beginning of the scope, when condition is omitted). There are seven possibilities for the timing field: *immediately*, *never*, *eventually*, *always*, *within n* time units, *for n* time units[5], and *after n* time units, the latter meaning: not within n time units and at the $n+1^{st}$ time unit. When timing is omitted, it is taken to mean *eventually*. To specify that the component shall satisfy R at

---

4 Actually the first occurrence of a last time in the mode; see Sect. 4.
5 The *timing* field possibilities correspond to the absence, existence and universality occurrence patterns of [8] and the bounded response and invariance patterns of [16].

all times where C holds, one can use Boolean implication in combination with timing *always*, as done in requirement [**AP-001**] (Sect. 6).

To summarize, we currently support 8 values for field mode (including global scope), 2 values for field condition (condition included or omitted), and 7 values for field timing, for a total of $8 \times 2 \times 7 = 112$ semantic templates. Each template is designated by a *template key*; for example, [*in, null, always*] identifies requirements of the form *In M mode, the software shall always satisfy R*; *null* means the optional condition has been omitted (as opposed to *regular* when a condition is included). The classic response pattern: *always (condition implies eventually response)*, is captured by the key [*null, regular, eventually*]; *null* means scope is omitted, which corresponds to global scope.

4   Compositional Formalization

Our approach to formalization is compositional: rather than creating a dedicated formula for each semantic template, we build formulas by putting together subformulas corresponding to the types of the template fields. For each semantic template key of FRETISH, we generate an fmLTL and a pmLTL formula; these formulas contain variables that get instantiated for each particular requirement. For example, the template for the key [*in, null, immediately*] of our example requirement [**AP-003b**] is: H(Fin_scope_mode $\rightarrow$ $post_condition$), and gets instantiated as shown in the last row of Table 5.

Our formalization algorithms produce SALT formulas, and invoke the SALT tool to convert these formulas into nuXmv format. This paper focuses on finite traces so we generate future-time formulas that only check up to the last point of a finite trace, denoted LAST. Due to limited space, we only present our construction of pmLTL formulas; the structure for fmLTL generation is similar but simpler, since it can directly incorporate SALT's support for expressing scope.

Scope. The scope of a requirement characterizes a set of disjoint finite intervals where the requirement must hold, and as such defines a high-level template for the generated formulas. Our approach treats a scope interval as an abstract interval between endpoints LEFT (inclusive) and RIGHT (exclusive), with two semantic options: if LEFT occurs but is never followed by RIGHT, then the interval (1) is not defined (*between* semantics) or (2) is defined and spans to the end of the finite trace (*after-until* semantics). Figure 2(a) illustrates after-until semantics for scope: "in MODE". It characterizes the types of intervals where requirements must hold: (1) intervals defined between *any* point (denoted by the box on the top line of the diagram) where MODE becomes true and the first subsequent point where MODE becomes false; and (2) an interval where MODE is true to the end of the execution. Our pmLTL formulas have the following high-level template:

```
generalform = (g-a) and (g-b)
g-a = historically (RIGHT implies previous BASEFORM_TO_LEFT)
g-b = ((not RIGHT) since inclusive required LEFT)
       implies BASEFORM_TO_LEFT
BASEFORM_TO_LEFT = (BASEFORM [since inclusive required LEFT]*)
```

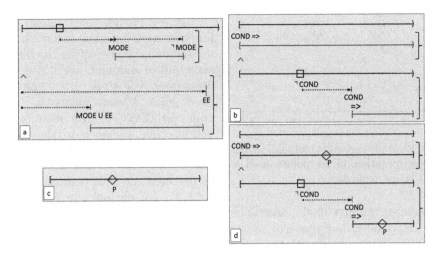

Fig. 2. RTGIL semantics: (a) "in MODE"; (b) "when condition COND"; (c) "eventually P". Our semantics is compositional: the blue interval of a diagram can be replaced by another diagram. For example, (d) illustrates the combined result of (b) and (c), i.e., "when COND, eventually P". EE (end of execution) denotes time point LAST+1. (Color figure online)

The template is a conjunction of two formulas. In formula **g-a**, historically imposes the requirement on all intervals of the target scope; previous is needed because intervals are open on the right; BASEFORM_TO_LEFT is the formula BASEFORM that must be checked back to, and including, the left endpoint of each interval. BASEFORM is defined later in the section, and expresses the requirements that must hold within each scope interval; the part within BASEFORM enclosed in []* is omitted in some cases, as discussed later. Formula **g-b** is applicable only with the *after-until* option; it similarly imposes BASEFORM_TO_LEFT on intervals that span to the end of the execution (i.e., RIGHT never occurs).

The endpoints LEFT and RIGHT in our general template get instantiated depending on the type of scope. Table 1 defines scope endpoints in terms of abbreviations (left), each characterized by a logical formula that tracks changes in the values of mode variables M (right). We use abbreviations FiM/LiM: first/last state in mode; FNiM/LNiM: first/last state not in mode; FFiM/FLiM: first occurrence of FiM/LiM in execution; FTP: first time point in execution; LAST: last time point in execution. FiM and LiM are used with scope key *in*; they are characterized by M becoming true (from false) and vice versa, respectively. Endpoint formulas may involve checking whether endpoints occur at state FTP (e.g., when (M **and** FTP) is true, FiM holds).

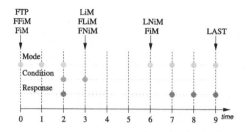

Fig. 3. Example execution including graphical representation of endpoints used in pmLTL scope semantics

Figure 3 provides an example system execution including mode-related information, and depicting the different types of endpoints used in defining scopes. For scope *after*, LEFT is time point 3, and RIGHT is time point 10 (LAST+1). As mentioned, our intervals are open to the right: [LEFT, RIGHT); this is because the RIGHT endpoint of scopes can only be detected one time point later (see Table 1). For example, in Fig. 3, the last point in the first mode interval is 2, but LiM is detected at time point 3, where M is false, but was true at the previous time point. As mentioned in Sect. 2, qualifier *only* expects the requirement to *not* hold outside of the specified scope. This means two things: (1) scope interval endpoints must be selected accordingly (Table 1), and (2) the base formula must be negated.

Note that for scopes *null*, *after*, and *only before*, the right endpoint of their associated intervals is LAST+1 (see Table 1). Since past-time formulas get evaluated backwards starting at the last point in an execution, we do not need to provide a formula for LAST+1. Rather, for these cases, we simplify the general template to the following: **generalform = (once LEFT) implies BASEFORM_TO_LEFT**.

Table 1. (left) Scope endpoints. (right) pmLTL formulas associated with each endpoint. LAST+1 is not provided because our formulas do not use it.

Scope	LEFT	RIGHT	Symbol	Formula
null	FTP	LAST+1	FFiM	FiM and previous (historically (not M))
before	FTP	FFiM	FLiM	LiM and previous (historically (not LiM))
after	FLiM	LAST+1	FiM	M and (FTP or (previous not M))
in	FiM	LiM	LiM	not M and previous M
notin, onlyin	FNiM	LNiM	FNiM	not M and (FTP or previous M)
only before	FFiM	LAST+1	LNiM	M and previous (not M)
only after	FTP	FLiM	FTP	not previous true

Base Formulas. BASEFORM describes the expectations of the requirement within each scope interval. We remind the reader that all BASEFORM formulas appear in the context of **generalform** and are interpreted starting at the RIGHT of each scope. A base formula is determined by whether a condition exists, the timing, and the type of response.

Table 2 illustrates the base formulas that correspond to various timings, without, and with conditions. A base formula f enclosed in $[f]^*$ indicates that the part in BASEFORM_TO_LEFT similarly enclosed in $[]^*$ must be omitted; for example, eventually formulas cannot be checked at each point of the interval. Some

Table 2. BASEFORMS without and with conditions. since_ir/since_er denote since inclusive/exclusive required, respectively.

Timing	BASEFORM	BASEFORM with conditions
immediately	LEFT implies RES	TRIGGER implies RES
always	[RES since_ir LEFT]*	NOCONDITION or (RES since_ir TRIGGER)
never	[always(not RES)]*	always(COND, (not RES))
eventually	[not ((not RES) since_ir LEFT)]*	[NOCONDITION or not ((not RES) since_ir TRIGGER)]*
for n	(once timed[$\leq n$] LEFT) implies RES	F_1 and F_2 $F_1 \equiv (((\text{not LEFT}) \text{ since\_er TRIGGER}) \text{ and }$ $(\text{once timed}[\leq n] \text{ TRIGGER})) \text{ implies RES}$ $F_2 \equiv (\text{COND and LEFT}) \text{ implies RES}$
within n	((not RES) since_ir LEFT) implies (once timed[$<n$] LEFT)	(previous timed[$=n$] (TRIGGER and not RES)) implies (once timed[$<n$] (LEFT or RES))
after n	for(n, not (RES)) and within(n+1, RES)	for(COND, n, not (RES)) and within(COND, n+1, RES)

timings are expressed in terms of others (e.g., never); we use a function-like notation to denote that. Timed cases have special treatment when the remaining interval in scope is too short to cover their duration. Take the trace of Fig. 3, for example. At time point 8: (1) *for* 3 time units imposes RES to the end of the execution; (2) *within* 3 time units is trivially true; (3) *after* 3 time units imposes that RES *not* occur until the end of the execution.

There are several options for interpreting conditions: is a requirement triggered by a condition *being* or *becoming* true? We currently only support the latter option, as illustrated in Fig. 2: we check requirements when a condition becomes true (from false) or is true at the first point where the requirement is in scope, as expressed by a trigger formula: TRIGGER = (COND and previous not(COND)) or (COND and LEFT). We can easily add support for different options by providing alternative trigger formulas. When conditions never occur in a scope of interest, then the requirement is true trivially. Base formulas with conditions therefore typically contain a disjunction with NOCONDITION (Table 2), where NOCONDITION = (not COND since inclusive required LEFT).

Finally, note that negating base formulas in *only* scopes does not always consist of wrapping the formula in a logical *not*. For this reason, negations of timings are specified explicitly in our approach (not illustrated for lack of space).

5   Verifying Formalizations

We provide assurance that formulas generated by our approach capture the intended semantics through a modular and extensible verification framework. For each template key and its corresponding fmLTL and pmLTL formulas ϕ_{ft}

and ϕ_{pt}, our framework (1) checks that ϕ_{ft} and ϕ_{pt} conform to the template key RTGIL semantics, and (2) verifies for a specified trace length that ϕ_{ft} and ϕ_{pt} are equivalent. Our verification framework consists of the following components:

- TRACE_GENERATOR produces traces, i.e., example executions such as the one illustrated on Fig. 3: mode M holds in intervals $\{[0..2], [6..9]\}$, condition COND holds in the interval $\{[2..3]\}$, and response RES holds in intervals $\{[2..2], [7..9]\}$.
- FORMULA_RETRIEVER produces the set of all possible verification tuples $\langle t, \phi_{ft}, \phi_{pt} \rangle$, where t is a template key, and ϕ_{ft} and ϕ_{pt} are its corresponding fmLTL and pmLTL formulas, respectively. This component establishes the set of formulas that must be checked by our framework.
- ORACLE takes a trace and a verification tuple $\langle t, \phi_{ft}, \phi_{pt} \rangle$, and computes the truth value of t on the trace, in terms of RTGIL semantics. For example, for template key [in, null, always] and the trace of Fig. 3, the expected value is false, because when M is active in interval $[0..2]$, RES does not hold on the entire interval.
- SEMANTICS_EVALUATOR receives a trace, a verification tuple $\langle t, \phi_{ft}, \phi_{pt} \rangle$, and an expected value e (provided by ORACLE), and checks whether ϕ_{ft} and ϕ_{pt} evaluate to e on the trace. In other words, it checks if, in the context of the particular trace, the generated formulas conform to the template key semantics.
- EQUIVALENCE_CHECKER receives a verification tuple $\langle t, \phi_{ft}, \phi_{pt} \rangle$, and checks whether ϕ_{ft} and ϕ_{pt} are equivalent formulas, thus ensuring consistency between different formalizations of the same template key.

5.1   Trace Generation

We support two approaches for trace generation: the first targets interesting relationships between mode, condition, response, and duration (for metric timing), while the second uses a random approach. Our framework is designed in a highly modular way, so additional strategies can easily be incorporated.

The first approach uses boundary value analysis and equivalence class strategies similar to [22], with the difference that we generate traces automatically as opposed to manually, and we additionally deal with durations for metric timing. We base trace generation on specifying numerical constraints on endpoints for mode, condition, and response. We then use constraint logic programming[6] to compute all solutions satisfying the constraints. These solutions define concrete traces used by our framework.

A trace spans between time points 0 and Max. We first select a point x where a condition trigger is imposed, with $0 \leq x \leq Max$. We optionally add another trigger point a fixed distance away. Condition intervals are currently of length 1 (for example, $[5..6]$). We then generate a mode interval $[x_1..x_2]$ where $0 \leq x_1 \leq x_2 \leq Max$ around the first trigger point according to boundary value and equivalence class testing strategies. In particular, we generate constraints on

---

[6] We use clp(fd) in SWI-Prolog: https://www.swi-prolog.org/.

x_1 and x_2 where $x_1 = x$, or $x_1 + 1 = x$ (boundary cases), or x is the midpoint of x_1 and x_2 (to represent the equivalence class of interior points between x_1 and x_2), or $x_2 = x$ (another boundary case).

We also generate traces with a second scope interval $[x_3..x_4]$ (where $x_3 > x_2 + 1$) based on a selected duration n. There are several cases for time point $x + n$: it could lie between x_1 and x_2, be x_2, be between x_2 and x_3, be x_3, be between x_3 and x_4, be x_4, or be greater than x_4. Next, we explore response intervals that implement each of the Allen interval relationships [1] to each mode interval, merging pairs of response intervals that are not separated. This process generates, for example: 1908 traces with $Max = 6$ and duration= 2; 12562 traces with $Max = 9$ and duration $= 4$ (the example of Fig. 3 is one of those); and 32717 traces with $Max = 12$ and duration $= 4$.

Random trace generation constructs a random number, between 0 and 3, of random, disjoint, non-consecutive intervals between 0 and Max, for each of mode, condition, and response. It also generates a random duration for metric timings. We used thus produced 60000 different random traces in the range $[0..12]$.

5.2   Test Oracles

ORACLE interprets the RTGIL semantics of a template key on a trace generated as above and produces an expected value of `true` or `false`. It performs this in a compositional fashion, which reflects the way in which the corresponding RTGIL semantics is defined. More specifically, fields scope and condition determine the intervals within a trace where the template is relevant, and fields timing and response determine the corresponding `true` or `false` value, as follows.

The first step consists of establishing the scope of the requirement as a set of intervals where the requirement must be evaluated. This is performed based on the trace and the type of field *scope*. Take, for example, the trace illustrated in Fig. 3, where M holds in intervals $\{[0..2], [6..9]\}$. If the scope field is *after* or *in*, then the scope of the requirement is $\{[3..9]\}$ or $\{[0..2], [6..9]\}$, respectively.

If the condition field is *regular*, then the intervals where the requirement must be evaluated get modified accordingly, based on the trigger point for the condition. The trigger point is computed as the first point where a scope interval intersects some condition interval. This could be the left endpoint of the scope interval, some other point within the interval, or no point, if the condition never holds within that interval. For example, in Fig. 3 where COND holds in the interval $\{[2..3]\}$, if the scope is $\{[0..2], [6..9]\}$, the condition triggers are time point 2 for $[0..2]$, and none for $[6..9]$. As a consequence, the requirement must only be evaluated in interval $[2..2]$; this is established by truncating interval $[0..2]$ to start at the condition trigger 2, resulting in interval $[2..2]$.

Timing and response fields determine the `true` or `false` value produced by the oracle through appropriate interval operations for each of the timing operators. Note that the timing constraints are applied to *each* interval in the scope, and the results are combined to establish the returned value. At a high level, our approach is based on interval operations, which we have implemented in a generic interval logic class. We discuss a few examples here to provide the intuition behind this step. For the trace illustrated in Fig. 3 and for a template key with scope field *in*, requirements must be evaluated in intervals $\{[0..2], [6..9]\}$. Let us focus on interval $[0..2]$, where similar steps are applied to the second interval $[6..9]$.

First, consider the case where the condition is *null*, i.e., the requirement must hold unconditionally. For timing *always*, our algorithm checks whether there exists some interval in the set of response intervals that includes interval $[0..2]$, resulting in `false` (since RES holds in intervals $\{[2..2], [7..9]\}$). For *eventually*, it checks whether there exists some interval in the set of response intervals that is not disjoint with interval $[0..2]$, resulting in `true`. For timing field *within* and duration 1, we truncate $[0..2]$ to interval $[0..1]$ that has the specified duration, and within which we expect the response to occur. We then check whether there exists some interval in the set of response intervals that is not disjoint with the truncated interval $[0..1]$, resulting in `false`.

If the condition field is *regular*, then we need to take the condition trigger into consideration. If there exists no condition trigger in the scope interval (e.g., $[6..9]$), then the result is vacuously `true`. For interval $[0..2]$, the trigger is 2. As mentioned, the scope interval is then truncated to start at the condition trigger, meaning to $[2..2]$, and timing operators are applied similarly as before, but this time on interval $[2..2]$. For timing field *always* and *eventually*, our algorithm returns `true`; *within* with duration 1 falls outside the range of the original scope interval, and hence also returns `true` (i.e., the remaining interval in scope is too short to cover duration).

Since requirements are expected to hold in all scope intervals, our oracle computes the expected result as the conjunction of the results obtained for each interval. For example, in the case of template key $[in, null, always]$, the result is `false` for scope interval $[6..9]$, and `false` for $[0..2]$, so the expected value is `false`.[7] Note that *only* scopes involve negating the body of the requirement, which our ORACLE also supports.

5.3   Testing and Verification

Components SEMANTICS_EVALUATOR and EQUIVALENCE_CHECKER use the model checker nuXmv. Given a trace and a verification tuple $\langle t, \phi_{ft}, \phi_{pt} \rangle$, SEMANTICS_EVALUATOR encodes the trace in nuXmv and evaluates the truth value of formulas ϕ_{ft} and ϕ_{pt} on the trace. Our framework subsequently checks if the truth values of ϕ_{ft} and ϕ_{pt} agree with the expected value computed by ORACLE.

The code listing below is the nuXmv code generated for the trace of Fig. 3. The intervals for mode, condition and response involved in a trace correspond in nuXmv to definitions of propositions (see lines 7 through 22 in Listing 1.1). Following the define clause are future-time and past-time formalizations of each template key to be checked, represented as $\phi(arguments)$ in Listing 1.1. The future-time formulas are evaluated at the beginning of time ($t = 0$) at line 24, and the past-time formulas are evaluated at the end of time ($t = 9$) at line 26.

---

[7] Had the scope interval $[6..9]$ been $[7..9]$ instead, the result would have been `true` for that interval, but still `false` for the result.

Listing 1.1. nuXmv Input for $\phi(\cdot)$

```
1   MODULE main
2   VAR     t : 0 .. 10;
3   ASSIGN  init(t):=0;
4           next(t):=(t >= 10)?10:t+1;
5   DEFINE
6           LAST := (t = 9);
7           MODE := case
8               t < 0 : FALSE;
9               t <= 2 : TRUE;
10              t < 6 : FALSE;
11              t <= 9 : TRUE;
12              TRUE : FALSE; esac;
13              COND := case
14                  t < 2 : FALSE;
15                  t <= 3 : TRUE;
16                  TRUE : FALSE; esac;
17              RES := case
18                  t < 2 : FALSE;
19                  t <= 2 : TRUE;
20                  t < 7 : FALSE;
21                  t <= 9 : TRUE;
22                  TRUE : FALSE; esac;
23  LTLSPEC NAME FO_ft_key :=
24      G((t=0)->φ_ft(LAST,MODE,COND,RES));
25  LTLSPEC NAME F1_pt_key :=
26      G((t=9)->φ_pt(MODE,COND,RES));
```

Given a verification tuple $\langle t, \phi_{ft}, \phi_{pt} \rangle$, EQUIVALENCE_CHECKER uses nuXmv to check $(G\,(LAST \Rightarrow \phi_{pt})) \Leftrightarrow \phi_{ft}$ over an unconstrained model of specified trace length (for example, length 10 in Listing 1.2. Formulas ϕ_{ft} and ϕ_{pt} are instantiated with the unconstrained nuXmv Boolean variables **mode**, **cond**, and **response**; moreover, a specific duration (say, 3) is chosen for metric timings.

Listing 1.2. Equivalence checking

```
1   MODULE main
2   VAR     t : 0 .. 10;
3           mode, cond, res : boolean;
4   ASSIGN  init(t):=0;
5           next(t):=(t >= 10)?10:t+1;
6   DEFINE LAST := (t = 9);
7   LTLSPEC NAME FO_key :=
8       G(LAST -> φ_pt(mode,cond,res))
9       <-> φ_ft(LAST,mode,cond,res);
```

Despite our high expertise with formal logics, our verification framework was central for detecting errors in our produced formalizations. The compositional nature of our algorithms simplifies formalization repairs: changes target particular fields and automatically affect all templates that include these fields. In the following, we describe a very subtle problem detected by our framework, concerning the formalization for conditions with *within* timing, for which the BASEFORM formula was originally:

$(((\text{not RES}) \text{ and } (\text{not LEFT})) \text{ since exclusive required } ((\text{not RES}) \text{ and TRIGGER})) \text{ implies } (\text{once timed}[<n] \text{ TRIGGER})$

In other words, if within the target scope interval, no RES occurs since and including TRIGGER, TRIGGER must occur less than n time points in the past, otherwise *within* is violated. The following discrepancy is reported by our verification framework for the pmLTL formula over a trace interval [0..12]:
Mode: $\{[0..1]|[5..10]\}$; Condition: $\{[1..2], [4..5]\}$; Duration: 4; Response: $\{[0..0], [6..10]\}$
Discrepancy *null, regular, within*: expected: false; nuXmv: true.

Scope *null* signifies that the requirement is evaluated in the entire trace interval. The condition is triggered at points 1 and 4. The trigger at point 1 requires RES to occur within 4 time points, i.e., by, or at, time point 5. Despite the fact that the response does not occur in that interval, the formula evaluates to true. The reason is that the above formula states that if RES does not hold since TRIGGER, then TRIGGER must occur in less than 4 time units. Unfortunately, since TRIGGER also holds at time point 4, it satisfies the formula. Indeed, it is not possible to identify which TRIGGER the formula refers to in order to avoid this problem. To address it, we used the timed equality operator **previous timed**$[=n]$. The formula of Table 2 removes all discrepancies associated with this error.

6   Lockheed Martin Cyber Physical Systems Challenge

We applied FRET to the publicly-available Lockheed Martin Cyber Physical Systems (LMCPS) challenge [9]. The requirements, given in natural language, were formulated in FRETISH. The Simulink models, included with the challenge, were verified against the formulas generated by FRET. The case study aimed to assess the expressiveness of FRETISH, the quality of produced formalizations, and the capability of FRET to drive analysis tools. Table 3 provides an overview of the detailed study [20]: we found that most requirements could be captured in FRETISH and FRET successfully produced formalizations for analysis tools.

We also studied the conciseness of formulas generated by FRET compared to equivalent[8] formulas produced by hand starting from the original natural language requirements. We observed that, for elaborate semantic templates, writing formulas was hard and error-prone; for simple semantic templates, hand-written formulas could be significantly more concise. Motivated by these findings, we implemented a rewriting engine that applies Boolean algebra and temporal logic simplifications to reduce the complexity and size of produced formulas.

Table 3. LMCPS summary. N_R: #requirements; N_F: #requirements expressed in FRETISH; N_A: #requirements for which FRET produced verification code.

Component	N_R	N_F	N_A
Triplex Signal Monitor (TSM)	6	6	6
Finite State Machine (FSM)	13	13	13
Tustin Integrator (TUI)	4	3	3
Control Loop Regulators (REG)	10	10	10
Nonlinear Guidance (NLG)	7	7	7
Feedforward Neural Network (NN)	4	4	4
Control Allocator Effector Blender (EB)	5	3	3
6DoF Autopilot (AP)	14	13	13
System Safety Monitor (SWIM)	3	3	3
Euler Transformation (EUL)	8	7	7

We discuss three requirements of increasing complexity. These are part of the "6DoF Autopilot" challenge, which concerns an aircraft autopilot (AP) system featuring several modes and commands under various conditions. The challenge includes components *Autopilot*, and the *RollAP* unit of the AP. In [**AP-001**] (Table 4), signal `ap_engaged` indicates whether the AP is active (engaged) or not; `roll_act_cmd` denotes the numeric output signal to the aircraft control surfaces for roll. The last row of Table 4 illustrates the significantly more concise formula produced by the rewriting engine as compared to the original formula above it.

---

[8] Equivalence of formulas was checked with Kind2. [5].

Table 4. [AP-001]: natural language, FRETISH, pmLTL, simplified pmLTL

When roll AP is not engaged, the command to the roll actuator shall be zero.
RollAP shall always satisfy !ap_engaged $\Rightarrow$ roll_act_cmd = 0.0
`(!ap_engaged → roll_act_cmd = 0.0) S` `((!ap_engaged → roll_act_cmd = 0.0) & FTP)`
`H(!ap_engaged → roll_act_cmd = 0.0)`

Requirement [**AP-003b**] (Table 5, Fig. 1) describes the conditions that must be satisfied in the *roll hold* mode of operation and belongs to the [*in, null, immediately*] template key. Here, *Fin_roll_hold, Lin_roll_hold* are as described in Table 1 for $M = roll\_hold$. The *immediately* timing was used to specify that the response must be satisfied at the time of roll hold mode engagement. For this template key, the complicated pmLTL formula is equivalent to the formula in the last row of the table. We could not devise rewriting rules to achieve this result, so we added a special case in the formula generation algorithms. Finally, [**AP-004a**] (Table 6) talks about conditions that must be satisfied when commands

Table 5. [AP-003b]: natural language, FRETISH, fmLTL, pmLTL, equivalent pmLTL

The roll hold reference shall be set to zero if the actual roll angle is less than 6 degrees, in either direction, at the time of roll hold engagement.
In roll_hold mode RollAP shall immediately satisfy abs(roll_angle) < 6.0 $\Rightarrow$ roll_hold_reference = 0.0
`((LAST V ((! (Fin_roll_hold & (! LAST)))	(X (abs_roll_angle < 6.0 → roll_hold_reference = 0.0)))) & (roll_hold → (abs_roll_angle < 6.0 → roll_hold_reference = 0.0)))`

`((H ((Lin_roll_hold & (! FTP)) → (Y ((Fin_roll_hold → (abs_roll_angle < 6.0 → roll_hold_reference = 0.0)) S ((Fin_roll_hold → (abs_roll_angle < 6.0 → roll_hold_reference = 0.0)) & Fin_roll_hold)))) &`
`(((! Lin_roll_hold) S ((! Lin_roll_hold) & Fin_roll_hold)) →`
`((Fin_roll_hold→ (abs_roll_angle < 6.0 → roll_hold_reference = 0.0)) S ((Fin_roll_hold → (abs_roll_angle < 6.0 → roll_hold_reference = 0.0)) & Fin_roll_hold))))`

`(H (Fin_roll_hold → (abs_roll_angle < 6.0 → roll_hold_reference = 0.0)))`

Table 6. [AP-004a]: natural language, FRETISH, pmLTL

Steady state roll commands shall be tracked within 1 degree in calm air.
When in roll_hold mode when steady state & calm air AP shall always satisfy abs(roll_err) $\leq$ 1.0
`(H ((Lin_roll_hold & (!FTP)) → (Y ((((!(steady_state & calm_air)) SI Fin_roll_hold)	((abs(roll_err) <=1.0) SI (((steady_state & calm_air) & (Y (!(steady_state & calm_air))))	((steady_state & calm_air) & Fin_roll_hold)))) SI Fin_roll_hold)))) & (((!Lin_roll_hold) SI Fin_roll_hold) → ((((!(steady_state & calm_air)) SI Fin_roll_hold)	((abs(roll_err) <=1.0) SI (((steady_state & calm_air) & (Y (!(steady_state & calm_air))))	((steady_state & calm_air) & Fin_roll_hold)))) SI Fin_roll_hold))`

are sent in the *roll_hold* mode. The displayed pmLTL formula using operator SI is over 3x shorter than the corresponding formula using operator S.

7   Conclusions

We presented a compositional approach for generating and verifying formalizations of structured natural language requirements. Such modularity is key for maintainability and extensibility. We have also developed an automated verification framework for the formulas that we generate. Despite our high degree of expertise in temporal logics, automated verification has been key for detecting subtle errors in our algorithms. Our approach may produce more complex formulas than could be custom-written for individual template keys. We implement several formula simplification steps, which we will further improve in the future; in particular, we will focus on templates that occur most often in practice.

We plan to extend FRETISH with responses that involve ordering of actions, and conditions that persist for some time interval. Moreover, we intend to support customization of FRETISH to fit domain-specific styles and towards including other requirement notations such as tables or finite-state machines. Finally, we are exploring natural-language processing in order to fit existing requirements within the templates supported by FRET. We are also extending FRET towards providing user-support in correcting requirements.

Acknowledgements. We gratefully acknowledge the NASA ARMD System-Wide Safety Project for funding this work.

References

1. Allen, J.F.: Maintaining knowledge about temporal intervals. CACM **26**(11), 832–843 (1983)
2. Badger, J., Throop, D., Claunch, C.: VARED: verification and analysis of requirements and early designs. In: RE 2014, pp. 325–326 (2014)
3. Bauer, A., Leucker, M.: The theory and practice of SALT. In: Bobaru, M., Havelund, K., Holzmann, G.J., Joshi, R. (eds.) NFM 2011. LNCS, vol. 6617, pp. 13–40. Springer, Heidelberg (2011). https://doi.org/10.1007/978-3-642-20398-5_3
4. Bloem, R., Cavada, R., Pill, I., Roveri, M., Tchaltsev, A.: RAT: a tool for the formal analysis of requirements. In: Damm, W., Hermanns, H. (eds.) CAV 2007. LNCS, vol. 4590, pp. 263–267. Springer, Heidelberg (2007). https://doi.org/10.1007/978-3-540-73368-3_30
5. Champion, A., Mebsout, A., Sticksel, C., Tinelli, C.: The KIND 2 model checker. In: Chaudhuri, S., Farzan, A. (eds.) CAV 2016. LNCS, vol. 9780, pp. 510–517. Springer, Cham (2016). https://doi.org/10.1007/978-3-319-41540-6_29
6. Cobleigh, R.L., Avrunin, G.S., Clarke, L.A.: User guidance for creating precise and accessible property specifications. In: Proceedings of SIGSOFT 2006/FSE 2014. ACM (2006)
7. Crapo, A., Moitra, A., McMillan, C., Russell, D.: Requirements capture and analysis in ASSERT(TM). In: RE 2017, pp. 283–291 (2017)

8. Dwyer, M.B., Avrunin, G.S., Corbett, J.C.: Patterns in property specifications for finite-state verification. In: Proceedings of ICSE 1999, pp. 411–420. ACM (1999)
9. Elliott, C.: An example set of cyber-physical V&V challenges for S5. Lockheed Martin Skunk Works. In: Proceedings of S5 2016. AFRL (2016). http://mys5.org/Proceedings/2016/Day_2/2016-S5-Day2_0945_Elliott.pdf
10. Fifarek, A.W., Wagner, L.G., Hoffman, J.A., Rodes, B.D., Aiello, M.A., Davis, J.A.: SpeAR v2.0: formalized past LTL specification and analysis of requirements. In: NfM 2017, pp. 420–426 (2017)
11. Gacek, A., Katis, A., Whalen, M.W., Backes, J., Cofer, D.: Towards realizability checking of contracts using theories. In: Havelund, K., Holzmann, G., Joshi, R. (eds.) NFM 2015. LNCS, vol. 9058, pp. 173–187. Springer, Cham (2015). https://doi.org/10.1007/978-3-319-17524-9_13
12. Gallegos, I., Ochoa, O., Gates, A., Roach, S., Salamah, S., Vela, C.: A property specification tool for generating formal specifications: Prospec 2.0. In: SEKE 2008, pp. 273–278 (2008)
13. Ghosh, S., Elenius, D., Li, W., Lincoln, P., Shankar, N., Steiner, W.: ARSE-NAL: automatic requirements specification extraction from natural language. In: Rayadurgam, S., Tkachuk, O. (eds.) NFM 2016. LNCS, vol. 9690, pp. 41–46. Springer, Cham (2016). https://doi.org/10.1007/978-3-319-40648-0_4
14. Jeannet, B., Gaucher, F.: Debugging embedded systems requirements with STIM-ULUS: an automotive case-study. In: ERTS 2016 (2016)
15. Konrad, S., Cheng, B.H.C.: Facilitating the construction of specification pattern-based properties. In: Proceedings of RE 2005, pp. 329–338. IEEE (2005)
16. Konrad, S., Cheng, B.H.C.: Real-time specification patterns. In: Proceedings of ICSE 2005, pp. 372–381. ACM (2005)
17. Kupferman, O., Vardi, M.Y.: Vacuity detection in temporal model checking. Int. J. Softw. Tools Technol. Transf. **4**(2), 224–233 (2003)
18. Lúcio, L., Iqbal, T.: Formalizing EARS - first impressions. In: 1st International Workshop on Easy Approach to Requirements Syntax (EARS), pp. 11–13 (2018)
19. Mavin, A.: Listen, then use EARS. IEEE Softw. **29**(2), 17–18 (2012)
20. Mavridou, A., Bourbouh, H., Garoche, P.L., Hejase, M.: Evaluation of the FRET and CoCoSim tools on the ten Lockheed Martin cyber-physical challenge problems. Technical report, TM-2019-220374, NASA (2019)
21. Moser, L.E., Melliar-Smith, P.M., Ramakrishna, Y.S., Kutty, G., Dillon, L.K.: The real-time graphical interval logic toolset. In: Alur, R., Henzinger, T.A. (eds.) CAV 1996. LNCS, vol. 1102, pp. 446–449. Springer, Heidelberg (1996). https://doi.org/10.1007/3-540-61474-5_99
22. Salamah, S., Gates, A., Roach, S., Mondragon, O.: Verifying pattern-generated LTL formulas: a case study. In: Godefroid, P. (ed.) SPIN 2005. LNCS, vol. 3639, pp. 200–220. Springer, Heidelberg (2005). https://doi.org/10.1007/11537328_17

Using Eye Tracking Data to Improve Requirements Specification Use

Maike Ahrens$^{(\boxtimes)}$ and Kurt Schneider

Software Engineering Group, Leibniz Universität Hannover,
Welfengarten 1, 30167 Hannover, Germany
{maike.ahrens,kurt.schneider}@inf.uni-hannover.de

Abstract. [**Context and motivation**] Software requirements specifications are the main point of reference in traditional software projects.
Especially in large projects, these documents get read by multiple people,
multiple times. [**Question/problem**] Several guidelines and templates
already exist to support writing a good specification. However, not much
research has been done in investigating how to support the use of specifications and help readers to find relevant information and navigate in
the document more efficiently. [**Principal ideas/results**] We used eye
tracking data obtained from observing readers when using specifications
to create three different attention transfer features to support them in
this process. In a student experiment, we evaluated if these attention
visualizations positively affect the roles software architect, UI-designer
and tester when reading a specification for the first time. The results
show that the attention visualizations did not decrease navigation effort,
but helped to draw the readers' attention towards highlighted parts and
decreased the average time spent on pages. [**Contribution**] We explored
and evaluated the approach of visualizing other readers' attention focus
to help support new readers. Our results include interesting findings
on what works well, what does not and what could be enhanced. We
present improvement suggestions and ideas on where to focus follow-up
research on.

Keywords: Attention transfer · Software requirements specification ·
Requirements document · Eye tracking · Visualization · Empirical
study

1 Introduction

Specifications are the most important documents to ensure effective transfer of
requirements and knowledge to developers and other project participants in traditional, non-agile software projects [8]. After eliciting, interpreting and possibly
negotiating requirements, they are documented in a specification. These documents are read by a variety of roles: customers, software architects, UI-designers,
testers, etc. They read, review, and use the specification throughout the project
for several purposes [18]. Due to the variety of readers, specifications are mostly

© Springer Nature Switzerland AG 2020
N. Madhavji et al. (Eds.): REFSQ 2020, LNCS 12045, pp. 36–51, 2020.
https://doi.org/10.1007/978-3-030-44429-7_3

written in natural language to ensure common understandability. A good structure and writing style is essential for an efficient use. Several guidelines and heuristics already exist to support writing specifications. Templates provide useful structures and serve as a checklist to cover all important aspects. However, not enough research has yet been done in investigating how specifications are actually *used* and how this process can be improved.

We apply the approach of *attention transfer* to reading specifications to counteract this lack of focus on the process of using specifications and how to provide support for it. In a previous study we observed by eye tracking how readers use specifications and where they primarily focus on depending on their role in the project [3]. Now we use these data to generate helpful visualizations to support others when getting familiar with the same specification and help them to find relevant information more efficiently. In this paper, we report on an experiment with 29 student participants that we conducted to investigate the effect of three different attention visualization features in requirements specifications: (1) quick access buttons to quickly navigate to important sections, (2) heatmap bars to subtly visualize reading intensity next to paragraphs and (3) role icons to indicate relevance differences between roles.

All these visualizations were automatically generated based on the previously recorded eye tracking data, i.e., in this approach we use eye tracking operationally and not just for analysis. We measured how these features influenced the reading process of different readers with regard to their role: software architect, UI-designer and tester.

Main research question: Do visualizations of other readers' attention help developers to find relevant information for their task in requirements documents faster and navigate more efficiently?

The results show:

- The quick access buttons did not decrease the time spent on scrolling, but were, nevertheless, perceived as valuable by the participants.
- The heatmap bars decreased the average time spent per page and seemed to provide a good indicator of what is important on a fine-grained level.
- The role icons drew the readers' attention more towards sections highlighted by the buttons for their role and decreased attention on sections that were indicated as less relevant by the icons.

This paper is structured as follows: Sect. 2 gives an overview of related work. Section 3 describes our approach of creating attention visualizations on requirements specifications. The design of our conducted experiment is covered in Sect. 4, followed by the analysis and results in Sect. 5. In Sect. 6 the threats to validity that apply to our experiment are presented. Finally, Sect. 7 discusses our results and presents suggestions for future work and Sect. 8 concludes this paper.

2   Related Work

Software requirements specifications are read with different purposes, either to gain knowledge, detect defects, or to implement a design [18]. Several reading techniques already exist to support the reader in finding defects, such as ad-hoc reading, checklist-based reading, defect-based reading, perspective-based reading, or usage-based reading [18]. Guidelines and templates (e.g., Volere [13]) support writing and structuring specifications. However, only few authors have looked at the general reading and use of specifications. Gross et al. [10] conducted three explorative studies to investigate the information needs of different roles when reading a specification based on the TORE framework [1] and introduced the vision of *view-based requirements specifications*. Ahrens et al. [3] partially replicated their study and used eye tracking to observe readers with different roles when reading a specification created with a slightly adapted version of the Volere template [13]. Gotel and Marchese [9] suggested using visual representations of specifications, e.g., with word clouds, for a preliminary quality check.

   In this paper, we build on the findings where different readers focus on in specifications, and evaluate the approach to visualize their attention focus recorded by eye tracking in order to support new readers to use requirements specifications more efficiently and effectively. Hill and Hollan [11] introduced the terms *edit wear* and *read wear* to describe the history of modifying or looking at a document. They suggested to visualize this information with *attribute-mapped scroll bars* that show most edited or read areas by horizontal marks on the scroll bar. Based on that, DeLine et al. [7] developed the idea of *wear-based filtering*, i.e., filtering out parts that were less interacted with. They applied this approach to UML diagrams by highlighting class names with a heatmap, as well as to code by hiding less frequently accessed classes based on interaction history. Similarly, the Eclipse Plugin Mylyn [12] hides infrequently accessed classes dependent on the user's task based on a *task context model*. In addition to these approaches that make use of interaction history, some also use eye tracking to record and guide developer's attention. Eye tracking data provides richer and more fine-grained information about what people focus on than interaction contexts [5]. Hence, it can track attention on a more detailed level. However, so far these applications are limited to software maintenance [2], programming [6], code comprehension [15] and localization of bugs [16]. We explore the benefit of this approach for reading and using specifications.

3   Attention Visualizations on Requirements Specifications

Eye tracking can provide detailed insight about where people focus their attention on when working with a document or artifact [5]. Our approach is to use this information to generate helpful visualizations to guide readers on where to look at first, thereby support them to get familiar with the document and give them an indicator on what is most important. At the same time, this visualization of others' attention focus can also indicate what information has been overlooked so far and thus identify neglected requirements. Using eye tracking data of reading and using requirements specifications, we developed the following three different attention visualization features that aim at supporting new readers. Figure 1 shows a screenshot of each of them.

Quick Access Buttons: To ease navigation in the document and prevent time loss on scrolling and searching in the document, we analyzed between which distanced sections readers switch most often. These sections were provided as quick access buttons next to the document, so that when the reader clicked on the button with the respective section's heading, they could reach the position in the document directly without needing to scroll to it.

Heatmap Bars: We represented the reading intensity within sections using small heatmap bars next to the text to visualize not only an entire section's relevance, but also highlight focused parts within a section. These were calculated by counting the number of fixations in small, fixed-sized horizontal intervals and then interpolating these numbers using cubic spline interpolation. Finally, we used the interpolated values to calculate an RGB color from green (zero fixations) to yellow (50% of fixations) to red (maximum number of fixations within an interval in the document) for each pixel to create the heatmap bars. To mitigate the effect of outliers with an extremely high number of fixations, we reduced the maximum from 95 to 70 to get a more adequate distribution of red, yellow and green areas.

Role Icons: By considering the reader's role, we identified sections that significantly differed in reading intensity between the roles. Those were marked with attached role icons whose border was colored on a heatmap scale representing the reading time on a scale from green (short) to yellow (medium) to red (long).

Using Eye Tracking Data of a Previous Experiment: In a prior eye tracking experiment [3], we recorded the gaze data of ten subjects (8 computer science students, 2 professional developers) while reading two requirements specifications: one on screen and one on paper. The participants in that experiment

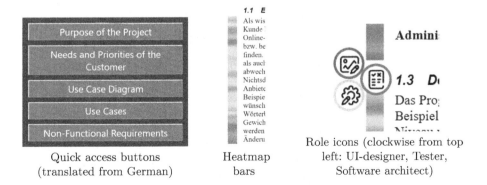

Quick access buttons (translated from German)   Heatmap bars   Role icons (clockwise from top left: UI-designer, Tester, Software architect)

Fig. 1. Attention visualizations based on eye tracking (Color figure online)

were assigned one of the following roles: software architect, UI designer, tester or developer. They were given a role-specific task to work on while reading the specification with a time limit of 20 min per specification. The software architect had to design a general architecture of the described software and draw a UML class diagram for it. The tester had the task to create test cases for the application, each specified with a setup, input and expected output. The UI-designer had to design mockups for the user interface and the participants with the developer role should work on all three tasks. For both the quick access buttons and the heatmap bars, we used the data of all four roles. For the quick access buttons, we focused on the data of the specification on paper because it gave the readers the option to freely switch and sort pages in an arbitrary order. For the role icons, we analyzed and represented the data of each role separately.

4   Experiment Design

Following the GQM paradigm [4], we started our experiment design by defining our research goal and refining it to questions and metrics. To ensure that the goal of our experiment is well-defined, we applied the goal template provided by Wohlin et al. [17].

> **Research Goal:**
> *Analyze* the effect of attention data representations based on eye tracking
> *for the purpose of* evaluation
> *with respect to* the efficiency of reading and using requirements specifications
> *from the point of view of* software architects, testers and UI designers
> *in the context of* a controlled experiment with computer science students.

4.1   Research Questions and Metrics

After defining the research goal, we formed research questions and refined these through metrics and hypotheses. Our three research questions are concerned with testing the three attention representations. We wanted to find out whether the features actually help the readers of requirements specifications or whether they have no or even a negative effect on them. We consider reading efficiency in terms of the two aspects navigating in the document and finding relevant information in it.

RQ1: Does a selection of quick access buttons help developers to navigate faster in specification documents?

RQ2: Does the visualization of reading intensities in the form of heatmap bars next to requirement specification sections help developers to find relevant information in the document faster?

RQ3: Do role dependent gaze time visualizations in the form of role icons attached to requirements specification sections help developers identify relevant sections for their particular task faster?

Table 1 shows an overview of all metrics that we took into account for each research question. The three metrics in the rightmost column were influenced by all three attention transfer features and were therefore analyzed collectively.

Table 1. Overview of questions and applied metrics

Research question	Metrics	
RQ1 Quick access buttons	Time spent on scrolling	
	Total number of page switches	
	Number of button uses	
	Avg. time spent on page after button use	
	Perceived value	
	Perceived detriment	Ease of finding relevant information for respective task
	Preference to have option to hide buttons	
	Preference to show all sections instead	
RQ2 Heatmap bars	Understandability of heatmap bars	Perceived clarity of specification presentation
	Avg. dwell time per page longer than 3 s	
	Correlation of total dwell time on each page with heatmap intensity	
	Perceived value	Perceived ease of getting acquainted with the document
	Perceived detriment	
	Preference to have an option to hide heatmap	
RQ3 Role Icons	Understandability of role icons	
	Dwell times on pages with role icons for each role	
	Perceived value	
	Perceived detriment	
	Preference to have an option to hide icons	

4.2 Hypotheses

For each metric that compares quantitative data, we stated hypotheses up front. They were used as a point of reference to compare results to.

H_1: The availability of quick access buttons reduces the time spent on scrolling. Readers can quickly and directly jump to often visited sections without needing to scroll and search for them and are hence assumed to save scroll time.

H_2: The availability of quick access buttons reduces the number of page switches. The buttons allow farther jumps through the document without going over each page in between.

H_3: Readers spend more time on pages that are directly accessed with the quick access buttons than on other pages. These are pages that were previously frequently accessed and are therefore assumed to be highly relevant.

H_4: The heatmap bars reduce the time spent on each page on average. Being provided the reading intensity of others, readers are assumed to find relevant parts and the information they are looking for more quickly.

H_5: Pages with a high heatmap intensity are visited longer than the same pages shown without the heatmap visualization. Analogously, pages with a low heatmap intensity are read less.

H_6: Role Icons lead to an increase (respectively decrease) of reading time from persons where the icon indicates a high (or low) relevance for their role.

4.3   Design

We conducted the study as a controlled experiment with between-group design with two groups. The control group read the specification as a normal PDF file without any attention transfer features. The treatment group read the same specification including all three features. All subjects were assigned one of the three roles that were also addressed in the initial study from which the eye tracking data were taken: software architect, tester and UI-designer [3]. Accordingly, they were assigned the same tasks to either create class diagrams of the application's architecture, specify test cases or design mock ups of the user interface.

4.4   Material

As study material, we used an 18-page long specification that was created in a four-month student software project. The template was a slightly adapted, mainly simplified version of the Volere template by Robertson and Robertson [13]. The software that is described in the specification is an application that is supposed to provide multiple translations and synonyms for a given word based on a number of online dictionaries.

We displayed the document in the browser using the PDF viewer script PDF.js[1] in order to provide a realistic environment to read the specification with still being able to track metrics automatically in the background. Figure 2 shows the experiment environment for the treatment group. As described above, the role icons were only displayed at sections where the reading intensity significantly differed between the roles. So in this example the second section in the screenshot has no icons attached because the reading intensities between all three roles were too similar. The environment for the control group looked exactly the same, except for the omitted quick access buttons on the top right and the heatmap bars and icons next to the paragraphs. Both were shown a timer with the remaining experiment time in the upper left corner of the web page. Underneath, there was a button to end the experiment prematurely.

4.5   Collecting Data for Metrics

The web page that displayed the specification tracked all quantitative raw data for our defined metrics automatically. This was done by creating a log in the background that kept track of information about page switches, as well as time-stamps of quick access button clicks, the time that the page was opened and the

---

[1] https://github.com/mozilla/pdf.js (accessed 07/16/2019).

time when the session ended. As soon as the subject opened the specification, a timer counted down to display the remaining time to read the specification. Once the timer hit zero or the participant ended the experiment, the log file was automatically retrieved.

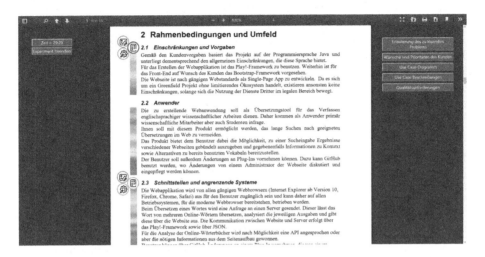

Fig. 2. Screenshot of experiment environment with attention visualizations

4.6   Subjects' Demography

Our sample consisted of 35 participants from which six data sets had to be excluded due to technical difficulties or unsuitability for the experiment because of a color vision deficiency or lack of knowledge of the German language. Since it was crucial to be able to distinguish red and green in the attention visualizations and the used specification was in German, we did not include the data of these subjects in our analysis. This left us with 29 subjects (23 male, 6 female). Most students were undergraduate computer science or technical computer science students and three were graduate electrical engineering and information technology students. All students successfully completed a preliminary course including theoretical knowledge about specifications, its contents and role in the development process. All subjects had at least an average level of knowledge of their task in the study as they stated in an initial questionnaire.

4.7   Setting and Procedure

The study was conducted as part of a course teaching software quality principles. Students could voluntarily take part in the experiment and as incentive they received a bonus point for the final exam of the course in return for participating in the experiment. However, getting the bonus point was in no way connected to how they performed in the experiment and students were informed that they could quit the experiment at any time without experiencing any disadvantage.

The participants were assigned as evenly as possible to the control and treatment group, as well as the three roles. That is, for both groups we had five participants per role except for the role UI-designer in the treatment group which was only represented by four participants. This inequality was caused by the necessary exclusion of data sets in the subsequent analysis process (see above).

Figure 3 shows the procedure of the experiment. Each session took about 40 min. For the treatment group, the task assignment additionally gave an explanation of the three attention transfer features. To bias participants as little as possible, it only stated that the visualizations are based on where others looked, not that they had to be used or necessarily indicate relevance.

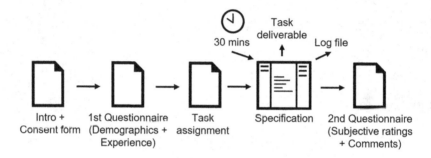

Fig. 3. Experiment process

5   Analysis and Results

Before analyzing and interpreting the results, we made sure that all completely and successfully recorded data are valid by manually checking subjects' deliverables, comments and log files. During this process, the above mentioned six participants were excluded from the analysis. The results of the analysis of the data sets of the remaining 29 subjects are described in this section.

Table 2 shows an overview of the results of the quantitative metrics for the control and treatment group. The rightmost column gives the U and p-values of performing an unpaired nonparametric Mann-Whitney test to test the hypotheses that we defined beforehand. We treated all Likert scales in our questionnaire as interval data because we only labeled the lowest and highest option. Since the options in between did not have a label, they were equidistant which allowed us to compute the mean and use statistical tests suitable for interval scaled data.

We divide the presentation of results according to the three research questions. Regarding the three metrics "ease of finding relevant information for the respective task", "perceived clarity of the specification representation" and "perceived ease of getting acquainted with the document", we did not find any effect.

RQ1 Quick Access Buttons: The quick access buttons were used by 12 of 14 participants of the treatment group for an average of 6.25 times (min = 1, max = 18). As shown in Table 2, the buttons did neither decrease the time spent on scrolling (**H1**), nor the total amount of page switches made during the 30 min of the experiment (**H2**). Apart from those metrics, we analyzed how long participants spent on pages they accessed over the quick access buttons. Since these are paired values we used a Wilcoxon signed rank test to test whether these pages are read longer than the pages accessed over normal page switches. We only considered subjects that used the quick access buttons more than twice to obtain representative values and no outliers. Pages accessed over the buttons were read for an average of 44.41 s $(SD = 29.17)$ and all the remaining pages were read for an average of 23.65 s $(SD = 10.74)$. In this case the Shapiro-Wilk test indicated a normal distribution with $p = .757$ and $p = .849$ respectively. Hence, we could perform a t-test resulting in $t(7) = 2.25$ and $p = .030$. With a significance level of 5%, we could thus reject the null hypothesis and show that

Table 2. Metrics results: perceived value from 1 = helpful to 5 = not helpful, perceived detriment from 1 = not annoying to 5 = annoying, preference to have option to hide the respective feature from 1 = yes to 5 = no; dashes denote not applicable metrics.

Metrics	Control group		Treatment group		Statistics	
	Mean	SD	Mean	SD	U	p
Scrolling time (Sum of page visits <3 s) [s]	37.14	16.59	40.49	19.03	94	.690
Total number of page switches	67.67	17.5	82.86	43.04	79	.876
Avg. number of quick access button uses	-	-	5.36	4.99	-	-
Perceived value of quick access buttons	-	-	1.93	1.21	-	-
Perceived detriment of quick access buttons	-	-	1.64	1.01	-	-
Preference to have an option to hide buttons	-	-	3.21	1.72	-	-
Preference to show a button for every section	-	-	3.07	1.64	-	-
Understandability of heatmap bars [1 = easily understandable, 5 = difficult to understand]	-	-	1.46	0.52	-	-
Avg. dwell time spent per page >3 s [s]	66.58	17.90	64.72	31.40	134	.109
Perceived value of heatmap bars	-	-	2.86	1.03	-	-
Perceived detriment of heatmap bars	-	-	2.62	1.12	-	-
Preference to have an option to hide heatmap	-	-	2.79	1.63	-	-
Understandability of role icons [1 = easily understandable, 5 = difficult to understand]	-	-	1.79	0.98	-	-
Perceived value of role icons	-	-	2.71	1.14	-	-
Perceived detriment of role icons	-	-	1.93	1.14	-	-
Preference to have an option to hide icons	-	-	3.14	1.75	-	-
Ease of finding relevant information for respective task [1 = easy, 10 = difficult]	4.60	2.85	4.86	1.75	95.5	.670
Perceived clarity of specification presentation [1 = clear, 10 = unclear]	3.87	1.92	3.79	2.01	109.5	.588
Perceived ease of getting acquainted with the document [1 = fast, 10 = slow]	3.93	2.02	4.21	2.72	103.5	.535

pages accessed over the quick access buttons are read longer than pages accessed over normal page switches (**H3**).

Although they did not decrease navigation effort, the participants still rated the quick access buttons as rather helpful and hardly annoying on average. When being asked if they wanted an option to be able to hide the buttons on demand or have all sections available as buttons instead of only most accessed ones, the responses were rather undecided. There were barely any ratings in the middle and the answers were almost evenly split between yes and no. Moreover, it can be noted that the treatment group spent more time on the last page that could be switched to with a button. This page was further away from the pages that readers tended to dwell on, i.e., the buttons helped to access it without the need to scroll through many pages.

RQ2 Heatmap Bars: As stated in the questionnaire, the heatmap bars were fairly easy to understand and their meaning was intuitively clear to the subjects. The results (see Table 2) also show that they decreased the average time spent on each page, even though not in a significant way (**H4**). This indicates that participants could find the information that they were looking for on each page faster than without the attention visualizations.

As an additional metric to evaluate the effect of the heatmap bars, we compared the total dwell time on each page for both groups. The values are shown in the bar chart in Fig. 4. Page 3 had a very high heatmap intensity and pages 5, 7, 8 and 14 had a medium heatmap intensity (i.e., some yellow areas), whereas for all remaining pages the heatmap bars were mostly green indicating a low intensity. Pages 3, 6, 7 and 14 were the pages that were accessible over the quick access buttons. As you can see in the diagram, pages 3 and 14 were looked at longer by the treatment group, while pages 5, 6, 7 and 8 were looked at longer by the control group on average. However, none of these differences is significant. That is, the heatmap bars do not generally increase the time spent on pages with many yellow areas, but they do increase the time spent on pages with many red areas (**H5**). Moreover, the subjective assessments of the metrics value and detriment of the heatmap bars were mostly somewhere in the middle between "helpful" and "not helpful" and "annoying" and "not annoying". Yet none of the subjects rated them as "not helpful" or "annoying".

RQ3 Role Icons: The role icons were rated as fairly easy to understand by the subjects, i.e., their meaning was intuitively clear to them. To quantitatively assess the effect of the role icons, we compared the average reading times of pages with role icons with the sections' relevance indicated by them. We took the reading times for both treatment and control group into account to determine whether the feature had an increasing or decreasing influence on the page's dwell time. To factor out the slightly differing total reading times of the specifications, we normalized the reading times for each participant for this purpose. These are shown in Fig. 5 and the relevance indicated by the icons on those pages is given in Table 3. By comparing the dwell times on the pages with role icons for the

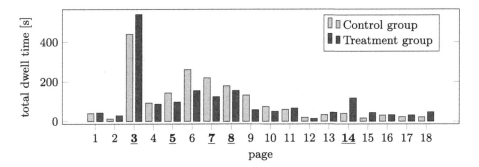

Fig. 4. Summarized time spent on each page (pages with high or medium heatmap intensity are marked with underlined bold page numbers)

two groups, you can see that they mostly had the intended effect to increase awareness on highlighted sections for the respective role and decrease attention on sections ranked as less relevant (**H6**). The only exceptions for this effect are pages that were generally looked at very long (see pages 5 and 6 for the role "software architect") or very briefly already (see pages 14, 15 and 17). However, these differences could not be proven significant given the small number of four or five subjects per role.

The ratings of the perceived value of the icons were mostly in the middle between "helpful" and not "helpful". Regarding the perceived detriment they were rated as hardly annoying on average. The option to be able to hide role icons on demand was favored by about half the participants.

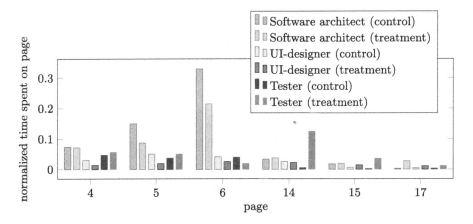

Fig. 5. Normalized average time spent on pages with role icons per role

Table 3. Relevance indicated by role icons (low = green, medium = yellow, high = red)

Page	Software architect	UI-designer	Tester
4	Medium	Low	High
5	Medium	Low	High
6	Medium	Low	Low
14	Low	Low	Medium
15	Low	Low	Medium
17	Medium	Low	Low

6   Threats to Validity

We distinguish threats to validity according to Wohlin et al. [17]:

Conclusion validity was ensured by testing on a 5% significance level and always making sure that required preconditions for statistical tests were given. To gain a high level of *internal validity*, all subjects read the same specification and got all introduction in written form to make sure they receive exactly the same information. However, the number of page switches or the time spent on each page might also be influenced by other unobserved, more individual factors. We tried to counteract this threat by choosing a homogeneous group and having multiple subjects for each role in the control and treatment group. Besides, we only considered dwell times longer than three seconds to measure the effect of the heatmap bars to exclude scrolling or mislead page switches.

One threat to *construct validity* might be that due to the design of our experiment, we cannot always clearly tell by which attention transfer feature an effect was caused since the treatment group was provided with all three of them and the control group with none. E.g., page 3 and 14 were highlighted by the quick access buttons and the heatmap bars. However, we assume that the reading time increase on page 14 was caused by the quick access buttons since to be affected by the heatmap bars, subjects had to already access that page in the first place. Page 3 on the other hand was in the beginning of the document, so readers usually came across that page anyway. We made this decision to also observe how the combination of multiple attention transfer features affect readers.

Regarding the *external validity*, it can be noted that our results are probably generalizable to other specification templates as well, as long as they contain mostly natural language. However, since we only considered student participants over a short period of time, the experiment should be replicated with people from industry with measuring the effect for longer than 30 min to ensure generalizability.

7 Discussion

The experiment that we conducted investigated the effect of three attention data representations. The quick access buttons did not have the intended effect to reduce time spent on navigation. Interestingly, they were still perceived as helpful by most subjects. Particularly, they increased attention to otherwise rather neglected specification parts further back in the document. That is, such a selection of quick access buttons can help to draw attention to relevant parts on back pages that otherwise might get overlooked. Since there was no clear preference on whether all sections should be accessible over buttons and if the participants want an option to hide the buttons on demand, we recommend providing both options to the specification readers, let them decide and investigate the usage in further research. Another option could also be to show all options and then highlight the most accessed ones.

The heatmap bars decreased the average time spent per page which indicates that they helped to directly focus on more relevant parts and spend less time reading rather irrelevant information. They also increased the dwell time on the page with many red highlighted areas, but not on the ones with many yellow areas consisting mostly of the pages with the use case diagram and the use case descriptions. This could mean that these artifacts are less suitable for this kind of attention visualization because the use case fields already give a suggestion of what is most important and the readers can easily filter themselves.

Regarding the role icons, it can be stated that for pages with an average reading time they had the intended effect of drawing the reader's attention to parts highlighted by the icon for their role or otherwise decrease the reading time if not highlighted for their role. However, some participants remarked that the icons' value was fairly limited due to the small number of them in the document. One subject also said that they "overloaded" the document. An alternative could be to show role-dependent heatmap bars instead of the icons. Generally, the results for this feature were neither clear-cut positive nor negative and their effect and perception need further investigation over longer periods of time.

For both the heatmap bars and the role icons it must be noted that they are supposed to serve as an entry point to ease getting acquainted with the specification, especially under time pressure. Hence, it is important that they are understood as such. It might make sense to offer an option to switch the features off in either case because once the reader is completely familiar with the document, the visualizations might be more distracting than helpful. However, this hypothesis still requires validation. Furthermore, the visualizations are based on where others looked at. Besides showing what is most relevant and where to start reading, this could also serve as an indicator to look at the parts that were not focused on yet to detect possibly neglected requirements.

In addition, further ways and visualizations of attention transfer should be explored to see if there are other options to guide the requirements document reading process by making use of others' attention data. One factor that should also be looked at is the effect on the reader's deliverables. It could be interesting to see whether their focus on artifacts change depending on what is highlighted and whether they save time overall. It might also be beneficial to use eye tracking to observe what the readers focus on with the attention representations in more detail. Moreover, other usage scenarios are possible as well, such as using attention visualizations to see what reviewers focused on to improve inspection. Since all these features can be generated automatically in a "By-Product Approach" [14], they could support the reader at a very low cost. With an option to switch them off on demand, users could evaluate for themselves whether they are of benefit for them and let them switched off otherwise.

8   Conclusion

In this work we explored the approach to transfer attention on requirements specifications and tested three attention representation features that were created based on eye tracking data: quick access buttons to most accessed sections, heatmap bars to visualize reading intensity and role icons to indicate a section's differing relevance for the roles software architect, UI-designer and tester. We evaluated their effect in an experiment with 29 computer science students reading a specification. Our results indicate different benefits from the three mechanisms investigated.

So far, eye tracking is yet too expensive and out of reach for everyday use. However, decreasing prices and sizes of eye tracking devices may soon make attention transfer features a valid choice for making requirements engineering work more productive.

References

1. Adam, S., Riegel, N., Doerr, J.: TORE - a framework for systematic requirements development in information systems. Requir. Eng. Mag. **4** (2014)
2. Ahrens, M., Schneider, K., Busch, M.: Attention in software maintenance: an eye tracking study. In: Proceedings of the 6th International Workshop on Eye Movements in Programming, pp. 2–9. IEEE (2019)
3. Ahrens, M., Schneider, K., Kiesling, S.: How do we read specifications? Experiences from an eye tracking study. In: Daneva, M., Pastor, O. (eds.) REFSQ 2016. LNCS, vol. 9619, pp. 301–317. Springer, Cham (2016). https://doi.org/10.1007/978-3-319-30282-9_21
4. Basili, V.R., Caldiera, G., Rombach, D.H.: The Goal Question Metric Approach, vol. I. Wiley, Hoboken (1994)
5. Bednarik, R.: Expertise-dependent visual attention strategies develop over time during debugging with multiple code representations. Int. J. Hum Comput Stud. **70**, 143–155 (2012)
6. Deitelhoff, F., Harrer, A.: Towards a dynamic help system: support of learners during programming tasks based upon historical eye-tracking data. In: 2018 IEEE 18th International Conference on Advanced Learning Technologies (ICALT), pp. 77–78. IEEE (2018)
7. DeLine, R., Khella, A., Czerwinski, M., Robertson, G.: Towards understanding programs through wear-based filtering. In: Proceedings of the 2005 ACM symposium on Software visualization - SoftVis2005, pp. 183–192. ACM, New York (2005)

8. Fricker, S.: Requirements value chains: stakeholder management and requirements engineering in software ecosystems. In: Wieringa, R., Persson, A. (eds.) REFSQ 2010. LNCS, vol. 6182, pp. 60–66. Springer, Heidelberg (2010). https://doi.org/10.1007/978-3-642-14192-8_7

9. Gotel, O.C.Z., Marchese, F.T.: Scouting requirements quality using visual representations. In: 13th International Conference on Information Visualization, pp. 519–526. IEEE (2009)

10. Gross, A., Doerr, J.: What you need is what you get!: the vision of view-based requirements specifications. In: 2012 20th IEEE International Requirements Engineering Conference (RE), pp. 171–180. IEEE (2012)

11. Hill, W.C., Hollan, J.D., Wroblewski, D., McCandless, T.: Edit wear and read wear. In: Proceedings of the SIGCHI conference on Human factors in Computing Systems, pp. 3–9. ACM (1992)

12. Kersten, M., Murphy, G.C.: Mylar: a degree-of-interest model for IDEs. In: Proceedings of the 4th International Conference on Aspect-Oriented Software Development, pp. 159–168. ACM, New York (2005)

13. Robertson, S., Robertson, J.: Mastering the Requirements Process. Addison-Wesley Professional, Boston (2012)

14. Schneider, K.: Rationale as a by-product. In: Dutoit, A.H., McCall, R., Mistrík, I., Paech, B. (eds.) Rationale Management in Software Engineering, pp. 91–109. Springer, Heidelberg (2006). https://doi.org/10.1007/978-3-540-30998-7_4

15. Schulte, C., Heinemann, B., Vrzakova, H., Budde, L., Bednarik, R.: Eye-movement modeling examples in source code comprehension: a classroom study. In: Proceedings of the 18th Koli Calling International Conference on Computing Education Research, pp. 1–8. ACM (2018)

16. Stein, R., Brennan, S.E.: Another person's eye gaze as a cue in solving programming problems. In: Proceedings of the 6th International Conference on Multimodal Interfaces - ICMI 2004, pp. 9–15 (2004)

17. Wohlin, C., Runeson, P., Höst, M., Ohlsson, M.C., Regnell, B., Wesslén, A.: Experimentation in Software Engineering. Springer, Heidelberg (2012). https://doi.org/10.1007/978-3-642-29044-2

18. Zhu, Y.M.: Software Reading Techniques. Springer, Heidelberg (2016)

Requirements Documentation

Hearing the Voice of Software Practitioners on Causes, Effects, and Practices to Deal with Documentation Debt

Nicolli Rios[1], Leonardo Mendes[2], Cristina Cerdeiral[2], Ana Patrícia F. Magalhães[8], Boris Perez[3,4], Darío Correal[3], Hernán Astudillo[5], Carolyn Seaman[6], Clemente Izurieta[7], Gleison Santos[2], and Rodrigo Oliveira Spínola[8(✉)]

[1] Federal University of Bahia, Salvador, BA, Brazil
nicollirioss@gmail.com
[2] Federal University of the State of Rio de Janeiro, Rio de Janeiro, RJ, Brazil
{leonardo.cabral,gleison.santos}@uniriotec.br,
cerdeiral@gmail.com
[3] University of Los Andes, Bogota, Colombia
{br.perez41,dcorreal}@uniandes.edu.co
[4] University Francisco de Paula Santander, Cúcuta, Colombia
[5] Univ. Técnica Federico Santa María, Valparaíso, Chile
hernan@inf.utfsm.cl
[6] University of Maryland Baltimore County, Baltimore, MD, USA
cseaman@umbc.edu
[7] Montana State University, Bozeman, MT, USA
clemente.izurieta@montana.edu
[8] Salvador University, Salvador, BA, Brazil
{ana.fontes,rodrigo.spinola}@unifacs.br

Abstract. **[Context and Motivation]** It is common for teams to take shortcuts during software development that, in the future, will lead to maintainability issues and affect productivity and development cost. Different types of technical debt may affect software projects, including those associated with software documentation. Although there are many studies on technical debt, few focus on documentation debt in an industrial environment. **[Question/Problem]** We aimed to identify how software practitioners perceive the occurrence of documentation debt in their projects. We present a combined analysis of the results from two complementary studies: a survey (*InsightTD*) and an interview-based case study. **[Principal Ideas/Results]** We provide a list of causes and effects of documentation debt, along with practices that can be used to deal with it during software development projects. **[Contribution]** We find that documentation debt is strongly related to requirements issues. Moreover, we propose a theoretical framework, which provides a comprehensive depiction of the documentation debt phenomenon.

Keywords: Documentation debt · Causes of documentation debt · Effects of documentation debt · Technical debt · InsightTD

N. Madhavji et al. (Eds.): REFSQ 2020, LNCS 12045, pp. 55–70, 2020.
https://doi.org/10.1007/978-3-030-44429-7_4

1 Introduction

The technical debt (TD) metaphor describes a daily challenge that software development teams face in their projects: balancing the costs for properly performing short-term product development activities with its long-term quality [1]. When the TD items incurred in a software project are identified, development teams will be able to understand their possible benefits or drawbacks to the project [3].

Different types of TD may affect software projects [4]. Some examples include design, architecture, testing, and documentation debt (DD). The latter is perceived as one of the four most important types in the embedded systems industry [5]. According to Seaman and Guo [7], DD refers to problems encountered in software project documentation looking for missing, inconsistent, outdated, or incomplete documentation.

Despite the growing number of studies in the area [8, 9], and particularly in the software industry [18, 19], little is still known about the impacts of TD [4]. Analyzing the TD phenomenon from the perspective of its causes, effects, and control practices deserves investigation because it is expected that TD prevention could sometimes be cheaper than TD repayment. Besides, when TD is prevented as much as possible, it also helps other TD management activities, and setting up TD prevention practices helps especially in catching inexperienced developers' not-so-good solutions [11]. Knowing the causes for TD can support development teams in defining actions that could be taken to prevent the occurrence of debt items. From the effects perspective, implications of TD can affect projects in different ways. Having this information could aid in prioritization of TD items to pay off, by supporting a more precise impact analysis and also the definition of corrective actions to minimize possible negative consequences for the project [12].

This paper contributes to this discussion from the perspective of DD. Defining, documenting and maintaining requirements is an important step in software engineering, and these critical activities form an integral part of producing high quality software. Thus, understanding DD will lead to decidedly better software. Although the lack of direct perceived benefits of a document to its producer is considered a base reason for many issues in software documentation [20, 21], it is also necessary to investigate other factors that can influence software documentation.

We investigate the causes, effects, and practices that can be employed to deal (prevent or pay the debt off) with this type of debt in the software industry. The research strategy adopted is based on the triangulation of the results of two complementary studies. The first study, *InsighTD*, is a globally distributed family of industrial surveys on TD [12]. For this article, we considered the data sets from Brazil, Chile, Colombia, and the United States. Although significant analysis has already been conducted over the available *InsighTD* data [12–14, 17], much still remains to be studied. The second study is an interview-based case study with practitioners from a large organization.

We provide a list of the top 10 DD causes (deadline being the most cited) and effects (low maintainability being the most cited) from *InsighTD* data. From the case study we identified 15 practices that can be used to deal with DD during a software development project, which corroborate with *InsightTD* participants' opinion that DD can be prevented. The case study provided six additional causes and one effect associated with DD. Results from both studies indicated a strong relationship between this type of debt and requirements issues in software projects. Moreover, based on the evidence we gathered from the data triangulation, we present a theoretical framework that depicts the DD phenomenon.

This paper is organized as follows: Sect. 2 presents a brief introduction to TD and the *InsighTD* project history, Sect. 3 presents the research strategy adopted, Sects. 4 and 5 describe and present our results, Sect. 6 discusses our main findings, Sect. 7 presents threats to the validity of the study, and finally, Sect. 8 presents our final considerations and next steps.

2 Background

2.1 Technical Debt

TD contextualizes the problem of pending software development tasks (for example, inexistent software documentation, tests not performed, non-adoption of good practices) as a type of debt that brings a short-term benefit to the project (usually in terms of higher productivity or shorter release times), but that may have to be paid later with interest in the development process (for example, the evolution of a poorly designed class tends to be more costly than if it was implemented considering good object-oriented design principles) [1, 7].

Alves *et al.* [9] identified that TD can occur in several artifacts throughout the life cycle of a software product. This paper focuses on the study of DD. The existing knowledge in the technical literature about this type of debt is still scarce, restricting itself to recognizing its existence and importance [4, 9]. In one of the few studies that specifically considered this type of debt, Spínola *et al.* [2] identified that DD cannot be automatically identified by current TD identification strategies based on the use of metrics. This paper sheds some light on this discussion by analyzing the causes and effects of DD, and practices that can be employed to prevent or address its existence.

2.2 The *InsighTD* Project

InsighTD is a globally distributed family of industrial surveys initiated in 2017. Planned cooperatively among TD researchers from around the world, the project aims to organize an open and generalizable set of empirical data on the state of practice and industry trends in the TD area. This data includes the causes that lead to TD occurrence, the effects of its existence, how these problems manifest themselves in the software development process, and how software development teams react when they are aware of the presence of debt items in their projects. Its design establishes the foundations for the survey to be continuously replicated in different countries. Up to date, researchers from 11 countries (Brazil, Chile, Colombia, Costa Rica, Finland, India, Italy, Norway, Saudi Arabia, Serbia, and the United States) have joined the project. At the moment, we have concluded data collections of the *InsighTD* replications in Brazil, Chile, Colombia, and the United States.

Rios *et al.* [12] discussed the basic survey design and the preliminary results of the first round of *InsighTD*. In that paper, the authors focused on the discussion on the top 10 causes and effects of TD, regardless the type of debt. *Rios et al.* [13] complemented the discussion of the previous work, focusing specifically on the causes and effects of TD in agile software projects. Rios *et al.* [14] proposed the use of cross-company probabilistic cause-effect diagrams to represent information about the TD causes and effects being analyzed. More Recently, Freire *et al.* [17] investigated preventive actions that can be used to curb the occurrence of TD and the impediments that hamper the use of those actions.

In this work, we go further into the analysis of *InsighTD* data by considering the point of view of the respondents about DD.

3   Research Strategy

3.1   Research Questions

We defined the following main Research Question (RQ) "How do software development teams perceive the occurrence of DD in their projects?" The goal of this RQ is to gather information on how practitioners face DD in their daily activities. To investigate it, we broke down this question into the following sub-questions:

RQ1: What are the main causes that lead development teams to incur DD in their projects? This question investigates the possible causes that contribute to the insertion of DD in software projects.
RQ2: What effects does DD have on software projects? This question is aimed at identifying the main effects felt by development teams due to the presence of DD.
RQ3: How often is the occurrence of DD items seen as preventable in software projects? Although DD can be incurred by choice –for example, to reduce costs or speed a release, it still has decidedly negative consequences on a project. In this question we explore our pre-conception that DD can be prevented, given a choice to do so, regardless of whether the DD item is intentional or unintentional. Through it, we explore practitioners' responses and have an indication on how often TD items could be prevented in their scenarios.
RQ4: What stage of a software development life cycle is most affected by the presence of DD? The documentation of a software project is a broad area, ranging from requirements specification to code comments. The purpose of this question is to investigate which stage of a software development life cycle has been more commonly seen as affected by DD.
RQ5: How can development teams react to the presence of DD? This question is aimed at identifying actions that can be used to deal (prevent or pay the debt off) with DD.

3.2   Method

The method is based on the combined analysis of the results from two complementary studies: a survey (*InsighTD*) and an interview-based case study, both with a population of software practitioners. While *InsighTD* allowed us to achieve a broad audience and collect answers to support the answering of RQ1, RQ2, RQ3, and RQ4, the interview study served to check and complement, through data triangulation, the findings from *InsighTD* and, also, to gather more contextual information to answer the RQ5. We chose to perform triangulation because it is an important tool for confirming the validity of conclusions [15].

Sections 4 and 5 describe the data collection and analysis procedures of each study as well as the obtained results. Then, Sect. 6 combines the results to answer the posed research questions. The empirical package of the survey and interview study containing their questions, answers/transcriptions, and codes are available at http://bit.ly/2uHv8x9.

4 Surveying Software Practitioners on Causes and Effects of Documentation Debt (*InsighTD*)

4.1 Data Collection

The data were collected in the context of the *InsighTD* project. The *InsighTD* questionnaire consists of 28 questions, previously described in [12]. Table 1 presents the subset of the survey's questions related to the context of this work. Q1 to Q8 capture the characterization questions, Q13 asks participants to provide an example of a TD item that occurred in their project and Q15 asks participants about the representativeness of that example. In Q16 to Q18 and Q20, the participants answer questions about causes and effects, respectively, considering the example provided in Q13. Finally, Q22 asks participants if the TD item (from Q13) could be prevented.

Table 1. Subset of the *InsighTD* survey questions considered in this paper.

No.	Question (Q)	Type
Q1	What is the size of your company?	Closed
Q2	In which country you are currently working?	Closed
Q3	What is the size of the system being developed in that project? (LOC)	Closed
Q4	What is the total number of people of this project?	Closed
Q5	What is the age of this system up to now or to when your involvement ended?	Closed
Q6	To which project role are you assigned in this project?	Closed
Q7	How do you rate your experience in this role?	Closed
Q8	Which of the following describes the development process model you follow on this project?	Closed
Q13	Give an example of TD that had a significant impact on the project that you have chosen to tell us about:	Open
Q15	About this example, how representative it is?	Closed
Q16	What was the immediate, or precipitating, cause of the example of TD you just described?	Open
Q17	What other cause or factor contributed to the immediate cause you described above?	Open
Q18	What other causes contributed either directly or indirectly to the occurrence of the TD example?	Open
Q20	Considering the TD item you described in question 13, what were the impacts felt in the project?	Open
Q22	Do you think it would be possible to prevent the type of debt you described in question 13?	Closed

The questionnaire was sent to only practitioners, because the objective of *InsighTD* is to investigate the state of the practice of TD. Some keywords related to software development activities and roles were used in LinkedIn to identify the participants. Also, invitations were sent to industry-affiliated member groups, mailing lists, and industry partners. The same strategy was applied in Brazil, Chile, Colombia, and the United States.

4.2 Data Analysis

The survey questionnaire consists of closed and open-ended questions. Therefore, it is necessary to adopt a series of different procedures to analyze the data. For the answers to the closed questions, descriptive statistics were used to understand the data, and then mode and median statistics were used for the central tendency of ordinal and interval data. For nominal data, the number of participants' choices about each option was calculated.

Qualitative data analysis techniques [15, 16] were applied to open-ended questions about causes and effects of TD. As the answers were unrelated to any previous expectations, an inductive logical approach was adopted. Then, manual coding was applied to the open questions as follows: initially, two researchers from each country (BR: authors N.R. and R.S., CH: B.P. and H.A., CO: B.P. and D.C., and US: N.R. and C.S.) individually coded the set of all answers for two subsets of related questions (RQ1: Q16 + Q17 + Q18 and RQ2: Q20). This involves open coding as described in [16] and axial coding to derive higher level categories. They then discussed possible differences in their coding until they reached consensus. Thus, the answers were coded and the emerged concepts (causes/effects) were organized into a hierarchy of categories. This process was performed until the point where no new code or category was identified.

4.3 Results

Characterization of the Participants. In total, 39 participants from *InsighTD* replications in Brazil, Chile, Colombia, and the United States answered questions about DD. Participants are well distributed among small (28%), medium (41%), and large (31%) companies. Looking at the data in more detail, we can see that most (mode) participants work in organizations with more than 2,000 employees (9 participants) and 11–50 employees (9), closely followed by 51–250 companies (7), and 251–500 employees (7). The average size of organizations is 251 to 500 employees. Therefore, participants tend to work in larger companies, but there are representatives of companies of all sizes.

Responses to Q3 on the system size, most participants indicated that the systems had between 10–100 KLOC (36%), followed by smaller systems (<10 KLOC - 26%). The results also indicated a significant sample of responses for larger systems (1–10 MLOC - 18%) (>10 MLOC - 5%). Responses to Q4 on the size of development teams that participants tend to work, most (31%) reported working in teams 5–9 people, followed by less than five members of staff (26%). There is also a good sample in teams of 10–30 people (20%) and larger development teams with more than 30 professionals (23%). Responding to Q5 about the age of the system developed in the project, most indicated age 2 to 5 years (33%). There are also a significant number of systems represented from 1 to 2 years (26%), closely followed by less than one year (20%). About 18% of participants indicated working on projects for more than 10 years.

Regarding the role assumed by the participants in their projects (Q6), several types of project roles were indicated in the results. Most of them work as a developer (46%), followed by project leader/project manager (18%), architect software (7%), test manager/tester (7%), and requirements analyst (7%). In response to Q7, results show that a significant portion of the sample is Proficient, Competent or Expert (92% of the total), indicating that, in general, the questionnaire was answered by professionals with experience in their roles. On the other hand, answers from professionals with low experience level (8%) were also obtained.

Finally, the responses to Q8 indicate that of the 39 respondents, 15 participated in projects that adopted agile process models (38%) and 15 indicated the use of hybrid process models (38%). Less common is the use of a traditional process (24%).

Thus, in general, although it is not possible to guarantee that the participants represent all the professionals in the software industry from Brazil, Chile, Colombia, and the United States, respondents characterize a broad and diverse audience that spans different functions and participant experience levels, different sizes of organizations and projects of different ages, sizes, team sizes, and process models.

What are the main causes that lead development teams to incur DD in their projects (RQ1)? In total, as informed by the participants in Q16–18, there are 37 causes that lead development teams to incur DD in their projects. The ten most commonly cited causes are displayed in Table 2 (the complete list can be accessed at http://bit.ly/2BtHglx). *Deadline* is the most cited cause. This indicates that it is a factor that normally contributes to the occurrence of DD items. The *company does not give importance to documentation* and *non-adoption of good practices* are other causes cited by at least 13% of the participants.

Table 2. Top 10 documentation debt causes cited.

Rank	Documentation debt cause	# of citations	Confirmed in interview based case study?
1st	Deadline	12	Yes
2nd	The company does not give importance to documentation	6	Yes
3rd	Non-adoption of good practices	5	Yes
4th	Inaccurate time estimate	4	Yes
5th	Inappropriate planning	4	Yes
6th	Outdated/incomplete documentation	4	Yes
7th	Team Overload	4	Yes
8th	Nonexistent documentation	3	Yes
9th	Not effective project management	3	Yes
10th	Poor allocation of resources	3	Yes

We can also observe in Table 2 that practitioners also commonly cited other causes like *inaccurate time estimate*, *inappropriate planning*, *outdated/incomplete documentation*, and *team overload*. The results of the data triangulation with the interview-based case study, partially presented in the fourth column, is discussed in Sect. 5.3.

What effects does DD have on software projects (RQ2)? In total, as informed by the participants in Q20, there are 24 effects of DD in software projects. Table 3 shows the ten most commonly cited effects (the complete list can be accessed at http://bit.ly/2BtHglx). Two effects stood out: *low maintainability* and *delivery delay*. *Low maintainability* encompasses problems that occur during software maintenance activities, such as an increased effort to fix bugs as well as limitations in system evolution. *Delivery delay* refers to the non-fulfillment of the deadlines agreed upon with the customer.

We can also observe in Table 3 that, in the point of view of the practitioners, *rework*, *low external quality* and *inadequate/nonexistent/outdated documentation* are issues that commonly affect software projects in the presence of DD. Also, there are three effects related to relations among people: *developer dependency* and *stress with stakeholders*. Thus, practitioners see that the presence of DD can harm the work environment.

How often is the occurrence of DD items seen as preventable in software projects (RQ3)? Answers to Q22 (yes/no question) of *InsighTD* indicated that DD could be prevented for most of the cases (95%). The two participants that reported that their DD items could not be prevented indicated cost as the main reason: *"the development team does not have the documentation updated because it needs to be more productive to do not lose the contract"* and that *"the effort needed to be invested to maintain the documentation updated is too high."*

Table 3. Top 10 documentation debt effects cited.

Rank	Documentation debt effects	# of citations	Confirmed in interview based case study?
1st	Low maintainability	9	Yes
2nd	Delivery delay	8	Yes
3rd	Rework	5	Yes
4th	Low external quality	4	Yes
5th	Inadequate/nonexistent/outdated documentation	3	Yes
6th	Developer Dependency	2	Yes
7th	Difficulty conducting tests	2	Yes
8th	Increased effort	2	Yes
9th	Need of refactoring	2	No
10th	Stress with stakeholders	2	Yes

Answers to RQ5 in the interview-based case study, discussed in Sect. 5.3, complement this result by indicating some practices that can be used to prevent DD.

What stage of a software development life cycle is most affected by the presence of DD (RQ4)? Results from *InsighTD* indicate a strong relationship between DD and requirements issues. By analyzing the answers of participants to Q13, about 53% of them reported requirements issues in their examples of DD. Some examples are: *"Little clarity and specificity in the definition of requirements," "Having to create code that* *was not stipulated, since the requirement was not considered in the documentation,"* and *"The lack of documentation and understanding of the requirements in the analysis and design activities caused rework in the construction of the prototypes."* Besides, all participants reported in Q15 that those instances of debt occur often or very often in their projects.

Other commonly cited software development areas (in Q13) affected by the presence of DD are design (10%), code comment (7%), testing (5%), and architecture (2%). We could not identify the specific area for 23% of the responses because they were about documentation in general (e.g.: *"hard maintenance and future change due to poor documentation from the development team"* and *"do not keep the documentation updated"*).

5 Interview-Based Case Study

This study complements the results obtained with *InsighTD* by (i) identifying new evidence to confirm causes and effects, and (ii) identifying practices that can be employed to prevent or deal with DD in software projects.

5.1 Data Collection

Data collection was performed through face-to-face interviews considering four open-ended questions. All interviews were recorded, with previous authorization of the participants, and then transcribed. Next, the transcripts were validated by their corresponding interviewees through peer reviews. The interviews were performed in Portuguese as well as their data analysis. Only the results were translated to English. The author L.M. translated the results (and also the text fragments used in this article), which were reviewed by the author G.S.

The first three questions address the characterization of the organization's development process: (P1) *"Does the organization adopt any project management methodology (traditional/agile)? If so, which one?"*; (P2) *"Did the organization define processes for software development? How are they performed?"*; (P3) *"How is the documentation process carried out in the organization and how are the documents prepared for each phase of the software life cycle?"* Finally, we characterized the issues found in the execution of processes in the organization: (P4) *"Are those involved in the software development process aware of the problems that may arise from not adopting adequate documentation? If so, could you cite possible causes and effects?"*

5.2 Data Analysis

The data analysis began with transcription of interviews and approval by participants. Then, we coded the content of the transcripts [16]. The coding considered excerpts of the transcriptions containing evidence on causes, effects and practices to deal with DD. Then, we grouped the identified causes, effects and practices.

The following example illustrates how we performed the coding of causes: *"We need to go fast with the development process, so we went directly to the testing phase.*

As consequence, the <u>documentation of the project was inappropriate</u>." The underlined fragments support the codes: *inappropriate documentation* and *focus on producing more at the expense of quality.*

The coding was done by the author L.M. The author G.S. reviewed all citations and codes. Participants were also asked to validate the results obtained. In the end, the codes identified for causes and effects were standardized considering the nomenclature obtained from the *InsighTD* results. This standardization was performed by the authors L.M. and R.S., who were involved in each of the studies.

5.3 Results

Execution. Participants were advised to feel free to talk about work processes and documentation issues. Participants allowed the interviews to be recorded and signed a Consent and Participation document. Each participant was interviewed individually, and the interviews took about 30 min.

The defined questions (P1–4) were performed sequentially. The researcher responsible for conducting the interviews complemented the questions with brief comments to adapt them to the working reality of the interviewees. During the interviews, new questions were formulated for gathering more details as needed (e.g.: "*Is there any practical situation that generated a problem with the documentation?*").

Characterization of the Participants. Four software practitioners who have worked as project manager, systems analyst, developer, and tester for 7, 2, 1 and 14 years, respectively, participated in the study. The selection of participants was made by convenience. Our main selection criterion was having answers from practitioners with different responsibilities in the development process and with different levels of experience. The four participants worked on the same development team and reported their experiences with both traditional and agile methods. All participants also indicated that the existing development processes are not followed.

The software organization where the study was conducted operates in the public health area. The study was conducted specifically in one of the software development areas. We selected the organization by convenience. The second author works in the organization, but in a different unit from the interviewees. In addition, we chose a public organization because the staff had little turnover so that we could better observe the influence of organizational culture on development processes.

The product used as a reference by the participants was an academic management system of the organization. The organization started the development of the product in 2009 and it has been maintained by the organization since 2014. The system is currently in production, but some of its modules are being refactored.

What are the main causes that lead development teams to incur DD in their projects (RQ1)? The participants reported 23 causes that contribute to the occurrence of DD. Participants reported, for example, the situation of a specific project that had three consecutive management changes during its implementation. The changes were mainly characterized by unsuccessful attempts to implement different development methods (agile and traditional). These consecutive management changes were characterized as one possible cause and were coded as *changes in management during the project*. The interviewed project manager, systems analyst, and developer stated that the organization did not have well-defined processes (*lack of a well-defined process*). *Deadline*, one of the causes reported by all participants, is considered responsible for most of the problems faced by the teams.

Participants were unanimous in stating that all team members were aware of documentation problems in their projects. The systems analyst said that, while practitioners are aware of the problems, there were negligence in not trying to solve them (*the company does not give importance to documentation*).

Table 2 presents ten of the causes identified in this study that are among those most commonly cited by *InsighTD* participants. The complete list of all identified causes can be accessed at http://bit.ly/2BtHglx. Seventeen common causes were identified between the two studies, and six were uniquely identified in the interviews: *inappropriate documentation, unknown legal requirements that affect the existing documentation, delays in the project, tacit knowledge not documented, changes in management during the project,* and *political issues.*

What effects does DD have on software projects (RQ2)? Participants reported 15 effects of DD. Nine of them are among those most cited by *InsighTD* participants as can be observed in Table 3. Only one of the reported effects had not been previously identified in *InsighTD*: *communication issues among team members.*

Some of the most critical effects reported by participants in this study were: *project does not serve customer, developer dependency, difficulty in project development, lack of understanding,* and *increased effort to maintain the product.*

How can development teams react to the presence of DD (RQ3 and RQ5)? We identified 15 practices (Table 4) that have been used by the organization to address software documentation issues and could be employed to deal with (prevention or payment) DD.

Most of the identified practices refer to preventive actions, as can be seen in the second column of Table 4. This result complements the indication provided by *InsighTD* participants that DD can be prevented. We can also observe that, from the point of view of the participants, the preventive actions usually have a well-defined documentation process. We also highlight the need of having the commitment from people responsible for documenting activities. To improve the commitment, one possible solution would be to increase the incentives to produce the documentation, and further, developers must feel how these improvements are a benefit to themselves [20, 21]. From Table 4, we see that only three practices are focused on debt payment.

What stage of a software development life cycle is most affected by the presence of DD (RQ4)? The interview-based case study confirmed the results from *InsighTD* for this question. Thus, participants also indicated during the interviews that DD is related to several areas of software development (requirements, design, coding, test, and maintenance). Particularly, the identified causes (~91% of them), effects (~80%), and practices (~87%) are almost all related to requirement issues as confirmed by the participants after we reported the results to them.

Table 4. List of practices.

Practices	Prevention/payment
Adopt TD payment prioritization criteria	Payment
Comment the code	Prevention
Create tutorials on how to fill in the documentation	Prevention
Define process and good practices for documentation	Prevention
Define roles concerning the documentation process	Prevention
Document the project since its begin	Prevention
Have a documentation repository	Prevention
Improve commitment of the team concerning documentation	Prevention
Involve several roles in documenting the project	Prevention
Keep the documentation updated	Payment
Penalties if not follow the documentation process	Prevention
Review outdated documentation	Payment
Training on the problems by don't document	Prevention
Use of Peer review	Prevention
Use of UML to document and share information	Prevention

6 Discussion

There is a clear need for research that consolidates data collected from empirical studies in the software industry. Results from both studies presented in this paper indicate that, from the point of view of software practitioners, DD can be prevented. Further, although practitioners are particularly concerned about requirements issues, we also found that DD can affect other areas of software development projects.

The aforementioned results stimulated us to organize the data (causes, effects, and practices) collected from both studies into a theoretical framework of DD, which is presented in the next subsection.

6.1 Theoretical Framework of Documentation Debt

Figure 1 summarizes the theoretical framework developed from this research. The framework aims to provide a comprehensive depiction of the DD phenomenon. It consists of causes that can lead development teams to incur DD in their projects, effects that can be felt in its presence, and, also, practices that can be employed to prevent or eliminate items of debt present in projects. The organization of causes and effects into groups (e.g.: development issues, methodology, people issues, external quality issues) followed the categories proposed by Rios *et al.* [12].

As a conceptual device, the framework can be employed to inform action in response to perceived DD, and as a comprehensive guide when assessing software development

Fig. 1. Theoretical framework of documentation debt.

practices. The framework facilitates more effective identification and acknowledgement of DD by highlighting aspects of software development that impact or is impacted by the presence of the debt.

By assisting in making the DD visible, as a communication device, the framework can be used to support development teams to more effectively communicate technical problems to management, and for managers to make better-informed decisions concerning DD.

7 Threats to Validity

As in any empirical study, there are threats to validity [6] in this work. We attempted to remove them when possible and mitigate their effect when removal was not possible. In this work, the primary threat to conclusion validity arises from the coding process as coding is mainly a creative task. To mitigate this threat, in *InsighTD*, the coding process was performed individually by two researchers and reviewed by one experienced researcher. In the interview-based case study, the coding process was performed by one researcher and reviewed by one experienced researcher. The recording/transcription process could raise threats too. We reduced them by validating the transcriptions with a peer review process involving the corresponding interviewees. Lastly, the data triangulation activities were performed by one researcher from each study, who also discussed their results until consensus was reached.

Concerning the internal validity, the questionnaire represents the main threat that could affect *InsighTD*. As indicated in [12], the questionnaire has direct questions, avoiding misunderstanding that could lead to meaningless answers. Besides, the questionnaire has passed through successive validation tasks (three internal and one external) and a pilot study to detect any inconsistencies or misunderstandings before executing the survey.

Finally, we reduced the external validity threats by targeting industry professionals and seeking to achieve participant diversity among the respondents. In *InsighTD*, we approached 39 practitioners from replications of the questionnaire in Brazil, Chile, Colombia, and the United States. The interview-based case study had the participation of four practitioners with different roles and levels of experience. Although the population provides interesting results on DD, we still cannot generalize the results. In search of more generalizable results, the *InsighTD* is now being replicated in Finland and Costa Rica.

8 Final Remarks

Documentation debt is a type of debt that still suffers from a lack of empirical evidence from software industry. This article approached this gap by triangulating results from two complementary studies with software practitioners. Results include the indication that we can prevent DD and that it affects several software development areas but specially requirements. Moreover, we defined a theoretical framework of DD, which presents the DD phenomenon in a more complete and comprehensive form.

For the practitioner community, the framework helps to realize the utility of technical debt as a tool for conceptualization, communication, and management. It can be used as tool to understand the reasons that lead development teams to incur in debt, which are the possible effects of its presence, and what actions can be taken to prevent or pay the debt off.

The next steps of this research include the analyses of *InsighTD* data collected from replications in Costa Rica and Finland. We also intend to run a follow up study in one of our industry partners based on the results reported in this article. Lastly, based on the conceptual framework presented in Fig. 1, we are also planning to look into relating causes, effects, and practices more directly to each other.

Acknowledgements. This work was partially supported by the Coordination for the Improvement of Higher Education Personnel - Brazil (Capes), under the Capes/IIASA Sandwich Doctoral Program, process n° 88881.189667/2018-01. This research was also supported in part by funds received from the David A. Wilson Award for Excellence in Teaching and Learning, which was created by the Laureate International Universities network to support research focused on teaching and learning. For more information on the award or Laureate, please visit www.laureate.net.

References

1. Kruchten, P., Nord, R., Ozkaya, I.: Technical debt: from metaphor to theory and practice. IEEE Softw. **29**(6), 18–21 (2012). https://doi.org/10.1109/MS.2012.167
2. Spínola, R.O., Zazworka, N., Vetro, A., Shull, F., Seaman, C.: Understanding automated and human-based technical debt identification approaches-a two-phase study. J. Braz. Comput. Soc. **25** (2019). https://doi.org/10.1186/s13173-019-0087-5
3. Ernst, N.A., Bellomo, S., Ozkaya, I., Nord, R.L., Gorton, I.: Measure it? Manage it? Ignore it? Software practitioners and technical debt. In: Proceedings of the 2015 10th Joint Meeting on Foundations of Software Engineering, ESEC/FSE 2015, pp. 50–60. ACM, New York (2015). https://doi.org/10.1145/2786805.2786848
4. Rios, N., Mendonça, M.G., Spínola, R.O.: A tertiary study on technical debt: types, management strategies, research trends, and base information for practitioners. Inf. Softw. Technol. **102**, 117–145 (2018). https://doi.org/10.1016/j.infsof.2018.05.010. ISSN 0950-5849
5. Ampatzoglou, A., et al.: The perception of technical debt in the embedded systems domain: an industrial case study. In: 8th International Workshop on Managing Technical Debt. IEEE (2016)
6. Wohlin, C., Runeson, P., Höst, M., Ohlsson, M.C., Regnell, B., Wesslén, A.: Experimentation in Software Engineering: An Introduction. Springer, Heidelberg (2012). https://doi.org/10.1007/978-3-642-29044-2
7. Seaman, C., Guo, Y.: Measuring and monitoring technical debt. Adv. Comput. **82**, 22 (2011)
8. Li, Z., Avgeriou, P., Liang, P.: A systematic mapping study on technical debt and its management. J. Syst. Softw. **101**, 193–220 (2015)
9. Alves, N.S.R., Mendes, T.S., de Mendonça, M.G., Spínola, R.O., Shull, F., Seaman, C.: Identification and management of technical debt: a systematic mapping study. Inf. Softw. Technol. **70**, 100–121 (2016). https://doi.org/10.1016/j.infsof.2015.10.008
10. Avgeriou, P., Kruchten, P., Ozkaya, I., Seaman, C.: Managing technical debt in software engineering (dagstuhl seminar 16162). In: Dagstuhl Reports, vol. 6, no. 4. Schloss Dagstuhl-Leibniz-Zentrum fuer Informatik (2016)
11. Yli-Huumo, J., Maglyas, A., Smolander, K.: How do software development teams manage technical debt? An empirical study. J. Syst. Soft. **120**, 195–218 (2016)
12. Rios, N., Spínola, R.O., Mendonça, M.G., Seaman, C.: The most common causes and effects of technical debt: first results from a global family of industrial surveys. In: The Proceedings of the 12th International Symposium on Empirical Software Engineering and Measurement, Oulu, p. 10. ACM, New York (2018). https://doi.org/10.1145/3239235.3268917. Article no. 39
13. Rios, N., Mendonça, M., Seaman, C., Spínola, R.O.: Causes and effects of the presence of technical debt in agile software projects. In: The Americas Conference on Information Systems (AMCIS), Cancun (2019)
14. Rios, N., Spínola, R.O., Mendonça, M.G., Seaman, C.: Supporting analysis of technical debt causes and effects with cross-company probabilistic cause-effect diagrams. In: Proceedings of the Second International Conference on Technical Debt (TechDebt 2019), pp. 3–12. IEEE Press, Piscataway (2019). https://doi.org/10.1109/techdebt.2019.00009
15. Seaman, C.: Qualitative methods in empirical studies of software engineering. IEEE Trans. Softw. Eng. **25**(4), 557–572 (1999). https://doi.org/10.1109/32.799955

16. Strauss, A., Corbin, J.M.: Basics of Qualitative Research: Techniques and Procedures for Developing Grounded Theory. Sage Publications, Thousand Oaks (1998)
17. Freire, S., et al.: Actions and impediments for technical debt prevention: results from a global family of industrial surveys. To appear in the Proceedings of the 35th ACM/SIGAPP Symposium on Applied Computing
18. Klotins, E., et al.: Exploration of technical debt in start-ups. In: Proceedings of the 40th International Conference on Software Engineering: Software Engineering in Practice (ICSE-SEIP 2018), pp. 75–84. ACM, New York (2018)
19. Nayebi, M., et al.: A longitudinal study of identifying and paying down architecture debt. In: Proceedings of the 41st International Conference on Software Engineering: Software Engineering in Practice, pp. 171–180. IEEE Press (2019). https://doi.org/10.1109/ICSE-SEIP. 2019.00026
20. Arkley, P., Riddle, S.: Overcoming the traceability benefit problem. In: The Proceedings of the 13th IEEE International Conference on Requirements Engineering (RE 2005), Paris, France (2005). https://doi.org/10.1109/re.2005.49
21. Berry, D.M., Czarnecki, K., Antkiewicz, M., Abdelrazik, M.: The problem of the lack of benefit of a document to its producer. In: Proceedings of the IEEE International Conference on Software Science, Technology and Engineering, Beer-Sheva, Israel (2016). https://doi.org/ 10.1109/swste.2016.14

Innovation Workshop Documentation for Following Software Engineering Activities

Patrick Mennig[(⊠)] and Claudia Nass

Fraunhofer IESE, Fraunhofer-Platz 1, 67663 Kaiserslautern, Germany
{patrick.mennig,claudia.nass}@iese.fraunhofer.de

Abstract. [**Context & motivation**] Requirements engineering (RE) can be seen as creative problem solving (CPS), overlapping with user experience (UX) and design activities. Creative processes, such as innovation workshops (IWs), are often facilitated group activities. They provide an understanding of challenges and user needs, leading to increased software quality. A large number of results from IWs needs to be documented in a suitable manner for later use, as not all results can be followed up upon immediately. [**Question/problem**] With current means of IW documentation, it is hard to extract the required information (e.g., photo minutes), or they are inefficient to produce or digest (e.g., audio and video recordings, textual documentation). Documentation of only the results leads to the loss of any discussions, decisions, reasons, and discarded alternatives, as these are usually not written down during an IW. The interpretation of the documentation depends on the viewer's memory and understanding of the IW and the results, which is prone to misinterpretation and errors unless enriched with context information from the IW planning. [**Principal ideas/results**] We explored the limitations of IW documentation during a workshop with 29 experts from the usability and UX domain. Problems with using the results in later software engineering (SE), RE, and UX activities arise from misalignment between IW result documentation and activity requirements. The experts created a set of initial solution ideas, but no concrete solutions. [**Contributions**] We address the need for reasonable methods for documenting the results of IWs so that they can be used efficiently in later activities. The design and preliminary results of the expert workshop are presented. Furthermore, we discuss a research roadmap towards making targeted improvements to IW documentation by understanding subsequent activities.

Keywords: Requirements engineering · Documentation · Creative problem solving · Innovation workshop · Creativity workshop

1 Creative Problem Solving

Many activities in software engineering (SE) are related to creative problem solving (CPS) [10]. Requirements engineering (RE) and user experience (UX) rely

© Springer Nature Switzerland AG 2020
N. Madhavji et al. (Eds.): REFSQ 2020, LNCS 12045, pp. 71–77, 2020.
https://doi.org/10.1007/978-3-030-44429-7_5

on an increasing number of methods that involve interdisciplinary teams engaging in collaborative face-to-face activities [6]. Design thinking, design sprints and innovation workshops (IWs) [4,11] provide methodologies for solving business and design problems alike [3]. These involve many different methods (e.g., affinity diagrams, card sorting, brainstorming, brainwriting, storyboarding, low-fidelity prototypes, etc.) centered around face-to-face communication and the use of analog materials. Their success lies in their ease of application, as a team of professionals from disciplines such as RE, UX, and design can follow a structured approach to solving complex problems. IWs help to understand challenges, user needs, and requirements. One aspect that we think deserves more attention from both research and practice is the integration of these methods' results into subsequent SE, RE, and UX activities. Karras et al. mention that written requirements specifications lack communication richness and effectiveness, and propose the use of videos in RE [7], especially for communicating project visions. Ideas found in IW an to be used in subsequent SE activities, are often expressed as concepts or goals, rather than concrete requirements, and need to be transformed [12]. Barrios et al. note that, in order to be capitalized on, results from IW need to be formalized and conserved [2].

2   Problem

In our business practice, we have conducted more than 40 IWs with different clients from research and industry in various domains, and have observed that many organizations struggle with actually implementing solutions found in CPS activities in later project stages. Actually utilizing the results in subsequent activities highly depends on whether they have been documented in a suitable manner. Typically, results created in IWs are built on initial hypotheses (e.g., problem statements, user needs, solution approaches) that need to be verified later on. Potential solutions need to be tested for their feasibility and applicability. Hence, appropriate documentation of workshop results and its availability is crucial for facilitating later processing and later application.

During an IW, participants create a large number of different artifacts. Within a typical two-day workshop, interdisciplinary teams compile a list of challenges (typically 30–60), analyze some of these challenges in detail (3–9), come up with many different initial solution ideas (approx. 600), select a subset of promising ideas, create storyboards or low-fidelity prototypes, and assess the solutions through presentations and discussions [1]. During face-to-face group activities, participants discuss the problems, ideas, and solutions, form mental models, bring in their own professional experience and background knowledge, and reason about the inclusion and exclusion of aspects found during and before the workshop. Even though many results are written down on sticky notes, paper cards, flipchart paper, and whiteboard walls, we observe that these often lack detail and only serve as mental anchors during the IW. Participants are busy following the creative process. Writing down details of their discussions that are not of immediate use slows down their thought processes, hence these are usually omitted.

Memories of details known during an IW fade with the time passing until its results are picked up or until subsequent activities are to be performed. One obvious means of documenting IWs is to take pictures of any results created, but these can only cover what is actually written down. Dedicating one participant to the documentation pulls her out of the group activity. Having a separate person (e.g., a co-moderator) doing the documentation can impose feelings of being observed or monitored. Audio and video recordings would provide the most detailed form of documentation, but a typical two-day IW with three sub-groups leads to about 42 h of recorded material. In order to make it usable, it has to be processed after the IW, either manually, increasing the cost (in person-hours) of the workshop by a large amount, or with the help of automation [8].

A more effective way of documenting IW results would enable them to be used more efficiently in subsequent activities, and in turn increase the applicability of IWs in RE. Understanding the requirements of the subsequent activities using these outcomes allows making targeted improvements to the way IW are documented. To collect initial evidence in support of this idea, we conducted an expert workshop.

3   Method

A workshop with usability and UX experts was held in which they discussed and analyzed the challenge and came up with initial solution ideas by applying CPS methods themselves. The workshop took place at the 2019 "Mensch und Computer (MuC)" conference held in Hamburg, Germany, and was part of the Usability Professionals (UP) track. Twenty-eight experts (23 female, 5 male) and two moderators were present throughout the 90-min workshop. One expert (female) joined later. Twenty-one disclosed their affiliation with a professional organization or company, two with a research institute or university, and six did not disclose their affiliation.

Session 1: At first, the problem of incomplete documentation was presented to the attendants in order to establish a common understanding of the goal of this expert workshop. In a twenty-minute presentation, we presented our typical approach to structuring two-day creativity processes [1,4]. We used the photo minutes of an example IW held in October 2018 about a ridesharing solution in small communities, and showed images from the photo minutes for each phase of the IW. During the ridesharing IW, we had applied creativity methods to explore the problem space, analyze details of high-priority problems, come up with a large number of ideas, build solution scenarios, reiterate them with transformational methods, and conclude with prototyped solutions. The experts were able to understand the structure and creativity methods applied in the ridesharing example through the images shown and the explanations given. For their own reference and to support further discussion, a hand-out was prepared. The actual results of the ridesharing example were not explained in detail, as we wanted the experts to express their own experiences and knowledge rather than discuss our example. We highlighted the documentation problem and concluded the presentation with the key takeaways: 1. Pictures of IW results only show content that is written down, drafted, drawn, or built. 2. Pictures do not show artifacts that are not used or are deemed unusable for the IW topic. 3. Photo minutes cannot convey discussions between participants that may lead to important decisions; only their outcomes. 4. The full context of an IW cannot be reflected completely in photo minutes, as it also includes the background and knowledge of the participants, often embedded into an organizational body of knowledge. **Session 2:** Directly after the presentation, we had the participants reflect on the presentation and share their own knowledge. The experts could contribute their own experiences with either CPS methods or with documentation of their outcomes. This was done to ensure that the presented problems were understood by all participants. For **Session 3**, the experts were randomly divided into five groups. Each group was assigned one step of the presented creative process. The experts were given the task to 1. discuss which creativity methods they typically use in their group's respective step, 2. write down a short summary of how the methods are performed, 3. analyze the types of results the method typically produces, 4. discuss in which activities after the creative process the results are typically used, and finally 5. what problems arise during later usage. The goal of this session was twofold: On the one hand, it should allow all the experts in a group to understand how they all apply creativity methods and form a rapport. On the other hand, we confronted them with the challenge that results of creative processes are used in later activities and the related assumption that this is difficult due to documentation problems. This implicitly includes our claim that proper documentation of IWs is important, as it allows their results to be used in later activities. The experts analyzed nine different CPS methods. **Session 4** was concerned with finding possible solution approaches to the challenges identified in the preceding session, which was again done in the subgroups. We allowed the experts to follow any ideation strategy they deemed suitable. Twenty problems (16 distinctive ones) with using the results of creative processes were identified and written down by the experts (e.g., "insights are not transferred", "other ideas are lost", "assumptions, reasons, decisions are lost due to swarm intelligence"). **Session 5:** The expert workshop concluded with a group discussion between all participants, allowing them to share their findings and elaborate on the problems of documentation, respectively the use of results for later activities.

4   Initial Results

The notion that there is a challenge with documentation in CPS activities was shared by all workshop participants. The experts agreed with our idea that later activities determine the requirements for the documentation. One expert group analyzed the brainstorming method to collect problems. Osborn's rules for brainstorming lead to a large number of results that are neither judged nor relate exclusively to the initial challenge, but are often based on associations that participants follow. The advantage of this approach is that it allows arriving at findings and insights that might have been overlooked or never uttered due to social pressure. But this leads to disadvantages for the documentation. The reasoning behind a single note is not part of it, hence it is lost once the participant forgets it. Additionally, the documentation can get unwieldy due to the large number of different notes, at varying levels of readability. The "Moonshot" or "Think Big" method [5] was analyzed by another group of experts. This method is used to work on product strategy and roadmaps in order to determine long-term goals. Many ideas for potential product features are created, of which only few are further elaborated. Assumptions and decisions made by the participants are not documented well through the "Moonshot" method itself. According to the experts, this happens due to the effects of swarm intelligence: During an IW, assumptions and reasons for decisions are shared, hence not written down. The results of the "Affinity Diagram" method [14] are used in conception, UX design, and implementation, according to the experts. They mentioned problems when using the results in later activities: The method builds empathy with the user, which degrades after an IW. Participants gain insights into the problem space, especially the user's needs, which are lost due to not being documented well, leading to the potential risk of implementing improper solutions. The "Crazy Eights" is a method [9] that helps to quickly come up with variants of ideas. Within eight minutes, participants draw or describe eight alterations of an initial idea that can be used for comparing solutions and assessing feasibility. The results are low-fidelity due to time constraints and missing descriptions, which makes it hard to use them in later activities.

One solution that might spring to mind is the use of a specific room for groups over the course of working on a topic or project, where all results can stay visible for an extended period of time, typically several weeks, so people do not lose track of any spatial interrelations formed in their mind. Notes can be rearranged to improve readability. Assumptions stay visible until rejected or confirmed. Such spaces can be referred to as "creativity rooms" [13] and provide a good context for projects incorporating CPS methods, but they are seldom available. Only one of the 29 participants has permanent access to such a room for their work. All others need to clean and remove all results from the physical collaboration space after an IW.

5   Further Research Plan

The initial results obtained from the expert workshop support our idea that the documentation of CPS activities, especially IWs, needs improvement. Though the expert workshop provided some insights into the problem of CPS documentation, the initial ideas and proposed solutions are not sufficient for solving the challenges of IW documentation. However, the experts' first insights into the problems of IW documentation motivate further research to fully understand the challenges and to come up with adequate solutions. The experts came up with an initial set of problems regarding the use of IWs results in later activities. This indicates that IW results do indeed need to be made available in a suitable manner for subsequent SE activities. A better understanding of which activities require input from IW will lead to a clearer scope of relevant subsequent activities. Analyzing different approaches to SE, RE, and UX processes will provide a comprehensive list of activities performed. We plan to elaborate on the analysis of how individual results of IWs can be used best in later activities from different angles.

To understand how the documentation of IW results can be improved, it would be beneficial to understand how it is used. Each subsequent activity should be analyzed in terms of the individual actions performed and the types of input required, such as information about the system to be built, the maturity of the requirements, or user needs. The input types then need to be categorized and condensed in order to be matched with the actual output of IWs. Not all information needs of later activities should be fulfilled by IWs, hence an understanding of result types is also necessary.

A large set of documentations on CPS activities and IW results should be obtained (e.g., existing photo minutes). If available, the documents used for planning the IWs will provide insights into the utilized methods and additional semantic information that might be useful for enriching available documentations. They should be analyzed and the output should be categorized by the type of output created (e.g., problems, ideas, scenarios, prototypes). According to our experience, different methods will provide the same type of output, even though the physical form of how the output is represented differs. On the other hand, one method might produce several types of output, either implicitly (e.g., assumptions uttered during discussions among CPS method participants) or explicitly (e.g., a concrete scenario). The output types should then be matched with the input types of subsequent activities, leading to a subset of IW result types that actually need to be preserved. For these, existing and novel approaches to documentation should be applied and evaluated. Not all means of documentation might be applicable.

Creative methods for groups collaborating face-to-face impose their own restrictions on possible means of documentation. They should not hinder the flow of ideas by overburdening the participants of IWs, neither by forcing them through seemingly unrelated activities nor by adding a feeling of being under surveillance. These constraints should be identified through literature research as well as experimental setups. Methods from IWs can be performed with static challenges and varying types of documentation (e.g., automatically analyzed audio recordings, team members facilitating the documentation, photo minutes). The quantity and quality of the results produced should provide an indication of problems arising from incorporating documentation into the CPS method. Possible documentation methods could be tailored specifically to the input needs of SE, RE, and UX processes, adapted to the given outputs, and incorporate the constraints of CPS methods. We envision different documentation approaches for different methods, which the facilitator will have to choose from, leading to better incorporation of IW results into later SE, RE, and UX activities.

Acknowledgements. Parts of this work have been funded by the "EnStadt: Pfaff" project (grants no. 03SBE112D and 03SBE112G) of the German Federal Ministry for Economic Affairs and Energy (BMWi) and the German Federal Ministry of Education and Research (BMBF).

References

1. Adam, S., Trapp, M.: Success factors for creativity workshops in RE. In: CEUR Workshop Proceedings, vol. 1342, pp. 54–61 (2015)
2. Barrios, P.C., Monticolo, D., Sidhom, S., Gabriel, A.: An organizational model to understand the creativity workshop. In: 2017 13th International Conference on Signal-Image Technology Internet-Based System, pp. 496–502. IEEE, December 2017. https://doi.org/10.1109/SITIS.2017.87. http://ieeexplore.ieee.org/document/8334793/
3. Brem, A., Spoedt, H.: Same same but different: perspectives on creativity workshops by design and business. IEEE Eng. Manag. Rev. **45**(1), 27–31 (2017). https://doi.org/10.1109/EMR.2017.2667143
4. Kerkow, D., Adam, S., Riegel, N., Ünalan, Ö.: A creativity method for business information systems. In: 16th International Working Conference on Requirements Engineering: Foundation for Software Quality, Proceedings of the Workshop CreaRE, PLREQ, RePriCo RESC, pp. 8–20 (2010)
5. Haigh, T.: Hey Google, what's a moonshot? How Silicon Valley mocks Apollo. Commun. ACM **62**(1), 24–30 (2018)
6. Inayat, I., Salim, S.S., Marczak, S., Daneva, M., Shamshirband, S.: A systematic literature review on agile requirements engineering practices and challenges. Comput. Hum. Behav. **51**, 915–929 (2015). https://doi.org/10.1016/j.chb.2014.10.046
7. Karras, O.: Software professionals' attitudes towards video as a medium in requirements engineering. In: Kuhrmann, M., et al. (eds.) PROFES 2018. LNCS, vol. 11271, pp. 150–158. Springer, Cham (2018). https://doi.org/10.1007/978-3-030-03673-7_11
8. Karras, O., Kiesling, S., Schneider, K.: Supporting requirements elicitation by tool-supported video analysis. In: Proceedings of the 2016 IEEE 24th International Requirements Engineering Conference, RE 2016, pp. 146–155 (2016). https://doi.org/10.1109/RE.2016.10
9. Knapp, J., Zeratsky, J., Kowitz, B.: Sprint: how to solve big problems and test new ideas in just five days. Simon and Schuster (2016)
10. Maiden, N., Jones, S., Karlsen, K., Neill, R., Zachos, K., Milne, A.: Requirements engineering as creative problem solving: a research agenda for idea finding. In: Proceedings of the 2010 18th IEEE International Requirements Engineering Conference, RE 2010, pp. 57–66 (2010). https://doi.org/10.1109/RE.2010.16
11. Maiden, N., Manning, S., Robertson, S., Greenwood, J.: Integrating creativity workshops into structured requirements processes. In: Proceedings of the 2004 Conference on Designing Interactive Systems: Processes, Practices, Methods, and Techniques, DIS 2004, p. 113. ACM Press, New York (2004). https://doi.org/10.1145/1013115.1013132. http://portal.acm.org/citation.cfm?doid=1013115.1013132
12. Maiden, N., Ncube, C., Robertson, S.: Can Requirements Be Creative? Experiences with an Enhanced Air Space Management System Centre for HCI Design, City University, London, UK Atlantic Systems Guild, London, UK Abstract (2007)
13. Mennig, P., Trapp, M.: Designing flexible creative spaces. In: CEUR Workshop Proceedings, vol. 2376 (2019). http://ceur-ws.org/Vol-2376/CreaRE_paper2.pdf
14. Plain, C.: Build an affinity for KJ method. Qual. Prog. **40**(3), 88 (2007)

Industrial Practices on Requirements Reuse: An Interview-Based Study

Xavier Franch$^{(\boxtimes)}$ (iD), Cristina Palomares (iD), and Carme Quer (iD)

Universitat Politècnica Catalunya (UPC-BarcelonaTech), Barcelona, Spain
{franch,cpalomares,cquer}@essi.upc.edu

Abstract. **[Context and motivation]** Requirements reuse has been proposed as a key asset for requirements engineers to efficiently elicit, validate and document software requirements and, as a consequence, obtain requirements specifications of better quality through more effective engineering processes. **[Question/problem]** Regardless the impact requirements reuse could have in software projects' success and efficiency, the requirements engineering community has published very few studies reporting the way in which this activity is conducted in industry. **[Principal ideas/results]** In this paper, we present the results of an interview-based study involving 24 IT professionals on whether they reuse requirements or not and how. Some kind of requirements reuse is carried out by the majority of respondents, being organizational and project-related factors the main drivers. Quality requirements are the type most reused. The most common strategy is find-copy-paste-adapt. Respondents agreed that requirements reuse is beneficial, especially for project-related reasons. The most stated challenge to overcome in requirements reuse is related to the domain of the project and the development of a completely new system. **[Contribution]** With this study, we contribute to the state of the practice in the reuse of requirements by showing how real organizations carry out this process and the factors that influence it.

Keywords: Requirements reuse · Requirements elicitation · Requirements documentation · Requirements engineering · Survey · Interview-based study

1 Introduction

Requirements reuse is the practice of systematically eliciting and specifying requirements not starting from scratch, but from already available artefacts. These artefacts range from requirements appearing in previous requirement specification documents, to templates stored in some sort of catalogue, adapted to every new project.

As reported in Sect. 3, there is a good number of research works addressing software reuse in the scientific literature. Still, not many of them report on the state of the practice. Questions as: is requirements reuse an extended practice among requirements engineers in industry?, if so, how is it implemented?, what are the challenges to overcome and the perceived benefits?, require further field investigation through empirical studies with practitioners. In this paper, we report the results of a study in this direction.

© Springer Nature Switzerland AG 2020
N. Madhavji et al. (Eds.): REFSQ 2020, LNCS 12045, pp. 78–94, 2020.
https://doi.org/10.1007/978-3-030-44429-7_6

The rest of the paper is organized as follows. Sections 2 and 3 describe the background and related work on requirements reuse that contextualizes our study. Section 4 describes the methodological aspects of the study, including the research questions, population and analysis procedures. Sections 5 and 6 present the results and their discussion organized according to the research questions. Finally, Sect. 7 concludes the paper and outlines some lines of future work.

2 Background

Two recent papers described in detail the background needed in this study. In a previous paper [1], we included a detailed description of background on requirements reuse until December 2015. In a paper published one year after [2], Irshad et al. presented a systematic literature review on requirements reuse based on publications previous to March 2016. The classification criteria that appear in both papers and that help to characterize better the reuse approaches are: the type of reusable artefacts and the means to retrieve the reusable artifacts from a repository. In this section, we classify the background according these criteria. The background consists on approaches identified in [1, 2] enriched with a search of approaches published after March 2016 in the three main RE-specific scientific venues: RE, REJ and REFSQ.

The type of reusable artifacts that are mainly used in the existing proposals are: requirements in natural language that can comply or not a certain form or template [3, 4]; domain models [5, 6]; and use cases [7, 8]. Other artifacts that are not strictly requirements but that are also reused are: ontologies [9, 10]; classifications of requirements in requirement specification or specification templates [11–14] and relationships or dependencies among requirements or models for reuse [11, 15, 16].

The means to retrieve the reusable artifacts that are mainly proposed in the existing proposals are: pattern based, using information embedded in the pattern (e.g., its goal) [11, 17]; matching based, comparing and matching with existing requirements [8, 18]; analogy based, searching for similar cases for applying requirements to be reused from past projects [19]; and ontology based, which in this case use ontologies not as reuse artifact but as a way to facilitate the retrieval of requirements to reuse suitable for a project [20, 21].

Other criteria that can be mentioned are: the existence of a process prescribing the reuse strategy; the existence of tool support; the elaboration of the structure of the repository. For details, we refer again to the two papers mentioned above [1, 2].

3 Related Work

In this section, we identify existing studies with similar aims than ours. We can consider two different types of studies.

Type 1: papers with requirements reuse proposals applied and validated in an industrial context. We already found out through a systematic search of publications (see [1] for more details) that there is a low percentage of papers on requirements reuse that conduct an experimental validation. Complementing this information, Irshad et al. reported that from the 69 papers analysed in their review, only 22 were validated in industry [2].

Remarkably, after the validation, the papers only describe positive results with respect to requirements reuse, and do not mention the possible negative aspects. The main result reported is the decrease of effort.

Type 2: papers presenting the state of the practice of requirements reuse in industry through surveys or interviews. We identified in [1] two secondary studies that present surveys or interviews fully focused on requirements reuse [22, 23]. Applying the same systematic search used in [1], we have found one new paper published after 2016 in the context of ERP implementations [24]. The works reported in [22, 23] address four aspects of reuse in practice, the level of application, the benefits, obstacles and critical factors. As levels of reuse the results of both surveys give a level of reuse from 59% to 72%. Benefits reported from reuse are: the improved performance of requirements engineering; reduced projects costs; and requirements easier to understand. Regarding obstacles, they mention: the risk of low maintenance of the reuse repository and difficulty of identifying requirements to reuse. Furthermore, a critical factor that was observed is the existence of tool support for reuse. The work in [24] is not relevant for the work presented here, since it has a different goal, namely to identify reusable requirement artifacts used in the ERP implementation industry, and to define metrics to measure reusability of artifacts.

4   The Study

In this section we summarize the study protocol; full details are given in the document available at [25]. As a preamble, it is necessary to say that the results reported in this paper are part of a broader study that includes research questions not only on requirements reuse but also on requirements elicitation and documentation. For the sake of clarity, we present the part related to reuse as if it were an independent study.

Research Questions. This study aims at investigating the state of the practice on requirements reuse. To conduct this investigation, we identified the research questions (RQs) shown in Table 1. The overall question is to investigate how extended is requirements reuse in industry (**RQ1**). Since we do not expect this RQ to have an uncontextual answer, we inquiry next what factors may influence in reusing or not reusing (**RQ2**). Also, from former studies, we are aware that some types of requirements may be more prone to reuse than others, motivating (**RQ3**). We are also interested in knowing the

Table 1. Research questions of the study.

RQ1	Is requirements reuse a usual practice in industry?
RQ2	What factors influence the level of adoption of requirements reuse?
RQ3	What types of requirements are subject of reuse?
RQ4	What is the process followed to implement requirements reuse?
RQ5	What are the benefits brought by requirements reuse?
RQ6	What are the challenges to overcome in requirements reuse?

way in which requirements reused is implemented in practice (**RQ4**). Last, we want to understand the benefits (**RQ5**) and challenges (**RQ6**) brought by reuse as perceived by practitioners, since the final decision will be a trade-off of both.

Population. We interviewed 24 subjects coming from 12 companies working in different domains. Although our aim was having 2 subjects per company, we finally had one

Table 2. Subjects, companies and projects of the study

ID	Exper.	Comp.	Years	Project domain	Methodology
S1	15	A	3	Messaging System	Waterfall
S2	15	A	10	Website	Waterfall
S3	20	B	≈9	Website	Agile
S4	13	B	13	Website	Agile
S5	25	C	4	Mobile OS	Waterfall
S6	20	D	20	Machine to Machine Internal System	Agile
S7	19	D	19	Carrier Business/Internal System	Agile
S8	15	E	15	Energy Measurement System	Waterfall
S9	20	E	6	Business Support System	Waterfall
S10	16	F	9	Carrier Business/Internal System	Agile
S11	17	F	0	Website	Agile
S12	12	G	≈9	Carrier Business/Internal System	Waterfall
S13	23	G	14	Carrier Business/Internal System	Waterfall
S14	10	H	5	Embedded System	Waterfall
S15	10	H	4.5	Embedded System	Waterfall
S16	25	I	19	Embedded System	Agile
S17	8	I	8	Embedded System	Waterfall
S18	9	J	2	Embedded System	Waterfall
S19	3	J	2	Embedded System	Waterfall
S20	23	J	16	Embedded System	Waterfall
S21	21	K	12	Mobile App	Waterfall
S22	9	K	9	Mobile App, Website	Agile
S23	15	L	4.5	Construction	Waterfall
S24	26	L	3.5	Construction	Waterfall

Exper.: Years in Industry; Comp.: Company ID; Years: Years in Organization company with only 1 subject (company ID = C) and another one with 3 (company ID = J). Details are provided in Table 2. For brevity, we only include information that is referred to in Sects. 5 and 6.

Procedure and Instruments. In order to gather data from the target population, we designed a semi-structured interview guide following the guidelines stated by Oates [26]. We asked the respondents to focus on one single project in order to gain as much insights as possible. The interview guide is available at [25]. The guide was piloted. The results were recorded but not transcribed according to the respondents' request.

Data Analysis. We applied coding techniques [27] with the support of the Atlas.ti[1] tool. We used multiple coding techniques in different steps, see details in [25]. We also applied some statistical techniques to look for associations among variables, remarkably Chi-square test of independence [28] (considering statistical significance if p-value < 0.05) and Cramer's V to estimate the strength of the association (strong association if V is $\geq$ 0.5, moderate if V $\geq$ 0.3) [29]. Not all correlations neither all significant correlations are reported, but only those that we think are interesting and eventually explainable. Therefore, some characteristics of the participants of projects that one might thought might influence the results (such as the years of experience or the development methodology used) are only mentioned in the results when it showed interesting insights.

Threats to Validity. We outline threats to validity and outline strategies used to deal with them. Again we refer to the protocol document for complete explanations [25].

- *Construct Validity.* The study was supported by two main principles: rigorous planning and the establishment of protocols for data collection and data analysis as suggested in [30]. Additionally, the interview guide was designed and piloted. Finally, both in the interview guide and during the actual interview, the subjects were aware that the data and information they provided would be confidential, anonymised, and aggregated with the rest of interviews, so the subjects could freely share their real experiences and perceptions.
- *Conclusion Validity.* Throughout the coding, many concepts and their relationships were identified. Traceability from the raw data to the categories, and their relationships, was preserved. Different coding techniques (theory triangulation) were used to capture various aspects of the reuse phenomenon.

Given that some respondents didn't really apply reuse in the selected project or even in any other project (see RQ1 results), some of the responses given in RQ2–RQ6 are more based on educated opinions than in past experiences. We opted by not considering some of these responses if we thought they were too vague or too speculative.

- *Internal Validity.* We focused most of the questions on a single software development project. In this way, it was possible to further inquire and analyse specific contexts that generated a particular decision. To avoid subsequent threats: (1) the interview

---

[1] http://atlasti.com/.

guide was sent in advance to the respondents so they rarely had difficulties remembering project details; (2) to minimize the risk of selecting only successful projects, we remarked that the study was not focused on analysing "wrong practices" but on knowing "how it is done in industrial practices".

To address single researcher bias in the coding process, we applied triangulation in different forms. Selected interviews were analysed independently by two researchers and the results were discussed to identify and eliminate any individual biases. Responses were triangulated too. In addition, the generated categories were analysed, discussed and reviewed by the team to ensure their accuracy, understanding and agreement.

- *External Validity.* Qualitative studies rarely attempt to make universal generalizations beyond the studied setting. Instead, as Robson explains [31], they are more concerned with characterizing, explaining and understanding the phenomena under the contexts of study. Still, we took some actions to strengthen external validity: (1) combination of convenience sampling and maximum variation sampling to select the companies; (2) freedom for respondents to choose the project for the interview. In addition, also a third party involved in the study had contacts with the companies, she did not knew about their way of working with respect to requirements engineering, so no pre-selection criteria was applied to choose the companies involved in the study. To support replication and validation by independent researchers, we are making available not just the protocol but all the coding results for the answers to research questions [32].

5 Results

In this section we report the results obtained for the 6 research questions. As general strategy, we applied content analysis to identify categories and subcategories. We usually present the results with bar graphics where the values are the number of respondents who answered in this category; the total number of respondents is explicitly stated given that usually it will be lower than the sum of respondents per category. To present the results, we have followed a narrative style integrating quasi-quotes from the respondents[2] in the general explanations. These quasi-quotes include the identifier of the subjects between curly braces.

5.1 RQ1. Is Requirements Reuse a Usual Practice in Industry?

A slight majority of respondents (14) stated that there was some kind of reuse in the projects that they reported in the survey (see Fig. 1, left).

The level of reuse was quite balanced among them, with almost the same amount of respondents reporting high level of reuse (5 respondents informing up to 85%) and low level of reuse (6 respondents down to only 5%). The interpretation of "high" and "low"

---

[2] With "quasi-quotes" we mean syntactical adaptations of the sentences to make them fit to the story (e.g., including missing context in the sentence, aligning verb tenses, …).

is quite consistent and the frontier seems to be in the interval [30%–50%], which was qualified as High percentage by one respondent, compared to [30%–40%] qualified as Low by another. Even the only respondent who qualified the level of reuse as Medium provides a consistent interval [60%–70%]. Effort reduction also oscillates, ranging from 5% to 80%. This effort reduction is focused on the requirements engineering stage: *less effort would have been put into the project, less time would have been needed for the elicitation of requirements, and less errors would have been made on the requirements* {S13}. As expected, there is a strong correlation among the level of the reuse and the effort reduction (see Fig. 1, right). It is interesting to quote the observation made by {S04} saying that in their case "more reuse would not have been more beneficial as they already reused as much as they could".

As a follow-up question, to those respondents who reported lack of reuse in the selected projects, we raised some additional questions that allowed to see that 3 of them have reused requirements in other projects, while 5 others were expecting to start reuse in a near future. Overall, only 2 respondents reported complete lack of reuse.

Fig. 1. Requirements reuse in industry (left) and relation among level of reuse and effort reduction (right).

We explored the possible impact of demographic factors into software reuse adoption. We found an interesting statistically-relevant association with the project domain (p-value = 0.020; V value = 0.746), so that some domains seem more prone to reuse than others. As an extreme case, all 7 respondents who selected projects developing embedded systems did reuse requirements, while none of the 5 respondents who selected projects related to internal systems reused requirements.

5.2 RQ2. What Factors Influence the Level of Adoption of Requirements Reuse?

Given that 2 out of the 14 respondents that reported reuse in the selected projects in RQ1 were not able to identify factors influencing reuse, the answer to this research question is based on the responses given by 12 respondents only. From these interviews, we identified four big categories of factors (Fig. 2).

Organizational. Up to 7 respondents reported factors related to the organization. Among them, the most mentioned one (5 respondents) was organizational culture, e.g.

reuse seen as positive in the organization {S19}. Also, a couple of respondents mentioned unavailability of previous specification documents for different reasons, like *not having any more intellectual rights of the previous documents (because the organization has been purchased by another)* {S18}. Finally, one respondent highlighted maturity of the organization, because *they have a quite mature requirements process that allows that the requirements of other projects are good enough to be reused* {S04}.

Project-Related. The same number of respondents as above justified the adoption of requirements reuse upon the similarity of the selected project to similar previous projects. As obvious as it can seem, *if there is no previous system with some similar functionality or part that you can reuse, then it is impossible to reuse* {S03}.

Human. Only mentioned by 3 respondents, who justified the adoption of reuse upon the engagement and personal attitude of the requirements engineer who *put the extra effort to apply some requirements reuse* {S11}.

Technical. Also mentioned only by 3 respondents who provided a varied set of reasons, like *compliance to a new standard to be fulfilled by the platform* {S18} or impediments for tool support (*Electra was not used before, so not too many requirements were in Electra at the start of the project and they could not be reused* {S18}).

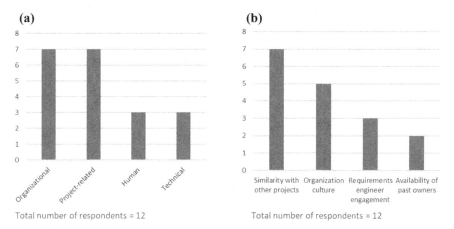

Fig. 2. Requirements reuse in industry: (a) categorization; (b) most frequent answers.

5.3   RQ3. What Types of Requirements Are More Prone to Reuse?

The majority of respondents (up to 20) provided information related to this research question; only 4 of them didn't make it.

We got two categories of answers: types of requirements that are prone to be reused and types of requirements that are prone not to be reused. The majority of answers (from 19 respondents) come from the first category (see Fig. 3) and, in fact, one type (not surprisingly) prevails: non-functional/quality requirements (NFRs), reported by 10

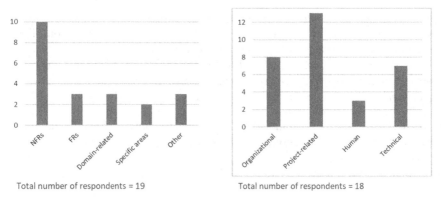

Total number of respondents = 19   Total number of respondents = 18

Fig. 3. Types of requirements prone to reuse. **Fig. 4.** Benefits brought by requirements reuse.

respondents (e.g. *infrastructure requirements such as performance and network capacity* {S08}) *because these ones might be common to other projects* {S10}. Still 3 respondents mentioned functional requirements (FRs) when *they weren't the innovative part of the project* {S05} and therefore *they didn't change from previous projects* {S18}. The same number of respondents mentioned also reuse for domain-related requirements like *a search engine* {S03} or requirements related to a specific part of the system like *the client environment (operating systems, browsers, screen sizes, etc.)* {S11}. Remarkably, only one respondent mentioned reuse related to standards, namely for *health & safety issues* {S15} (Fig. 4).

Types that prevent reuse were very different. For instance, {S23} identified as difficult to reuse the requirements that evolve too much technologically, whilst {S18} was more specific to a certain category, *the group that manages the requirements of the hardware used to activate it [a particular embedded subsystem] because from project to project what changes most is the hardware.*

5.4 RQ4. What Is the Process Followed to Implement Requirements Reuse?

Again, we had 20 respondents providing details on the process followed, and this number increased until 22 considering some additional information related to the process itself, like techniques, artefacts and tools used during requirements reuse.

Similar to RQ3, a prevalent response emerged (see Fig. 5, a): the most popular process (10 respondents) was to search similar requirements in past requirements specification documents, copy them into the current specification and then adapt to the new project. This find-copy-paste-adapt strategy at the requirements level, was applied by 3 respondents at the software requirements specification document level by *looking at other projects, finding the most similar one, duplicating it and work in the parts as needed* {S05}.

Another approach to the reuse process followed by 4 respondents was the use of catalogues as central asset, i.e. *a kind of requirements repository, and user can check the repository by systems, subsystems, keywords, etc. and reuse something if necessary by linking to the source and copy and pasting to the new project* {S12}.

Some artefacts or concepts were mentioned when describing the process. Remarkably, three respondents talked about traceability to the source *having a link from where the requirements came from* {S18}. The use of tags or design rules (*set of requirements that all the projects/products have to comply with* {S07}) was also reported.

Last, we inquired the respondents about tool support (see Fig. 5, b). The majority of respondents (12) did not use tool support, but the rest did at some extent, in all cases using *the same tool as the one used for managing the requirements* {S24}. Half of them (4) reported a tool-centric approach to the reuse process, e.g. *Jira allows reusing requirements by having a main ticket (requirement) to which you can link from a new system by creating a new ticket in another project that links to that main ticket* {S10}.

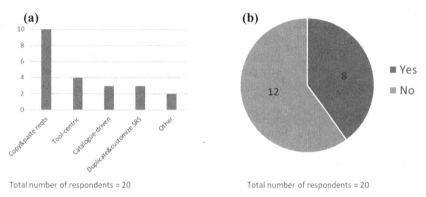

Total number of respondents = 20   Total number of respondents = 20

Fig. 5. (a) Processes followed to implement requirements reuse; (b) Existence of tool support.

5.5 RQ5. What Are the Benefits Brought by Requirements Reuse?

Most of the respondents (22) considered reuse as a beneficial practice independently of whether they were reusing or not in the selected project (*it was beneficial* {S05} vs. *it would have been beneficial* {S01}). Only one respondent was absolutely negative because at the end *it was too much time to look for something, to reuse just a small part* {S03} while the other provided a contextual answer (*requirements reuse is not beneficial in my organization because everything we create is new* {S06}). Statistical analysis showed a moderate correlation (p-value = 0.037; V value = 0.426) between the perception of reuse being not beneficial and the type of project: the only 2 people not seeing reuse as beneficial work in projects following agile methodologies.

From those 22 respondents, 18 provided some justification to sustain their opinion. We classified the answers into the same categories as in RQ2 (see Fig. 3).

Organizational. 7 of the respondents reported causes related to the organization, in terms of *less effort needed for eliciting and specifying the requirements* {S02}. An additional reason given by {S11} only is that a reuse infrastructure makes it possible *not having to rely that much on people experience and knowledge*, making thus the organization less vulnerable. A moderate correlation (p-value = 0.020; V value = 0.473) informs that people perceiving organizational benefits also perceives project-related benefits (7 out of 8 respondents).

Project-Related. Up to 12 respondents mentioned gain of efficiency in the RE process as the main benefit brought by reuse, mainly because *less time is needed for eliciting and specifying requirements* {S23}; more specifically, *if there is a high-level set of requirements already defined [...] to start the discussion, you could get faster to the key points* {S09}. The second reason given by only one respondent is that reuse can bring *a standard way of specifying requirements... including the level of detail and abstraction you should arrive* {S01}. We remark that we found a strong correlation (p-value = 0.030; V value = 0.612) among this type of benefits and years in the organization: while 12 out of the 13 respondents who worked in the organization less than 15 years reported these benefits, only 1 out of 5 working more of 15 years reported them too. Another correlation was only moderate (p-value = 0.043; V value = 0.414) but also interesting: project-related benefits was mostly perceived by respondents working in projects that follow a waterfall methodology (11 out of 13 people).

Human. As happened with RQ2, this was the least influential category. Two respondents argued that reuse may ease communication inside the development team by *helping to put everyone together in the same page, from developers to testers* {S01}. An additional respondent highlighted that reuse was beneficial in front of customers *because it was easier to have something ready to introduce to customers* {S04} and get feedback from them earlier.

Technical. Some of the respondents argued that requirements reuse is beneficial from a technical perspective. One reason mentioned by 4 subjects was that with reuse *in general, you get more quality [in requirements], and because of that less errors* {S19}; only {S22} mentioned a more concrete quality criterion (*it is easier to write unambiguous requirements*). Other reasons were mentioned by one respondent each, e.g. *not only to reuse the requirements, but also the information about the effort and the historical data associated to the requirements (problems encountered, etc.)* {S16}, or also (and related) *the reuse of requirements implies for them also the reuse of code, tests, etc.* {S17}. It is worth to mention a statistically significant strong correlation here (p-value = 0.001; V value = 0.772): technical benefits are mostly perceived by people working in industry less than 10 years (and in fact, the 4 respondents in this situation reported technical benefits for reuse).

5.6 RQ6. What Are the Challenges to Overcome in Requirements Reuse?

Remarkably enough, 8 respondents didn't identify any challenge to overcome related to requirements reuse. Answers given by the remaining 16 respondents showed two different strengths on the opinion. On the one hand, 11 respondents reported reasons that, either as an observation from the selected project or as an educated opinion, absolutely prevent the adoption of reuse practices, related to three of the categories mentioned in RQ2 and RQ5 (see Fig. 6, left):

Organizational. 2 respondents reported organizational challenges of different type:

- Immature organization: *If the organization is not mature, they do not put that much effort on requirements and they think that the effort is not worthwhile* {S10}.
- Siloed projects: *They don't work enough together between projects because they have too many projects at the same time* {S01}.
- Focus on short-term benefits only (and *reusing requirements produces benefits only in the long term* {S01}).
- Cost of licenses of the tools required to implement a reuse infrastructure: *without having Jira free of cost, we would have not tried* {S10}.

Project-Related. 9 respondents informed about project-related challenges responding to two causes:

- Developing a new type of system (5 responses): reuse is not applicable in *a totally new platform; there was anything before, it was totally blank* {S01}.
- Developing a system in a new domain (5 responses): it can be related to the application domain but also *a new domain for the requirements engineer* {S24}, meaning that she has difficulties on reusing from a domain she does not master.

We found a strong correlation (p-value $= 0.028$; V value $= 0.547$) showing that most of the respondents having project-related reasons to not reuse requirements (8 out 9 people) are not reusing requirements now.

Technical. 4 respondents mentioned as technical challenges:

- Difficulty to access previous requirement specifications (3 respondents): in the extreme case, *no requirements were available of the old system to be replaced* {S13}.
- Lack of agreed standards: this causes that *everyone writes requirements in a different way [...] so it becomes really hard to take over somebody else requirements* {S01}.
- Low support from the requirements management tool: the tool their used was not used *for specifying the requirements of the system; it is used for other systems* {S02}.

On the other hand, 5 respondents communicated obstacles that made reuse challenging but still possible (see Fig. 6, right). The only category mentioned by more of one respondent was organizational, and among them, low consideration of RE in the company was cited by 3 respondents (*not too much attention is put into requirements* {S08}). Interestingly, {S03} stated as obstacle that *reusing is not fun (it will cut the creativity part of the projects) [...] people likes to do new things.*

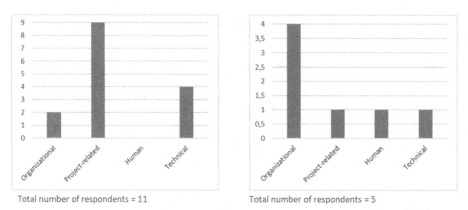

Total number of respondents = 11   Total number of respondents = 5

Fig. 6. Challenges to overcome in requirements reuse: preventing (left) or interfering (right).

6   Discussion

Observation 1. *Requirement reuse is part of the requirements engineer toolbox.* RQ1 reports that a slight majority of respondents have reused requirements either in the project selected for this study or in the past. This observation aligns well with previous studies in the field [1, 22, 23]. Putting this fact together with the factors reported as barriers or incentives to reuse, we may conclude that reuse shall be considered not as a universal principle that needs to be always pursued, but as yet-another-technique in the requirements engineer toolbox. For instance, the benefits of reuse in elicitation reported by several respondents point out that reuse can be viewed as an additional technique supporting requirements elicitation, as interviews, focus groups and others, with its own selection criteria [33]. Adding to this observation, the significantly statistical correlation informed in Sect. 5.1 (use in embedded systems) and Sect. 5.5 (use in agile projects) may hint that reuse may be more useful for some kind of projects than others.

Observation 2. *Requirement engineers have a positive perception about software reuse.* Even not being used in all projects, respondents clearly consider benefits outweighing challenges. Only one respondent was absolutely skeptical about requirements reuse. The difference among this positive consideration and the real extent and level of reuse reported in the study has to be attributed as said in Observation 1: reuse is not for every project but when contextual conditions apply, it will bring benefits.

Observation 3. *Organizational and project-related factors are determinant to reuse, over human and technical factors.* Connecting with Observation 1 again, it is clear that requirements reuse is hindered by new types of systems and new domains, although the fact that non-functional requirements have been identified as the most reusable artefact opens the door for their reuse at least at a high abstraction level even if this situation. About human factors, they are recognized to be capital for RE as a discipline, given the central role that stakeholders play. However, the study shows that this is not the case when it comes to requirements reuse. In fact, the only factor that is mentioned by some is the requirements engineer attitude towards adopting reuse and positive impact on human communication.

Observation 4. *Requirements reuse is still implemented in a very simple way.* As the answer to RQ4 shows, copy-and-paste based solutions are largely dominant as reuse technique, which fully aligns to our previous questionnaire-based study [2]. This dominance has a negative effect in the reuse level, as indicated by a statistically significant correlation (p-value = 0.008; V value = 0.807) that we found: most of the respondents using this approach to reuse report Low or Medium level of reuse. The main reason behind the dominance of copy-and-paste solutions can be the absence of tool support and the lack of well-established methods in the organization. The first candidate reason is supported by another significant correlation (p-value = 0.002; V value = 0.632): all respondents using catalogues for requirements reuse have tool support (i.e., the catalogue is not a separate, ad-hoc instrument but it is integrated somehow in the requirements management tool).

Comparing to the related work reported in Sect. 3, we can observe how some findings in our study are aligned with their observations (reuse level and benefits), but not all of them (neither obstacles nor adoption influencing factors) (Table 3):

- The level of reuse found in this study (14 respondents reusing in their selected projects, i.e. 58%) is in the lower range of the interval [59%–72%] reported in [22, 23].
- Related work mentions three benefits. One of them, efficiency in the RE process, is the main benefit uncovered by our study. Another benefit, reduced project costs, is directly related to the decrease in cost identified as second main benefit in our study. Instead, the third benefit, better understanding of requirements, is only marginally mentioned by our respondents.
- The two obstacles identified in the related work are just marginally mentioned in our study. Instead, the main challenges and obstacles that we report in this paper are not identified in the previous work.
- Last, the existence of tool support was not a major influencing factor in our study.

Table 3. Comparison of this study and the previous questionnaire-based study reported in [1]

Observations in the questionnaire-based study	This study
A significant percentage of the respondents practice requirements reuse	PA
The level of requirements reuse is usually low	PA
Participants of larger organizations declare a higher level of reuse	NE
Requirements reuse techniques most commonly used are those based on textual copy and subsequent modification of requirements from previous projects	FA
There is a correlation between the level of requirements reuse and the requirements reuse techniques used	PA
Organizations with more established software processes and methods are the ones that declare a higher level of requirements reuse	NE
NFRs are more likely to be similar or recurrent among projects	FA
Ignorance of reuse techniques and processes is the main reason for the lack of reuse adoption	NE

To finalize this discussion, we compare the observations reported in our previous questionnaire-based study [1] with those uncovered in this current study. For each observation in [1] related to reuse, we assign as value: if the current study is fully aligned (FA), partially aligned (PA), misaligned (MA) or does not provide any evidence in this direction (NE). It is worth to mention that none of the 8 findings in [1] is contradicted in this study, but on the other side, only 2 of them are fully endorsed by ours, with 3 others partially aligned and 3 for which we did not get any evidence. This last statement, together with the slight misalignments with related work mentioned above, calls for more empirical studies to gather more evidence to build a theory on requirements reuse.

7   Conclusions and Future Work

In this study, we have presented an empirical study based on interviews with practitioners on the adoption level of requirements reuse and the practices, benefits and challenges related. We responded six research questions, which results are:

- **RQ1**: Moderate adoption of reuse practices by practitioners
- **RQ2**: Prevalence of organizational and project-related factors influencing reuse adoption.
- **RQ3**: Non-functional requirements as the type of requirement more prone to reuse.
- **RQ4**: Find-copy-paste-adapt the most popular approach to implement reuse.
- **RQ5**: Prevalence of organizational and project-related benefits stemming from reuse adoption.
- **RQ6**: Prevalence of project-related challenges to overcome when reusing.

In addition to giving answer to the research question, we found some interesting insights. We found that requirement reuse is quite a common practice for requirements engineers and that they have a positive perception of reuse, since it usually leads to benefits. However, the determinant factors to reuse are associated to organizational and project-related issues, and requirements reuse is still implemented in a very simple way.

Finally, we compare our results with the related work and a previous questionnaire-based study. In both cases, we can observe how some results from our study are aligned with their observations, but not all of them (mainly because we did not get enough evidence to consider it a result as such).

Future work moves on the direction of replicating these studies in other settings in order to find further evidence that may help in establishing a theory on the topic.

Acknowledgements. This work has been partially funded by the Horizon 2020 project OpenReq, which is supported by the European Union under the Grant Nr. 732463.

References

1. Palomares, C., Quer, C., Franch, X.: Requirements reuse and requirement patterns: a state of the practice survey. Empirical Softw. Eng. **22**(6), 2719–2762 (2017). https://doi.org/10.1007/s10664-016-9485-x

2. Irshad, M., Petersen, K., Poulding, S.: A systematic literature review of software requirements reuse approaches. Inf. Softw. Technol. **93**, 223–245 (2018)
3. de Gea, J.M.C., Nicolás, J., Alemán, J.L.F., Toval, A., Vizcaíno, A., Ebert, C.: Reusing requirements in global software engineering. In: Maalej, W., Thurimella, A. (eds.) Managing Requirements Knowledge. Springer, Heidelberg (2013). https://doi.org/10.1007/978-3-642-34419-0_8
4. Pacheco, C., Garcia, I., Calvo-Manzano, J.A., Arcilla, M.: Reusing functional software requirements in small-sized software enterprises: a model oriented to the catalog of requirements. Requirements Eng. J. **22**(2), 275–287 (2017)
5. Haeng-Kon, K.: Effective domain modeling for mobile business AHMS (Adaptive Human Management Systems) requirements. In: SNPD 2014 (2014)
6. Veleda, R., Cysneiros, L.M.: Towards a tool to help exploring existing non-functional requirements solution patterns. In: REW 2017 (2017)
7. Chung, L., Supakkul, S.: Capturing and reusing functional and non-functional requirements knowledge: a goal-object pattern approach. In: IRI 2006 (2006)
8. Kundi, M., Chitchyan, R.: Use case elicitation with FrameNet frames. In: REW 2017 (2017)
9. Salini, P., Kanmani, S.: A knowledge-oriented approach to security requirements for an E-voting system. Int. J. Comput. Appl. **49**(11), 21–25 (2012)
10. de Brock, B.: Towards pattern-driven requirements engineering: development patterns for functional requirements. In: MoDRE 2018 (2018)
11. Franch, X., Quer, C., Guerlain, C., Renault, S., Palomares, C.: Constructing and using software requirement patterns. In: Maalej, W., Thurimella, A. (eds.) Managing Requirements Knowledge. Springer, Heidelberg (2013). https://doi.org/10.1007/978-3-642-34419-0_5
12. Renault, S., Méndez-Bonilla, O., Franch, X., Quer, C.: PABRE: pattern-based requirements elicitation. In: RCIS 2009 (2009)
13. Panis, M.C.: Reuse of architecturally derived standards requirements. In: RE 2015 (2015)
14. Darimont, R., Zhao, W., Ponsard, C., Michot, A.: Deploying a template and pattern library for improved reuse of requirements across projects. In: RE 2017 (2017)
15. Srivastava, S.: A repository of software requirement patterns for online examination system. Int. J. Comput. Sci. **10**(3), 247 (2013)
16. Chen, X., Han, L., Liu, J., Sun, H.: Using safety requirement patterns to elicit requirements for railway interlocking systems. In: REW 2016 (2016)
17. Knote, R., Söllner, M., Leimeister, J.M.: Towards requirement patterns for smart physical work assistants. In: REW 2017 (2017)
18. Niu, N., Savolainen, J., Niu, Z., Jin, M., Cheng, J.R.C.: A systems approach to product line requirements reuse. IEEE Syst. J. **8**(3), 827–836 (2014)
19. Chiang, C.C., Neubart, D.: Constructing reusable specifications through analogy. In: SAC 1999 (1999)
20. Bonilla, B., Crespo, S., Clunie, C.: Reuse of Use Cases Diagrams: An Approach based on Ontologies and Semantic Web Technologies. Int. J. Comput. Sci. **9**(1), 24–29 (2012)
21. Carvalho, R.M., Andrade, R.M.C., Oliveira, K.M., Kolski, C.: Catalog of invisibility requirements for UbiComp and IoT Applications. In: RE 2018 (2018)
22. Chernak, Y.: Requirements reuse: the state of the practice. In: SWSTE 2012 (2012)
23. Bakar, N.H., Kasirun, Z.M.: Exploring software practitioners perceptions and experience in requirements reuse: an empirical study in Malaysia. Int. J. Softw. Eng. Technol. **1**(2), 33–42 (2014)
24. Baig, J.J.A., Al Fadel, M.A.: Measuring reusability during requirement engineering of an ERP implementation. In: ICICIS 2017 (2017)
25. Palomares, C., Franch, X., Quer, C.: Industrial practices on requirements reuse: an interview-based study – research protocol. http://tiny.cc/reuse-protocol

26. Oates, B.J.: Researching Information Systems and Computing. SAGE Publications, Thousand Oaks (2006)
27. Saldana, J.: The Coding Manual for Qualitative Research. SAGE Publications, Los Angeles (2009)
28. Field, A.: Discovering Statistics Using SPSS. SAGE Publications, London (2009)
29. Cohen, J.: Statistical Power Analysis for the Behavioral Sciences, 2nd edn. Lawrence Erlbaum Associates, Hillsdale (1988)
30. Runeson, P., Höst, M.: Guidelines for conducting and reporting case study research in software engineering. Empirical Softw. Eng. **14**(2), 131 (2009)
31. Robson, C.: Real World Research: A Resource for Social Scientists and Practitioner-Researchers. Blackwell Publishers Inc., Oxford (2002)
32. Franch, X., Palomares, C., Quer, C.: Industrial practices on requirements reuse: an interview-based study – coding results. http://tiny.cc/reuse-replication-package
33. Carrizo, D., Dieste, O., Juristo, N.: Systematizing requirements elicitation technique selection. Inf. Softw. Technol. **56**(6), 644–669 (2014)

Privacy and Legal Requirements

Disambiguating Requirements Through Syntax-Driven Semantic Analysis of Information Types

Mitra Bokaei Hosseini[1]([⊠]), Rocky Slavin[2], Travis Breaux[3], Xiaoyin Wang[2], and Jianwei Niu[2]

[1] St. Mary's University, San Antonio, TX, USA
mbokaeihossein@stmarytx.edu
[2] University of Texas at San Antonio, San Antonio, TX, USA
{rocky.slavin,xiaoyin.wang,jianwei.niu}@utsa.edu
[3] Carnegie Mellon University, Pittsburgh, PA, USA
tdbreaux@andrew.cmu.edu

Abstract. [Context and motivation] Several state laws and app markets, such as Google Play, require the disclosure of app data practices to users. These data practices constitute critical privacy requirements statements, since they underpin the app's functionality while describing how various personal information types are collected, used, and with whom they are shared. [Question/Problem] When such statements contain abstract terminology referring to information types (e.g., "we collect your device information"), the statements can become ambiguous and thus reduce shared understanding among app developers, policy writers and users. [Principle Ideas/Results] To overcome this obstacle, we propose a syntax-driven method to infer semantic relations from a given information type. We use the inferred relations from a set of information types (i.e. lexicon) to populate a partial ontology. The ontology is a knowledge graph that can be used to guide requirements authors in the selection of the most appropriate information type terms. [Contributions] Our method employs a shallow typology to categorize individual words in an information type, which are then used to discharge production rules in a context-free grammar (CFG). The CFG is augmented with semantic attachments that are used to generate the semantic relations. This method is evaluated on 1,853 unique information types from 30 privacy policies to yield 0.99 precision and 0.91 recall when compared to human interpretation of the same information types.

Keywords: Privacy policy · Abstraction · Ontology

1 Introduction

Mobile and web application (app) companies manage data practice requirements concerning information collection, use, and sharing. These requirements are communicated to users through privacy policies [1,18]. When describing data practices, privacy policies often use vague, high-level terms with unclear conditions

© Springer Nature Switzerland AG 2020
N. Madhavji et al. (Eds.): REFSQ 2020, LNCS 12045, pp. 97–115, 2020.
https://doi.org/10.1007/978-3-030-44429-7_7

to generalize a wide range of information types [29]. To be comprehensive, the language used in these policies tends to be ambiguous, which consequently leads to multiple, unwanted interpretations [25]. Ambiguity can also reduce the shared understanding among app developers, policy writers, and regulators who need to support privacy compliance and data transparency [7]. Such misunderstanding has consequences, such as the recent $5 billion settlement of Federal Trade Commission with Facebook [16]. This penalty arose from poor data practices resulting in leaking the personal information of 87 million users to third parties.

To ensure data transparency and compliance, methods have been proposed to analyze data practices in privacy policies. For example, Breaux et al. formalized data practice requirements from privacy policies using Description Logic [6], to automatically detect conflicting requirements across interacting services [8]. Tracing privacy requirements across policies can enhance developers' understanding of third-parties' data practices and comply with legal requirements, such as General Data Protection Regulation (GDPR), Articles 13.1 and 14.12. Other researchers have proposed techniques to trace requirements from privacy policies to app code using lookup tables, platform permissions, and information flow analysis [28, 33]. These methods were based on a manually-compiled lexicon (i.e. set of information types), wherein information types were grouped into categories tagged by keywords, such as "location", "contact", or "identifier" [33]. Coarse categorization can lead to inaccuracies, e.g., the phrase "WiFi SSID" can be construed to be a type of location information [33], perhaps because the corresponding technology can be used to infer device locations; however, this type does not constitute a location.

Hypernymy occurs when a more abstract or general information type is used instead of a more specific information type (e.g., the broader term "device information" used in place of "mobile device identifier") [3]. Hypernymy permits multiple interpretations of words and phrases, which leads to ambiguity and inconsistency in traceability.

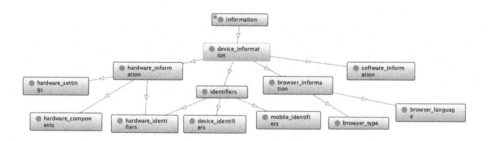

Fig. 1. Ontology example

Consider the following snippet from EA Games' privacy policy[1] stating, "We collect other information automatically [...], including: [...]; Mobile and other

---

[1] https://www.ea.com/legal/privacy-policy.

hardware or device identifiers; Browser information, including your browser type and the language you prefer; [...]; Information about your device, hardware and software, such as your hardware settings and components [...]". In this example, an analyst may make several inferences: (1) that "mobile identifiers", "hardware identifiers", and "device identifiers" are all kinds of "identifiers" that EA collects; (2) that "browser type" and "browser language" are both kinds of "browser information"; (3) "hardware information" and "software information" can be inferred as specific kinds of "device information"; and (4) that "hardware settings and components" are a specific kind of "hardware information". The analyst can infer such hypernymy relationships between information types intuitively by applying their domain knowledge and experience. An analyst who documents these inferences could create a reusable ontology, shown in Fig. 1, to illustrate each term and it's semantic relationships to other terms via hypernymy.

Ontologies are useful in dealing with requirements that are presented in potentially abstract human language. Without an ontology, analysts may be inconsistent in their interpretations by inconsistently applying heuristics in an ad hoc manner. In contrast, ontologies enable precise, reusable and semi-automated analysis of requirements [8,9,31,32].

Prior work on ontology construction has relied on manual comparison of information types [31], which is tedious and still susceptible to human error due to fatigue and gaps in analyst domain knowledge. Furthermore, the language use evolves, requiring ontology reconstruction. Two recent studies employed regular expressions that were hand-crafted from individual policy statements to extract hypernymy [12,21]. These approaches require a new analysis for each new policy, which does not generalize well.

To summarize, the research has shown the significance of utilizing ontologies in disambiguating vague and abstract requirements [8,9,31,32]. However, the current ontology construction methods rely on manual analysis, lack scalability or validation on information types from various domains (e.g., app categories and data practices). To address these issues and enable easier, more consistent ontology construction, we propose a syntax-driven semantic analysis method to construct an ontology. This method is evaluated on information types from six domains of mobile and web-based privacy requirements considering various data practices. The contributions of this paper are two-fold: (1) a syntax-driven method to infer semantic relations from a given information type. This method is based on the principle of compositionality, which states the meaning of each phrase can be derived from the meaning of its constituents [15,23]. Using this principle, we developed a context-free grammar (CFG) augmented with semantic attachments [2] over typed constituents of an information type to infer semantic relations between the information type and its constituents. (2) an empirical evaluation of our syntax-driven semantic analysis method on sample set of 1,138 information types from 30 mobile and web-based apps' requirements in six domains, including shopping, telecommunication, social networks, employment, health, and news.

This paper is organized as follows. In Sects. 2 and 3, we discuss important terminology and related work. In Sect. 4 we introduce our method. In Sect. 5, we present the evaluation and results, followed by threats to validity and concluding remarks in Sects. 6 and 7.

2 Background

In this section, we introduce terminology, datasets, and research method used throughout this paper.

Hypernymy: a relationship between two noun phrases where the meaning of one (hypernym) is more generic than the other (hyponym), e.g., "device information" is a hypernym of "device ID".

Meronymy: a part-whole relationship between two noun phrases, e.g., "device ID" is a part of "device".

Synonymy: a relationship between two noun phrases with a similar meaning or abbreviation, e.g., "IP" is synonym of "Internet protocol".

Lexicon: a collection or list of noun phrases that are information type names.

Ontology: an arrangement of concept names in a graph in which terms are connected via edges corresponding to semantic relations, such as hypernymy and synonymy, among others [24]. In this paper, we only consider information type names.

Morphological Variant: a concept name that is a variant of a common lexeme, e.g., "device ID" is a morphological variant of "device".

In the definitions above, we assume that noun phrases expressed in text have a corresponding concept and that the text describes one name for the concept. This relationship between the phrase and concept is also arbitrary, as noted by Saussure in his theory of the signifier, which is the symbol that represents a meaning, and the signified, which is the concept or meaning denoted by the symbol [11]. Peirce defines a similar relationship between sign-vehicles and objects, respectively [20].

Context-free Grammar: a set of production rules, expressing the way that symbols of a language can be grouped and ordered together [24].

Semantic Attachment: each production rule in a grammar is mapped to its semantic counterpart, called semantic attachment [2].

Lexicon L_1: a previously published lexicon containing 351 platform-related information types (e.g., "IP address") defined as "any information that the app or another party accesses through the mobile platform that is not unique to the app." The information types were extracted from collection data practices of 50 mobile app privacy policies [21,31].

Lexicon L_2: a previously published lexicon containing 1,853 information types related to any data collection, use, retention, and sharing practices, extracted from 30 mobile and web app privacy policies across six domains (shopping, telecommunication, social networks, employment, health, and news) [12].

Grounded Theory: a qualitative inquiry approach that involves applying codes to data through coding cycles to develop a theory grounded in the data [30]. We describe three applications [10] in this paper: (1) codes applied to phrases in Lexicon L_1 to construct a context-free grammar; (2) memo-writing to capture results from applying the grammar and its semantic attachments to infer relations from L_1; and (3) theoretical sampling to test the proposed method on a sample set of information types in lexicon L_2.

3   Related Work

Lexicons play an important role in reducing ambiguity and improving the quality of specifications [17]. Boyd et al. proposed to reduce ambiguity in controlled natural languages by optimally constraining lexicons using term *replaceability* [5]. Our proposed method improves lexicon development through automation to account for discovering new, previously unseen terms. By incorporating semantic relationships between terms, a lexicon can be expanded into an ontology. Breitman and do Prado Leite describe how ontologies can be used to analyze web application requirements [9]. Breaux et al. use an ontology to identify conflicting requirements across vendors in a multi-stakeholder data supply chain [8]. Their proposed ontology was formalized for three apps (i.e., Facebook, Zynga, and AOL) and contains hierarchies for actors roles, information types, and purposes. Their work motivates the use of ontologies in requirements analysis, yet relies on a small set of policies and has not been applied at scale.

Oltramari et al. propose using a formal ontology to specify privacy-related data practices [27]. The ontology is manually populated with practice categories, wherein each practice has properties, including information type. While the ontology formalizes natural language privacy requirements, there are no semantic relations formalized among information types, thus the ontology does not encode hypernymy.

Zimmeck et al. proposed an approach to identify the misalignments between data practices expressed in privacy requirements and mobile app code [33]. The approach uses a bag-of-words for three information types: "device ID", "location", and "contact information". For example, "IP address" is contained in the bag-of-words associated with device ID. Without an ontology, this approach cannot distinguish between persistent and non-persistent types, which afford different degrees of privacy risk to users.

Slavin et al. identify app code that is inconsistent with privacy policies using a manually constructed ontology [22,31]. The approach overcomes the limitation of Zimmeck et al. [33] and exemplifies the efficacy of ontologies for requirements traceability. However, it is costly and lacks scalability due to: (1) the time spent by analysts to compare information types, and (2) errors generated by analysts during comparison [22].

Hosseini et al. [21] proposed 26 regular expression patterns to parse the information types in lexicon L_1 (see Sect. 2) and to infer semantic relations based on their syntax. The discovered patterns fail to cover all the information types in lexicon L_1 and the approach requires extending the pattern set for new policies. To address this problem, we propose a context-free grammar to formally infer all the information types in L_1 with regard to pre-defined inference heuristics that are policy-independent.

Lexical ontologies, such as WordNet, can be used in requirements analysis. WordNet contains English words grouped into nouns, verbs, adjectives, adverbs, and function words [13,26]. Within each category, the words are organized by their semantic relations, including hypernymy, meronymy, and synonymy [13]. However, only 14% of information types from a privacy policy lexicon [22] are found in WordNet, mainly because the lexicon is populated with multi-word, domain-specific phrases. Therefore, finding an information type can be a challenging task for requirement analysts. We aim to address this limitation and facilitate automated analysis of data requirements.

4   Ontology Construction Method

Figure 2 presents our method overview given a privacy policy lexicon. This figure is summarized as follows: in step 1, information types in a lexicon are pre-processed and reduced; in step 2, an analyst manually assigns semantic roles to the words in each reduced information type, a step that is linear in effort in the size of the lexicon; in step 3, a context-free grammar (CFG) and its semantic attachments are used to automatically infer morphological variants and <u>candidate</u> ontological relations.

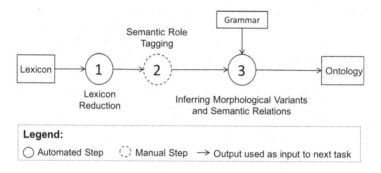

Fig. 2. Ontology construction method overview

The production rules that comprise the CFG and that are introduced in this paper are used to formalize and analyze the syntax of a given information type. To infer semantic relations, we implement the rule-to-rule hypothesis [2] by mapping each production rule in the CFG to its semantic counterpart, presented using λ-calculus.

4.1   Lexicon Reduction

In step 1, the information types from the input lexicon are reduced as follows: (1) plural nouns are changed to singular nouns, e.g., "peripherals" is reduced to "peripheral"; (2) possessives are changed to non-possessive form, e.g., "device's information" is reduced to "device information"; and (3) suffixes "-related", "-based", and "-specific" are removed, e.g., "device-related" is reduced to "device";

4.2   Semantic Role Tags

Given the reduced lexicon as input, step 2 consists of tagging each word in a phrase with one of five semantic roles: *modifier* (m), which describe the quality of a head word, such as "mobile" and "personal"; *thing* (t), which is a concept that has logical boundaries and can be composed of other things; *event* (e), which describe action performances, such as "usage", "viewing", and "clicks"; *agent* (a), which describe actors who perform actions or possess things; *property* (p), which describe the functional feature of an agent, place or thing such as "date", "name", "height"; and (x) which is an *abstract tag* indicating any general category of information, including "information", "data", and "details," among others. In an ontology, the concept that corresponds to x (e.g., "information") is the most general, inclusive concept in the hierarchy [21]. The roles are the result of grounded analysis on lexicon L_1 conducted by Hosseini et al. [21].

Part-of-speech (POS) is commonly used to tag natural language phrases and sentences [24]. *event* (e) words, for example, often correspond to noun-forms of verbs with special English suffixes (e.g., "usage" is the noun form of "use" with the suffix "-age"), and *things* (t) and *actors* (a) are frequently nouns. However, the analysis of lexicon L_1 shows that only 22% of tagged sequences can be identified using POS and English suffixes [21]. Therefore, we rely on manual tagging of words using five semantic roles by two analysts. The effort required for this task is linear in the size of lexicon.

The information type tagging is expressed as a continuous series of letters that correspond to the semantic roles. Figure 3 shows an example information type, "mobile device identifier" that is decomposed into the atomic words: "mobile", "device", and "identifier", and presented with tag sequence *mtp*. The intuition behind step 2 in the overall approach is based on the observation that information types are frequently variants of a common lexeme.

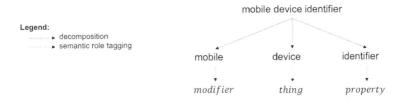

Fig. 3. Example of lexicon phrase, tokenized and tagged

4.3 Syntactic Analysis of Information Types Using Context-Free Grammar

A context-free grammar (CFG) is a quadruple $G = \langle N, V, R, S \rangle$, where N, V, and R are the sets of non-terminals, terminals, productions, respectively and $S \in N$ is the designated start symbol.

Step 3 (Fig. 2) begins by processing the tagged information types from the reduced lexicon using the CFG in Table 1. The CFG represents the antecedent and subsequent tags used to infer morphological variants from a given information type. The grammar is yielded by applying grounded analysis to the tag sequences of all information types in lexicon L_1. Notably, the grammar distinguishes between four kinds of tag sub-sequences: (1) a type that is modified by a modifier, called *Modified1*; (2) a type that is modified by an agent (e.g., "user" or "company") or event (e.g., "click" or "crash"), called *Modified2*; (3) a *Final* type that describes the last sequence in a typed string, which can end in a part, an information suffix, or an empty string; (4) for any parts of a whole (*Part*), these may be optionally described by modifiers, other parts, or things; and (5) *Info*, including those things that are described by information (e.g., "device information").

Table 1. Context-free grammar for syntax analysis

$<S> \rightarrow <Modified1> \mid <Modified2> \mid <Final> \mid x$
$<Modified1> \rightarrow m<Modified1> \mid m <Modified2> \mid m <Final> \mid mx$
$<Modified2> \rightarrow a <Final> \mid e <Final> \mid a <Info>$
$<Final> \rightarrow t <Part> \mid t <Info> \mid e <Info> \mid p$
$<Part> \rightarrow <Modified1> \mid <Modified2> \mid <Final>$
$<Info> \rightarrow x \mid \epsilon$

Figure 4 shows the parse tree for the phrase "mobile device identifier" with type sequence *mtp*. Next, we discuss how these productions are extended with semantic attachments to infer ontological relationships.

4.4 Inferring Morphological Variants and Semantic Relations

Based on the compositionality principle, the meaning of a sentence can be constructed from the meaning of its constituents [15, 23]. We adapt this principle to infer semantics between an information type and its constituent morphological variants by extending the CFG production rules with semantic attachments.

Each production $r \in R, r : \alpha \rightarrow \beta_1 ... \beta_n$ is associated with a semantic rule $\alpha.sem : \{f(\beta_1.sem, ..., \beta_n.sem)\}$. The semantic attachment $\alpha.sem$ states: the representation assigned to production r contains a semantic function f that maps semantic attachments $\beta_i.sem$ to $\alpha.sem$, where each $\beta_i, 1 \leq i \leq n$ is a

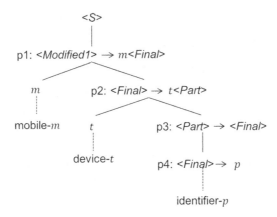

Fig. 4. Parse tree for "mobile device identifier" with tag sequence "*mtp*"

constituent (terminal or non-terminal symbol) in production r. The semantic attachments for each production rule is shown in curly braces {...} to the right of the production's syntactic constituents. Due to space limitations, we only present the semantic attachments of four production rules used in Fig. 4 in Table 2. The full table is published online[2]. We first introduce λ-calculus functions used in Table 2, before presenting an example where semantic attachments are applied to the tagged information type "mobile device identifier-*mtp*".

In λ-calculus, functions are represented by symbolic notations called λ-expressions. *Variables* and *constants* are atomic constituents of λ-expressions. Complex λ-expressions can be built from variables based on their application and abstraction [19].

Unary function $WordOf(y)$ maps a non-terminal to its tagged phrase sequence. For example, $WordOf(Final)$ returns "device identifier-*tp*" in Fig. 4. In this example, *Final* refers to the left-side non-terminal of *Modifier1*.

$Concat(y, z)$ is a binary function used to concatenate two tagged phrase sequences, for example $Concat$(mobile-m, information-x) produces "mobile information-mx".

$SubVariant(y)$ is a higher-order function accepting other functions like $Concat$ as an argument. It returns a list of variants that can be constructed using the input argument, e.g., $SubVariant$(mobile device identifier-*mtp*) returns the following list of variants: [mobile device identifier-*mtp*, device identifier-*mtp*, identifier-p].

$IsInfo$(y) is a unary function on a tagged phrase sequence, returning an empty list if the input sequence matches "information-x" and $Eqv(y,$ information-x), otherwise. For example, $IsInfo$(data-x) returns Eqv(data-x, information-x), since "data-x" and "information-x" do not match.

---

[2] http://galadriel.cs.utsa.edu/~rslavin/ontology-grammar/.

$KindOf(y, z)$, $PartOf(y, z)$, and $Eqv(y, z)$ are higher-order functions that map two tagged phrases to a single-element list containing a candidate hypernymy, meronymy, and synonymy axioms, respectively.

$Map(y, z)$ is a binary higher-order function that distributes the application of a function over a list of tagged phrases. More precisely, it can be shown as:

$$Map(f, [E_1, ..., E_n]) = [(f)E_1, ..., (f)E_n]$$

Table 2. Rules and semantic attachments for "mobile device identifier-mtp"

	Production	Semantic attachments	Line
p1	$<Modified1> \rightarrow m<Final>$	$\{\lambda y.\lambda m. Final.\text{sem}(\text{Concat}(y, m));$	1
		$\lambda m.\text{KindOf}(\text{WordOf}(Modified1), \text{Concat}(m, \text{information-}x));$	2
		$\text{KindOf}(\text{WordOf}(Modified1), \text{WordOf}(Final))\}$	3
p2	$<Final> \rightarrow t <Part>$	$\{\lambda y.\lambda t. Part.\text{Sem}(\text{Concat}(y, t));$	1
		$\text{KindOf}(\text{WordOf}(Final), \text{WordOf}(Part));$	2
		$\text{Map}(\lambda z.\text{PartOf}(\text{Concat}(z, \text{WordOf}(Part)),z))\lambda y.\lambda t$ $\text{SubVariant}(\text{Concat}(y, t))\}$	3
p3	$<Part> \rightarrow <Final>$	$\{\lambda y. Final.\text{sem}(y)\}$	1
p4	$<Final> \rightarrow p$	$\{(\text{Map}(\lambda p.\lambda z.\text{PartOf}(p, z)))\lambda y.\text{SubVariant}(y);$	1
		$\lambda y.\lambda p.\text{PartOf}(\text{Concat}(y,p),y)\}$	2

We now describe step 3 (Fig. 2) using the tagged information type "mobile device identifier-mtp". The tagged information type is first parsed using the grammar in Table 1. Its semantics are computed by visiting the nodes of the parse tree in Fig. 4 and applying the corresponding semantic attachments from Table 2 during a single-pass, top-down parse. Following this order, the semantics of production rule p1 is mapped to the following λ-expressions, where l in p1.l refers to line l in Table 2:

p1.1 represents an abstraction with two lambda variables, where y refers to the inherited tagged phrase from the right and top of the parse tree and m refers to the tagged phrase "mobile-m" read through the lexical analyzer. In this case, variable y refers to an empty string, since no tagged phrase precedes "mobile-m". Therefore, the first λ-expression can be reduced to $Final.sem(\text{"mobile-}m\text{"})$. In this λ-expression, "mobile-m" is inherited by non-terminal $Final$ in the parse tree. Based on the principle of compositionality, the semantics of a phrase depends on the order and grouping of the words in a phrase [23]. An unambiguous grammar like the CFG cannot infer all possible variants, such as "mobile device" and "device identifier", by syntax analysis alone, because the input phrase "mobile device identifier" would require both left- and right-associativity to be decomposed into these two variants. We overcome this limitation by introducing an unambiguous right-associative grammar and utilize λ-calculus to ensure that each non-terminal node inherits the sequence of words from the node's parents and siblings.

p1.2 represents an abstraction which reduces to a list containing a semantic relation: [KindOf("mobile device identifier-mtp", "mobile information-mx")] through reading variable m from the lexical analyzer. One might raise a point that "mobile information" is not a valid phrase. We acknowledge this fact, however, applying this rule to phrases such as "unique device identifier", "anonymous device information", and "anonymous demographic information" will results in creation of "unique information", "anonymous information", and "demographic information", which are meaningful phrases. We emphasize that the variants and relations generated through our method are only *candidates* and might not be semantically sound.

p1.3 represents a λ-expression which is the application of $KindOf$ on two operands, which reduces to a single element list [KindOf("mobile device identifier-mtp", "device identifier-tp")]. In the next step, we analyze the semantics of production rule p2 that are presented using three λ-expressions:

p2.1 represents a λ-expression to concatenate tagged phrases associated with the inherited variable y and variable t and passes the concatenation result ("mobile device-mt") to direct descendants of this node.

p2.2 represents the application of $KindOf$ function on "device identifier-tp" and "identifier-p", resulting a hypernymy relation in a single element list.

p2.3 is an application that maps a λ-expression to a *list* of variants. This list is constructed using a λ-abstraction that can be reduced to Sub-Variant("mobile device-mt"), producing [mobile device-tp, device-t]. Finally, Map applies $PartOf$ function on all the elements of this list resulting in [PartOf("mobile device identifier-mtp", "mobile device-mt"), PartOf("device identifier-tp", "device-t")].

Without inheriting "mobile-m" from the ancestors, we would not be able to infer the meronymy relationships between "mobile device identifier-mtp" and "mobile device-mt". Moreover, variant "mobile device-mt" is generated using syntax analysis of the tagged phrase sequence and semantics attached to the syntax. In contrast, other tagged phrases like "device identifier-tp" are solely generated through syntax analysis of "mobile device identifier-mtp". By augmenting syntax analysis with semantic attachments, we capture the ambiguity of natural language as follows. If we show the grouping using parenthesis, we can present the phrase associated with "mobile device identifier-mtp" as (mobile (device identifier)) which means mobile is modifying device identifier, e.g., an IP address as a kind of device identifier that changes based on location which makes it mobile. Another possible grouping is ((mobile device) identifier) which is interpreted as an identifier associated with a mobile device, e.g., a MAC address associated with a mobile phone, tablet or laptop. Therefore, grouping of words in "mobile device identifier-mtp" helps us consider all the possible semantics associated with an ambiguous phrase.

p3.1 is used to pass the inherited tagged phrase "mobile device-mt" to *Final* as the right-hand side, non-terminal. The semantics of production rule p4 as the last node visited in the parse tree is mapped to the following attachments:

p4.1 is the application of Map to a variant list constructed from a λ-abstraction. This abstraction is reduced to SubVariant("mobile device-mt"), returning the following variant list: ["mobile device-mt", "device-t"]. Finally, Map applies $PartOf$ function on all the elements of this list resulting in [PartOf("identifier-p", "mobile device-mt"), PartOf("identifier-p", "device-t")].

p4.2 represents an abstraction that reduces to [PartOf("mobile device identifier-mtp", "mobile device-mt")].

All the above production rules and semantic attachments yield a collection of candidate relations contained in multiple lists. As the final procedure in step 3, we merge the lists and add the relations to the output ontology.

5   Evaluation and Results

We answer the following research questions as part of our evaluation:

RQ1: How much, and to what extent, does the grammar generate the relationships between information type pairs in Lexicon L_1?

RQ2: Which semantic relations are missed by the method in comparison with the ground truth ontology?

RQ3: What level of effort is required to maintain the method for each new lexicon addition, considering the type of apps and data practices the lexicon is constructed from?

RQ4: How reliable is the method with respect to a new lexicon addition?

Research questions RQ1 and RQ2 evaluate the ontology construction method using lexicon L_1, discussed in Sect. 5.1. Research questions RQ3 and RQ4 evaluate the generalization and coverage of our method using lexicon L_2, discussed in Sect. 5.2.

5.1   Evaluation Using Lexicon L_1

We evaluate ontology construction method using lexicon L_1 to answer RQ1 and RQ2. L_1 contains 351 information types which are used to develop the context-free grammar (CFG) in Sect. 4.3. We acquired the reduced and tagged information types in L_1 online[3]. Given 335 reduced tagged information types, the CFG and semantic attachments yield 4,593 relations between phrases that share at least one word, which we published here (See Footnote 2).

We require a ground truth (GT) ontology containing the relations between information types in lexicon L_1 to evaluate the accuracy of the inferred relations

---

[3] http://gaius.isri.cmu.edu/dataset/plat17/study-platform-lexicon-typedPhrases-reduced.csv.

to answer RQ1. We acquired the results of a study published by Hosseini et al. [21][4] and followed their approach to construct the GT. This study contains 2,253 information type pairs which is the result of pairing all the information types that share at least one word in the reduced version of lexicon L_1 (based on step 1). Further, the study contains the relations assigned to each pair by 30 human subjects (called participant preferences). The participants were recruited from Amazon Mechanical Turk, had completed over 5,000 HITs, had an approval rating of at least 97%, and were located within the US [21].

Due to the diversity of participant experiences, which allows participants to perceive different phrase senses, participants can assign different semantic relations to the same pair, e.g., "mac" can refer to both a MAC address for Ethernet-based routing, and a kind of computer sold Apple. In another example, "email" can refer to three different senses: a service or program for sending messages; a message to be sent via the SMTP protocol; or to a person's email address, which is the recipient address of an email message. Therefore, participants may conclude "email address" is a part of "email", or is equivalent to "email" which are both valid interpretations. To avoid excluding valid interpretations, we follow Hosseini et al.'s approach to build a multi-viewpoint GT that accepts multiple, competing interpretations [21]. Valid interpretations for a pair are the ones that the observed number of responses per category exceeds the expected number of responses in a Chi-square test, where $p < 0.05$. This threshold means that there is at least a 95% chance that the elicited response counts are different than the expected counts [21]. The expected response counts for a relation are based on how frequently participants chose that relation across all participant comparisons. Finally, we constructed a multi-viewpoint GT as follows: for each surveyed pair, we add an axiom to the GT for a relation category, if the number of participant responses is greater than or equal to the expected Chi-square frequency; except, if the number of unrelated responses exceeds the expected Chi-square frequency, then we do not add any axioms.

We compared the inferred relations with the relations in the GT. An inferred relation is a true positive (TP), if it is logically entailed by GT, otherwise, that relation is a false positive (FP). Overall, 980 inferred relations are logically entailed in the GT. We use logical entailment to identify TPs, because subsumption is transitive and whether a concept is a hypernym of another concept may rely on the transitive closure of that concept's class relationships in the GT. We only found two inferred relations as FPs. An unrelated information type pair in the GT is considered as true negative (TN), if we cannot match any inferred relation with it. We found 805 pairs as TNs. For all information type pairs with valid interpretations (i.e., hypernymy, meronymy, and synonymy) in GT that do not match an inferred semantic relation, we count these as false negatives (FN). We found 466 of the related pairs in the GT that cannot be logically entailed in the ontology fragments inferred through our method.

We computed $Precision(Prec.) = TP/(TP + FP)$ and $Recall(Rec.) = TP/(TP + FN)$ for the ontology construction method using CFG and semantic

---

[4] http://gaius.isri.cmu.edu/dataset/plat17/preferences.csv.

attachments, presented in Table 3. We also compare the results of our method to the previously proposed ontology construction method using 26 regular expression patterns by Hosseini et al. [21]. Our model outperforms the 26 regular expression patterns, by decreasing the number of FNs and improving the recall.

Table 3. Performance Measures for Lexicon L_1

Method	Prec	Rec
26 regular expression patterns	0.99	0.56
CFG and semantic attachments	0.99	0.67

RQ2 concerns the type of relations that cannot be inferred using our syntax-driven method. To answer this question, we open coded the 466 FNs and identified four codes that explain the reasons that our method could not infer the relations:

(1) *Tacit Knowledge:* The relation requires tacit knowledge to be inferred and may not be inferred using syntax analysis of phrases, alone. For example, the hypernymy relation between "crash events" and "device event information" requires knowing that a crash is a software or hardware failure on a device, which is tacit knowledge that our method lacks. We identified 404/466 of the FNs that fall into this category.

(2) *Parse Ambiguity:* Our method analyzes phrases by grouping words from the right and left using the CFG and inherited variants in semantic attachments, respectively. However, we have observed 17/466 of FNs that disregard this grouping and therefore, cannot be inferred by our method. For example, an equivalence relation between "device unique identifier" and "unique device identifier" would be inferred as two kinds of "device identifier", but not as equivalent concepts.

(3) *Modifier Suppression:* Participants may ignore modifier roles in a phrase and thus prefer an equivalent relation between a pair of phrases. For example, "actual location" and "approximate location" are identified equivalent in the GT ontology. This phenomenon was also reported by Hosseini et al. [21]. We identified 34/466 phrase pairs and their relations that fall into this category.

(4) *Unjustifiable:* We identified 11/466 phrase pairs in the GT that we cannot justify despite the participant preference for these relations. For example, individuals identified "general demographic information" as a kind of "general geographic information". In another example, "mobile device type" is identified as a kind of "mobile device unique identifier" by the individuals.

5.2   Evaluation Using Lexicon L_2

RQ3 and RQ4 ask about the level of effort to maintain the method, and the method's reliability. We pre-processed 1,853 information types in lexicon L_2

using the strategies mentioned in Sect. 4.1, yielding 1,693 information types. In the four steps presented in Fig. 2, only step 2 involves manual effort for semantic tagging. During this step, two analysts individually assigned tags to information types in L_2. We calculated the inter-rater agreement for the assigned tags using Fleiss' Kappa co-efficient, which is a chance-corrected measure of agreement between two or more raters on a nominal scale [14]. The comparison resulted in 518 disagreements with Kappa = 0.704. After reconciling the disagreements, we increased Kappa to 0.917 and randomly selected tag assignments from one of the analysts.

To address RQ4 on method reliability, we require a ground truth for relations in L_2. For this reason, we selected information type pairs that share at least one word, yielding 1,466,328 pairs. Due to this large number, we sampled the pairs by creating strata that represent comparisons between tag sequences as follows:

Phase A: Each information type pair is mapped to their respective tag sequence pair, e.g., pair (mobile device, device name) is mapped to (mt, tp), yielding 974 unique tag sequence pairs, which we call the strata.

Phase B: Proportional stratified sampling is used to draw *at least* 2,000 samples from all strata with layer size range 1–490. The wide range in layer sizes implies unbalanced strata; e.g., strata that contain 1–3 pairs when divided by the total number of information type pairs yields zero. Therefore, we select all the pairs from strata with size one to ensure strata coverage. For strata of size two and three, one random information type pair is selected. For the remaining strata with sizes greater than three, sample sizes are proportional to the strata size, yielding one or more pairs per stratum. For each stratum, the first sample is drawn randomly. To draw the remaining samples, we compute a similarity distance between the already selected pairs and remaining pairs in each stratum: First, we create a *bag-of-lemmas* by obtaining word lemmas in the already selected pairs. Next, in each stratum, the pairs with the least common lemmas with the bag-of-lemmas are selected. We update the bag-of-lemmas after each selection by adding the lemmas of the selected pairs. This strategy ensures the selection of pairs with lower similarity measure, resulting in a broader variety of words in the sampled set.

Further, we ensure that each tag sequence is represented by at least one sampled item, and that sequences with a larger number of examples are proportionally represented by a larger portion of the sample. Using the initial sample size of 2,000, we captured 2,283 samples from 1,466,328 phrase pairs. Our samples contain 1,138 unique information types from Lexicon L_2. Using the pairs, we published a survey that asks subjects to choose a relation for pair (A, B) from one of the following six options [21]:

s: A is a kind of B, e.g., "mobile device" is a kind of "device."
S: A is a general form of B, e.g., "device" is a general form of "mobile device."
P: A is a part of B, e.g., "device identifier" is a part of "device."
W: A is a whole of B, e.g., "device' is a whole of "device identifier."
E: A is equivalent to B, e.g.,"IP" is equivalent to "Internet protocol."
U: A is unrelated to B, e.g., "device identifier" is unrelated to "location".

We recruited 30 qualified Amazon Mechanical Turk participants following the criteria mentioned in Sect. 5.1. We constructed a multi-viewpoint ground truth (GT) containing 2,283 semantic relations (See Footnote 2). Application of the CFG and semantic attachments on sampled information types from L_2 results in 21,745 inferred relations (See Footnote 2). To compute Precision and Recall, we compare the inferred relations with the multi-view GT. Overall, the method correctly identifies 1,686/2,283 of relations in the GT. We also compare the inferred relations using 26 regular expression patterns [21] with the GT. The performance measures in Table 4, suggest that our proposed CFG and semantic attachments reduce the number of false negatives (FNs). FNs are the semantic relations between information type pairs in the GT that do not match inferred semantic relations. By reducing the number of FNs, our proposed method improves the recall compared to the 26 patterns.

Table 4. Performance measures for lexicon L_2

Method	Precision	Recall
26 regular expression patterns	0.99	0.62
CFG and semantic attachments	0.99	0.90

6 Threats to Validity

Internal Validity - Evaluating semantic relations depends on reliable tagging of information types by analysts. Changes in tags affect the performance of the method when compared to the ground truth (GT). In Sect. 5.1, we identified four categories reflecting the relations that cannot be inferred when compared with ground truth (GT) for lexicon L_1. During second-cycle coding of Tacit Knowledge category, we observed a potential explanation for why individuals prefer a relation that differs from our results. The terms in "application software" were tagged tt, which is used to entail that "software" is part of an "application". However, we believe that participants recognize that "application software" is a single entity or thing. We also believe this explanation applies to 20 phrases and 69 semantic relations in the GT. We revised the tag sequences for these phrases and inferred relations based on this revision. Applying our method on the set of revised tagged types results in an additional 74 FNs compared to the original tagged information types. For example, the method cannot infer the relations between the following pairs: ("application software", "software information"), ("page view order", "web page"). Therefore, semantic ambiguity in tokenization and tagging can result in changes to the inferred relations, which is a shortcoming of the method.

For lexicon L_2, two analysts individually assigned tags to information types with an initial Kappa = 0.70. The analysts reconciled their differences to reach a Kappa = 0.92.

External Validity - The CFG is constructed on lexicon L_1 containing 351 platform-related information types defined as "any information that the app or another party accesses through the mobile platform that is not unique to the app." The information types were extracted from collection data practices of 50 mobile app privacy policies [21,31]. To study generalizability beyond lexicon L_1, we utilize lexicon L_2 for evaluation. Lexicon L_2 contains 1,853 information types related to collection, usage, retention, and transfer data practices, extracted from 30 mobile and web app privacy policies [12]. Further study is needed to determine how well the method extends beyond these datasets.

7   Conclusion and Future Work

Privacy policies are expressed in natural language and thus subject to ambiguity and abstraction. To address this problem, we propose a method to infer semantic relations between information types in privacy policies and their morphological variants based on a context-free grammar and semantic attachments. This method is constructed based on grounded analysis of information types in 50 privacy policies and tested on information types from 30 policies. Our method shows an improvement in reducing the number of false negatives, the time, and effort required to infer semantic relations, compared to previously proposed methods by formally representing the information types. Evidence from Bhatia et al. shows that between 23–71% of information types in any new policy will be previously unseen [4], which further motivates the need for a high-precision, semi-automated method to infer ontological relationships.

In future work, we plan to augment our method with a neural network classification model to infer semantic relations that are independent of syntax and purely rely on tacit knowledge, such as hypernymy relation between "phone" and "mobile device".

Acknowledgment. This research was supported by NSF #1736209 and #1748109.

References

1. Anton, A.I., Earp, J.B.: A requirements taxonomy for reducing web site privacy vulnerabilities. Requir. Eng. **9**(3), 169–185 (2004)
2. Bach, E.: An extension of classical transformational grammar (1976)
3. Bhatia, J., Breaux, T.D.: Towards an information type lexicon for privacy policies. In: RELAW, pp. 19–24. IEEE (2015)
4. Bhatia, J., Breaux, T.D., Schaub, F.: Mining privacy goals from privacy policies using hybridized task recomposition. TOSEM **25**(3), 22 (2016)
5. Boyd, S., Zowghi, D., Gervasi, V.: Optimal-constraint lexicons for requirements specifications. In: Sawyer, P., Paech, B., Heymans, P. (eds.) REFSQ 2007. LNCS, vol. 4542, pp. 203–217. Springer, Heidelberg (2007). https://doi.org/10.1007/978-3-540-73031-6_15
6. Breaux, T.D., Antón, A.I., Spafford, E.H.: A distributed requirements management framework for legal compliance and accountability. Comput. Secur. **28**(1–2), 8–17 (2009)

7. Breaux, T.D., Baumer, D.L.: Legally "reasonable" security requirements: a 10-year FTC retrospective. Comput. Secur. **30**(4), 178–193 (2011)

8. Breaux, T.D., Hibshi, H., Rao, A.: Eddy, a formal language for specifying and analyzing data flow specifications for conflicting privacy requirements. Requir. Eng. **19**(3), 281–307 (2013). https://doi.org/10.1007/s00766-013-0190-7

9. Breitman, K.K., do Prado Leite, J.C.S.: Ontology as a requirements engineering product. In: Proceedings. In: 11th IEEE International Requirements Engineering Conference, pp. 309–319. IEEE (2003)

10. Corbin, J., Strauss, A.: Basics of Qualitative Research: Techniques and Procedures for Developing Grounded Theory. Sage Publications (2014)

11. De Saussure, F., Harris, R.: Course in General Linguistics. (Open Court Classics). Open Court, Chicago and La Salle (1998)

12. Evans, M.C., Bhatia, J., Wadkar, S., Breaux, T.D.: An evaluation of constituency-based hyponymy extraction from privacy policies. In: RE, pp. 312–321. IEEE (2017)

13. Fensel, D., McGuiness, D., Schulten, E., Ng, W.K., Lim, G.P., Yan, G.: Ontologies and electronic commerce. IEEE Intell. Syst. **16**(1), 8–14 (2001)

14. Fleiss, J.L.: Measuring nominal scale agreement among many raters. Psychol. Bull. **76**(5), 378 (1971)

15. Frege, G.: Über begriff und gegenstand (1892)

16. FTC: FTC's $5 billion Facebook settlement: record-breaking and history-making (2019)

17. Gervasi, V., Zowghi, D.: On the role of ambiguity in RE. In: Wieringa, R., Persson, A. (eds.) REFSQ 2010. LNCS, vol. 6182, pp. 248–254. Springer, Heidelberg (2010). https://doi.org/10.1007/978-3-642-14192-8_22

18. Harris, K.D.: Privacy on the go: recommendations for the mobile ecosystem (2013)

19. Henk, B.: The lambda calculus: its syntax and semantics. Stud. Logic Found. Math. (1984)

20. Hookway, C.: Peirce-Arg Philosophers. Routledge, Abingdon (2010)

21. Bokaei Hosseini, M., Breaux, T.D., Niu, J.: Inferring ontology fragments from semantic role typing of lexical variants. In: Kamsties, E., Horkoff, J., Dalpiaz, F. (eds.) REFSQ 2018. LNCS, vol. 10753, pp. 39–56. Springer, Cham (2018). https://doi.org/10.1007/978-3-319-77243-1_3

22. Hosseini, M.B., Wadkar, S., Breaux, T.D., Niu, J.: Lexical similarity of information type hypernyms, meronyms and synonyms in privacy policies. In: AAAI Fall Symposium (2016)

23. Janssen, T.M., Partee, B.H.: Compositionality. In: Handbook of Logic and Language, pp. 417–473. Elsevier (1997)

24. Jurafsky, D., Martin, J.H.: Speech and Language Processing, vol. 3. Pearson, London (2014)

25. Massey, A.K., Rutledge, R.L., Antón, A.I., Swire, P.P.: Identifying and classifying ambiguity for regulatory requirements. In: RE, pp. 83–92. IEEE (2014)

26. Miller, G.A.: WordNet: a lexical database for english. Commun. ACM **38**(11), 39–41 (1995)

27. Oltramari, A., et al.: PrivOnto: a semantic framework for the analysis of privacy policies. Semant. Web **9**(2), 185–203 (2018)

28. Petronella, G.: Analyzing privacy of android applications (2014)

29. Reidenberg, J.R., Bhatia, J., Breaux, T.D., Norton, T.B.: Ambiguity in privacy policies and the impact of regulation. J. Leg. Stud. **45**(S2), S163–S190 (2016)

30. Saldaña, J.: The Coding Manual for Qualitative Researchers. Sage, Thousand Oaks (2015)

31. Slavin, R., et al.: Toward a framework for detecting privacy policy violations in android application code. In: ICSE (2016)
32. Wang, X., Qin, X., Hosseini, M.B., Slavin, R., Breaux, T.D., Niu, J.: GUILeak: identifying privacy practices on GUI-based data (2018)
33. Zimmeck, S., et al.: Automated analysis of privacy requirements for mobile apps. In: NDSS (2017)

On Understanding How Developers Perceive and Interpret Privacy Requirements Research Preview

Mariana Peixoto[1][(✉)], Dayse Ferreira[1], Mateus Cavalcanti[1], Carla Silva[1], Jéssyka Vilela[1], João Araújo[2], and Tony Gorschek[3]

[1] Universidade Federal de Pernambuco (UFPE), Recife, Brazil
{mmp2,dmmf,mcl2,ctlls,jffv}@cin.ufpe.br
[2] Universidade Nova de Lisboa (UNL), Lisbon, Portugal
p191@fct.unl.pt
[3] Blekinge Institute of Technology (BTH), Karlskrona, Sweden
tony.gorschek@bth.se

Abstract. **[Context and motivation]** Ensuring privacy of users' data has become a top concern in software development, either to satisfy users' needs or to comply with privacy laws. The problem may increase by the time a new law is in the vacancy period, and companies are working to understand how to comply with it. In addition, research has shown that many developers do not have sufficient knowledge about how to develop privacy-sensitive software. **[Question/problem]** Motivated by this scenario, this research investigates the personal factors affecting the developers' understanding of privacy requirements during the vacancy period of a data protection law. **[Principal ideas/results]** We conducted thirteen interviews in six different private companies. As a result, we found nine personal factors affecting how software developers perceive and interpret privacy requirements. **[Contribution]** The identification of the personal factors contributes to the elaboration of effective methods for promoting proper privacy-sensitive software development.

Keywords: Privacy requirements · Software development · Qualitative study

1 Introduction

Data handled in software applications often reveal large quantities of personal information, which are sometimes used for other purposes than initially intended and constitutes, in many cases, an invasion of privacy [6,12]. In this sense, users'

Electronic supplementary material The online version of this chapter (https://doi.org/10.1007/978-3-030-44429-7_8) contains supplementary material, which is available to authorized users.

N. Madhavji et al. (Eds.): REFSQ 2020, LNCS 12045, pp. 116–123, 2020.
https://doi.org/10.1007/978-3-030-44429-7_8

privacy can be defined as the right to determine when, how and to what purpose information about them is communicated to others [6].

According to Spiekermann and Cranor [10], new regulatory demands and consumer concerns are driving companies to consider privacy-friendly policies. Face to this, it is necessary to consider privacy principles and apply them from the early stages of the Software Development (SE) process, i.e., from the Requirements Engineering (RE) phase [3,6].

One approach created for this purpose is called Privacy by Design (PbD) [2]. It begins with explicit recognition of the value and benefits of proactively adopting strong privacy practices at the early stages of software development [2,5]. PbD has been embraced by the European Union to create the European General Data Protection Regulation (GDPR) [4]. This regulation was applied in May 2018 and introduced rules regarding the protection and processing of personal data. In Brazil, the General Personal Data Protection Law 13.709/2018 (in Portuguese, Lei Geral de Proteção de Dados or LGPD) was approved in August 2018 and is in the vacancy period [7].

On the other hand, there is still limited awareness of the importance of privacy requirements. For example, people are not aware of how privacy can be used to mitigate the damage caused by a potential security violation. In addition, there is little research related to the fact that developers[1] do not have sufficient knowledge of how to develop software with privacy requirements [5]. In fact, to successfully deploy PbD, we need to know how developers understand privacy [5].

In this context, we take advantage of the LGPD vacancy period, when organizations are struggling to come into compliance, to perform a qualitative study to identify the personal factors that affect how developers interpret and perceive privacy requirements in their daily work. To achieve this, we conducted thirteen semi-structured interviews with developers from six different private organizations. Data analysis was performed in light of personal factors of the Social Cognitive Theory (SCT) [1]. In SCT, a personal factor can be characterized as an element that constitutes human cognition, that is, the ability of the human being to memorize, plan, judge, among others [1,5].

Next sections are organized as follows: Sect. 2 describes the research method. Section 3 presents the study results. Section 4 details the threats to validity. And, finally, Sect. 5 shows the final considerations.

2   Research Method

We summarize the goal of our research as follows: **Analyze** personal factors, **for the purpose of** understanding their influence, **with respect to** interpretation and perception of privacy, **from the point of view of** software developers, **in the context of** Brazilian software development companies, more specifically, at Recife. Based on our goals, and a previous study provided by Hadar et al. [5],

---

[1] We generalize the term developer to those who work in software development.

we aim to answer the following Research Question (RQ): *What personal factors influence developers' perception and interpretation of privacy requirements in software development?*

Design and Procedures. Grounded Theory (GT) [11] was performed in light of the personal factors of SCT [1]. It is composed of the findings related to developers' perceptions and their interpretation of privacy requirements. For data collection, we performed semi-structured interviews based on the questionnaire[2] provided by Hadar et al. [5]. We decided to use the questionnaire because it was already used in previous research and validated to observe how personal factors of SCT affect the understandings of privacy by software developers. We chose non-probabilistic convenience sampling because it would be challenging to identify all members of the target population (i.e., software developers). Therefore, our candidates' selection was based on our known industrial contacts who were available and willing to participate.

We previously had a pilot interview with a member of a software development company to verify comprehension of the questions and to measure the time spent. After that, two authors conducted thirteen detailed in-depth face-to-face interviews between January 2019 and May 2019. Each interview lasted an average of 37.46 min and resulted in 8 h and 11 min of audio time. At the beginning of each interview, the participant's verbal consent, as well as audio recording permission, were confirmed to continue the procedure of data collection.

After data collection, two authors transcribed all interviews. The data analysis was conducted by four authors, based on qualitative coding principles of GT [11]. We started the coding process by performing open coding, in which we created codes for extracts of the text. After that, in axial coding, we took further readings in the transcripts and the created codes (from open coding). Thus, we identified other text extracts and also group similar codes. Finally, in selective coding, we identified categories that codes could be linked to. These categories are the personal factors that affect how developers interpret and perceive privacy in RE. We present an example of coding in Fig. 1. The coding process was performed using atlas ti software (cloud.atlasti.com).

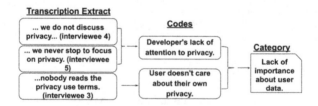

Fig. 1. Category creation.

---

[2] Supplementary Material: https://marianapmaia.github.io/REFSQ2020/.

3   Results and Analysis

We interviewed a total of thirteen developers from six private companies. Table 1 shows the sample characterization. The model presented in Fig. 2 explains the personal factors that play a role in developers' understanding of privacy. In the rectangles, we show nine categories as personal factors that affect positively (+) or negatively (−) how developers perceive and interpret privacy requirements. The arrows between categories (personal factors) represent that the related categories can influence each other. We also found some secondary factors (represented as a statement with an arrow to a category) which can influence positively (+), i.e., corroborate, or negatively (−), i.e., oppose the personal factors.

Table 1. Sample characterization.

Id cpy.	Cpy. size*	Domain	Role (years of experience)
1	Medium	Marketing	CEO (5)
2	Very small	Software factory	CEO (9)
3	Large	Several**	Soft. Engineer (5/5/16/10/3/4); Soft. Consultant (20)
4	Medium	Security	Soft. Analyst (3); Soft. Engineer (5)
5	Very large	Several	Developer (10)
6	Very small	Aug. reality	Developer (2)

*Number of employees: Very small < 10; Small < 100; Medium < 500; Large < 1000; Very Large > 1000. ** Offers services, maintenance, software creation, courses, etc.

Empirical knowledge about informational privacy is a positive personal factor which is corroborated by two secondary factors indicating that respondents had a practical knowledge about personal data. For example, interviewee 2 (from cpy 2) said: *"I have already served as an architect [...] that handle user data"*. This personal factor influences and is influenced by other positive personal factors. For example, **Experience in allowing the user to control their data stored by the system**, in particular, is corroborated by three secondary factors indicating that respondents concern about the need for transparency in the collection and use of personal information. For example, interviewee 12 (from cpy 3) said: *"I think all kinds of information I collect, the user has to give me consent"* .

Privacy decision depends on each development project is a positive personal factor that influences and is influenced by **Empirical knowledge about informational privacy** and **Lack of formal privacy knowledge**. This personal factor is corroborated by two secondary factors that allowed us to observe consistency among answers related to how privacy should be handled in each development project interaction. Indeed, interviewee 12 (from cpy 3) said: *"[...] it depends on each company, the way it deals with its users.*

Lack of formal privacy knowledge is a negative personal factor and it is corroborated by two secondary factors, indicating the unawareness regarding the laws and privacy definition. For example, interviewee 4 (from cpy 4) said,

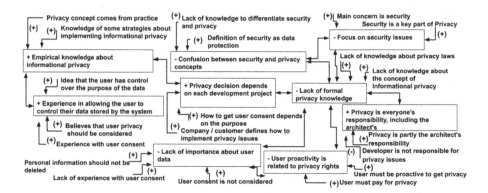

Fig. 2. Personal factors influencing interpretation and perception of privacy.

"I haven't had this contact [with the law] yet". This personal factor is related to **Confusion between security and privacy concepts**, also a negative personal factor because security and privacy have different meaning. This personal factor is corroborated by two secondary factors, indicating that respondents defined privacy using security-related terms. For example, interviewee 5 (from cpy 3) said: *"I think it's the data security part, refers to the protection of personal information"*. Other answer was provided by interviewee 13 (from cpy 3): *"When you give permission to use your data, and that application eventually leaks [...] it's also a matter of privacy, but I don't know if it's a security issue"*.

Confusion between security and privacy concepts also influences and is influenced by **Focus on security issues**. This factor is corroborated by two secondary factors, indicating the respondent's main concern is just security as well as privacy is all about security. For example, interviewee 4 (from cpy 4) said: *"We need to make sure our software is secure [...]"*.

Respondents mostly believe **Privacy is everyone's responsibility, including the architect's**. One secondary factor corroborates and one opposes to this personal factor. This category showed respondents think privacy responsibility should be shared between the architect, clients, or the team. For example, interviewee 12 (from cpy 3) said: *"It is not only the responsibility of [the architect]"*. Some respondents did not believe that the responsibility for privacy lies with the developer as, for example, interviewee 12 (from cpy 3): *"Privacy issues do not come [to the developer] very much. These security issues are linked to development, but privacy issues not"*.

User proactivity is related to privacy rights is a negative personal factor with two corroborations. In some cases, it was pointed out that the right to privacy is equally proportional to the user proactivity to achieve it. Interviewee 2 (from cpy 2) quoted: *"If the application is free, you have to accept that you are the product"*. This personal factor influences and is influenced by **Lack of importance about user data**, which is also a negative factor. It has three corroborations related to the belief that data should be kept into the system regardless users' consent and privacy breach risk. For example, interviewee 12 (from cpy 3) said: *"I don't think that storing personal information is privacy violation because with this I make user's life more comfortable"*.

Our findings indicate that developers have empirical knowledge of privacy, but most of them do not know how to interpret properly privacy requirements, as well as many of them do not know about formal privacy or LGPD. Empirical knowledge is a positive point, despite that, the fact of developers do not have formal knowledge can be seen as problematic because it is a period of privacy law vacancy. They generally understand that privacy could be implemented by using practices for implementing security because they make confusion between privacy and security. This finding is similar to the findings provided by Hadar et al. [5], that developers use the vocabulary of security to address privacy challenges, and this vocabulary limits their perceptions of privacy. In addition, some respondents do not intend to use privacy practices (for example, delete personal data when it is no longer needed) even recognizing their importance. They believe privacy is a trade-off, that the lack of privacy is justified by the provision of the service. Also, there was no concern to restrict the collection of personal data to only those necessary for the software operation. In fact, unrestricted data collection can become a bigger problem if a security problem occurs. This findings may be a negative factor for the acceptance and incorporation of PbD, that is, the implementation of privacy practices since the beginning of software development.

4 Threats to Validity

In the validity threats, we considered the indications provided by Runeson and Höst [9]. **Construct validity** reflects the extent to which operational measures represent what the researcher has in mind and what is investigated according to the RQs. We considered this threat by ensuring that the identities of participants and companies would not be disclosed. Besides that, prior to the interviews, we presented clarifications on the research reasons. In addition, we considered this validity when using a questionnaire already tested and validated for the same purpose (privacy point of view by developers).

Internal validity considers whether there are other factors that influence the results. To mitigate this type of threat, the sample was composed of individuals with different roles/years of experience and from companies of different sizes/domains. **External validity** is concerned with to what extent it is possible to generalize the results. We cannot assure the presented results can be generalized because the qualitative study was carried out with few participants. However, these results presented similar findings to that provided by Hadar et al. [5].

Reliability is concerned with to what extent the data and the analysis are dependent on the specific researchers. To mitigate this threat, we followed a clear method and we conducted several rounds of discussion among the involved researchers before the interviews. In addition, the interviews and data analysis were carried out by more than one researcher.

5   Final Considerations

This paper presented results of a qualitative study on how developers perceive and interpret privacy requirements. We showed nine personal factors that positively or negatively affect the developer's understanding of privacy requirements. We found that developers have practical knowledge of privacy, rather than theoretical knowledge. They often focus on security and this can compromise the resolution of privacy issues. Besides that, many developers recognize the importance of using privacy practices but some have no intention of using it.

As ongoing research, we are analysing other data collected in the interviews to observe the behavioral and environmental factors of SCT, and how they interact with personal factors and affect developers' understanding of privacy. We are also working on defining and evaluating a requirements specification method designed to guide developers to consider privacy from the beginning of agile software development [8].

Acknowledgments. This study was financed in part by the Coordenação de Aperfeiçoamento de Pessoal de Nível Superior - Brasil (CAPES) - Finance Code 001, supported by the S.E.R.T research profile, (see rethought.se, kks.se), and NOVA LINCS Research Laboratory (Ref. UID/CEC/04516/2019).

References

1. Bandura, A.: Social Foundations of Thought and Action. Prentice-Hall, Inc., Englewood Cliffs (1986)
2. Cavoukian, A.: Privacy by design: the 7 foundational principles. Inf. Priv. Commissioner Ontario Canada **5** (2009)
3. del Alamo, J.M., Martín, Y.-S., Caiza, J.C.: Towards organizing the growing knowledge on privacy engineering. In: Hansen, M., Kosta, E., Nai-Fovino, I., Fischer-Hübner, S. (eds.) Privacy and Identity 2017. IAICT, vol. 526, pp. 15–24. Springer, Cham (2018). https://doi.org/10.1007/978-3-319-92925-5_2
4. GDPR: General data protection regulation (2018). https://eugdpr.org/
5. Hadar, I., et al.: Privacy by designers: software developers' privacy mindset. Empir. Softw. Eng. **23**(1), 259–289 (2018)
6. Kalloniatis, C., Kavakli, E., Gritzalis, S.: Addressing privacy requirements in system design: the pris method. Requir. Eng. **13**(3), 241–255 (2008)
7. LGPD: General Law on Personal Data Protection/Lei Geral de Protecao de Dados n. 13.709 (2018). http://www.planalto.gov.br/ccivil_03/_ato2015-2018/2018/lei/L13709.htm
8. Peixoto, M., Silva, C., Lima, R., Araújo, J., Gorschek, T., Silva, J.: PCM tool: privacy requirements specification in agile software development. In: 10th Brazilian Software Conference: Theory and Practice (CBSoft 2019), pp. 108–113. SBC (2019)
9. Runeson, P., Höst, M.: Guidelines for conducting and reporting case study research in software engineering. Empir. Softw. Eng. **14**(2), 131 (2009)
10. Spiekermann, S., Cranor, L.F.: Engineering privacy. IEEE Trans. Software Eng. **35**(1), 67–82 (2008)

11. Strauss, A., Corbin, J.: Basics of Qualitative Research Techniques. Sage Publications, Thousand Oaks (1998)
12. Van Der Sype, Y.S., Maalej, W.: On lawful disclosure of personal user data: what should app developers do? In: International Workshop on Requirements Engineering and Law (RELAW), pp. 25–34. IEEE (2014)

A Methodology for Implementing the Formal Legal-GRL Framework: A Research Preview

Amin Rabinia[1]([✉]), Sepideh Ghanavati[1], Llio Humphreys[2],
and Torsten Hahmann[1]

[1] University of Maine, Orono, ME 04469, USA
`amin.rabinia@maine.edu`
[2] University of Torino, 10124 Turin, TO, Italy

Abstract. [**Context and motivation**] Legal provisions create a distinct set of requirements for businesses to be compliant with. Capturing legal requirements and managing regulatory compliance is a challenging task in system development. [**Question/problem**] Part of this task involves modeling legal requirements, which is not trivial for requirements engineers as non-experts in law. The resultant legal requirements models also tend to be very complex and hard to understand. [**Principal ideas/results**] To facilitate the modeling process, we propose a formal framework for modeling legal requirements. This framework includes a methodology that helps to resolve complexities of legal requirements models. [**Contribution**] In this paper, we outline this methodology and present a procedure that reduces modal and conditional complexities of legal models and facilitates automation of the modeling process.

Keywords: Goal model · Formal logic · Legal requirements · GDPR

1 Introduction

Analysts extract legal requirements from regulations and model them in a format to be used for compliance analysis. Due to the complexity of legal texts, the modeling process can be challenging. Moreover, the resultant legal requirements models usually contain the complexities inherited from the original texts.

To address regulatory compliance problems, goal- and non-goal-oriented methods have been used in requirements engineering [2]. While non-goal-oriented methods, such as some logic-based approaches, provide a stronger reasoning support on requirements models, goal-oriented approaches, with visual and natural language representations, are easier to understand and use [10]. In [12,13], we proposed a modeling framework that integrates a formal method for extracting legal requirements with an expressive representation in Goal-oriented Requirements Language (GRL) [4]. This framework, called Formal Legal_GRL (FLG), is composed of three phases: (A) a legal requirements extraction phase, where legal

© Springer Nature Switzerland AG 2020
N. Madhavji et al. (Eds.): REFSQ 2020, LNCS 12045, pp. 124–131, 2020.
https://doi.org/10.1007/978-3-030-44429-7_9

requirements are manually extracted by following the FLG procedure (Sect. 2); (B) a data storage and retrieval phase, where legal requirements are manually stored in a database and then automatically retrieved as an .xml/.grl file; and (C) a goal model generation phase, where a .grl file is imported into GRL's tool support, jUCMNav [5], to automatically create a goal model.

This paper focuses on Phase A, which employs a logic-based methodology to resolve modal and conditional complexities of legal models. Most logic-based modeling attempts mirror such complexities with the aim of preserving accuracy and isomorphism in their models. However, the resulting models are arguably too complex to be usable. In this paper, we describe our modeling approach, using an algorithm for resolving legal complexities. With this approach, we are able to simplify legal models without losing their validity. Our proposed algorithmic procedure is also a step towards increased automation of the FLG framework.

2   Legal Requirements Extraction (Phase A) - Overview

In Phase A, we extract legal requirements from regulations and annotate them based on the Deontic notions of obligation and permission [3]. Next, we reduce the modal and conditional complexity of legal statements by following the procedure described in Subsect. 2.1. Reducing these complexities helps (semi)-automating Phase B and Phase C of the FLG framework and in creating legal goal models which are more concise and understandable to human analysts.

Modal complexity relates to the difference between obligations and permissions, and the complication of different behaviors that satisfy them. To decrease the modal complexity of legal models, we keep obligations as-is and interpret prohibitions as negative obligations. On the other hand, we formalize permissions in an obligatory setting of the form $A \vee \neg A$. For example, this permissible clause, "the data protection officer [DPO] may fulfill other tasks and duties" [1], can be formulated as A: the DPO fulfills other tasks and duties OR $\neg A$: the DPO does NOT fulfill other tasks and duties. Where the clause is not originally an obligation, choosing between A or $\neg A$ is patently inevitable and thus convertible to obligation. With this technique, the final model only contains obligations (e.g. duties), negative obligations (e.g. prohibitions), and choices between obligations (e.g. permissible norms such as rights and powers).

Conditional complexity arises from legal statements that include (pre)-conditions or exceptions. To simplify conditional sentences, we convert them to equivalent disjunctive sentences by applying the implication rule (i.e. $A \rightarrow B \leftrightarrow \neg A \vee B$). Both humans and computers can more easily represent and process the simpler connective of disjunction as compared to a conditional.

After converting all legal statements to an obligatory format, we aggregate the obligations to form non-modal (descriptive) statements that utilize only simple connectives 'and', 'or', and 'xor'. The end result is then forwarded to Phase B.

2.1   The Procedure of Generating Non-modal Statements

We now describe our proposed procedure for modeling legal statements in Deontic logic and for converting them to non-modal statements.

First, we focus on the target stakeholder, who is supposed to satisfy the legal requirements, and convert the norms in a legal document to obligations or permissions for him. Next, we decompose the legal document based on its logical structure. A document's building blocks, or entities (i.e. paragraphs, sub-paragraphs, sentences, and phrases) are connected via logical connectives (and, or, if_then). Thus, we formalize these entities and connectives in a logical expression that represents how atomic entities of a legal document are connected to each other. Given such logical expressions, then, we follow a process defined in Algorithm 1, to resolve complexities and create non-modal statements. The procedure for modeling legal statements as logical expressions and resolving complexities consists of seven steps:

- **Step 1**– Convert the norms for the targeted stakeholders.
- **Step 2**– Identify entities (i.e. building blocks) of the document and label them as $E1, E2, ..., Ei$.
- **Step 3**– Identify connectives between the entities.
- **Step 4**– Model the set of entities in Deontic logic (using the modal operators 'O' for obligation and 'P' for permission) to create a logical expression.
- **Step 5**– Use Algorithm 1 to resolve complexities.
- **Step 6**– Document the output by replacing the Ei's with their natural language contents. For negations, we write the sentence in negative form.
- **Step 7**– Validate the result by analyzing non-compliance cases based on the original text, and examining whether resultant statements capture them.

Algorithm 1. Algorithm for Resolving Legal Complexities

```
1   FLG_Function(logical_expression) begin
2       if  the logical_expression contains modal complexity then
3           switch the logical_expression do
4               case unconditional obligation, OE do
5                 | keep the obligation as is;
6               case conditional obligation, E1 → OE2 do
7                 | factor out the obligation (O[E1 → E2]);
8               case unconditional permission, PE do
9                 | transform to obligatory form (O[E ∨ ¬E]);
10              case conditional permission, PE1 → E2 do
11                  | transform to conditional obligation (¬E2 → O¬E1);
12                  | factor out the obligation (O[¬E2 → ¬E1]);
13      if  the logical_expression contains conditional complexity then
14          factor out the obligations;
15          apply the implication rule, i.e. convert E1 → E2 to ¬E1 ∨ E2.
```

Algorithm 1, at this point, only provides a general guideline for manual process of logical expressions of generic and simplified cases. To extend and implement this algorithm, we need to articulate its data-flow and include more complex inputs.

3   An Example of Modeling with the FLG Procedure

In this section, we apply the procedure explained in Subsect. 2.1 to an excerpt of Article 15 of the General Data Protection Regulation (GDPR) [1] which is as follows:*(1) The data subject shall have the right to obtain from the controller confirmation as to whether or not personal data concerning him or her are being processed, and, where that is the case, access to the personal data. [The rest is removed]. (2) Where personal data are transferred to a third country or to an international organisation, the data subject shall have the right to be informed of the appropriate safeguards [cross-reference]. [Paragraph 3 and 4 are removed].*

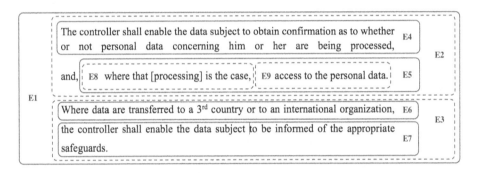

Fig. 1. Example of annotation for step 1 (*Ei* denote entities)

Step 1 (Extract obligations). Since the requirements model is made for the controller, we convert the data subject rights to obligations for the controller (shown in Fig. 1: E4, E7, and E9).

Step 2 (Identify entities) starts with identifying the building blocks of the document and decomposing them based on their logical structure. As shown in Fig. 1, E1 has two paragraphs (E2 and E3). Paragraph 1 has two parts (E4 and E5) connected with 'and'. E5 is a conditional statement, where E8 is its antecedent and E9 is its consequent. Same for E6 and E7, in Paragraph 2.

Step 3 (Identify the connectives): To satisfy the article, both the paragraphs are required. Therefore, E1 entails E2 AND E3; E2 entails E4 AND E5; E3 entails IF E6 THEN E7 (Note that E3 involves a conditional obligation, i.e. the obligation might not be in force if the precondition is not met. This is captured by the material conditional); E5 entails IF E8 THEN E9.

Step 4 (Formalize the entities). We annotate the obligations with 'O':

$E1 = E2 \wedge E3$
$\quad = (OE4 \wedge E5) \wedge (E6 \rightarrow OE7)$
$\quad = (OE4 \wedge [E8 \rightarrow OE9]) \wedge (E6 \rightarrow OE7).$

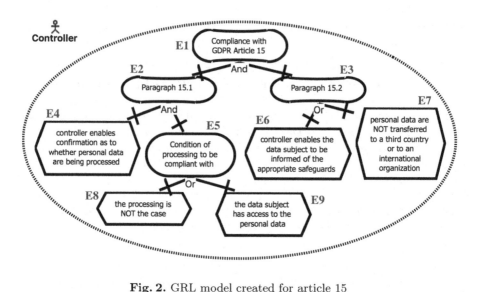

Fig. 2. GRL model created for article 15

Step 5 (Use Algorithm 1) resolves the modal complexity, by factoring out the obligations:

$= (OE4 \wedge O[E8 \rightarrow E9]) \wedge O(E6 \rightarrow E7)$ **line 7 of the algorithm**

$= O[(E4 \wedge [E8 \rightarrow E9]) \wedge (E6 \rightarrow E7)]$ **line 14**.

And conditional complexity, by using the implication rule:

$= O[(E4 \wedge [\neg E8 \vee E9]) \wedge (\neg E6 \vee E7)]$ **line 15**.

Step 6 (Document the output by replacing the Ei's with their content):

It shall be the case that [(the controller enables confirmation as to whether or not personal data concerning the data subject are being processed AND [either the processing is NOT the case OR the data subject has access to the personal data]) AND (either personal data are NOT transferred to a third country or to an international organization OR the controller enables the data subject to be informed of the appropriate safeguards)]

Step 7 (Validation): There are three cases of non-compliance based on the original text: (1) when the data subject cannot obtain the confirmation ($E4 = false$); (2) when the personal data is being processed but the data subject has no access ($E8 = true, E9 = false$); (3) when the data is transferred but the data subject cannot be informed of the safeguards ($E6 = true, E7 = false$). If any of the cases happens, the entire logical expression becomes *false*, which indicates non-compliance.

Figure 2, depicts the final model of the running example, created with the FLG methodology and represented in GRL. Entities are annotated in the figure based on the logical expression ($O[(E4 \wedge [\neg E8 \vee E9]) \wedge (\neg E6 \vee E7)]$).

4   Literature Review

Governatori and Rotolo [9] present a conceptual model for handling legal obligations for business process compliance. Their model includes a language based on Defeasible and Deontic logic for representing, and reasoning about legal obligations. Although the paper [9] focuses on complexities related to obligations, their approach influenced our method for dealing with various legal complexities. Torre et al. [15] propose a UML-based representation of the GDPR [1] with two generic and specialized tiers. The modeling process in their work relies heavily on the participation of legal experts, which limits its automation. Another approach [6] systematically extracts and represents requirements in a semi-formal notation. We follow their methodology to develop the FLG framework. However, their work [6] only provides textual requirements models, which reduces its flexibility for compliance analysis.

Nòmos 3, a goal-oriented modeling language for evaluating compliance [11], presents a sophisticated language for reasoning and representing rights and duties. However, Nòmos 3 lacks a detailed methodology for extracting and modeling legal requirements. Legal-URN [7,8], another goal-oriented framework for modeling legal requirements, extracts the natural language legal requirements and creates their corresponding goal models in Legal-GRL. Despite the expressiveness of Legal-GRL models, its modeling process is manual.

5   Evaluation Plan

To evaluate our framework, we plan to perform both conceptual and empirical evaluations. For the conceptual evaluation, we aim to demonstrate the soundness of theoretical and legal basis of the FLG methodology, based on Deontic logic and legal theories (such as [3,14]).

For the empirical evaluation, we aim to apply the proposed FLG methodology to various regulations, specifically comparing how experts and non-experts apply the method. Measuring the degree of consensus and dissensus between the resultant models indicates the reliability and replicability of the methodology. Our preliminary study shows that the degree of consensus will increase when (1) the methodology is accompanied by details of logical conventions and rules, and when (2) example patterns of modeling are provided.

We will also evaluate the validity and comprehensiveness of the produced models with participation of legal experts (and against the annotated documents as the gold standard). Although the FLG models seem intuitively and theoretically simpler, we need to also evaluate this empirically. This work will require participants (e.g. requirements engineers) to compare the FLG models versus the original regulations and also models from other approaches (e.g. Legal-GRL, Nòmos 3). For this evaluation, we will use our corpus of models created for 38 privacy-related articles of the GDPR.[1]

---

[1] Part of the corpus is accessible at: https://bit.ly/35znB0t.

6   Conclusion and Future Work

In this paper, we proposed a seven step procedure for the extraction of legal requirements as a step towards increased automation within the FLG framework. At the center of this procedure lies an algorithm that resolves modal and conditional complexities of a given legal text.

In future, we will elaborate on the proposed procedure to handle cross-references, ambiguities, and legal interpretations, and also on the algorithm to cover complexities beyond the generic cases. We also plan to expand our effort in implementing and automating Phases A of the FLG framework (using NLP techniques) and perform a detailed evaluation as outlined in Sect. 5.

References

1. The general data protection regulation (GDPR) (2018). https://gdpr-info.eu/
2. Akhigbe, O., Amyot, D., Richards, G.: A systematic literature mapping of goal and non-goal modelling methods for legal and regulatory compliance. Requirements Eng. **24**(4), 459–481 (2018). https://doi.org/10.1007/s00766-018-0294-1
3. Alchourrón, C.E.: Logic of norms and logic of normative propositions. Logique et analyse **12**(47), 242–268 (1969)
4. Amyot, D., Ghanavati, S., Horkoff, J., Mussbacher, G., Peyton, L., Yu, E.: Evaluating goal models within the goal-oriented requirement language. Int. J. Intell. Syst. **25**(8), 841–877 (2010)
5. Amyot, D., Mussbacher, G., Ghanavati, S., Kealey, J.: GRL modeling and analysis with jUCMNav. iStar **766**, 160–162 (2011)
6. Breaux, T.D., Antón, A.I.: A systematic method for acquiring regulatory requirements: A frame-based approach. RHAS-6), Delhi, India (2007)
7. Ghanavati, S.: Legal-URN framework for legal compliance of business processes. Ph.D. thesis, Université d'Ottawa/University of Ottawa (2013)
8. Ghanavati, S., Amyot, D., Rifaut, A.: Legal goal-oriented requirement language (legal GRL) for modeling regulations. In: Proceedings of the 6th International Workshop on Modeling in Software Engineering, pp. 1–6. ACM (2014)
9. Governatori, G., Rotolo, A.: A conceptually rich model of business process compliance. In: Proceedings of the Seventh Asia-Pacific Conference on Conceptual Modelling, vol. 110, pp. 3–12. Australian Computer Society, Inc. (2010)
10. Hashmi, M., Governatori, G., Lam, H.-P., Wynn, M.T.: Are we done with business process compliance: state of the art and challenges ahead. Knowl. Inf. Syst. **57**(1), 79–133 (2018). https://doi.org/10.1007/s10115-017-1142-1
11. Ingolfo, S., Jureta, I., Siena, A., Perini, A., Susi, A.: Nòmos 3: legal compliance of roles and requirements. In: Yu, E., Dobbie, G., Jarke, M., Purao, S. (eds.) ER 2014. LNCS, vol. 8824, pp. 275–288. Springer, Cham (2014). https://doi.org/10.1007/978-3-319-12206-9_22
12. Rabinia, A., Ghanavati, S.: FOL-based approach for improving legal-GRL modeling framework: a case for requirements engineering of legal regulations of social media. In: IEEE 25th International RE Conference Workshops (REW), pp. 213–218 (2017)
13. Rabinia, A., Ghanavati, S.: The FOL-based legal-GRL (FLG) framework: towards an automated goal modeling approach for regulations. In: 2018 IEEE 8th International Model-Driven Requirements Engineering Workshop (MoDRE), pp. 58–67 (2018)

14. Sartor, G.: Fundamental legal concepts: a formal and teleological characterisation. Artif. Intell. Law **14**(1–2), 101–142 (2006)
15. Torre, D., Soltana, G., Sabetzadeh, M., Briand, L., Auffinger, Y., Goes, P.: Using models to enable compliance checking against the GDPR: an experience report. In: Proceeding of the IEEE/ACM 22nd International Conference on Model Driven Engineering Languages and Systems (MODELS 19) (2019)

Stakeholders Feedback and Training

Towards Integrating Data-Driven Requirements Engineering into the Software Development Process: A Vision Paper

Xavier Franch[1], Norbert Seyff[2], Marc Oriol[1(✉)], Samuel Fricker[2], Iris Groher[3], Michael Vierhauser[3], and Manuel Wimmer[3]

[1] Universitat Politècnica de Catalunya, Barcelona, Spain
{franch,moriol}@essi.upc.edu
[2] University of Applied Sciences and Arts Northwestern Switzerland FHNW, Windisch, Switzerland
{norbert.seyff,samuel.fricker}@fhnw.ch
[3] Johannes Kepler University Linz & CDL-MINT, Linz, Austria
{iris.groher,michael.vierhauser,manuel.wimmer}@jku.at

Abstract. *[Context and motivation]* Modern software engineering processes have shifted from traditional upfront requirements engineering (RE) to a more continuous way of conducting RE, particularly including data-driven approaches. *[Question/problem]* However, current research on data-driven RE focuses more on leveraging certain techniques such as natural language processing or machine learning than on making the concept fit for facilitating its use in the entire software development process. *[Principal ideas/results]* In this paper, we propose a research agenda composed of six distinct research directions. These include a data-driven RE infrastructure, embracing data heterogeneity, context-aware adaptation, data analysis and decision support, privacy and confidentiality, and finally process integration. Each of these directions addresses challenges that impede the broader use of data-driven RE. *[Contribution]* For researchers, our research agenda provides topics relevant to investigate. For practitioners, overcoming the underlying challenges with the help of the proposed research will allow to adopt a data-driven RE approach and facilitate its seamless integration into modern software engineering. For users, the proposed research will enable the transparency, control, and security needed to trust software systems and software providers.

Keywords: Data-driven requirements engineering · Feedback gathering · Requirements monitoring · Model-driven Engineering

1 Vision

Software systems have an increasingly critical role in today's society. The efficient construction, operation, and evolution of software systems to satisfy the functionality and quality that users expect is key to success. This also includes to anticipate user expectations and provide functionality and qualities that users are unaware of and cannot communicate explicitly. Moreover, software systems that adapt to context changes need to

© Springer Nature Switzerland AG 2020
N. Madhavji et al. (Eds.): REFSQ 2020, LNCS 12045, pp. 135–142, 2020.
https://doi.org/10.1007/978-3-030-44429-7_10

gain users' trust. New approaches such as continuous software engineering [7, 15] have the potential to successfully keep the user in the loop, which is still a challenge in the requirements engineering discipline (RE) [6].

With this new demand, the so-called data-driven RE (DDRE) has emerged [9, 10]. DDRE proposes a paradigm shift in that RE is becoming a data-centred endeavour in support of the continuous evolution of software-intensive systems. Instead of letting a requirements engineer elicit, analyze, document, and validate requirements, (a crowd of) users generate data that leads to requirements as a result. This data can be provided by users either explicitly in the form of comments, ratings, and other kinds of feedback or implicitly through usage logs and monitoring data [7]. The realization of DDRE benefits from recent technological advancements, such as machine learning (ML) and natural language processing (NLP). In contrast to traditional RE techniques, DDRE enables the continuous elicitation of requirements directly from the (crowd of) end-users using the software. Although DDRE can only be applied to eliciting requirements from existing software, and must take into account regulatory and privacy concerns, the advent of Continuous Delivery, combined with techniques for privacy management, foster the applicability of DDRE and reduce those limitations. Furthermore, it is argued that software products' success depends on user feedback [9]. For instance, a recent survey with release engineers showed that 90% believed that users' feedback has the highest importance for evaluating success and failure of mobile apps [10].

While the general idea of DDRE is clear and increasingly accepted, its impact on software development and software systems is still an open question. Maalej et al. [9] have identified three directions for future research: more sophisticated ML and NLP techniques with analytic capabilities, integration of explicit and implicit feedback, and exploitation of data in release planning. While these three areas are subject of current research (e.g., [3, 12, 16]), we deem additional research directions crucial for the success of DDRE. These are the systematic development and integration of software development and runtime infrastructure required to implement DDRE, the integration of DDRE into a continuous software engineering process, and the trust of end-users in the responsible use of their data. Some research has started, e.g., with the integration of data-driven requirements management into rapid software development [5]. However, additional effort is needed considering the ongoing shift in software technologies (e.g., Cyber-Physical Systems) and software engineering (e.g., Agile/Lean and DevOps).

In this paper, we present our vision of enabling and integrating DDRE in continuous software engineering. Section 2 describes the challenges we deem important. Section 3 outlines our research roadmap alongside an introduction of an envisioned DDRE framework. Finally, Sect. 4 concludes the paper.

2   Research Challenges

In recent years, researchers have proposed adaptations of traditional RE with aspects of DDRE, such as user feedback and runtime monitoring [12, 16]. However, no holistic approach has been proposed for the integration of DDRE into software engineering. This goal would require flexible processes and tools that seamlessly integrate with existing environments and development processes. In the following, we describe the challenges we deem crucial for our vision coming to fruition. The identified challenges were obtained after studying the scientific state of the art and analyzing the limitations of current approaches.

Challenge 1: Seamless integration into existing development processes and software systems. Typically, the development of DDRE components (such as feedback forms or monitoring components) is done ad-hoc without considering the information needs of the different stakeholders in the development processes. Furthermore, the evolution and adaptation of these DDRE components is not always well-coordinated and aligned with the evolution of the system itself. This co-evolution process requires a flexible and configurable DDRE infrastructure incorporating different tools and interfaces to keep the system and the DDRE components in sync.

Challenge 2: Collection, processing, and integration of relevant heterogeneous information. The combination of user data from diverse sources into a consolidated source of feedback provides semantically richer information for decision-making [10, 12, 16]. The "diverse sources" comprise those mentioned above: data collected with feedback forms (e.g., ratings, text, images, or videos), logs of user interactions with the system, and quality-of-service data gathered through runtime monitoring of the system execution (e.g., response time, invalid accesses).

Challenge 3: Context-awareness and adaptability. The contexts in which users operate with the systems may change even during runtime when the system is being used. It is necessary to adapt the DDRE infrastructure to these changes. The context comprises several facets, for instance, locations, time of the day, environmental conditions, and user profiles [2].

Challenge 4: Provision of actionable feedback. Consolidated feedback needs to be analysed to inform decision-makers about the users' experience. The increasing popularity and adoption of software analytics [11], data science [4], and visualization approaches offer novel techniques to design methods supporting DDRE. Traceability to the requirements and design artefacts of the system is key, but often missing [14].

Challenge 5: Gaining users' trust. Information obtained via monitoring and collecting feedback from users is sensitive. The information may be misused for exposure, discrimination, and even identity theft. If such information concerns business affairs, it can expose a company to business intelligence and espionage. Hence, DDRE must win the users' trust in the responsible use of the collected data. It may do so by guiding developers in ethically sound use of data and help them to comply with regulations, e.g., by respecting the human users' privacy and the corporate users' business secrets.

Challenge 6: Provision of value for the entire life-cycle. So far, DDRE has mainly focused on the utilization of user data to support requirements elicitation, covering only a fraction of a system's life-cycle. We envision the same concepts being applied during system maintenance and evolution. E.g., before putting a release in operation, collected data could be leveraged to create realistic and lifelike simulations. This way, the DDRE infrastructure may be used for multiple ends and improve the return of investment in it.

Although we deem those six challenges as crucial for integrating DDRE into software engineering, it must be acknowledged that there might be additional issues that may require further research. For instance, analyzing the limitations and pitfalls of DDRE; defining types of systems or domains for which DDRE may be difficult to apply;

studying the possible combination of DDRE with traditional RE techniques; identifying the risks of misuse of DDRE (e.g., biased data or inappropriate choice of data sources); or challenges in upgrading the skills and training of RE practitioners.

3   Research Roadmap

In order to tackle the challenges presented in Sect. 2, we identify and elaborate respective research directions and propose a conceptual model-driven DDRE infrastructure (cf. Fig. 1). The infrastructure comprises five major parts: a family of domain specific languages (DSLs), the management of data sources, code generation, DDRE support components (such as monitoring and context-based feedback mechanisms), and components for analytics and decision support.

The first two parts are dedicated to the description and management of various different design time artifact that play a critical role in a data-driven RE process. This includes, for example, the requirements for the system, various design and context models, and monitoring or adaptation rules. In order to consolidate these diverse sources, we envision a family of DSLs facilitating the declarative description of these artifacts in a structured way. The third part of the infrastructure is dedicated to making use of these components at runtime. This is achieved by employing a model-driven approach that allows generating executable components based on the descriptions found in the DSL (e.g., monitors collecting certain information about the system). The data and user feedback collected by these components then needs to be consolidated and analysed. Finally, this will provide the foundation for the last part, supporting the decision-making process for new or changing requirements of the system. Related to these parts we have derived six distinct research challenges that drive our work on the DDRE infrastructure:

Research Direction 1: Specification and Generation of DDRE infrastructures. Bridging the gap between system development and infrastructure generation requires developing them from the same underlying basis, namely the system requirements. We think that system requirements provide valuable information to identify feedback needs and guide infrastructure development and customization. For instance, a non-functional requirement such as *"The system shall complete a user's purchase order in less than 2 s in 95% of the time"* points out the need for: (a) logging response times, (b) generating infrastructure code to aggregate all purchase order response times and check the stated condition, (c) generating context-based feedback forms to be shown to users for validating the requirement, and (d) mining suitable forums (blogs, twitters, ticketing systems) to gain additional information about user satisfaction or dissatisfaction. We anticipate employing a model-driven development approach [1] for generating DDRE infrastructure (cf. Fig. 1 – RD 1). A family of DSLs may allow specifying a DDRE infrastructure by, e.g., refining the requirements as formulas and linking them to the design of the system that receives the user data during runtime. An important milestone in this direction would be the availability of first DSLs for DDRE.

Research Direction 2: Embracing heterogeneous sources and feedback types. In order to collect valuable information for DDRE, the large variety of different sources and diverse types of feedback need to be taken into consideration [12, 16]. This in turn requires to identify relevant sources and to understand their information structure.

Again, dedicated DSLs are needed to describe different feedback types (cf. Fig. 1 – RD 2). Such descriptions allow for the structured combination of different kinds of feedback and are the basis for any form of subsequent data analysis. Bringing together heterogeneous feedback, therefore, is key to automatically uncover hidden requirements, identify problems to be solved, and improvement opportunities to be seized. Concrete outcomes regarding this second research direction could include advanced definitions of data sources and data sets in the form of data models. The availability of such models could be considered as important milestone in this direction.

Research Direction 3: Context-Aware Adaptation of the DDRE infrastructure. As a response to Challenge 3, we envision a certain degree of (self-)adaptability of the infrastructure to foresee, respond to, and learn about changing user contexts. This also means that this challenge includes two main aspects, context-awareness and adaptation. Analyzing usage contexts and being aware of the capabilities of DDRE components, we expect so-called context-awareness patterns to emerge that can be used to generate context-related code (cf. Fig. 1 – RD 3). These patterns will be bound to certain context dimensions and provide the necessary input for the adaptation of DDRE components in order to ensure the effective and efficient collection of data. Furthermore, the adaptation is needed to ensure that users' data is gathered accurately, efficiently, and in a non-intrusive way. For example, when a mobile device is running out of battery (a context change) the monitoring sampling rate could be reduced or monitoring could even be temporarily deactivated (adaptation of the DDRE components). This pattern may be always applied in systems deployed on a mobile device. The provision of advanced context models, the definition of context-awareness patterns and actual code generation to ensure the adaptation are important milestones for this research direction.

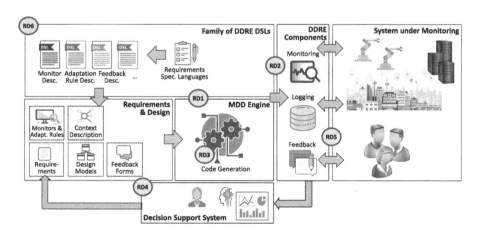

Fig. 1. Generation of the data-driven RE infrastructure: a model-driven vision.

Research Direction 4: Advanced Data Analysis capabilities and Decision Support Systems. We foresee the extensive use of analytics tools (such as SonarQube [13]) fed with the data collected by the DDRE infrastructure. Analytics may include indicators about customer satisfaction, risk, or time-to-market. They inform decision-makers and guide the evolution of the system by triggering requirement changes (cf. Fig. 1 – RD 4). As we perceive requirements to be the source for building the DDRE infrastructure, requirement changes also have an impact on this infrastructure. This self-adaptation enabling loop means that the infrastructure can co-evolve with the monitored system even at runtime. Providing first prototypes of DDRE infrastructures which are capable of co-evolving with the system itself, based on requirements for the system can be considered as key milestone here.

Research Direction 5: Ensuring Users' Trust in DDRE. Building and maintaining user trust requires an ethically and legally sound approach for collecting and processing data (cf. Fig. 1 – RD 5). In particular, DDRE should support privacy and business secrecy laws, such as the European General Data Protection Regulation 2016/679 (GDPR) and Trade Secrets Directive 2016/943. These will affect the DDRE technical architecture and DSL, the software lifecycle processes benefiting from DDRE, and the organisational structure of the data processors and users. Several aspects will need to be considered, such as purposeful data minimisation and safeguarding, end-user data governance with dynamic consent, and mobility of the collected data. Furthermore, any DDRE approach will need to be evaluated in terms of privacy and trust impact and in its ability to unlock data for supporting decisions in the software process. In general, a better understanding of user's trust in the context of DDRE and the documentation of this understanding, e.g., in the form of trust models can be considered important milestones.

Research Direction 6: Processes Integration of DDRE into existing software development lifecycles. DDRE needs to be smoothly integrated and exploited in rapid, even continuous software development (cf. Fig. 1 – RD 6). The support of all relevant activities in the end-to-end process should be studied, starting with the identification of user needs and ending with the addition of requirements to the product backlog. Knowing how and when data analysis is performed and by whom allows understanding the implications of DDRE in the software process. Furthermore, the DDRE infrastructure has to be validated before going into production. This is challenging considering the context-dependent nature of the infrastructure, which calls for a component able to generate contexts that are part of the infrastructure-testing process. Finally, DDRE needs to be aligned with existing paradigms and methods in software engineering and business modelling. E.g., online controlled experimentation is one such relevant method [8] that uses collected usage data, here for evaluating different implementations of a feature. The data-driven nature of such paradigms and methods calls for the exploration of possible synergies. In the previous paragraph, we have highlighted several important steps towards process integration of DDRE which represent key milestones in this regard.

4   Conclusion

Recent research in DDRE contributes important pieces of the puzzle. To be valuable and useful in real-world applications, these pieces need to be arranged so that they fit together seamlessly and automation possibilities need to be explored. This is particularly true for current user-driven approaches that are already delivering value to software producers but also face challenges which we have outlined in this paper. Although we expect DDRE to have a major impact on RE in the near future, RE as we know it will still be necessary when it comes to the development of entirely new systems where experiences and data cannot be sufficiently leveraged to "generate" requirements. Furthermore, DDRE does not limit creative developers but is intended to offer means that empower creativity. We are convinced that this novel RE paradigm will increase the effectiveness of RE, improve software quality, and eventually will help to increase the trust of users in software applications.

Acknowledgements. This work has been supported by: the Spanish project GENESIS (TIN2016-79269-R), the Christian Doppler Forschungsgesellschaft, the Austrian Federal Ministry for Digital and Economic Affairs, the National Foundation for Research, Technology and Development, and the Austrian Science Fund (FWF) under the grant numbers J3998-N31, P28519-N31, and P30525-N31.

References

1. Brambilla, M., Cabot, J., Wimmer, M.: Model-driven Software Engineering in Practice, 2nd edn. Morgan & Claypool Publishers, San Rafael (2017)
2. Cabrera, O., Franch, X., Marco, J.: 3LConOnt: a three-level ontology for context modelling in context-aware computing. Softw. Syst. Model. **18**(2), 1345–1378 (2017). https://doi.org/10.1007/s10270-017-0611-z
3. Dąbrowski, J., Letier, E., Perini, A., Susi, A.: Finding and analyzing app reviews related to specific features: a research preview. In: Knauss, E., Goedicke, M. (eds.) REFSQ 2019. LNCS, vol. 11412, pp. 183–189. Springer, Cham (2019). https://doi.org/10.1007/978-3-030-15538-4_14
4. Ebert, C., Heidrich, J., Martinez-Fernandez, S., Trendowicz, A.: Data science: technologies for better software. IEEE Softw. **36**(6), 66–72 (2019)
5. Guzmán, L., Oriol, M., Rodríguez, P., Franch, X., Jedlitschka, A., Oivo, M.: How can quality awareness support rapid software development? – a research preview. In: Grünbacher, P., Perini, A. (eds.) REFSQ 2017. LNCS, vol. 10153, pp. 167–173. Springer, Cham (2017). https://doi.org/10.1007/978-3-319-54045-0_12
6. Jarke, M., Loucopoulos, P., Lyytinen, K., Mylopoulos, J., Robinson, W.: The brave new world of design requirements. Inf. Syst. **36**(7), 992–1008 (2011)
7. Johanssen, J.O., Kleebaum, A., Bruegge, B., Paech, B.: How do practitioners capture and utilize user feedback during continuous software engineering? In: Proceedings of RE (2019)
8. Lindgren, E., Münch, J.: Raising the odds of success: the current state of experimentation in product development. Inf. Softw. Technol. **77**, 80–91 (2016)
9. Maalej, W., Nayebi, M., Johann, T., Ruhe, G.: Toward data-driven requirements engineering. IEEE Softw. **33**(1), 48–54 (2015)
10. Maalej, W., Nayebi, M., Ruhe, G.: Data-driven requirements engineering: an update. In: Proceedings of ICSE/SEIP, pp. 289–290. IEEE (2019)
11. Martínez-Fernández, S., et al.: Continuously assessing and improving software quality with software analytics tools: a case study. IEEE Access **7**, 68219–68239 (2019)
12. Oriol, M., et al.: FAME: supporting continuous requirements elicitation by combining user feedback and monitoring. In: Proceedings of RE, pp. 217–227. IEEE (2018)
13. SonarQube: https://www.sonarqube.org. Accessed 24 Jan 2020
14. Vierhauser, M., Cleland-Huang, J., Burge, J., Grünbacher, P.: The interplay of design and runtime traceability for non-functional requirements. In: Proceedings of the 10th International Workshop on Software and Systems Traceability, pp. 3–10. IEEE (2019)

15. Villela, K., Groen, E.C., Doerr, J.: Ubiquitous requirements engineering: a paradigm shift that affects everyone. IEEE Softw. **36**(2), 8–12 (2019)
16. Wüest, D., Fotrousi, F., Fricker, S.: Combining monitoring and autonomous feedback requests to elicit actionable knowledge of system use. In: Knauss, E., Goedicke, M. (eds.) REFSQ 2019. LNCS, vol. 11412, pp. 209–225. Springer, Cham (2019). https://doi.org/10. 1007/978-3-030-15538-4_16

Identifying and Classifying User Requirements in Online Feedback via Crowdsourcing

Martijn van Vliet[1], Eduard C. Groen[1,2(✉)], Fabiano Dalpiaz[1],
and Sjaak Brinkkemper[1]

[1] Department of Information and Computing Sciences,
Utrecht University, Utrecht, Netherlands
{m.vanvliet,f.dalpiaz,s.brinkkemper}@uu.nl
[2] Fraunhofer IESE, Kaiserslautern, Germany
eduard.groen@iese.fraunhofer.de

Abstract. [**Context and motivation**] App stores and social media channels such as Twitter enable users to share feedback regarding software. Due to its high volume, it is hard to effectively and systematically process such feedback to obtain a good understanding of users' opinions about a software product. [**Question/problem**] Tools based on natural language processing and machine learning have been proposed as an inexpensive mechanism for classifying user feedback. Unfortunately, the accuracy of these tools is imperfect, which jeopardizes the reliability of the analysis results. We investigate whether assigning *micro-tasks* to crowd workers could be an alternative technique for identifying and classifying requirements in user feedback. [**Principal ideas/results**] We present a crowdsourcing method for filtering out irrelevant app store reviews and for identifying features and qualities. A validation study has shown positive results in terms of feasibility, accuracy, and cost. [**Contribution**] We provide evidence that crowd workers can be an inexpensive yet accurate resource for classifying user reviews. Our findings contribute to the debate on the roles of and synergies between humans and AI techniques.

Keywords: Crowd-based requirements engineering · Crowdsourcing · Online user reviews · Quality requirements · User feedback analysis

1 Introduction

As a growing body of requirements engineering (RE) literature shows, substantial amounts of online user feedback provide information on user perceptions, encountered problems, suggestions, and demands [3,21,22]. Researchers have predominantly focused on analyzing user feedback about mobile apps. Of the various online sources of user feedback, they have emphasized app stores and Twitter because these readily offer large amounts of user feedback [23].

© Springer Nature Switzerland AG 2020
N. Madhavji et al. (Eds.): REFSQ 2020, LNCS 12045, pp. 143–159, 2020.
https://doi.org/10.1007/978-3-030-44429-7_11

The amount of feedback typically obtained for an app is too large to be processed manually [12,17], and established requirements elicitation techniques, such as interviews and focus groups, are not suitable for engaging and involving the large number of users providing feedback. Hence, user feedback analysis has become an additional elicitation technique [13]. Because most user feedback is text-based, natural language processing (NLP) techniques have been proposed to automatically—and thus efficiently—process user feedback [4,22,24,34].

However, although NLP approaches perform well for simple tasks such as distinguishing informative from uninformative reviews, they often fail to make finer distinctions such as feature versus bug, or privacy versus security requirements [5,34]. Also, most NLP techniques focus on functional aspects, while online user feedback has been found to contain much information on software product quality by which users are affected directly [11], such as usability, performance, efficiency, and security. Their correct identification is made more difficult by language ambiguity due to poor writing [34]. Extensive training and expert supervision are required to improve the outcomes of NLP techniques.

We surmise that a *crowdsourcing-based approach* to identifying and classifying user feedback could overcome the limitations of existing approaches that are NLP-based or reliant on expert analysts. The premise is to train crowd workers to perform the classification. Spreading the tagging workload over the members of an inexpensive crowd might make this approach a feasible alternative for organizations, with more accurate results than those obtained through automated techniques. Moreover, since the extraction is done by human actors, the results may in turn be used as training sets for NLP approaches [12,17,30].

The challenge is that the quality of the annotation results largely depends on the knowledge and skills of the human taggers. A crowdsourcing setting offers access to many crowd workers, but they are not experienced in requirements identification or classification. Hence, we employ strategies from the crowdsourcing field [18], including the provision of *quick training* to the workers [7], simplification of their work in the form of *micro-tasks*, and the use of redundant annotators to filter out noise and to rely on the predominant opinion.

Our main research question is: *"How can a method that facilitates the identification of user requirements[1] through a sizeable crowd of non-expert workers be constructed?"* Such a method should ease the removal of spam and other useless reviews, and allow laypeople to classify requirements aspects in user reviews. It also needs to be feasible and cost-effective: The quality of the tagging should be regarded sufficiently high by the app development company to justify the investment, also thanks to the time saved by crowdsourcing tasks that would otherwise be performed by employees. We make the following contributions:

1. We present *Kyōryoku*: a crowdsourcing method for eliciting and classifying user requirements extracted from user feedback. Our method aims to allow laypeople to deliver effective outputs by simplifying tasks.

---

[1] In this paper, *user requirements* are understood as "a need perceived by a stakeholder", as per one sub-definition of *requirement* in the IREB Glossary [9].

2. We report on a validation of the method performed on a sample of 1,000 app store reviews over eight apps, which attracted a large crowd and provided good results in terms of processing speed, precision, and recall.
3. We provide the results from the crowd workers and our gold standard as an open artifact [33] that other researchers can use for training automated classifiers that rely on machine learning (ML) or for assessing the quality of human- or machine-based classification methods.

Organization. After reviewing related work in Sect. 2, we describe our method in Sect. 3. We present the design of our experiment in Sect. 4, and report and analyze the results in Sect. 5. We review the key threats to validity in Sect. 6, while Sect. 7 presents conclusions and future directions.

2   Related Work

Crowd involvement in RE has been studied by various researchers over the past decade, especially through the proposal of platforms that allow the crowd of stakeholders, users, and developers to actively participate in the communication of needs for creating and evolving software systems [20,29]. The *Organizer & Promoter of Collaborative Ideas* (OPCI; [1]) is a forum-based solution that supports stakeholders in collaboratively writing, prioritizing, and voting for requirements. Through text analysis, initial ideas of the stakeholders are clustered into forums, and a recommender system suggests further potentially relevant forums. Lim and Finkelstein's *StakeRare* method includes an online platform for identifying stakeholders via peer recommendation, and for eliciting and prioritizing the requirements they suggest [20]. *REfine* [29] is a gamified platform based on idea generation and up-/downvoting mechanisms through which stakeholders can express their needs and rank their priority. A similar idea forms the basis of the *Requirements Bazaar* tool [26]. All these platforms offer a public space for stakeholders to interact and express their ideas.

Other researchers have investigated the adequacy of crowd workers in acting as taggers in requirements-related tasks. This has been explored, for example, in the context of user feedback collected from app stores. The Crowd-Annotated Feedback Technique (CRAFT) [16] is a stepwise process that creates micro-tasks for human taggers to classify user feedback at multiple levels: (i) category, e.g., bug reporting vs. feature request; (ii) classification, e.g., whether a bug regards the user interface, error handling, or the control flow; and (iii) quality of the annotated feedback and confidence level of the tagger. CRAFT inspires our work because it aims to provide empirical evidence regarding the actual effectiveness of such annotation techniques in practice. Stanik, Haering and Maalej [30] recently employed crowdsourcing to annotate 10,000 English and 15,000 Italian tweets to the support accounts of telecommunication companies, which in turn served as part of their training set for ML and deep learning approaches.

User feedback classification has seen a rapid rise of automated techniques based on NLP and ML. Research on the automatic classification of feedback has given rise to alternative taxonomies; for example, Maalej and Nabil [22] tested the performance of classic ML algorithms with different feature sets to distinguish bug reports, feature requests, ratings, and user experience. Panichella *et al.* [24] took a similar approach but included slightly broader classes, like information seeking and information giving. Guzmán and Maalej [14] studied how the polarity of sentiment analysis can be applied to classify user feedback.

Automated classification techniques deliver good results in terms of precision and recall, but they are inevitably imperfect. This is largely due to the noise inherently present in user-generated feedback [34], which leads to imperfect classifications that decrease the trust of the user in the algorithm and the platform in which the outputs are embedded [4]. Furthermore, these approaches achieve their best results when using supervised ML algorithms, which require extensive manual work and expensive tagging to train the algorithms. This led to approaches like that of Dhina *et al.* [5], which aims to diminish human effort by employing strategies like active learning. In our work, we want to assess the adequacy of inexpensive crowd workers for the task.

Performing RE activities through crowdsourcing is part of Crowd-based RE (CrowdRE) [13], which includes all approaches that engage a crowd of mostly unknown people to perform RE tasks or provide requirements-relevant information [10]. CrowdRE aims to involve a large number of stakeholders, particularly users, in the specification and evolution of software products. To realize this vision, it is key to understand for which tasks CrowdRE is (cost-)effective. This is one of the goals of our paper, which aligns with the results of Stol and Fitzgerald's [31] case study, which showed that crowdsourcing in software engineering is effective for tasks with low complexity and without interdependencies, such as tagging of user reviews, but less suited for more complex tasks.

3   Kyōryoku: Crowd Annotation for Extracting Requirements-Related Contents from User Reviews

We propose Kyōryoku[2], a method for crowd workers to identify requirements-related contents in online user reviews. In particular, we describe an annotation process that focuses on the separation of useful and useless reviews, and on the identification of reviews that mention requirements-related aspects such as features and qualities. This process can be viewed as a *complex task* (cf. [28]), which crowd workers cannot generally perform because they lack the required level of expertise in RE. For example, laypeople who act as crowd workers are not familiar with the distinction between features and the qualities of these features.

Complex tasks can be outsourced to a large crowd of laypeople by decomposing these tasks into so-called *micro-tasks*; the dominant form of directed crowdsourcing [32]. Micro-tasks involve simpler and more routine data extraction decision workflows that are performed by laypeople in return for relatively small rewards. The difficulty lies in how such a complex task can be structurally

---

[2] Kyōryoku (協力) is a Japanese term for *collaboration*: literally, it combines *strength* (力) with *cooperation* (協).

transformed into a set of simpler tasks. This involves the definition of effective workflows to guide paid, non-expert workers toward achieving the desired results that are comparable to those that experts would attain [27].

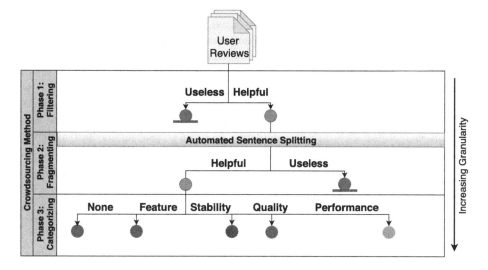

Fig. 1. Overview of the Kyōryoku crowd-based annotation method.

Kyōryoku consists of a stepwise classification process with three phases, as visualized in Fig. 1. In line with the *CrowdForge* framework [19], each phase is conceived as a micro-task, each being more granular than the preceding phase. Our design approach was iterative and based on empirical evidence: Each micro-task was discussed extensively among three of the authors, and then tested internally with master's degree students in order to maximize the probability that the micro-tasks were defined in a way that they can be executed well by laypeople in a crowdsourcing marketplace. We defined the following phases:

P1: Filter user reviews. Following the principle of increasing granularity [19], crowd workers should first analyze the nature of the data itself before classifying the requirements-relevant aspects. In this phase, crowd workers distinguish between user reviews that are "helpful" to software developers from those that are "useless", i.e., spam or irrelevant. "Spam" is any ineligible user review that is not written with good intent, while a user review is "irrelevant" if it does not contain useful information from an RE perspective. The input for Phase 1 is a set of unprocessed user reviews; crowd workers are presented with the entire body text of each user review.

P2: Filter fragments. Via a text processor, the reviews classified as "helpful" are split into sentences, which we call fragments. The crowd workers perform the same task as in Phase 1, except that they handle one-sentence fragments of helpful user reviews. One-sentence reviews from Phase 1 that are not split up can be kept in the dataset to improve filtering effectiveness.

P3: Categorize. The fragments classified as "helpful" in Phase 2 undergo a more fine-grained classification into five categories. This is a more demanding task for the crowd workers, so it calls for a clear job description with good examples. The category "Feature Request" applies to fragments addressing functional aspects. Three categories are included to denote software quality aspects, and "None of the Above" is used for aspects such as general criticism and praise. Our categories of software product qualities are based on Glinz' taxonomy [8], which we modified to ease the task and maximize comprehensibility by laypeople. The category "Performance Feedback" reflects the quality "performance". To help crowd workers understand better how "reliability" is distinct, we named it "Stability Feedback", reflecting the reliability aspect most commonly addressed in user feedback [11]. To limit the number of categories, several qualities – including "usability", "portability", and "security" – have been combined into "Quality Feedback".

Description

In this job, you will be presented with text from user reviews from mobile app stores such as the Google Play Store or the Apple App Store. The goal of this job is to filter out the spam and to remove useless reviews.

Steps

1. Read each user review carefully.
2. Determine whether the review could be of any help to a developer based on the guidelines and examples listed below.
3. Mark the reviews as helpful or useless.

Guidelines

- **Useless Reviews**
  - Contain spam or other unrequested or unwanted messages.
  - Their content does not relate to the app and its functions.
- **Helpful Reviews**
  - Specifically mention aspects of the apps, that is, functions, features and behaviour of an app.
  - Report bugs and performance issues that the user encountered.

Examples

- **Useless Reviews**
  - *"I Really Like This!"*
  - *"My kids love it. Thanks"*
- **Helpful Reviews**
  - *"Newest version crashes when opening"*
  - *"Buggy and unreliable. Does not work often. Signs me out regularly. Won't download movies onto my iPad. Disappointing."*

Fig. 2. Abridged job description for the crowd workers in Phase 1.

Our approach emphasizes proper training because crowd workers base the decisions they make during the categorization work on our instructions in the job description. We paid attention to balancing clarity with brevity, both essential properties of a job, i.e., a task assigned to a crowd worker.

Figure 2 shows an abridged version of the job description for Phase 1, with the template we used for the job description of each phase. All job descriptions are available in our online appendix [33]. The *introduction* triggers the participants' attention, followed by the *steps*, *guidelines*, and *examples*. The guidelines cover the core principles of each answer category, while in the examples, we provide a selection of actual reviews that are representative of these categories. Drafts were tested in two pretests, which showed that the job description required improvements to better guide crowd workers towards the correct decision.

Following the job description, crowd workers are presented with an *eligibility test* that serves two purposes: First, the crowd workers can practice the job, and after the test read the explanations for the items they categorized incorrectly, so they can learn from these mistakes and improve their decision-making. Second, it allows us to ensure that only well-performing crowd workers can participate. The *annotation task* itself is like an eligibility test, with a page presenting a number of items for the crowd workers to categorize.

4   Experiment Design and Conduction

To validate Kyōryoku, we designed a single group experiment for which we recruited crowd workers through the online crowdsourcing marketplace *Figure Eight*[3] to annotate a set of 1,000 user reviews in the three phases shown in Fig. 1. Through our experiment, we sought to confirm the following hypotheses:

H1. Crowd workers can distinguish between useful and useless reviews.
H2. Crowd workers can correctly assign user reviews to different requirement categories.
H3. Extracting RE-relevant contents from online user feedback through crowd-sourcing is feasible and cost-effective.

H1 focuses on Phases 1–2, and H2 focuses on Phase 3 of Kyōryoku. H3 is a more general hypothesis regarding the method as a whole.

The *Figure Eight* platform allows crowd workers to perform jobs by assigning micro-tasks in exchange for fixed-price monetary rewards. We set the reward for Phase 1 to $0.03 per user review, based on a pretest in which the participants took an average of 9.3 min to classify 50 user reviews. This means that the hourly remuneration is similar to the minimum wage in the United States [15].

In order to test the ability of individual workers to follow Kyōryoku, we decided to offer individual micro-tasks rather than collaborative tasks where crowd workers can assess the contributions of others. However, collaboration and peer reviewing are important research directions to explore in future work.

---

[3] https://www.figure-eight.com/.

We opted for an open crowd selection policy: candidates qualify for partic-ipation through an eligibility test. We saw no need to add further restrictions such as native language or reputation. Rather, we found it realistic to expect non-native English-speaking crowd workers to be capable of performing such a task. If confirmed, this expectation would greatly expand the size of the available crowd and thus the number of crowd workers participating in our micro-tasks.

We selected *Figure Eight* because of its support for data categorization tasks and its many embedded quality control mechanisms, including eligibility test questions defined by the crowdsourcer that crowd workers must pass to con-tribute, control questions throughout the actual task, and a reputation system.

Our reviews are a sample of Groen *et al.*'s dataset [11]. We omitted the "Smart Products" category, which refers to a combination of hardware and soft-ware, and the "Entertainment" category, whose reviews were found not to be rep-resentative of the general population of app store reviews in an earlier study [11]. We also discarded the reviews from Amazon's app store, from which reviews can no longer be retrieved, limiting its potential for use in future studies. From the resulting dataset, we took a systematic stratified sample of 1,000 user reviews, in accordance with the job size limit of a *Figure Eight* trial account. The reviews were stratified across apps and app stores, but we limited the proportion of reviews about the Viber app to $\leq$30%. The sample resembled the characteris-tics of the whole dataset with respect to the distribution of stars, sentiment, and years, while the disparity of average app ratings was negligible (maximum +0.16 for TweetCaster Pro).

A gold standard for this dataset was created based on the work of this paper's first author and feedback from other researchers on selected samples. We will compare the crowd work against the gold standard on two different levels of strictness, with the first (*strict*) being the gold standard defined a priori, and the second (*lenient*) being a revision that takes into account potential errors by the researcher, as well as commonly misclassified reviews that can be attributed to ambiguities for which the job description did not provide guidance. The lenient gold standard was constructed after examining the answers by the crowd work-ers, taking the perspective of the crowd workers, who neither have information regarding the apps to which the reviews refer, nor access to the entire review once it is chunked after Phase 1.

The tags *app reviews*, *spam detection*, and *user reviews* were applied to each test as a means of generating visibility and interest among crowd workers. A total of 45 test questions were constructed to provide 15 unique test questions per phase for quality control purposes. We constructed our test questions to equally represent all possible tagging categories (e.g., all five aspects in Phase 3). For each phase, ten test questions were randomly allocated to the eligibility test. Seven of them had to be answered correctly in order to pass, while the remaining five were used as control questions during the actual task. The workers were presented with pages containing ten items, nine of which were randomly selected fragments of the dataset, and one a control question. A micro-task was limited to five pages, for a total of 50 items, to prevent all the work being done by a small group of early responders. The crowd workers could abandon their job every time they finished a page. We included a setting that disqualified a crowd worker from further participation if they completed a ten-item page too quickly (<20 s for Phases 1 & 2; <30 s for Phase 3). Average time per judgment varied between 23 (Phase 3) and 14 (Phases 1 & 2) s. The test questions along with the job descriptions can be viewed in the online appendix [33].

Table 1. Summary of the configuration of *Figure Eight* per phase.

Phase-session	Jobs	Judgments per review	Required judgments	$ per judgment
1-1	200	3	600	0.04
1-2	800	3	2400	0.03
2-1	242	3	726	0.02
2-2	1000	3	3000	0.02
3-1	683	6	4098	0.02

As Table 1 shows, Phases 1 and 2 were carried out in two different sessions. Due to the experimental nature and the limited budget, Phase 1 commenced with a trial job of only 200 reviews to detect possibly overlooked faults or flaws in the process. We were required to split Phase 2 between two accounts because *Figure Eight*'s trial accounts are limited to 1,000 tasks, but we obtained 1,242 fragments from splitting the helpful reviews from Phase 1 into individual sentences. For Phases 1 and 2, three judgments from three different crowd workers were required to reach a satisfactory classification. For Phase 3, we raised this number to six due to the increased complexity of the task with a larger number of categories. Six annotations across five categories moreover precluded a balanced outcome with several categories getting tagged only once. Remuneration varied slightly between the different sessions. Participants in the first session of Phase 1 received a reward that was slightly above average because we had underestimated the efficiency of crowd workers on the platform. Due to budget constraints, Phase 3 offered remunerations slightly below minimum wage for the length of the task.

5 Results

We have organized the results of our experiment as follows: First, we will describe the crowd that we assembled through *Figure Eight* (Sect. 5.1), then present some statistics regarding job duration and cost (Sect. 5.2), and finally report on the outcome of the jobs in terms of precision and recall (Sect. 5.3).

5.1 Demographics of the Gathered Crowd

We gathered a large worldwide crowd through multiple crowd work channels associated with *Figure Eight*. A total of 603 unique crowd workers commenced participation in the five sessions listed in Table 1, 422 of whom passed the eligibility test and quality checks. These 422 workers can be considered contributors. They were from 42 different countries, with the highest number of contributors coming from Venezuela (36.7%), probably due to the current economic situation [25], followed by Ukraine (11.6%), Russia (7.8%), Egypt (6.6%), and Turkey (6.4%).

An automatically deployed contributor survey showed that the contributors deemed the test questions fair, the tasks not too difficult to complete, and the remuneration satisfactory. However, the overall rating did decrease from 4.3/5 in Phase 1 to 3.7/5 in Phases 2 & 3, probably due to the increasing overall difficulty of the task or the reduced compensation.

The total number of annotations to user reviews or fragments amounted to 10,555. Each contributor classified 24.8 items on average, with the vast majority of crowd workers either tagging the minimum of 10 or the maximum of 50 contributions. On average, 16.4% of the crowd workers failed the eligibility test to perform the job. The failure rates for Phase 1 (9.6%), Phase 2 (11.7%), and Phase 3 (27.4%) highlight the increasing difficulty of the tasks.

5.2   Job Statistics

Table 2 shows that the total cost of our experiment was $354.72, which includes *Figure Eight*'s 20% usage fee. Because we reduced the remuneration due to the tagging of shorter text fragments, Phase 2 was the cheapest. In total, the jobs were active for a total of 323 min before reaching full completion. Phase 3 had the highest workload, and therefore took the longest time to reach completion. Phase 2 amassed a large group of contributors the quickest, and therefore achieved completion in the least amount of time.

Table 2. Launch time and completion statistics for all the launched jobs.

Phase-session	Launch (CET; 2019)	Duration (min.)	Contributions	Test question judgments	Total judgments	Judgments per min.	Time per judgment	Total cost ($)
1-1	May 7, 10:47	29	600	477	1086	38	13.7	33.60
1-2	May 15, 11:27	82	2400	1437	3855	46	12.6	97.20
2-1	May 23, 11:21	28	726	665	1463	42	12.3	21.36
2-2	May 29, 16:40	44	3000	2091	5250	113	10	84.96
3-1	June 13, 11:04	140	4098	1943	6311	43	23.6	117.60
Total & Micro-Avg		323	10824	6613	17965	56	15.9	354.72

As shown in Fig. 3, the jobs ramped up slowly in the beginning, followed by a period of intense contributions, and finally a long tail for the unfinished jobs to be completed. The average number of judgments per minute was 56, and varied from 38 judgments in session 1-1 to 113 judgments in session 2-2. In the intense contribution phase, which we set as the center 90% contributions in each distribution so as to remove the initial slower phase and the long final tail, the average number of judgments per minute varied from 54 for session 1-1 to 373 for session 2-2. The not-so-steep activity for session 3-1 can be explained by the higher number of contributors failing the eligibility test. The contributors required significantly more time per judgment in Phase 3 (23.6 s) than in Phases 1 & 2 (between 10 and 13.7 s).

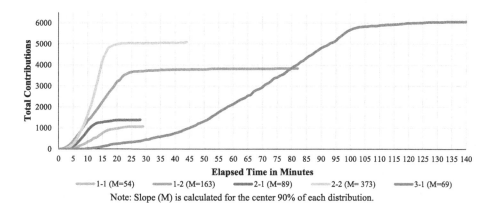

Fig. 3. Total number of contributions received over the course of each session.

5.3   Outcome of the Crowd Work

As summarized in Fig. 4, the crowd workers processed 1,000 reviews from app stores, in which they *identified* 683 requirements-relevant fragments, which they then *classified* into five RE-relevant categories.

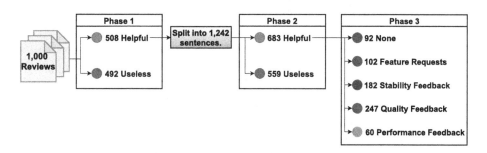

Fig. 4. Overview of the course of the user reviews through the different phases.

Table 3 compares the crowd judgments against the gold standard. In Phase 1, the crowd was able to classify the reviews with a precision of 93%, meaning that only 7% of helpful reviews were misjudged as useless by the crowd. Depending on the strictness of the gold standard (strict or lenient, see Sect. 4), the crowd

Table 3. Detailed comparison of the results of the crowd for Phases 1 & 2.

Phase	Positives: useless (Gold Std)	Negatives: helpful (Gold Std)	True positives	True negatives	False positives	False negatives	Precision	Recall
1 (strict)	620	380	459	347	33	161	0.93	0.74
1 (lenient)	547	453	460	421	32	87	0.93	0.84
2 (strict)	679	563	478	482	81	201	0.86	0.70
2 (lenient)	609	633	493	566	66	117	0.88	0.81

was able to correctly identify either 74% or 84% of the useless reviews from the dataset (recall)[4].

In Phase 2, the crowd was able to classify useless results with a precision of 88%, meaning that 12% of helpful fragments were discarded incorrectly. The crowd was able to identify 81% of all useless fragments. This constitutes effective filtering, although 19% of the useless fragments still remained in the dataset. Fragments that received the same judgments from all three contributors (61.4% of all cases) were more often classified correctly, reaching 87% accuracy, while accuracy dropped to 64% for the cases in which only two contributors agreed.

As Table 4 shows, the crowd workers reached an average accuracy of 78% (lenient) in Phase 3. The confusion matrix in Table 5 reveals that there was some misalignment between categories, mainly between "None" and "Quality" and, to a lesser degree, "Performance". Crowd workers were the most precise in classifying "Stability" issues, while reaching the highest recall on "Feature Requests". They were the least precise on "None" and "Performance" issues, and reached the lowest recall on "Performance" issues. Further investigation of the agreement between the six contributors per review fragment (Table 4) revealed a meaningful impact of the level of agreement on the accuracy of the classification. Accuracy ranged from 100% for fragments that the six contributors classified unanimously, down to 49% when only two contributors picked the same category.

Table 4. Accuracy for the different levels of agreement between contributors.

Agreement	Frequency	Correct	Incorrect	Accuracy
Six out of six	85 (12%)	85	0	100%
Five out of six	144 (21%)	131	13	91%
Four out of six	170 (25%)	145	25	85%
Three out of six	196 (29%)	128	68	65%
Two out of six	88 (13%)	43	45	49%
Total	**683 (100%)**	**532**	**151**	**78%**

---

[4] Note: because Phases 1 and 2 focus on filtering out irrelevant reviews, we take the *useless* category as our positives.

6   Threats to Validity

Despite our efforts to carefully design Kyōryoku, not every aspect could be accounted for due to the experimental nature of this research. Kyōryoku relies on several assumptions due to the scarcity of literature on how to assemble effective micro-tasks. Thus, we have no way of knowing whether Kyōryoku reached its highest or lowest potential, which makes it harder to put the results into context. Furthermore, it is currently impossible to trace back potential flaws to individual design decisions, because only one such experiment was conducted and no variations have been tested so far. However, the effectiveness of the training method seems to be the most crucial aspect, due to the high number of participants who failed the eligibility test.

Table 5. Confusion matrix for the results of the crowd in Phase 3 (lenient).

Crowd	Gold Standard					Precision	Recall
	None	Feature	Stability	Performance	Quality		
None	67	5	3	3	14	0.57	0.73
Feature	4	94	1	1	2	0.83	0.92
Stability	14	8	134	6	20	0.93	0.80
Performance	4	5	3	29	19	0.63	0.41
Quality	28	1	3	7	208	0.80	0.84
Average						0.75	0.74

The tests were conducted with only limited experience with the *Figure Eight* platform, and without prior experience in outsourcing tasks to the crowd. No restrictions were in place to exclude countries or channels that might provide results with significantly lower quality. The analysis of the results currently does not account or compensate for possible influences from these sources. Comparing the results against the gold standard, however, did not reveal significant discrepancies for any particular country or channel in terms of accuracy.

Each phase of our experiment utilized inputs from the preceding phases; thus, errors by crowd workers were perpetuated in all subsequent phases. Although this affected the cumulative results, we decided to examine the performance of the whole method performed sequentially, not that of individual phases. Testing each phase separately might lead to slightly different results. An inherent shortcoming of this approach is furthermore that the classifications are left to a very small subset of the crowd, with only three judgments in Phases 1 & 2, and six in Phase 3. As Table 4 corroborates, the quality of the results can be improved by involving more crowd workers, although this also increases costs. Finally, the dataset contains user reviews from 2011–2015; due to the rapid evolution of the app landscape, results may differ with more recent user feedback.

The creation of the gold standard and the review of the crowdsourcing task's outputs relied mostly on a single researcher, with other researchers cross-checking samples. Thus, although we transparently share our materials publicly, only samples of the gold standard classification have been reviewed. It is not unreasonable to assume that some errors were introduced into the gold standard that may affect the validity of the results.

Finally, the quality control mechanisms that we deployed into the *Figure Eight* platform have an effect on the results, for they determine the inclusion or exclusion of crowd workers. Despite our efforts to make it as robust as possible, this quality control mechanism is imperfect. This might especially affect the potential accuracy by incorrectly excluding good workers or by improperly detecting poor workers.

7   Conclusion and Future Work

We have presented Kyōryoku, a crowdsourcing method for identifying and classifying user requirements – more precisely, requirements-relevant information – in online user feedback through crowd work. Kyōryoku was tested on 1,000 app store reviews, which were analyzed and classified by over 400 crowd workers.

Based on the outcomes of Phases 1 & 2 of Kyōryoku, we can confidently state that crowd workers are able to distinguish between useful and useless reviews (**H1**). The crowd workers achieved precision rates of 93% and 88% and recall rates of 84% and 81%, respectively, in these phases. Although there is no automated technique that serves as a baseline, further research is needed to compare against algorithms based on automated spam detection in app reviews [2].

When we consider the ability of the crowd workers to correctly assign user reviews to different requirement categories (**H2**), the results are positive, but inevitably not as good as the binary useful/useless classification. The overall accuracy was 74% for the five categories that we deemed suitable for crowdsourced classification: "Feature", "Stability", "Performance", (other) "Quality", and "None". Interestingly, for the 85 fragments with perfect agreement among all six taggers, we could observe 100% accuracy. We have not tested Kyōryoku against automated classifiers yet. These results seem to be at least as good as optimized automated classifiers of NFRs [21], which achieve an accuracy of ∼70%.

H3 concerned the feasibility and cost-effectiveness of Kyōryoku to extract RE-relevant contents from online user feedback. We were able to show the feasibility of such a method through the tasks we composed for the crowd workers to carry out. In terms of cost-effectiveness, 1,000 reviews were fully processed through crowdsourcing for approximately $350 and in 5.4 h for all phases and sessions combined. On the other hand, creating a gold standard, i.e., tagging the data without crowd workers, required circa 20–30 person-hours. Although we cannot provide a conclusive answer to H3, the results suggest that Kyōryoku might be suitable for companies who wish to analyze user reviews about their products, but who do not have sufficient resources to hire an expert assessor.

This work presents a novel method for engaging a crowd to elicit user requirements from online user feedback, and paves the way for future work in this direction. Kyōryoku, which includes openly available task descriptions [33], can be taken as is and used by organizations who would like to classify a reviews dataset. Kyōryoku can be improved by changing the wording of the job description, the examples, and the classification taxonomy. To do so, it is imperative to complement our quantitative results with a qualitative analysis that reveals which utterances are most likely to lead to false positives and false negatives. We hope that future studies will take Kyōryoku as a baseline to improve upon; researchers can directly compare their automated or human-driven method using the gold standard we make available. Alternatively, it is possible to use this gold standard to train approaches based on ML. Also, it would be interesting to investigate whether the crowd can effectively use fine-grained taxonomies of quality requirements. It is essential to test the approach on larger datasets that contain recent user reviews. The outcomes of such an analysis might also have financial consequences: Is Kyōryoku feasible for companies whose products receive thousands of user reviews per day? Moreover, different aggregation techniques can be studied to reconcile the taggers' opinions. Finally, in the context of adopting crowdsourcing for analyzing large-scale industrial datasets requires assessing the ethical concerns [6] that crowd work entails, since most contributors originate from countries with a complex social and political situation.

More generally, this research advocates the use of crowdsourcing for *complex tasks* in RE or other disciplines. Our results warrant increased exploration of the applicability of crowdsourcing to similar challenges that revolve around large volumes of data with a difficult nature. This research has shown that crowd workers are able to deal with perhaps more complex problems than anticipated, provided they receive proper instruction.

References

1. Castro-Herrera, C., Duan, C., Cleland-Huang, J., Mobasher, B.: Using data mining and recommender systems to facilitate large-scale, open, and inclusive requirements elicitation processes. In: Proceedings of the RE, pp. 165–168 (2008)
2. Chandy, R., Gu, H.: Identifying spam in the iOS app store. In: Proceedings of the WebQuality, pp. 56–59 (2012)
3. Chen, N., Lin, J., Hoi, S.C., Xiao, X., Zhang, B.: AR-miner: mining informative reviews for developers from mobile app marketplace. In: Proceedings of the ICSE, pp. 767–778 (2014)
4. Dalpiaz, F., Parente, M.: RE-SWOT: from user feedback to requirements via competitor analysis. In: Knauss, E., Goedicke, M. (eds.) REFSQ 2019. LNCS, vol. 11412, pp. 55–70. Springer, Cham (2019). https://doi.org/10.1007/978-3-030-15538-4_4
5. Dhinakaran, V.T., Pulle, R., Ajmeri, N., Murukannaiah, P.K.: App review analysis via active learning. In: Proceedings of the RE, pp. 170–181 (2018)
6. Fort, K., Adda, G., Cohen, K.B.: Amazon mechanical turk: gold mine or coal mine? Comput. Linguist. **37**(2), 413–420 (2011)

7. Gadiraju, U., Fetahu, B., Kawase, R.: Training workers for improving performance in crowdsourcing microtasks. In: Conole, G., Klobučar, T., Rensing, C., Konert, J., Lavoué, É. (eds.) EC-TEL 2015. LNCS, vol. 9307, pp. 100–114. Springer, Cham (2015). https://doi.org/10.1007/978-3-319-24258-3_8

8. Glinz, M.: On non-functional requirements. In: Proceedings of the RE, pp. 21–26 (2007)

9. Glinz, M.: A glossary of requirements engineering terminology. Version 1.7. International Requirements Engineering Board (IREB) (2017). https://www.ireb.org/en/cpre/cpre-glossary/

10. Glinz, M.: CrowdRE: achievements, opportunities and pitfalls. In: Proceedings of the CrowdRE, pp. 172–173 (2019)

11. Groen, E.C., Kopczyńska, S., Hauer, M.P., Krafft, T.D., Doerr, J.: Users—The hidden software product quality experts? A study on how app users report quality aspects in online reviews. In: Proceedings of the RE, pp. 80–89 (2017)

12. Groen, E.C., Schowalter, J., Kocpzyńska, S., Polst, S., Alvani, S.: Is there really a need for using NLP to elicit requirements? A benchmarking study to assess scalability of manual analysis. In: Proceedings of the NLP4RE (2018)

13. Groen, E.C., et al.: The crowd in requirements engineering: the landscape and challenges. IEEE Softw. **34**(2), 44–52 (2017)

14. Guzman, E., Maalej, W.: How do users like this feature? A fine grained sentiment analysis of app reviews. In: Proceedings of the RE, pp. 153–162 (2014)

15. Horton, J.J., Chilton, L.B.: The labor economics of paid crowdsourcing. In: Proceedings of the EC, pp. 209–218 (2010)

16. Hosseini, M., Groen, E.C., Shahri, A., Ali, R.: CRAFT: a crowd-annotated feedback technique. In: Proceedings of the CrowdRE, pp. 170–175 (2017)

17. Hosseini, M., Phalp, K.T., Taylor, J., Ali, R.: Towards crowdsourcing for requirements engineering. In: Proceedings of REFSQ Workshops (2014)

18. Howe, J.: The rise of crowdsourcing. Wired **14**(6), 1–4 (2006)

19. Kittur, A., Smus, B., Khamkar, S., Kraut, R.E.: CrowdForge: crowdsourcing complex work. In: Proceedings of the UIST, pp. 43–52 (2011)

20. Lim, S.L., Finkelstein, A.: StakeRare: using social networks and collaborative filtering for large-scale requirements elicitation. IEEE Trans. Softw. Eng. **38**(3), 707–735 (2012)

21. Lu, M., Liang, P.: Automatic classification of non-functional requirements from augmented app user reviews. In: Proceedings of the EASE, pp. 344–353 (2017)

22. Maalej, W., Nabil, H.: Bug report, feature request, or simply praise? On automatically classifying app reviews. In: Proceedings of the RE, pp. 116–125 (2015)

23. Nayebi, M., Cho, H., Ruhe, G.: App store mining is not enough for app improvement. Empir. Softw. Eng. **23**(5), 2764–2794 (2018). https://doi.org/10.1007/s10664-018-9601-1

24. Panichella, S., Di Sorbo, A., Guzman, E., Visaggio, C.A., Canfora, G., Gall, H.C.: How can I improve my app? Classifying user reviews for software maintenance and evolution. In: Proceedings of the ICSME, pp. 281–290 (2015)

25. Posch, L., Bleier, A., Flöck, F., Strohmaier, M.: Characterizing the global crowd workforce: a cross-country comparison of crowdworker demographics. arXiv preprint arXiv:1812.05948 (2018)

26. Renzel, D., Behrendt, M., Klamma, R., Jarke, M.: Requirements bazaar: social requirements engineering for community-driven innovation. In: Proceedings of the RE, pp. 326–327 (2013)

27. Retelny, D., et al.: Expert crowdsourcing with flash teams. In: Proceedings of the UIST, pp. 75–85 (2014)

28. Schenk, E., Guittard, C.: Towards a characterization of crowdsourcing practices. J. Innov. Econ. Manag. **1**(7), 93–107 (2011)
29. Snijders, R., Dalpiaz, F., Brinkkemper, S., Hosseini, M., Ali, R., Ozum, A.: REfine: a gamified platform for participatory requirements engineering. In: Proceedings of the CrowdRE, pp. 1–6 (2015)
30. Stanik, C., Haering, M., Maalej, W.: Classifying multilingual user feedback using traditional machine learning and deep learning. In: Proceedings of the AIRE (2019)
31. Stol, K.J., Fitzgerald, B.: Two's company, three's a crowd: a case study of crowdsourcing software development. In: Proceedings of the ICSE, pp. 187–198 (2014)
32. Valentine, M.A., Retelny, D., To, A., Rahmati, N., Doshi, T., Bernstein, M.S.: Flash organizations: crowdsourcing complex work by structuring crowds as organizations. In: Proceedings of the CHI, pp. 3523–3537 (2017)
33. van Vliet, M., Groen, E., Dalpiaz, F., Brinkkemper, S.: Crowd-annotation results: identifying and classifying user requirements in online feedback (2020). https://doi.org/10.23644/uu.c.4815591.v1. Zenodo
34. Williams, G., Mahmoud, A.: Mining Twitter feeds for software user requirements. In: Proceedings of the RE, pp. 1–10 (2017)

Designing a Virtual Client for Requirements Elicitation Interviews

Sourav Debnath$^{(\boxtimes)}$ and Paola Spoletini$^{(\boxtimes)}$

Kennesaw State University, Marietta, USA
sdebnath@students.kennesaw.edu, pspoleti@kennesaw.edu

Abstract. [**Context and motivation**] Role-playing offer experiential learning through the simulation of real-world scenarios; for this reason, it is widely used in software engineering education. In Requirements Engineering, role-playing is a popular way to provide students hands-on experience with requirements elicitation interviews. [**Problem**] However, managing a role-playing activity to simulate requirements elicitation interviews in a class is time consuming, as it often requires pairing students with student assistants or fellow classmates who act as either customers or requirement analysts as well as creating and maintaining the interview schedules between the actors. To make the adoption of role-playing activities in a class feasible, there is a need to develop a solution to reduce instructors' workload. [**Principal ideas**] To solve this problem we propose the use of VIrtual CustOmer (VICO), an intent-based, multimodal, conversational agent. VICO offers an interview experience comparable to talking to a human and provides a transcript of the interview annotated with the mistakes students made in it. The adoption of VICO will eliminate the need to schedule interviews as the students can interact with it in their free time. Moreover, the transcript of the interview allows students to evaluate their performance to refine and improve their interviewing skills. [**Contribution**] In this research preview, we show the architecture of VICO and how it can be developed using existing technologies, we provide an online rule-based initial prototype and show the practicality and applicability of this tool through an exploratory study.

Keywords: Requirements elicitation interview · Role-playing · Requirements engineering education and training · Intelligent agent

1 Introduction

The goal of requirements elicitation is to discover requirements for a system by communicating with the stakeholders and exploring available information. Among the variety of available elicitation techniques, requirements elicitation interviews are the most used [1, 6, 11] and among the most effective [5, 6, 14]. While often perceived by students and young analysts as an easy technique to master, the success of requirements elicitation interviews depends on many (soft) skills, such as the ability to create a relationship with the interviewee to ease the process, formulate questions properly, and introspect or probe into the customers' needs. The importance of these skills and the level of effort required to acquire them are difficult to communicate in a convincing way through traditional lectures but are immediately perceived by students through practice. For this reason, role-playing is a popular pedagogical approach to teach these skills [15].

As a class activity, role-playing for requirements elicitation interviews can be performed by pairing students with each other [16] or with student assistants acting as either customers or requirements analysts [9]. Despite the positive results obtained by using role-playing activities to teach requirements elicitation interviews [15, 16], such activities are not often adopted since they can be cumbersome to manage in a standard classroom setting. Indeed, scheduling students for the interview activity (with either peers or student assistants) and maintaining the schedule are time and resource consuming activities. Furthermore, role-playing does not provide all students with an experience of comparable quality: some students may be partnered with someone motivated and talented who plays her role well, while others may be partnered with someone who has no interest in the activity and so underperforms. Also, students can usually role-play only one or two interviews which may not provide them with enough experience to realize their mistakes and improve their interviewing skills.

To overcome these limitations, and consequently support the diffusion of role-playing activities to teach requirements elicitation interviews and to train young analysts, similarly to what is done in other fields [2, 10, 8, 12, 13] we propose the use of VIrtual CustOmer (VICO), an intent-based, multimodal, conversational agent, able to offer an interview experience comparable to the one provided by a human. In addition, VICO also provides the users with a transcript of the interview annotated with the mistakes that the user made in the interview. Given its double contribution, the adoption of VICO has the potential not only to resolve the problems connected to organize role-playing interviews, but also to allow students to evaluate and reason on their performance to refine and improve their interviewing skills. Our research towards the development of VICO has the goal to answer to the following research questions:

RQ1: Can the use of an agent-based solution statistically significantly improve interviewing skills of novice analysts?

RQ2: How comparable can an agent-based solution be to real human interaction in terms of (**2.1**) usability, (**2.2**) learning experience, (**2.3**) engagement?

Because of the ambitious nature of our research, we are planning to develop a series of prototypes with increasing level of intelligence and building on the evaluation of each prototype to develop the subsequent one using more advanced algorithms and architectures. In particular, we are planning to produce three prototypes to evaluate our idea and results in a timely manner.

In the rest of the paper, we present an overview of the envisioned final version of VICO (Sect. 2), we outline our research agenda (Sect. 3), and we then describe our first prototype of VICO, V_0 and the results of an exploratory study aimed to initially answer to RQ2 (Sect. 4). Finally, Sect. 5 concludes the paper.

2 An Overview of VICO

VICO is defined as a multimodal intent-based conversational agent. Roughly speaking, this means that VICO can support different input and output modalities and is capable of processing natural language questions and building an adequate response to them.

VICO has two main goals: playing the role of a customer who wants to develop a product and is interviewed by a VICO's user, and producing a transcript annotated with the mistakes made by the user during the interview. To achieve these goals, VICO needs to be able to (1) listen to the interviewer and understand her questions, (2) appropriately react to them, generating a suitable answer, (3) communicate the answer to the interviewer, (4) keep track of the interview status, and (5) identify the mistakes the user made while conducting the interview.

The capabilities (1)–(3) are comparable to capabilities of virtual agents, such as Ellie, or the agents created with either TARDIS or Virtual People Factory, used for training purposes in specific fields. Ellie [8] is a virtual human, a fully animated face-to-face interviewer used to make automated healthcare decision after conversing with patients. It supports a pre-fixed number of sentences (and their variations) and can detect nonverbal behavior like distress, anxiety. This tool can show emotions like empathy and active engagement which builds trust with the patients. TARDIS [2] is, instead, a framework to create virtual agents that can be used to run social coaching workshops in which young adults are taught how to talk, behave and present themselves in job interviews. In this tool the scenes, dialogues and animations are predetermined by the authors. Similarly, to Ellie, also TARDIS agents have the capability to detect social cues of the participants and produce reactive animations in the virtual recruiter. Finally, Virtual People Factory [4] is a tool to create virtual humans whose conversational capabilities rely on a model built on real conversations. In [15], Virtual People Factory has been used to build virtual patients with stomachache capable of talking in natural language. The goal was to use these virtual humans to teach medical students how to interact with patients in realistic settings. To build the conversational model efficiently, Rossen et al. propose the use of crowdsourcing [15].

The above-mentioned tools suggest that constructing a virtual agent with human-comparable conversational capabilities using the existing technologies is a realistic goal. However, since these solutions are domain-specific and require building a specific model for each different type of human, adopting them in our case would require building a new model for each requirements elicitation interviewee. While our current prototype is also based on predefined knowledge, our plan for VICO is to create a tool that relies on a model independent from the domain of the interview built only on the structure of correct/incorrect interviews and correct/incorrect questions. The specific domain, separated by the model and provided as a knowledge base, will be used only to contextualize the answers of the agent, while their structure will be determined using an analysis of the question structure and the interview current state. To realize this separation, we will rely on the high-level architecture shown in Fig. 1.

VICO's users interact with it online through a user interface with an Embodied Agent. The inputs from the users will be analyzed using a Speech Synthesizer; which will extract the intents and entities. Intents are categorizations of the user's input that identify what the user wants from VICO and entities are keywords that determine what specific information a user is requesting. The intents and the entities are then combined with the interview status, a list of the past intents, entities, questions and answers of the current interview, received from the Interview Recorder. The combined information will then be sent to the answer generator. A part of the Speech Synthesizer could be built using DeepSpeech [7], an open-source speech recognition software.

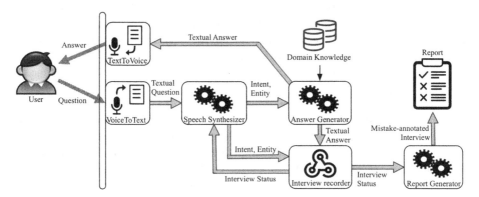

Fig. 1. Overview of VICO

The contextualized and structured information related to the current question are then sent to the Answer Generator that uses them and the domain knowledge in the knowledge base to formulate an appropriate answer to the question. This component is the core of VICO and will be developed to identify the structure of the response independently from the domain and to complete this response using the knowledge base separately. In this way, the only part to update, when a new domain for the interview is selected, is the domain base.

The response generated by the Answer Generator is then sent to the user through the Embodied Agent and to the Interview Recorder, an aggregator that keeps track of the interview from its beginning to its current state. The status, as explained above, is used in the Speech Synthesizer, and is also sent to the Report Generator, which analyzes the questions to identify the user's mistakes. The complete recorded interview annotated with the mistakes identified by Report Generator is provided to the user.

3   Research Agenda

Because of the ambitious nature of the proposed idea, before developing the agent with all the characteristics described in Sect. 2, we plan to develop two prototypes with increasing level of intelligence and, by building on the evaluation of each prototype, to construct the subsequent one using more advanced algorithms and architectures. This will allow us to evaluate our idea in a timely manner.

The goal of the first prototype, V_0, is to evaluate the potential of our idea. V_0 is designed as a basic online multiple-choice text adventure software that uses an open-source interactive non-linear story-telling tool to simulate a requirements elicitation interview. V_0 is evaluated through an exploratory study to investigate the perception of users while using V_0 and its potential impact on their performance. More details on V_0 and the results of the exploratory study are briefly V_0 presented in Sect. 4.

As intermediate prototype, we plan to develop a tool with similar capability of the tool described in Sect. 3, with the only difference that this prototype will have limited ability to formulate answers. Its Answer Generator will act exactly as the agents produced by TARDIS and Virtual People Factory and will use the input from the Speech Synthesizer to select the appropriate response from a knowledge corpus. This corpus will contain a comprehensive set of responses related to the domain of the interview. These responses are primarily extracted from role-played interviews and manual entries from domain experts. To evaluate this prototype, we plan to run two controlled experiments, one to answer to RQ1 and one to answer to RQ2. In the first experiment, the control group will only be taught how to run interviews and will be then asked to execute one as interviewer, while the experimental group will use the tool before running the interview. The interviews of both groups will be independently analyzed by two experts to measure the effectiveness of VICO in improving the quality of the interviews. During the analysis of the interviews, the experts will be blind with respect to the group in which participants belong. The second experiment, to evaluate RQ2, compares the impact of the training with a human with the impact of the training with VICO. So, the control group will be first role-playing with a human, while the experimental group will be role-playing with VICO, then they both run a second interview with a human. The participants in both groups will be asked to fill out a follow-up questionnaire, aimed to investigate how the groups perceived the effect of the training. Also, as done for the interview in the first experiment, the second interview of both groups will be analyzed to have an objective measure of the effectiveness of VICO compared with the human-based experience.

The final product of VICO will be evaluated in a similar way. Moreover, we will analyze the required time to build knowledge bases to evaluate the time needed to build new customers. Finally, we will ask members of our institution's industry advisory board to evaluate the tool with their younger analysts to explore the opportunity to use it in industry settings as a training tool for freshly hired analysts.

4   Initial Prototype and Exploratory Study

The initial prototype[1] for VICO, V_0, simulates a virtual customer, who wants to build a software system for her ski resorts. It has been developed using Twine, an open-source tool for creating non-linear stories. When using V_0, at each step, the user is given three options of questions to ask the customer. Once the user selects a question, V_0 provides a suitable predefined answer. Each question has different levels of mistakes associated with it. The questions and responses were developed by examining 80 interview recordings collected from role-playing interview activity and cover 12 types of mistakes, selected from the 34 mistake types described in [3]. At the end of the interview, the participants are given the full list of questions they asked and the associated mistakes.

We performed an initial exploratory study with 17 undergraduate junior students majoring in software engineering to evaluate the potential of V_0. The participants were

---

[1] Available at http://www.interviewsim.com.s3-website.us-east-2.amazonaws.com/.

divided into 2 groups. Both groups initially watched a 20 min video on how to conduct elicitation interviews [9]. Then the participants in the first group were given an initial description of a ski resort project and were asked to use the tool and analyze their mistakes. The second group skipped this step. Then, both groups were given the description of another project for a hair salon and performed interview as interviewers on this topic with a human fictional customer. The interviews were recorded and analyzed independently by the authors to identify the mistakes in the asked questions using an evaluation sheet provided in [9]. To ensure a unbiased review of the interviews the assignment of the participants to each group was performed by an external researcher and not shared with the authors. This preliminary informal analysis shows that the participants who used V_0 before conducting the interview with the customer made less mistakes than the participants who did not use the prototype. In particular, they avoided the majority of the mistake types embedded into V_0.

Moreover, 25 participants used V_0 and evaluated its engagement, helpfulness and level of difficulty, with the following results: 73% of the participants rated the engagement positively, 81% found V_0 helpful and 77% found it easy to use.

5 Conclusion

In this research preview, we introduced our idea and research agenda to develop a human-comparable agent-based customer to train analysts to perform requirements elicitation interviews and save the resources needed to manage the same activity with human participants. We have also presented our initial prototype, V_0, and the preliminary results obtained by using it. Notice that some of the user of V_0 sent us verbose positive feedback that encourages us to further evaluate V_0 and move forward with our research agenda.

Acknowledgment. The authors thank Kim Hertz for her support in the enrollment of the participants that guaranteed that the authors were blind with respect to the participants' assigned group, the graduate and undergraduate research assistants in the Tiresias Lab for beta testing V_0, and all the participants for their time. This work was partially supported by the National Science Foundation under grant CCF-1718377.

References

1. Agarwal, R., Tanniru, M.R.: Knowledge acquisition using structured interviewing: an empirical investigation. JMIS **7**(1), 123–140 (1990)
2. Anderson, K., et al.: The TARDIS framework: intelligent virtual agents for social coaching in job interviews. In: Proceedings of International Conference on Advances in Computer Entertainment, pp. 476–491 (2013)
3. Bano, M., Bano, M., Zowghi, D., Ferrari, A., Spoletini, P., Donati, B.: Learning from mistakes: an empirical study of elicitation interviews performed by novices. In: IEEE 26th International Requirements Engineering Conference (RE), pp. 182–193 (2018)
4. Carnell, S., Lok, B., James, M.T., Su, J.K.: Predicting student success in communication skills learning scenarios with virtual humans. In: 9th International Conference on Learning Analytics & Knowledge, pp. 436–440. ACM (2019)

5. Coughlan, J., Macredie, R.D.: Effective communication in requirements elicitation: a comparison of methodologies. Requirements Eng. **7**(2), 47–60 (2002)
6. Davis, A.M., Tubío, Ó.D., Hickey, A.M., Juzgado, N.J., Moreno, A.M.: Effectiveness of requirements elicitation techniques: empirical results derived from a systematic review. In: 14th IEEE International Requirements Engineering Conference, pp. 179–188 (2006)
7. DeepSpeech. https://github.com/mozilla/DeepSpeech
8. DeVault, D., et al.: SimSensei Kiosk: a virtual human interviewer for healthcare decision support. In: Proceedings of the 13th International Conference on Autonomous Agents and Multiagent Systems (AAMAS 2014), Paris, France, 5–9 May 2014, pp. 1061–1068. International Foundation for Autonomous Agents and Multiagent Systems, Richland (2014)
9. Ferrari, A., Spoletini, P., Bano, M., Zowghi, D.: Learning requirements elicitation interviews with role-playing, self-assessment and peer-review. In: IEEE 27th International Requirements Engineering Conference (2018)
10. Gratch, J., Wang, N., Gerten, J., Fast, E., Duffy, R.: Creating rapport with virtual agents. In: Pelachaud, C., Martin, J.-C., André, E., Chollet, G., Karpouzis, K., Pelé, D. (eds.) IVA 2007. LNCS (LNAI), vol. 4722, pp. 125–138. Springer, Heidelberg (2007). https://doi.org/10.1007/978-3-540-74997-4_12
11. Hickey, A.M., Davis, A.M.: Elicitation technique selection: how do experts do it? In: 11th IEEE International Requirements Engineering Conference, pp. 169–178 (2003)
12. Kleinsmith, A., Rivera-Gutierrez, D., Finney, G., Cendan, J., Lok, B.: Understanding empathy training with virtual patients. Comput. Hum. Behav. **52**, 151–158 (2015)
13. Rossen, B., Lind, S., Lok, B.: Human-centered distributed conversational modeling: efficient modeling of robust virtual human conversations. In: Ruttkay, Z., Kipp, M., Nijholt, A., Vilhjálmsson, H.H. (eds.) IVA 2009. LNCS (LNAI), vol. 5773, pp. 474–481. Springer, Heidelberg (2009). https://doi.org/10.1007/978-3-642-04380-2_52
14. Sutcliffe, A., Sawyer, P.: Requirements elicitation: towards the unknown unknowns. In: RE 2013, pp. 92–104. IEEE (2013)
15. Svensson, R.B., Regnell, B.: Is role playing in requirements engineering education increasing learning outcome? Requirements Eng. **22**(4), 475–489 (2017)
16. Zowghi, D., Paryani, S.: Teaching requirements engineering through role playing: lessons learnt. In: 11th IEEE International Requirements Engineering Conference, pp. 233–241 (2003)

Agile Methods and Requirements Comprehension

Explicit Alignment of Requirements and Architecture in Agile Development

Sabine Molenaar[1]([✉]), Tjerk Spijkman[1,2], Fabiano Dalpiaz[1], and Sjaak Brinkkemper[1]

[1] Department of Information and Computing Sciences, Utrecht University, Utrecht, The Netherlands
{s.molenaar,f.dalpiaz,s.brinkkemper}@uu.nl
[2] fizor., Soest, The Netherlands
tjerk@fizor.io

Abstract. [**Context & Motivation**] Requirements and architectural components are designed concurrently, with the former guiding the latter, and the latter restricting the former. [**Question/problem**] Effective communication between requirements engineers and software architects is often experienced as problematic. [**Principal ideas/results**] We present the Requirements Engineering for Software Architecture (RE4SA) model with the intention to support the communication within the development team. In RE4SA, requirements are expressed as epic stories and user stories, which are linked to modules and features, respectively, as their architectural counterparts. Additionally, we provide metrics to measure the alignment between these concepts, and we also discuss how to use the model and the usefulness of the metrics by applying both to case studies. [**Contribution**] The RE4SA model employs widely adopted notations and allows for explicitly relating a system's requirements and architectural components, while the metrics make it possible to measure the alignment between requirements and architecture.

Keywords: Requirements Engineering · Software Architecture · User stories · Alignment · Metrics · Case study · Agile RE

1 Introduction

Requirements and design are interdependent and cannot be conducted as separate activities [28]. The Twin Peaks model describes how requirements and architecture are defined concurrently, yet being separate activities, with the former guiding the latter and the latter constraining the former [28]. Extending Nuseibeh's model, the Reciprocal Twin Peaks model [22] focuses on agile development and discusses why the synergy between requirements and architectural elements matters. Throughout the development process, one has to manage a continuous flow of requirements, as well as a continuously changing architecture.

Since software engineering is essentially a social activity among collaborating humans [36], communication within and across the various disciplines of software

© Springer Nature Switzerland AG 2020
N. Madhavji et al. (Eds.): REFSQ 2020, LNCS 12045, pp. 169–185, 2020.
https://doi.org/10.1007/978-3-030-44429-7_13

engineering (requirements analysis, architectural design, development, testing, etc.), is of primary importance [25]. In Requirements Engineering (RE), flawed communication within the development team is a common cause of project failure [15]. Furthermore, client wishes and needs change continuously, leading to volatile requirements that are hard to cope with [13,39].

While RE is still mostly rooted in a written set of requirements, the lack of proper documentation is a serious problem in Software Architecture (SA), which creates high risks of architectural drift and erosion, as well as increased costs and a decrease in software quality [34]. Inaccurate or missing documentation leads to difficult to maintain software. To make matters worse, the impact of new requirements are uncertain and reuse of components is nearly impossible [21].

The challenge that we tackle in this paper is how to keep RE and SA aligned in the context of agile development. While both Nuseibeh [28] and Lucassen [22] identified challenges and explained how RE and SA can support each other, they did not specify *how* to tackle them. What makes the problem hard is that a good solution should not increase stakeholders' workload or costs, in line with the principles of ubiquitous traceability [9]. Furthermore, Cleland-Huang *et al.* [10] identified seven challenges concerning the Twin Peaks model, of which we aspire to address five: lack of in-depth communication between requirements analysts and architects, lack of requirements/architectural knowledge, lack of architectural visualization and explicit traceability between the two domains.

As a solution, we present explicit concepts and relationships that link functional requirements and functional architectural components in order to achieve alignment, among other purposes. While this solution requires some upfront work, aimed at creating or recovering the architecture and linking the requirements, we expect it to decrease rework in the subsequent development phase. Furthermore, to minimize the extra effort, we make use of notations that are widely adopted in agile development and in software architecture. Specifically, we make the following contributions:

- We present a refined version of the RE4SA model [32], which includes notations and relationships for linking RE and SA in agile development;
- We introduce metrics that allow quantifying the relationship between the two domains. While meant for RE4SA, the metrics can be applied more in general to other notations for expressing requirements and architectures;
- We report on two case studies that apply RE4SA for the purpose of architecture discovery and architecture recovery, respectively.

The rest of the paper is structured as follows. Section 2 discusses background work. In Sect. 3 we present the RE4SA model, followed by the alignment metrics in Sect. 4. Section 5 illustrates how the model and its metrics can be applied in practice, using two case studies. Limitations, expected benefits and future work are discussed in Sect. 6, followed by the conclusion in Sect. 7.

2   Background

The rise of agile development created new challenges for the RE and SA disciplines. Requirements documentation changed from long, detailed specifications to less detailed documentation and increased face-to-face contact [8]. The most common notation for requirements in agile development is user stories, a concise notation that captures only the essential elements of a requirement [23]. Regarding the SA discipline, agile practices require the incremental, step-wise construction of a product's functionality, which calls for modular architectures that require minimal coordination with other modules and are easy to extend [12]. This dynamic context is the one within which this paper is positioned.

Keeping software artifacts aligned falls under the umbrella term of software traceability [9], which includes techniques for establishing and maintaining trace links between different artifacts like requirements, architecture, code, and tests. Among the open challenges that pertain to our work, *ubiquitous traceability* [17] is especially important, as it stresses the need of tools and techniques that minimize the required human effort to create and keep the trace links up to date.

Many automated tools exist for the automated establishment of trace links. Trace Analyzer [14] uses certain or hypothesized dependencies between artifacts and common ground and then considers nodes that contain overlapping common ground to establish a trace link. The common ground they use, however, is source code, which is unusable when the system is still under design. Zhang *et al.* [38] use an ontology-based approach to recover trace links, but only link the source code to documentation. Traceability links have also been explored in agile development, with a focus on establishing links between commits and issues [30].

The systematic mapping by Borg *et al.* [4] shows that the most frequently studied links in information retrieval-based traceability are the links between requirements and between requirements and source code. Other popular links are between requirements and tests, and other artifacts and code. Linking requirements and architectures is a less studied topic.

Tang *et al.* [33] study the creation of traces between requirements and architecture. They provide an ontology for annotating manually specifications and architectural artifacts, which are then documented in a semantic wiki. This wiki shows which architectural design outcome realizes which requirement, which decisions have been made, and the links to quality requirements.

Rempel and Mäder [31] are among the first ones to propose traceability metrics in the context of agile development. They propose graph-based metrics that link requirements and test cases. Numerous researchers in the field of software maintenance proposed metrics, starting from the seminal work by Pfleeger and Bohner [29]. Our work, however, focuses solely on metrics between requirements and architectures in the context of agile development for software products.

Recently, Murugesan *et al.* [27] presented a hierarchical reference model to capture the relationship between requirements and architecture. Their goals are similar to those of this research, but they focused on *technical* architectures.

Our work, instead, investigates *functional* architectures and suggests the use of specific artifacts to formulate more specific guidelines, as opposed to a generally applicable requirement-to-component connection model.

3   The RE4SA Model

To facilitate good communication within the development team and support consistency, we propose the Requirements Engineering for Software Architecture (RE4SA) model. Figure 1 shows the four core concepts of the RE4SA model, and an example for each of the concepts from a case study [32]. RE4SA was assembled on the basis of tight collaboration with industrial partners in the software products domain and combines artifacts that we often found employed in their agile practices [24,32]. Like the Twin Peaks model, RE4SA links the RE and SA domains. More specifically, it relates Epic Stories (ESs) [24] and User Stories (USs) [11] in the requirements domain, and modules and features from the functional architecture model [7]. The problem space, which describes the intended behavior through requirements, is related to the solution space that defines how such intended behavior is implemented, i.e., how the requirements are satisfied [2]. Note that the model is only concerned with horizontal traceability [18].

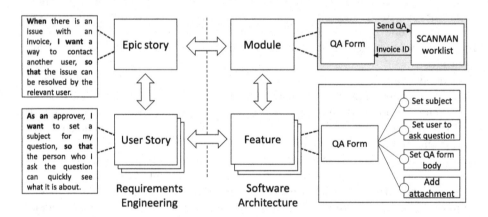

Fig. 1. The Requirements Engineering for Software Architecture (RE4SA) model.

3.1   Representing Requirements and Architecture

The concepts that are part of the RE4SA model encompass notations that are highly adopted in the industry, in an attempt to minimize the need for change and training of professionals. USs, for example, are often found to be among the requirements documents used in agile methods [20], and a US describes a requirement for one feature [23]. Features are often represented using feature diagrams, a graphical language for organizing features hierarchically [19]. By focusing on the details, USs and features make it hard for the stakeholders to obtain an overview of the system that is necessary for clear and easy communication within the development team, thereby calling for a higher level of abstraction.

In practice, USs are grouped together using themes, epics or 'large USs' [35]. However, themes and epics tend to consist of one or a few words and thus lack the rationale that justifies why a requirement should be satisfied by the system [37]. Therefore, we propose the use of ESs [24], which make use of a clear template including both a motivation aspect and an expected outcome. From the architectural standpoint, we take the notion of 'module' from the functional architecture framework [7] as a grouping of features, that also allows for the visualization of usage scenarios through information flows [5].

3.2 Relationships Between the RE4SA Concepts

The RE4SA model supports the establishment of relationships between the four concepts in two ways: (i) Architecture Discovery (AD) is a top-down process that takes the requirements as input in order to create an architecture; (ii) Architecture Recovery (AR) is a bottom-up process that extracts the architecture from an implemented system [1]; then, the architectural components can be linked to the requirements. Figure 2 illustrates the four types of relationships between the concepts of RE4SA. The solid arrows indicate relationships in an AD process, while dashed arrows indicate an AR process. Furthermore, the relationships can be classified depending on whether they affect the *granularity* of the specification (refinement and abstraction) or they support the *alignment* between requirements and architecture (allocation and satisfaction).

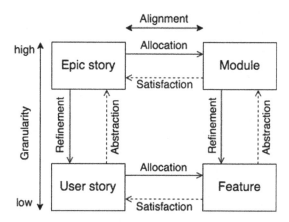

Fig. 2. Relationships between the RE4SA concepts.

Refinement. According to the SWEBOK guide *"decomposition centers on identifying the major software functions and then elaborating and refining them
in a hierarchical top-down manner"* [6]. In an AD process, the major functions are described first, in ESs and modules, and subsequently refined into
more specific functions and descriptions (here, in USs and features).

Abstraction. *"[...] refers to both the process and result of generalization by
reducing the information of a concept, a problem, or an observable phenomenon so that one can focus on the "big picture""* [6]. USs are grouped
together using ESs, while features are bundled together based on similar
functionality and placed in modules. The groupings of USs and features differ in the functionality they describe and the functionality they provide,
respectively. The process of placing these sets of USs and features in ESs and
modules we refer to as abstraction.

Allocation. The process of relating requirements to architectural components
is *"the assignment to architecture components responsible for satisfying the
requirements"* [6]. Since both requirements and architectural components
exist on two levels of granularity, this relationship is included on both levels.

Satisfaction. The SWEBOK guide states that *"the process of analyzing and
elaborating the requirements demands that the architecture/design components that will be responsible for satisfying the requirements be identified"* [6].
Therefore, we refer to this relationship from architectural components to
requirements as satisfaction.

Since this paper investigates requirements-architecture alignment, we leave
the study of refinement and abstraction to future research.

3.3   Architecture Discovery and Architecture Recovery

The AD process (solid arrows in Fig. 2) aims to design an intended architecture
based on the requirements. It is advisable to start at the highest level of granularity, for the collection of ESs describe the functionality of the entire system, while
USs specify the details of how such a high-level functionality is to be delivered.
Once the requirements have been defined, they can be allocated to architectural
components. W e suggest starting at the highest level: ESs are allocated to modules, then USs to features within the identified modules. Finally, it is useful to
check if the features included in the software architecture are all represented
in the requirements set. Features that cannot be linked to a requirement can
indicate missing requirements or unnecessary features.

The goal of an AR process (dashed arrows in Fig. 2), instead, is to recover the
implemented architecture from the system, using available documentation, such
as source code and a run-time version of the system, and linking the recovered
components to requirements. We suggest starting at the lowest level of granularity, and documenting the identified elements in a feature diagram. Different
modules can then be defined to group the features.

Then, the architectural components can be linked to requirements by creating
satisfaction links. We recommend starting at the highest level of granularity: the

ES-module alignment. If these relationships are established first, it should be easier to identify which feature satisfies which US, for the USs are abstracted to ESs. Optionally, missing ESs or USs can be formulated, if the module or feature they will be allocated to is still relevant and/or required. On the other hand, ESs or USs that cannot be allocated to an architectural component need to be assessed. If the functionality the requirement describes is not required or desired, the requirement can be removed. If the opposite is true, the implementation of the feature(s) that would satisfy the requirement can be added to the backlog.

4   Alignment Metrics

We introduce metrics that allow for quantitative investigation of the relationship between requirements and architecture through the lenses of the RE4SA model. To do so, we present the necessary formal framework the metrics build on. We use numbered definitions only for the core concepts of our framework.

Let $R = \{r_1, r_2, \ldots, r_n\}$ be a collection of requirements and $C = \{c_1, \ldots, c_m\}$ be a collection of architectural components. In the RE4SA model, a requirement can be either an Epic Story (ES) or a User Story (US), while a component can be either a module or a feature.

Since a requirement can denote multiple needs (e.g., using the conjunction 'and'), we introduce the function $needs : R \to 2^C$ that maps a requirement r to the needs it expresses. Formally, given a set of needs N, we have that for any $r \in R$, $needs(r) = \{n \in N. \; requested\_by(n, r)\}$, where $requested\_by(n, r)$ is true when n is expressed in the text of requirement r. In this paper, the identification of the needs that are requested by a requirement is left to human analysis.

We can now define the set $N_R = \bigcup_{r \in R} needs(r)$ as the collection of needs that are requested by individual requirements in the collection R.

Definition 1 (Alignment matrix). *A matrix A of size $|N_R| \times |C|$ such that $a_{ij} = 1$ if and only if the need $n_i \in N_R$ matches the component $c_j \in C$. Formally,*

$$a_{ij} = \begin{cases} 1, & \text{if } matches(n_i, c_j) \\ 0, & \text{otherwise.} \end{cases}$$

The alignment matrix is a key element of our framework that can be used to explore the mutual relationship between requirements and components. Based on the matrix, we define the function $allocation : R \to 2^C$ that returns the set of components that match the needs in a requirement. Formally, $allocation$ $(r) = \bigcup_{n_i \in needs(r)} \{c_j. \; a_{ij} = 1\}$. Conversely, we define a function $satisfaction :$ $C \to 2^R$ that returns all the requirements with needs matching a given component. Formally, $satisfaction(c_j) = \bigcup_{r \in R} \{n_i. \; a_{ij} = 1 \wedge n_i \in needs(r)\}$.

Based on the allocation function, we can partition the set of requirements into four non-disjoint subsets: $R = R_{not} \cup R_{under} \cup R_{exact} \cup R_{multi}$, defined as follows:

- $R_{not} = \{r \in R. \; allocation(r) = \emptyset\}$

- $R_{under} = \{r \in R.\ 0 < |allocation(r)| \wedge \exists n_i \in needs(r).\ (\sum_j a_{ij}) = 0\}$
- $R_{exact} = \{r \in R.\ \forall n_i \in needs(r).\ (\sum_j a_{ij}) = 1\}$
- $R_{multi} = \{r \in R.\ \exists n_i \in needs(r).\ (\sum_j a_{ij}) > 1\}$.

R_{not} is the set of requirements that are not allocated, R_{under} are those requirements with some but not all allocated needs, R_{exact} are those requirements with each need allocated to exactly one component, and R_{multi} are those requirements having at least one need allocated to multiple components. The four sets are not disjoint. For example, a requirement requesting needs n_1 and n_2, with n_1 matching components c_1 and c_2 and with n_2 matching no components would be both multi-allocated (because of n_1) and under-allocated (because of n_2).

Definition 2 (Allocation degrees). *The partitioning of R into R_{not}, R_{under}, etc. can be used to define metrics on the allocation degree of a set of requirements. We introduce three degrees, each in the $[0, 1]$ range:*

- *multi-allocation degree: $multi\_alloc_d = |R_{multi}|/|R|$*
- *exact allocation degree: $exact\_alloc_d = |R_{exact}|/|R|$*
- *under-allocation degree: $under\_alloc_d = (|R_{not}| + |R_{under}|)/|R|$*

The ideal case is one in which the exact allocation degree is close to 1 and the other two degrees are close to zero: in that case, indeed, each need in a requirement can be traced to exactly one architectural component. This situation is good because the needs are homomorphically mirrored in the architectural design, thereby facilitating the conversation between experts in either discipline. An exception to this case is when the system includes variability: in that case, it is desired to have a multi-allocation degree, for multiple components may be devised as alternative ways to fulfill one requirement.

Similar to the partitioning of requirements based on the allocation function, we can partition the set of components based on the satisfaction function. Specifically, the set of components is partitioned into two disjoint subsets: $C = C_{not} \cup C_{sat}$, where $C_{sat} = \{c \in C.\ satisfaction(c) \neq \emptyset\}$ and $C_{not} = C \setminus C_{sat}$.

Definition 3 (Satisfaction degree). *It defines the ratio of components that satisfy at least one need in a requirement as follows: $sat_d = |C_{sat}|/|C|$.*

When the satisfaction degree reaches the value of 1, all architectural components trace back to at least one requirement and, thus, their existence is justified. Unlike Definition 2, we do not include a notion of multi-satisfaction, for we are interested in assessing *whether* a component is justified or not, instead of *counting* how many needs the component accommodates.

To represent the combination of allocation and satisfaction, we introduce the metric of alignment which is a weighted arithmetic mean of the extent to which needs are allocated, and the extent to which components can be traced back to requirements. To do so, we first need to introduce the need allocation degree:

$$need\_all_d = \frac{|\{n_i \in N_R.\ (\sum_j a_{ij}) = 1\}|}{|N_R|}.$$

Definition 4 (Alignment degree). *It is a weighted arithmetic mean (with* $\alpha \in [0,1]$*) of the need allocation degree and the component satisfaction degree:* $align_d = \alpha \cdot need\_all_d + (1 - \alpha) \cdot sat_d$.

In this paper, we set $\alpha = 0.5$ and give equal weight to the requirements and architecture perspectives. Similar to the debate on the β in the F_β-score [3], in-vivo studies are necessary to tune our parameter based on the relative impact of need allocation degree and component satisfaction degree. However, our experience with the software production industry reveals that early product releases include several implicitly expressed needs (e.g., printing, storage, menu interaction), thereby requiring a high $\alpha > 0.5$, whereas later releases focus on explicit (customer) requirements allocation with $\alpha < 0.5$.

The concepts and definitions above apply to the generic notions of *requirement* and *component*. In RE4SA, as per Fig. 2, we can reason about alignment at two granularity levels: *high* and *low*. The definitions and metrics can therefore be applied at either level:

- *high*: the set R contains ESs, C includes modules, N consists of outcomes from an ES, and the function *needs* returns the set of outcomes of an ES;
- *low*: R contains USs, C consists of features, N includes actions from a US, and the function *needs* returns the set of actions of a US.

5   The RE4SA Model in Practice

To assess the feasibility and usefulness of RE4SA and our metrics, we apply them to two case studies. The first presents an AD process, while the second illustrates an AR process. After introducing each case, we discuss the granularity relationships in Sect. 5.1, and analyze the alignment metrics in Sect. 5.2.

VP. The discovery case concerns a portal for vendors to manage their open invoices through an integration with the customers' ERP system. Following a requirements elicitation session with the customer, a list of USs was created and then grouped in themes. We defined ESs from the themes by rewording them and by splitting one of them into two (based on the word "and"). The SA was created by transforming the requirements into an intended architecture following the AD process described in Sect. 3.3. The software architect was allowed to include his interpretation of the requirements, e.g., by adding missing features and modules.

YODA. The recovery case regards a research application called Your Data (YODA, https://github.com/UtrechtUniversity/). A rich collection of USs was available, already grouped in themes. We used these one-word themes to formulate ESs. The functional architecture had to be recovered. As described in Sect. 3.3, this was done using a bottom-up approach. Using the implemented system, in this particular case a web application, all features were recovered by modeling every user-interactive element in the GUI as a feature.

5.1   Granularity: Exploring Refinement and Abstraction

Descriptive statistics of both cases are shown in Table 1, including the arithmetic mean for the granularity. The average number of USs in an ES is shown on the

Table 1. Descriptive statistics of both the Vendor Portal (VP) and YODA case.

Case	Level of granularity	Requirements						Comp.		Granularity	
		R	$Needs$	R_{not}	R_{under}	R_{exact}	R_{multi}	C	C_{sat}	$\mu ES\text{-}US$	$\mu M\text{-}F$
VP	*ES-module*	8	9	1	0	4	3	14	11	3.8	3
	US-feature	30	37	2	2	17	9	43	35	1	1
YODA	*ES-module*	12	12	0	0	12	0	12	12	8	12.6
	US-feature	96	102	3	3	84	6	161	66	1	1

top row, while the number of ESs a US is abstracted to, on average, is shown below that. The same is done for the averages of modules and features.

VP. This collection of requirements has an average of 3.8 US per ES. Analyzing our artifacts, we see that one ES only contains a single US, four modules have a single feature, and five modules only have two features. On average, a module has three features. This may indicate either the existence of few requirements per ES, high modularity, or non-detailed requirements. Due to the use of Scrum in the project, it is likely that the number of requirements will grow during development. The ES with a single US can indicate missing requirements, that it should actually be a US, or that it is expected to be extended in later phases. On the SA side, the aforementioned modules with one or two features should be analyzed as they can indicate missing features, modules to be extended, or an incorrect organization of features.

YODA. While all ESs contain at least two USs, thereby representing a proper refinement, three of them are larger than average. Regarding the modules, three contain less than two features, and one contains far more features than the average. The YODA development team can use these results to analyze their architecture and code. The larger-than-average module, for instance, may include too much functionality. In addition, the three modules with zero or one feature may lead the team to consider removing these modules or expanding upon them in the future. After speaking with the lead developer, it turns out that they have recently been working on 'simplifying' the largest module, since it was difficult to maintain and complex to use. On the other hand, they have been adding features to the modules that are relatively small.

5.2   Alignment: Studying Allocation and Satisfaction

The alignment metrics for both cases are presented in Table 2, including the ES-module alignment and the US-feature alignment.

VP. On both levels of granularity, the under-allocation degree shows that *13% of the requirements contain needs that are not addressed* by architectural components. The exact allocation degree is 0.50 for ES-M and 0.57 for US-F; roughly half of all requirements have each of their needs allocated to exactly one SA element. The remaining requirements are multi-allocated, with a degree of 0.38 for ES-M and 0.30 for US-F, which could indicate duplicate features or inefficient solutions. Only *around 80% of the components satisfy a requirement*; the remaining components are not explicitly justified by the requirements.

Table 2. The alignment-related metrics applied to the VP and YODA cases.

Relationship	Metric	VP		YODA	
		ES-M	*US-F*	*ES-M*	*US-F*
Allocation	$multi\_alloc_d$	0.38	0.30	0.0	0.06
	$exact\_alloc_d$	0.50	0.57	1.0	0.88
	$under\_alloc_d$	0.13	0.13	0.0	0.06
Satisfaction	sat_d	0.79	0.81	1.0	0.41
Alignment	$need\_all_d$	0.89	0.86	1.0	0.94
	$\textbf{align}_d$	**0.84**	**0.84**	**1.0**	**0.68**

Since this is an AD process, we expect a high alignment degree, as the architecture is based on the requirements before taking implementation factors into account (as opposed to the AR process). The alignment degree is 0.84 on both granularity levels, indicating some discrepancies between the requirements and the architecture. Together with the multi-allocation degrees of 0.30 and 0.38, this seems to indicate *the requirements set is not sufficiently detailed*. The under-allocation degree indicates that the software architect either did not agree with certain requirements, or missed them during the AD process. The inexact allocation on the ES-M level can indicate an incorrect categorization of requirements, that the granularity of ES is not on a module level, or that the architect's categorization differs from that of the requirements engineer.

Figure 3 shows how USs can be allocated to features. The first US in the figure is multi-allocated, as it is linked to two features, specifically the need *"use password forgotten functionality"* is allocated to the features *"initiate password recovery"*, and *"send password recovery email"*. The other two USs are exact-allocated as they contain a single need and are allocated to a single feature.

The metrics from the VP case were discussed with the CEO of the company that developed the portal. He was *surprised by the low alignment score*, for the project was rather simple and the requirements were the basis for the architecture. The metrics were mentioned to be useful in highlighting potential issues with the requirements, and it was noted that the *requirements specification was not revisited after the SA creation*. Multi-allocation was seen as the most important allocation degree, as it *can indicate unnecessary costs*, while under-allocation was expected to be detected during use of the application, or denote

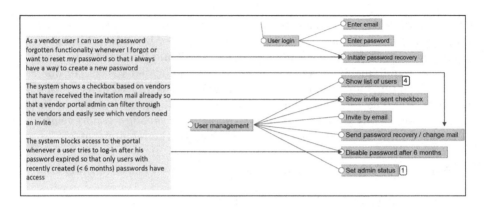

Fig. 3. Example of how USs were allocated to features.

missing features to add later. The modules that did not satisfy a requirement were judged to be a *result of missing requirements*. Finally, he mentioned the potential for making *agreements when outsourcing development*, e.g., requiring the architecture to have a 0.9 alignment degree with the requirements.

YODA. The ESs were allocated one-to-one to modules, while all modules satisfied exactly one ES; thus, these metrics are not further discussed. Nearly all USs were allocated to a feature in the architecture. Only three USs are missing completely and three others have not been fully implemented. The latter three USs contained two needs, of which only one was allocated to a feature. Regarding the features, instead, *not even half of the features satisfy at least one need*.

The missing satisfaction links may be due to a *granularity levels discrepancies*: the features are probably more specific than the USs. Also, since our feature recovery was based on exploring the GUI, some features (e.g., those related to navigation) might not need to be listed in a requirement.

According to the metrics, *not all requirements are currently allocated*: some features still need to be implemented. Moreover, since around 60% of the features do not satisfy a requirement, either the requirements are incomplete or unnecessary features exist. The lead developer explained that they *do not consider anything in retrospect*: when a US is considered completed, it is removed from the backlog. Thus, he was *unaware that six USs have not yet been fully implemented* in the system.

An example of how modules and features were recovered from the GUI is shown in Fig. 4. For the sake of brevity, the alternative features related to F2 and F3 were collapsed. The module satisfies an ES that was based on the "Metadata" theme: "When I am storing research data, I want to *include metadata about the content*, so that I can document my data." Only two of the features satisfy a US, features F3 and F4 (in Fig. 4) satisfy US3 and US4, respectively:

US3: "As a researcher, I want to *specify the accessibility of the metadata* of my dataset, so that access can be granted according to policy [...]."

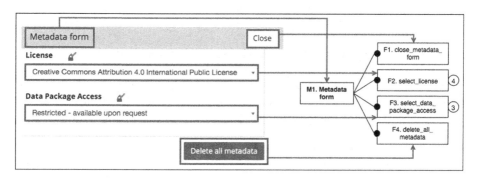

Fig. 4. Example of how architectural components were recovered from the GUI.

US4: "As a researcher, I want to be able to *discard existing metadata* and re-begin adding metadata, so that I can document a data package."

Therefore, F1 and F2 are part of the C_{not} count, while F3 and F4 are considered part of the C_{sat}.

YODA's lead developer expects the metrics to be useful, as they could help *foster the creation of trace links*, currently nonexistent. The situation is problematic when new colleagues join ("it takes approximately three months to get up to speed and be able to add something of value to the system") or when someone leaves the team, for their knowledge is lost. Also, team members often *do not know where features originate from*. To discover the rationale, the source code is checked to locate features; if unused, it is removed. This happens because the team sometimes adds features without defining the requirements first. Moreover, he expects under-allocation to be useful during development, e.g., during or at the end of every sprint, to *check whether all requirements were satisfied and if they were satisfied in full*. Finally, the multi-allocation metric may help identify duplicate features; the user stories often have overlap, causing the team to implement the same feature twice. The developer stated they are planning on *using the metrics in their next sprint aiming to improve their work efficiency and quality*.

6   Discussion

We present expected benefits from the use of RE4SA in practice, and present the validity threats to our study.

Expected Benefits. RE4SA can improve requirements-architecture communication in agile development product teams, which include product managers and product owners, through (1) simple communication means, (2) clear structural guidelines, and (3) consistent domain terminology. Combining the two granularity levels of the RE4SA model provides a shared context view of the software for the functional and technical experts. Functional experts tend to employ a high-level overview (ES-module), while technical experts are mostly focused on the detailed level (US-feature) [32].

The objective of the RE4SA model, however, is not limited to improving communication. Gayer *et al.* [16] argued for the need of dynamic architecture creation. This architecture allows for traceability that can make software more maintainable, changeable and sustainable. The alignment relationships in RE4SA support traceability, with little documentation and effort required.

We also surmise that RE4SA helps reason about the system, for all stakeholders know which parts of the system are being discussed. In addition, when requirements are changed (modified, added, or deleted), it is apparent which other parts of the system are affected, due to the explicit relationship between concepts. Obviously, some effort is required to maintain the artifacts updated.

The RE4SA model and its metrics can be utilized for communication outside of the development team as well, such as when interacting with clients. One expected benefit is the ability *provide proof for contractual obligations*, which could also be applied to ensuring requirements alignment when outsourcing development. Using the alignment metrics, a company can prove that its system complies with the contractual requirements they and the client agreed on for the project. Furthermore, the company can provide *feedback on its progress* in percentage of realized functionality or satisfied requirements. At times, customers will have requirements for a software product that form a risk to the maintainability of the product. In these cases, the architecture can be used to *visualize the risks* of these particular elements and ensure that the customer is aware and agrees to the risks before the requirement is accepted as part of the project.

Finally, RE4SA may support release planning. The architecture highlights feature dependencies, while the requirements show the priorities. Using both perspectives, the developers can determine the *top-priority* features and, optionally, the pre-requisite features. When customers have a customized version of a software product, the architecture of the new release can be compared to the architecture of the customer [32]. Through this comparison, *incompatibilities can be detected*, allowing for better planning in an upgrade project for a new release.

Validity Threats. Concerning *construct validity*, the formulation of ESs presents some difficulties; in RE practice, ESs are formulated using the US template (epics) or as themes. Although our re-formulation did not present particular difficulties, we need to acknowledge that the ES notation we suggest is not mainstream yet. All other concepts of RE4SA (user stories, modules, features) are adopted by the industry. An *internal threat* in using the RE4SA model is *determining the 'right' levels of granularity*. While USs should describe a requirement for exactly one (atomic) feature [23], this is often unfeasible or inefficient and a US might describe a composite feature instead. For example, a US like "As a user, I want to select a language." would result in one feature 'select language'. Depending on the chosen granularity level, this feature may either be atomic, or be a composite one that is refined into separate features to switch to each supported language. To minimize this threat, we used the same levels of granularity and metrics for both cases. *Conclusion validity* is indirectly affected by the granularity problem: should we have employed a different granularity level, the conclusions we have drawn may have differed. Regarding *external validity*, we considered only two case studies; nevertheless, the metrics are applied to real-world examples of documentation and cover common software applications.

7 Conclusion

In this study on requirements and architecture alignment, we presented the RE4SA model [26] that supports communication within the development team. We formalized the links between the four core concepts in RE4SA and we provided metrics to quantify the alignment between RE and SA. The results of these metrics can be used to analyze and improve the alignment. The metrics were applied in two industry provided cases and allow for detection of improvements in both the architecture and the requirements.

The results presented in this paper and in previous work regarding RE4SA [26,32] provide initial evidence on the suitability of our model for experimentation in practice. In particular, the AR process detailed in Sect. 3.3 allows for the RE4SA model to be used even if currently no architecture artifacts are in place.

This paper paves the way for various research directions. Firstly, we would like to study whether the linguistic structure of the artifacts, e.g., the specific words used, can help relate requirements with architectural components, and support the proper positioning of new functionality within an existing architecture. Moreover, using the sentence structures in USs, it might be possible to extract feature names from USs automatically. Secondly, evolution in agile environments [10] is a notable challenge that could benefit from the use of RE4SA. By capturing software changes introduced in extension, customisation and modification of a product in the architecture, the evolution of the product becomes visible and manageable. Utilizing the alignment relationships can be used to ensure that both the requirements and architecture stay up to date. Thirdly, we intend to apply the RE4SA model and its alignment metrics to additional cases, aiming to validate them and to determine best practices. One of the first steps in this direction is to formalize metrics for the granularity relationships, in the same manner as for the alignment relationships as presented in this paper. Finally, it is important to investigate how quality requirements are represented in agile development and how they are mapped to quality aspects in architectures.

Acknowledgements. We would like to thank Remmelt Blessinga, Abel Menkveld and Thijs Smudde for their contributions to an earlier version of this work.

References

1. Ali, N., Baker, S., O'Crowley, R., Herold, S., Buckley, J.: Architecture consistency: state of the practice, challenges and requirements. Empirical Softw. Eng. **23**(1), 224–258 (2018)
2. Apel, S., Kästner, C.: An overview of feature-oriented software development. J. Object Technol. **8**(5), 49–84 (2009)

3. Berry, D.M.: Evaluation of tools for hairy requirements and software engineering tasks. In: Proceedings of the RE Workshops, pp. 284–291 (2017)
4. Borg, M., Runeson, P., Ardö, A.: Recovering from a decade: a systematic mapping of information retrieval approaches to software traceability. Empirical Softw. Eng. **19**(6), 1565–1616 (2014). https://doi.org/10.1007/s10664-013-9255-y
5. Bosch, J.: Software architecture: the next step. In: Oquendo, F., Warboys, B.C., Morrison, R. (eds.) EWSA 2004. LNCS, vol. 3047, pp. 194–199. Springer, Heidelberg (2004). https://doi.org/10.1007/978-3-540-24769-2_14
6. Bourque, P., Fairley, R.E., et al.: Guide to the Software Engineering Body of Knowledge (SWEBOK (R)): Version 3.0. IEEE Computer Society Press (2014)
7. Brinkkemper, S., Pachidi, S.: Functional architecture modeling for the software product industry. In: Babar, M.A., Gorton, I. (eds.) ECSA 2010. LNCS, vol. 6285, pp. 198–213. Springer, Heidelberg (2010). https://doi.org/10.1007/978-3-642-15114-9_16
8. Cao, L., Ramesh, B.: Agile requirements engineering practices: an empirical study. IEEE Softw. **25**(1), 60–67 (2008)
9. Cleland-Huang, J., Gotel, O.C., Huffman Hayes, J., Mäder, P., Zisman, A.: Software traceability: trends and future directions. In: Proceedings of the FOSE, pp. 55–69 (2014)
10. Cleland-Huang, J., Hanmer, R.S., Supakkul, S., Mirakhorli, M.: The twin peaks of requirements and architecture. IEEE Softw. **30**(2), 24–29 (2013)
11. Cohn, M.: User Stories Applied. Addison-Wesley Professional, Boston (2004)
12. Coplien, J.O., Bjørnvig, G.: Lean Architecture. Wiley, Hoboken (2011)
13. Curtis, B., Krasner, H., Iscoe, N.: A field study of the software design process for large systems. Commun. ACM **31**(11), 1268–1287 (1988)
14. Egyed, A., Grünbacher, P.: Automating requirements traceability: beyond the record & replay paradigm. In: Proceedings of the ASE, pp. 163–171 (2002)
15. Fernández, D.M., et al.: Naming the pain in requirements engineering. Empirical Softw. Eng. **22**(5), 2298–2338 (2017). https://doi.org/10.1007/s10664-016-9451-7
16. Gayer, S., Herrmann, A., Keuler, T., Riebisch, M., Antonino, P.O.: Lightweight traceability for the agile architect. Computer **49**(5), 64–71 (2016)
17. Gotel, O., et al.: The quest for ubiquity: a roadmap for software and systems traceability research. In: Proceedings of RE, pp. 71–80 (2012)
18. Gotel, O., et al.: Traceability fundamentals. In: Cleland-Huang, J., Gotel, O., Zisman, A. (eds.) Software and Systems Traceability, pp. 3–22. Springer, Heidelberg (2012). https://doi.org/10.1007/978-1-4471-2239-5_1
19. Hubaux, A., Tun, T.T., Heymans, P.: Separation of concerns in feature diagram languages: a systematic survey. ACM Comput. Surv. (CSUR) **45**(4), 1–23 (2013)
20. Inayat, I., Salim, S.S., Marczak, S., Daneva, M., Shamshirband, S.: A systematic literature review on agile requirements engineering practices and challenges. Comput. Hum. Behav. **51**, 915–929 (2015)
21. Lindvall, M., Muthig, D.: Bridging the software architecture gap. Computer **41**(6), 98–101 (2008)
22. Lucassen, G., Dalpiaz, F., Van Der Werf, J.M., Brinkkemper, S.: Bridging the twin peaks: the case of the software industry. In: Proceedings of the TwinPeaks, pp. 24–28 (2015)
23. Lucassen, G., Dalpiaz, F., van der Werf, J.M.E., Brinkkemper, S.: Improving agile requirements: the quality user story framework and tool. Requirements Eng. **21**(3), 383–403 (2016)

24. Lucassen, G., van de Keuken, M., Dalpiaz, F., Brinkkemper, S., Sloof, G.W., Schlingmann, J.: Jobs-to-be-done oriented requirements engineering: a method for defining job stories. In: Kamsties, E., Horkoff, J., Dalpiaz, F. (eds.) REFSQ 2018. LNCS, vol. 10753, pp. 227–243. Springer, Cham (2018). https://doi.org/10.1007/978-3-319-77243-1_14

25. McChesney, I.R., Gallagher, S.: Communication and co-ordination practices in software engineering projects. Inf. Softw. Technol. **46**(7), 473–489 (2004)

26. Molenaar, S., Brinkkemper, S., Menkveld, A., Smudde, T., Blessinga, R., Dalpiaz, F.: On the nature of links between requirements and architectures: case studies on user story utilization in agile development. Technical report UU-CS-2019-008, Department of Information and Computing Sciences, Utrecht University (2019). http://www.cs.uu.nl/research/techreps/repo/CS-2019/2019-008.pdf

27. Murugesan, A., Rayadurgam, S., Heimdahl, M.: Requirements reference models revisited: accommodating hierarchy in system design. In: 2019 IEEE 27th International Requirements Engineering Conference (RE), pp. 177–186. IEEE (2019)

28. Nuseibeh, B.: Weaving together requirements and architectures. Computer **34**(3), 115–119 (2001)

29. Pfleeger, S.L., Bohner, S.A.: A framework for software maintenance metrics. In: Proceedings of Conference on Software Maintenance, pp. 320–327 (1990)

30. Rath, M., Rendall, J., Guo, J.L.C., Cleland-Huang, J., Mäder, P.: Traceability in the wild: automatically augmenting incomplete trace links. In: Proceedings of the ICSE, pp. 834–845 (2018)

31. Rempel, P., Mäder, P.: Estimating the implementation risk of requirements in agile software development projects with traceability metrics. In: Fricker, S.A., Schneider, K. (eds.) REFSQ 2015. LNCS, vol. 9013, pp. 81–97. Springer, Cham (2015). https://doi.org/10.1007/978-3-319-16101-3_6

32. Spijkman, T., Brinkkemper, S., Dalpiaz, F., Hemmer, A.F., van de Bospoort, R.: Specification of requirements and software architecture for the customisation of enterprise software. In: Proceedings of the RE Workshops, pp. 64–73 (2019)

33. Tang, A., Liang, P., Clerc, V., Van Vliet, H.: Traceability in the co-evolution of architectural requirements and design. In: Avgeriou, P., Grundy, J., Hall, J., Lago, P., Mistrík, I. (eds.) Relating Software Requirements and Architectures, pp. 35–60. Springer, Heidelberg (2011). https://doi.org/10.1007/978-3-642-21001-3_4

34. Venters, C.C., Capilla, R., Betz, S., Penzenstadler, B., Crick, T., Crouch, S., Nakagawa, E.Y., Becker, C., Carrillo, C.: Software sustainability: research and practice from a software architecture viewpoint. J. Syst. Softw. **138**, 174–188 (2018)

35. Wautelet, Y., Heng, S., Kolp, M., Mirbel, I., Poelmans, S.: Building a rationale diagram for evaluating user story sets. In: Proceedings of the RCIS, pp. 1–12 (2016)

36. Whitehead, J.: Collaboration in software engineering: a roadmap. In: Proceedings of FOSE, pp. 214–225 (2007)

37. Yu, E.S.: Towards modelling and reasoning support for early-phase requirements engineering. In: Proceedings of ISRE, pp. 226–235 (1997)

38. Zhang, Y., Witte, R., Rilling, J., Haarslev, V.: An ontology-based approach for traceability recovery. In: Proceedings of the ATEM, pp. 36–43 (2006)

39. Zowghi, D., Nurmuliani, N.: A study of the impact of requirements volatility on software project performance. In: Proceeding of the APSEC, pp. 3–11 (2002)

Applying Distributed Cognition Theory to Agile Requirements Engineering

Jim Buchan[1]([⊠]), Didar Zowghi[2], and Muneera Bano[3]

[1] Auckland University of Technology, Auckland, New Zealand
jim.buchan@aut.ac.nz
[2] University of Technology Sydney, Sydney, Australia
didar.zowghi@uts.edu.au
[3] Deakin University, Melbourne, Australia
muneera.bano@deakin.edu.au

Abstract. [**Context & Motivation**] Agile Requirements Engineering (ARE) is a collaborative, team-based process based on frequent elicitation, elaboration, estimation and prioritization of the user requirements, typically represented as user stories. While it is claimed that this Agile approach and the associated RE activities are effective, there is sparse empirical evidence and limited theoretical foundation to explain this efficacy. [**Question/problem**] We aim to understand and explain aspects of the ARE process by focusing on a cognitive perspective. We appropriate ideas and techniques from Distributed Cognition (DC) theory to analyze the cognitive roles of people, artefacts and the physical work environment in a successful collaborative ARE activity, namely requirement prioritization. [**Principal idea/results**] This paper presents a field study of two early requirements related meetings in an Agile product development project. Observation data, field notes and transcripts were collected and qualitatively analyzed. We have used DiCoT, a framework for systematically applying DC as a methodological contribution, to analyze the ARE process and explain its efficacy from a cognitive perspective. The analysis identified three main areas of cognitive effort in the ARE process as well as the significant information flows and artefacts. Analysis of these have identified that the use of *physical* user story cards, specific facilitator skills, and development of shared understanding of the user stories, were all key to the effectiveness of the ARE activity observed. [**Contribution**] The deeper understanding of cognition involved in ARE provides an empirically evidenced explanation, based on DC theory, of why this way of collaboratively prioritizing requirements was effective. Our result provides a basis for designing other ARE activities.

Keywords: Distributed Cognition · Agile · Requirements prioritization

1 Introduction

The development of a shared understanding of user requirements between the client and development groups is fundamental to the design and development of software that satisfies the stakeholders' needs. In Agile Requirements Engineering (ARE) the effort

© Springer Nature Switzerland AG 2020
N. Madhavji et al. (Eds.): REFSQ 2020, LNCS 12045, pp. 186–202, 2020.
https://doi.org/10.1007/978-3-030-44429-7_14

to collaboratively understand user requirements, generally represented as user stories, occurs frequently, in every sprint. Each sprint, the focus is given to identifying and deepening understanding of user stories that are high value and prioritizing them for development in the next sprint [1]. Regular ARE activities include team meetings for requirements prioritizing, elaboration, estimation and planning. The emphasis in Agile RE is on regular face-to-face communication and collaboration among the client stakeholders and development team to develop and deepen this shared understanding of the requirements [2]. While it is claimed that the Agile approach is effective in supporting the achievement of these RE goals, there is little detailed empirical evidence and limited theoretical foundations for these claims. This paper proposes viewing ARE as a collaborative distributed cognitive process and appropriates a multidisciplinary framework, Distributed Cognition theory (DC), as a theoretical foundation for understanding and explaining the efficacy of ARE activities. Viewing ARE as a collaborative cognitive (information processing) process is a natural perspective, given the emphasis on communication (information flows and processing), and the fundamental cognitive goals of shared user requirements understanding. DC is a good fit to describe and understand this since it provides a theoretical foundation for how work is done in complex, collaborative team-based activities such as ARE, where the cognitive activities are socially distributed and interactions with work objects and the work environment are important [3]. A DC analysis of such work can have the applied aim of explaining and understanding the efficacy and shortcomings of current workspaces, work practices and technologies used, as in our case.

Although RE is recognized as a complex socio-technical set of activities involving people, tools and artefacts, very few studies have attempted to understand the nature of RE activities through the lens of DC theories. The applications of DC have been demonstrated in areas such as creative requirements engineering [4], semi-structured creative processes in group work [5], knowledge management in requirements engineering [6], distributed requirements engineering [7], Model-Driven requirements [8], and open source software requirements [9, 10]. Although not focused solely on RE, Sharp and Robinson [11–13] used the DC framework to analyze the collaborative work in the XP team development process in order to highlight the potential problem areas in the activity. Outside RE the DC approach has been used to analyze the computer-supported co-operative work (CSCW) for discovering the effectiveness of collaborative technologies [14, 15], community of practice [16], effective design of teamwork systems [3, 17] and in the field of HCI to analyze the development of interactive systems [18, 19].

The existing literature justifies the use of the DC framework and its theoretical underpinning for understanding collaborative RE practices. Our study differs from existing DC literature by applying the DC analysis to the ARE context, applying it to a shorter time frame (specific time-boxed meetings), and how the achievement of the specific cognitive goals of the observed ARE activity are supported through distributed information processing as cognition. It can be expected that this detailed DC analysis explains the efficacy of some characteristics of the process involving interactions between people, the room layout and artefacts, and may also suggest some possible process improvements.

In our field study, a specific ARE activity, early requirements prioritization (RP), is chosen as the focus of our DC analysis, but the principles and research approach could be applied to any collaborative aspect of ARE, which is the aim of our future research. Early RP meetings were selected as an example of applying DC theory to ARE because, RP is iterative, frequent and central to the agile way of working. Agile RP is collaborative and, particularly in the early requirements phase, it can be complex and challenging cognitively. The RP process in practice can vary widely, with context-dependent adoption of many processes and techniques [20]. The cognitive complexity of Agile RP can be inferred from the plethora of RP processes and techniques described in the literature [21, 22].

In summary, this paper reports on an in-depth field study of an aspect of the collaborative Agile RE process taking a cognitive perspective. It is based on observational field work of two early-phase RP meetings in preparation for the first development sprint. The transcribed audio, video and field notes collected in the meetings are analyzed to understand the strengths and weaknesses of the observed RE activity from a distributed cognition perspective. Based on DC theory we identify the significant interactions between people, the physical work environment and work-related artefacts, viewed as a single extended information processing (distributed cognition) system. The system in our study comprises the people, space and artefacts involved in the two RP meetings observed.

In line with other DC researchers, we have utilized a specific DC framework, Distributed Cognition for Teamwork (DiCoT) [17], to guide what aspects of ARE work activities to focus on for the DC analysis as well as to provide a systematic approach to data collection and analysis. DiCoT was first described and applied in [17] to study the teamwork in the London Ambulance Service. Application of the DiCoT framework and its set of 18 cognitive principles and three themes has enabled us to describe three main areas of cognition involved in this area of ARE, as well as explain the efficacy and limitations of the observed ARE process in terms of the cognitive significance of particular people, artefacts, the work place and their interactions. The contributions of this study are twofold: (1) the first and novel application of DC and the DiCoT framework to analyze aspects of the collaborative ARE process is a contribution to RE research and practice, (2) the utility of DiCoT in the context of requirements engineering is a methodological contribution to DC research.

2 Background

Distributed Cognition (DC) is a theoretical and methodological framework [23] that describes an approach for studying the organization of cognition in collaborative group activities. In this framework, cognition is viewed as a system capability, extending beyond individual brains into the interaction between individuals in the group as well as interactions with artifacts and structure in the work environment as cognitive resources. This view is based on the observation that groups have cognitive properties that cannot be explained by simply aggregating the cognitive properties of the individuals in the group. The functional system, then, is the cognitive unit of analysis, where this system has cognitive properties different to the sum of the people in the system and solves cognitive problems differently to individuals [24]. In our case, the functional system is the people at the ARE meeting, artefacts used in the meeting, as well as characteristics of the room that may support or hinder the distributed cognition related to achieving the functional goal. The functional goal being the agreement on a priority order for working on the user stories presented.

Unlike the traditional view of cognition as symbol manipulation inside the heads of individuals, the distributed cognition is observable since the "computation" is the flow and transformation of information between the elements of the functional system ("*the propagation of representational states across representational media*" [23]). In this view, artifacts and structure in the workplace appropriated in the performance of work are more than "*mere stimuli for a disembodied cognitive system*" [18].

In the DC the emphasis is on uncovering the dynamics of how knowledge is propagated and transformed through the functional system by describing the subtasks and interactions at a high level of detail, identifying breakdowns and accomplishments in the functional system. Rogers [3] describes the initial approach as a "*micro-level analysis*" that distinguishes the flows of representational states by describing "*in increasing detail the seemingly trivial and the usually taken for granted aspects of actions and interactions.*" Vaesen [25] describes this analysis as reverse engineering in the sense that the task is to "*derive and model the system's information-transforming subfunctions and the particular ways in which these are organized so as to realize the system's functional goal*".

There are a number of possible levels of activity and cognitive perspectives a DC analysis could focus on when observing and analyzing a work activity: communication dynamics between people; information filtering or biases; collaborative manipulation of an artefact; and appropriation of structure to simplify information sharing, collective memory, or lessen the cognitive load on individuals. The DiCoT framework [17] provides a checklist of 28 DC principles to consider for a DC analysis of a collaborative team activity. The authors of [17] base the principles on their synthesis of those found in DC literature. In DiCoT, the principles are grouped into five broad themes, each of which represents a particular emphasis with which to view and analyze the collected data in multiple passes. The three themes reported in this paper are: (1) information flow (2) physical layout and (3) artifact details. The other two themes, related to social structure and temporal considerations, are also relevant to the overall study and will be reported in a later paper. DiCoT's tabular and diagrammatic approach to data collection and analysis was loosely followed in the field notes and were supplemented by content and interaction analyses of electronic recordings of meetings and their transcripts.

The information flow theme focuses on identifying what information flows and transformations are important to the ARE activity. Questions to be addressed include: What information is significant to whom for what purpose? What structures broadcast information relevant to the activities (information radiators), as a coordinating mechanism? What structures act as buffers to information flow to avoid constant interruptions to work from new information? What is limiting access to relevant information? What structures or activities are important for information coming together to make decisions (information hubs)?

The physical layout perspective considers the role of space, spatial structure and the arrangement of material objects in the workplace in supporting cognition and includes the possible role of physical bodily support (e.g. pointing). Mechanisms for how people are kept informed of what the current activity is, and what is planned, are considered (situational awareness), as well as limitations of the horizon of observation of group members. The focus of the physical layout perspective is to address the question of how well the physical layout of the workspace supports information flows and processing and whether it could be improved.

3   Research Design and Implementation

The main aim of this research was to understand the distributed cognition involved in the ARE process in practice. Two meetings aimed at prioritizing user stories in the early requirements phase of an Agile project were selected as examples of the ARE process. A DC analysis of the process begins with identifying the high-level cognition and functional sub-goals in the process, as well as the enabling information flows and transformations (RQ1). This cognitive description of the process is then analyzed using the principles from three themes from the DiCoT framework previously discussed (RQ2). Principles from DiCoT that are identified as being adhered to in the meetings provide a theoretical foundation for explaining the efficacy of the RE activities taking place in the meetings.

The two research questions we sought to answer, aligning with this approach, are:

RQ 1 What aspects of the of observed ARE process are cognitively significant?
RQ2 What principles from DiCoT are important in the observed ARE process?

The data for the DC analysis were gathered by observing two requirements prioritization meetings of an Agile product development project. The meetings occurred early in the project, before development had started, and involved a group of stakeholders collaboratively prioritizing sets of user stories, one at a time. The data collected comprised observational data (photographs of the workspace and copies of some artefacts), field notes and transcripts of audio recordings of the two meetings. The data were gathered by the first author as a non-intrusive observer. A qualitative analysis tool (NVivo) was used to support the analysis of the meeting transcripts. The field notes captured aspects of the ARE process being observed. The focus during data collection was to observe and note the immediate impressions of the cognition occurring in use of space, artefacts and people, based on researcher's understanding of DC theory. The field notes were time stamped periodically to enable easy cross-referencing with the audio transcripts, which were also time stamped.

Most of the DiCoT analysis was done after the meetings, based on a synthesis of photographs, field notes and the meeting transcripts. To answer RQ1, the data analysis involved reviewing the field notes and coding and categorizing snippets of the transcripts as different types of information being sought, challenged or shared. These types of information were then coded and grouped according to: (1) the purpose of the information (expected cognitive outcome or goal); and (2) an area of cognitive effort. For example, in one transcript the sales manager proposed that a specific user story be given high priority because she was losing sales as a result of its absence in the product line. This information was coded as relating to "requirements business value" (rather than "requirements meaning" for example). It was grouped in the general area of cognitive effort that related to "reasoning about the absolute value of a requirement", with the cognitive goal of "understanding multiple perspectives".

Answering RQ2 involved analysis of the photographs, field notes or coded sections of the meeting transcripts as suited the information sought for each DiCoT principle. For example, the information radiator principle from DiCoT was analyzed based on data from the transcripts – what information sources did team members refer to often; as observation in the field notes– what information sources were noted as being referred to frequently; as well as photographs of the information sources available easily around the room. The areas of the transcript to focus on were guided by the field notes which identified interactions of cognitive significance. On the other hand, descriptions of the perceptual principle and naturalness principle, for example, were based on photographs of the workplace and researcher's memory, reminded by re-reading parts of the transcripts and field notes.

4   The Context of the Field Work

The field work was conducted in a medium-sized organization in New Zealand in the Finance/Insurance sector with around 200 employees and 10 agile development teams. The organization represents the relatively common situation of an in-house software development department that uses agile development methods with a mixture of practices from Scrum and Extreme Programming. The software development project studied involved developing functionality for both internal and external clients.

The two observed RP meetings (P1 and P2) were one-hour long each, three days apart with the same participants and a very similar format. They took place during the early requirements phase of the project, prior to development starting but had 75 user stories in the product backlog (PB), some already prioritized. The functional goal of these meetings was to agree on the rough order of the large pieces of work (groups of functionally related requirements)to be done (one or more iterations each), and then order enough of the more valuable work for the development team to estimate and plan the first few sprints. Present at both meetings were two business analysts (BA1 and BA2), a Project Manager (PM), the Product Owner (PO), a Customer Services representative (CS), and the Sales Manager (SM). BA1 facilitated both prioritization meetings, set the room up and managed the sequencing of the activities in the meetings. The other members of the core development team (two testers and two developers) were not present at these meetings because they were still finishing off other projects.

In terms of the physical environment, the meetings took place in a meeting room with everyone sitting around a table. The significant cognitive artefacts were the whiteboard, the user story cards and the projected computer screen, which all acted as information radiators, filters and transformers, as described in the DiCoT framework, at different times.

5   Results of the Distributed Cognition Analysis

In this section the process is analyzed in terms of the significant cognitive goals (RQ1) and then the analysis using the DiCoT framework is presented (RQ2).

5.1   RQ 1: What Aspects of the Observed ARE Process Are Cognitively Significant?

The RP process observed involved repeatedly selecting an unprioritized user story and deciding on its position in the previously ordered part of the PB. Based on analyses of the transcripts and field notes of the meetings, three aspects the RP process that are cognitively significant can be distinguished: (C1) explain and reason about stakeholders' perspectives on the value of that user story; (C2) agree on a position for the user story in the ordered part of the PB; (C3) reasoning, questioning and explaining the meaning of user stories in order to develop (or confirm) a shared understanding of the meaning and context of the user story. For (C1), divergent thinking was prevalent, with different perspectives and information about the value of a user story being sought from team members. The type of cognition in (C2) was more convergent thinking, aiming to get consensus on the priority of the user story being discussed. The information sharing and cognition in (C3) were about verifying shared understanding of relevant user stories, mainly through question and answer interactions and re-statement of others' explanations. A summary of the important information processed and the cognitive outcomes for each area of cognitive effort is presented in Table 1.

Table 1. Analysis of each area cognitive effort in the observed process

Area of cognitive effort	Important information shared and processed	Cognitive outcomes
(C1) Reasoning about the absolute and relative value of the user story	- The high-level functional area or part of the wider product the requirement relates to - The main prioritization criteria - Which prioritization criteria are currently being applied - The value of other user stories as previously discussed	- Shared understanding of different perspectives on the value of the user story - Shared understanding of some explicit and tacit criteria for reasoning about the level of importance of a user story
(C2) Agreeing on the relative priority of the user requirement	- Previous decisions about priority of other user stories - Others' points of view on priority order - Which prioritization criteria are currently being applied - Current proposed priority and changes/alternative proposals	- Consensus on the priority position of the user story in relation to other ordered user stories
(C3) Reasoning about the meaning (functionality) of the user story	-The user story feature, the user type it is for and the expected value to the user -Domain knowledge about the current process relevant to the requirement -Domain knowledge about the expected change from the use of the proposed feature - The dependencies of the requirement on other requirements or vice versa	-Shared understanding of meaning of user requirement. Development of a Team Mental Model -Further development of a shared language -Uncovering tacit assumptions or misunderstandings about a user story

5.2 RQ 2: What Principles from DiCoT Are Important in the Observed ARE Process?

Having understood the main cognition in the RP process, this is then analyzed from a DC perspective using the DiCoT framework in the next section. Each DiCoT principle within the three DiCoT themes is described based on analysis of the data collected and the conceptualization of the cognition in the RP process.

Principles for the "Information Flows" Theme

Information Movement. The mechanics of information moving around the cognitive system (e.g. physical, verbal). Information movement is dense in the RP process, as identified in the second column of Table 1. This movement involves many information channels, including between individuals and other group members (verbal and visual); the writing on the whiteboard (visual and physical); the spatial arrangement of cards (visual and physical); the writing on story cards (visual); the contents of the projected screen ((visual, physical). This highlights the cognitive complexity of the interactions and information flows, which are coordinated and simplified through the use of the physical story cards complemented by the electronic versions.

Information Transformation. Transformation of information from one representational form to another. One key and directly observable information transformation was the transformation of the user story priority and value information in individual's minds (evidenced by what they said) to the visual spatial information (order) of user stories on the whiteboard or table. Conversely, this visual spatial information was transformed into information in people's minds for processing (e.g. verifying their view of what was agreed on, or challenging/strengthening their mental model of the situation). Also, the visual spatial information of story cards acted as an information filter to focus on order or categories and not on the written details of a user story. The meeting facilitator often acted as an information filter, transforming others' spoken views of value into a synthesized view or proposing a specific view as strongest. She was skilled at this and also had a certain power advantage as meeting facilitator, so her information filtering was often "deferred" to.

Information Hubs. Different information channels meet and information sources are processed together. Within the meeting the whiteboard with the spatial arrangement of story cards and writing was the central and most-used information hub. It brought together the information and information processing from individuals and previous prioritization work.

Buffering. New information is stored until an appropriate time to avoid interfering with the task at hand. Information buffers were important at different times in the meeting to avoid interruptions, but not lose the interrupting information. For example, the whiteboard was used as an information buffer. If information was needed about a requirement or its value, future information gathering task was noted on the whiteboard (and perhaps the relevant user story card) and the prioritization process continued with minimal interruption. The spatial arrangement of story cards could also act as a buffer. If a new idea came up about a user story other than the one being worked on, often this user story card would be put to one side spatially as a reminder to come back to it.

Communication Bandwidth. Face to face communications is richer than other means (exchanges more information). The face-to-face and co-located information channels were high bandwidth in their richness of visual and verbal interactions.

Behavioral Trigger Factors. Individuals respond to local factors rather than an overall plan. The start and end of the cognitive activities were generally signaled by a behavioral trigger from an individual team member, generally the meeting facilitator. The move to agreeing on the priority of a user story was generally signaled by the behavioral trigger of someone proposing the position of the user story being discussed, and this was either accepted or resulted in further discussion about value and possibly a counterproposal. The facilitator was central to the triggering a change in focus and achieving consensus through behavioral triggers and summarizing others' views and the prevailing accepted views. Sometimes there was no clear cognitive trigger to end some discussions about a requirement since sufficiency is uncertain (more time may uncover unknown unknowns, misunderstandings, or hidden assumptions to test). Often the facilitator would propose ending the discussion about a particular user story based on time urgency and others assented by silence.

Principles for the "Use of Space" Theme

Space and Cognition. The use of space to support cognition such as problem solving. The spatial arrangement of physical story cards is a visual information channel to convey functional relationships of requirements, priority order, previous decisions and understanding, and the requirement with attention. This was the key mediating artefact throughout the prioritization process and provided diverse cognitive support throughout the process. This approach to RP would have been cognitively much harder without physical cards to rearrange, and act as a dynamic, in-the-moment information radiator and visual "memory" of priority.

Perceptual Principle. The use of spatial representations with clear mapping of spatial layout to what is being represented. Physical manipulation of story cards simplified the cognition of proposing and testing a priority position or functional relationship of a requirements with other requirements. There was a clear mapping between the spatial distance and order of cards and the functional distance and priority order of requirements. This manipulation was cognitively important to the prioritization process, particularly during consensus development.

Naturalness Principle. The form of representation matches the properties of that being represented. The small size of a story card constrains the amount of detail about a user story that is documented, supporting its use as a reminder to have a conversation about the meaning and value of the user story when it is needed. The cognitive significance of this was – cards small enough to be manipulated but still readable (within the horizon of observation) of everyone – just enough info to need discussion.

Subtle Bodily Supports. The use of body movements for cognition (e.g. pointing). Pointing at user story cards or lifting them off the white board and raising them in the air was a common way for the facilitator to draw the group's attention, emphasize a point, or support a behavioral trigger to change tasks. Cognitively this may seem unimportant, but in fact it was a key mechanism to keep the group on-task, where there were potentially many information sources to distract them. Non-verbal information exchange through body language was rich and significant in the meetings. This included nodding and head shaking, eye contact, pointing and hand gestures. Example of information conveyed are agreement, disagreement, strength of conviction, attention or loss of it. It was clear that such visual cues were important cognitively as feedback and attention information for this group of people doing work together. This strengthens the argument for face-to-face meetings for this process.

Situation Awareness. Team members are aware of what has happened, is happening and what is planned. The user story cards on the whiteboard provided situational awareness because they were an information radiator of the current situation: what has been prioritized, what still needs to be prioritized, what is being proposed and what user story currently has attention. Sometimes the table was used to draw attention to a sub-set of user stories to manipulate and decide on priority order. This illustrates the diversity of the cognitive benefits of using physical user story cards in this way.

Horizon of Observation What Can be Seen and Heard by Team Members. The layout of the room as well designed to allow the main sources of information and information processing, other team members and the main artefacts, to be within the horizon of observation of everyone in the meeting without much effort or movement. Cognitively, this meant that the exchange of information was low effort and attention could be redirected easily.

Arrangement of Equipment. The effects of the physical layout of the workspace on information flows. The channels of information flow were not inhibited by the arrangement of equipment. The availability of the projected spreadsheet of user stories was important cognitively to the effectiveness of the meeting by providing a fast search mechanism for user stories.

Principles for the "Artefact" Theme

Mediating Artefacts. Artefacts that the team bring into coordination to complete their task. The user story cards on the whiteboard were the central mediating artefact for the cognitive effort in the process. The user story cards were brought into coordination (order) to complete the task of prioritization consensus. The order of other story cards also indicated the state of previous priority decisions. The story cards also coordinated the group's decisions and attention on a proposed priority order or changes to a proposal, for discussion and agreement or a counterproposal.

Creating Scaffolding. Team members appropriate parts of their environment as to simplify a task. The movement of user story cards on the whiteboard and table is an example of "external scaffolding to simplify our cognitive tasks". As previously discussed, the transformation of individual's mental cognition to visual cognition simplified the coordination of.

Representation-Goal Parity. An artefact explicitly represents the relationship between the current state and the goals state. The spatial arrangement of story cards closely represents a current state of unprioritized user stories (spatially separate) and the goal state of prioritized user stories (the card in the ordered column).

Coordination of Resources. Abstract information structures can be coordinated to support action or cognition (e.g. a plan or a goal). The pre-arrangement of the spatial arrangement of the user stories on the whiteboard was cognitively significant as an information radiator of what prioritization had been done and what needed to be done, giving the meeting a clear plan and goal. This information was updated as the story cards were moved around on the whiteboard, providing information about progress towards the goal and sometimes triggering a new plan for the meeting.

6   Discussion

Overall, analyzing this ARE activity through the lens of DC has highlighted the cognitive complexity of the process in terms of information sharing and processing, as well as information seeking and retrieval. The DiCoT analysis has provided a structure to analyze the web of interactions between the group members, the mediating artefacts and the workspace layout. The analysis has provided evidence to explain the strengths and weaknesses of this process from a cognitive perspective and evidenced the cognitive significance of aspects of the workspace, information flows and artefacts.

6.1   The Observed Agile Requirements Prioritization Process: A High-Level View

The observed ARP process cannot be characterized as a single named prioritization technique identified in the review by ([21] Fig. 5, p. 572). The observed process did not follow a predictable structure with clear prioritization criteria and did not have specific roles and information sources pre-planned. This aligns with the findings of [1] in their interview-based case study which found that the *"prioritization process itself varies significantly in terms of participants involved, prioritization criteria applied, purpose and frequency of the prioritization"*. Despite the observation that the process was cognitively complex and unpredictable, it was effective: the functional goal was achieved. The DC analysis provides an explanation of this success, suggesting that it can be attributed to the good use of space and artefacts and the diversity of participants as a distributed cognitive system to achieve this goal.

The ARP process conceptualized in a number of other papers (e.g. [1, 26, 27]) is generally broader in scope and level and does not consider the level of detail in specific RP meetings that our study has. Our study complements these models by focusing on this detailed process as well as considering *early* prioritization meetings. These early meetings are important because they lay the foundation for subsequent meetings in terms of planning (e.g. release goals and order of work), initial scope, stakeholder involvement, and the ARP process itself.

6.2   The Cognitive Role of the Prioritization Criteria

It can reasonably be expected that shared understanding of requirements and application of the prioritization criteria would be central to the RP process. The Scrum framework does not specify particular criteria to evaluate the value of PB items to order the PB, so it useful to see what happens in practice, with six different value criteria identified in this study: (PC1) the strategic value (to the case organization) of the requirement or its product functional area; (PC2) the strategic and operational value to the current or potential end-users; (PC3) the negative impact of not implementing the requirement; (PC4) the cost/effort versus the benefits of developing and deploying the requirement; (PC5) risk of negative impact on internal stakeholder with dependencies on changes related to the requirement; (PC6) the potential negative impact of dependencies between this requirement and others. Different team members tended to be biased towards the application of specific criteria For example, the PO (a manager also) tended to apply PC1 (*"this is part of a strategic initiative"*) and PC4 (*"it's cheaper to keep doing this manually than spending 5 sprints on it"*) when discussing priority. The sales manager SM (*"we are losing sales without this"*), BA3 (*"at installation the customer is surprised it can't do this"*) and CS1 (*"this is the most common feature request I get -, it's highest priority"*) often invoked PC2 and PC3. BA1 had the clearest "big picture" and would often bring up PC5 (*"we should check if this change will have a big impact on the BI people"*) and PC6 (*"If we do [this] then we have to send out comms quickly to all affected [customers]"*). These prioritization criteria have some overlap to those found in [26] in their multiple case study of agile requirements prioritization. While we found business value (PC1 and PC2), negative value (PC4), risk (PC5) and (limited) developer input were discussed in our study, project context, estimated size, external change and learning experiences were not involved in our ARP process. This may highlight some differences between early and later ARP meetings, but this needs more research. It will almost certainly be a function of the roles and value biases of those present. The criteria were often tacitly assumed and applied in a fairly ad hoc manner in the observed meetings. This could be an area of possible improvement: a mechanism to encourage explicit cognitive effort in developing shared understanding of the prioritization criteria and an associated information radiator.

6.3   The Cognitive Role of the User Story Cards

The DiCoT analysis provides a compelling argument, at least from a DC perspective, for the use of physical story cards and their spatial manipulation in RP. The DiCoT analysis shows that the story cards feature in almost all areas of DC and provide substantial cognitive benefit as information radiators, information buffers, information filters, information transformers, and attention coordinators. Importantly, the cards afford a significant cognitive load transfer from individual memory of priority to visual perception of order. Moreover, they were used by the facilitator in behavioral triggers to manage the flow of the work in the meeting, as well an information radiator for the meeting plan and progress. Transferring the cards to the development team's work board, in order, also served as a memory of the outcome of the process and an information radiator for others not at the meeting. As a cognitive artefact the user story cards could be used at different levels of cognition: reading the text, use of the label or manipulated as a card. The characteristics of the user story cards were well suited to the RP process: they were well sized to manipulate and carry around, yet still be read easily; they had sufficient requirements detail to act a reminder but encourage discussion; the information on the cards was useful for the process. The availability of the searchable spreadsheet of user stories complemented the story cards, although was not used often.

6.4 The Important Cognitive Role of the Meeting Facilitator

The DiCoT analysis highlighted the cognitive importance of a skilled facilitator in the process. The facilitator played a central role in information movement, filtering and processing. This can be both a strength and a weakness: the effectiveness of the process relied on the cognitive skills of the facilitator. In addition, the facilitator had more influence than others in the meeting in terms of the information filtering and flow of the meeting (changing the group's attention), because of the power attributed to the facilitator role.

6.5 The Importance of the Face-to-Face Meeting as an Information Hub

From a DC perspective the meetings can be conceptualized as an important information hub in the requirements management process. The meetings were a central focus where many information channels coincided. This information was processed by the group to make a decision about the requirements priority order. Without this meeting involving a diversity of stakeholders' perspectives it would have been difficult to achieve such high-quality decisions about the priority. The face-to-face interactions provided rich and immediate information communication channels (including non-verbal). In addition, the visual cognitive affordance of *physical* manipulation of user story cards would be difficult if the group were not co-located.

6.6 The Importance of the Room Layout

The DiCoT analysis identified that the room was well laid out for the cognition involved in the ARE process. The room was laid out so that important information sources (people and artefacts) were within everyone's horizon of observation and information flows were low effort. It is worth noting that the room was sufficiently isolated from outside to avoid distracting information unrelated to the meeting.

6.7 The Need for a Diversity of Perspectives on User Story Value

ARE promotes consideration of multiple stakeholders' views in the prioritization process and to some extent the DiCoT analysis justifies this. The broader perspectives of value and meaning for user stories resulted in decisions about priority that were better informed and benefited from the expanded cognitive base. For example, one set of user stories (previously a high priority), was discarded and another became high priority unexpectedly based on the views and arguments of some team members influencing those of others. This effect of diverse perspectives on team decision-making has a strong theoretical basis (e.g. [28]).

6.8 Secondary Cognitive Outcomes of the RP Process

The DC analysis has identified some significant cognitive outcomes of these early ARE meetings process, apart from the prioritized user stories, that were important in later collaborative requirements work. These include: a significant deepening of the shared understanding of some user stories; a broader view of requirements value from others' perspectives and criteria to judge value; significant development of shared language for the team to discuss, explain and reason about requirements; shared understanding and embedding of a collaborative process for RP.

7 Reflections on the Application of DiCoT

This study has demonstrated the usefulness of using the DiCoT framework to perform a DC analysis of collaborative work in ARE process. The analysis has provided a rich set of insights as a basis for understanding the strengths and weaknesses of the ARE process and reasoning about possible changes. However, the effort in collecting and analyzing the data was significant and may not be feasible to be conducted regularly. The framework itself was reasonably straightforward to apply with clear descriptions of the DiCoT principles. However, the themes were intertwined and sometimes it was difficult to know how to differentiate the artefact view and the information processing view. Starting the DiCoT analysis with a high-level cognitive description of the ARP process was needed to inform the DiCoT description.

This study suggests that the themes and principles of DiCoT could be used as a checklist to assess an ARE activity, the artefacts involved and the layout of the workspace. For example, the physical layout of the room can be checked as being suitable for smooth information movement between people, and to and from the significant artefacts. The horizon of observation can be checked as being suitable to provide situational awareness. This same approach of DiCoT could be used as an assessment tool if the RE process does not appear to be going well.

The DiCoT framework can also be used to reason about changes or redesign of the RE process. For example, it is common to have the user stories stored electronically. Given the understanding of the cognitive affordance of physical story cards, the positive and negative cognitive impact of replacing them with electronic versions of user stories, at least in the RP process, can be identified. Another common change to the RE process to consider is the situation where group members are geographically distributed and communicating electronically in real time.

8 Threats to Validity

Although it is not possible to cover every contextual factor in this study, we did take some steps to ensure internal validity. We used data triangulation between the two meetings throughout data analysis. To ensure continuity of data collection, all field work was conducted by the first author. It is possible that selection is a threat since the team was selected by one contact, although invitations were sent more widely. External validity is low and we cannot claim the results will apply to all Agile projects and teams, however, our aim was to uncover some useful insights that may resonate with other practitioners. DiCoT analysis of the ARP in different contexts to broaden the likely applicability is for future research.

The presence of the researcher in the meetings may have reduced reliability by changing the behavior of those being observed. To address this the observing researcher spent some time with the team prior to data collection and gained their trust and a degree of comfort with the researcher's presence in meetings. The meetings were transcribed word for word and the observing researcher identified the speakers. We discussed the resulting analysis with some team members. We tried to adhere to the explanations and structure of DiCoT in the original paper by Blandford and Furniss [17] closely but inevitably we may have made some subjective assumptions in doing this.

9 Conclusion

The novel application of DC theory through the use of DiCoT to the requirements prioritization as part of an ARE process has provided an empirically evidenced explanation of why this way of implementing the RP process was effective. In answering RQ1, three main areas of cognition were identified in the process. In addition, some insights were gained about the different perspectives on requirements value associated with different roles, as well as the six prioritization criteria applied. Application of the DioCoT framework (RQ2) also identified a number of aspects of the process that had cognitive significance to its success. For example, the DiCoT analysis provided substantial evidence that the use of physical story cards, a skilled facilitator, and a cognitive-friendly work environment were central to the success of this approach. This may provide a basis for others to design, modify and assess other activities in the ARE process.

Future work planned includes the extension of the DiCoT analysis to include the two DiCoT themes not included in this study and applying DiCoT analyses in other contexts. Also, the application of DiCoT to other Requirements Engineering activities will be explored.

References

1. Bakalova, Z., Daneva, M., Herrmann, A., Wieringa, R.: Agile requirements prioritization: what happens in practice and what is described in literature. In: Berry, D., Franch, X. (eds.) REFSQ 2011. LNCS, vol. 6606, pp. 181–195. Springer, Heidelberg (2011). https://doi.org/10.1007/978-3-642-19858-8_18
2. Inayat, I., Salim, S.S., Marczak, S., Daneva, M., Shamshirband, S.: A systematic literature review on agile requirements engineering practices and challenges. Comput. Hum. Behav. **51**, 915–929 (2015)
3. Rogers, Y., Ellis, J.: Distributed cognition: an alternative framework for analyzing and explaining collaborative working. J. Inf. Technol. **9**(2), 119–128 (1994)

4. Nguyen, L., Shanks, G.: A framework for understanding creativity in requirements engineering. Inf. Softw. Technol. **51**(3), 655–662 (2009)
5. Blackburn, T., Swatman, P., Vernik, R.: Cognitive dust: linking CSCW theories to creative design processes. In: 2006 10th International Conference on Computer Supported Cooperative Work in Design, pp. 1–6. IEEE (2006)
6. White, S.M.: Application of cognitive theories and knowledge management to requirements engineering. In: 2010 IEEE International Systems Conference, pp. 137–142. IEEE (2010)
7. Hansen, S.W., Robinson, W.N., Lyytinen, K.J.: Computing requirements: cognitive approaches to distributed requirements engineering. In: 2012 45th Hawaii International Conference on System Sciences, pp. 5224–5233. IEEE (2012)
8. Hundal, K.S., Mussbacher, G.: Model-based development with distributed cognition. In: 2018 IEEE 8th International Model-Driven Requirements Engineering Workshop (MoDRE), pp. 26–35. IEEE (2018)
9. Gopal, D., Lindberg, A., Lyytinen, K.: Attributes of open source software requirements– the effect of the external environment and internal social structure. In: 2016 49th Hawaii International Conference on System Sciences (HICSS), pp. 4982–4991. IEEE (2016)
10. Thummadi, B.V., Lyytinen, K., Hansen, S.: Quality in requirements engineering (RE) explained using distributed cognition: a case of open source development. In: Proceedings of JAIS Theory Development Workshop (2011)
11. Sharp, H., Robinson, H.: A distributed cognition account of mature XP teams. In: Abrahamsson, P., Marchesi, M., Succi, G. (eds.) XP 2006. LNCS, vol. 4044, pp. 1–10. Springer, Heidelberg (2006). https://doi.org/10.1007/11774129_1
12. Sharp, H., Robinson, H., Segal, J., Furniss, D.: The role of story cards and the wall in XP teams: a distributed cognition perspective. In: AGILE 2006 (AGILE 2006), pp. 11–75. IEEE (2006)
13. Sharp, H., Robinson, H.: Collaboration and co-ordination in mature eXtreme programming teams. Int. J. Hum Comput Stud. **66**(7), 506–518 (2008)
14. Halverson, C.A.: Activity theory and distributed cognition: or what does CSCW need to DO with theories? Comput. Support. Coop. Work (CSCW) **11**(1–2), 243–267 (2002). https://doi.org/10.1023/A:1015298005381
15. Jones, P.H., Chisalita, C.: Cognition and collaboration: analyzing distributed community practices for design. In: Extended Abstracts on Human Factors in Computing Systems, CHI 2005, p. 2120. ACM (2005)
16. Hoadley, C.M., Kilner, P.G.: Using technology to transform communities of practice into knowledge-building communities. ACM SIGGROUP Bull. **25**(1), 31–40 (2005)
17. Blandford, A., Furniss, D.: DiCoT: a methodology for applying distributed cognition to the design of teamworking systems. In: Gilroy, S.W., Harrison, M.D. (eds.) DSV-IS 2005. LNCS, vol. 3941, pp. 26–38. Springer, Heidelberg (2006). https://doi.org/10.1007/11752707_3
18. Hollan, J., Hutchins, E., Kirsh, D.: Distributed cognition: toward a new foundation for human-computer interaction research. ACM Trans. Comput. Hum. Interact. (TOCHI) **7**(2), 174–196 (2000)
19. Wright, P.C., Fields, R.E., Harrison, M.D.: Analyzing human-computer interaction as distributed cognition: the resources model. Hum. Comput. Interact. **15**(1), 1–41 (2000)
20. Racheva, Z., Daneva, M., Buglione, L.: Supporting the dynamic reprioritization of requirements in agile development of software products. In: 2008 Second International Workshop on Software Product Management, pp. 49–58. IEEE (2008)
21. Achimugu, P., Selamat, A., Ibrahim, R., Mahrin, M.N.: A systematic literature review of software requirements prioritization research. Inf. Softw. Technol. **56**(6), 568–585 (2014)
22. Riegel, N., Doerr, J.: A systematic literature review of requirements prioritization criteria. In: Fricker, S.A., Schneider, K. (eds.) REFSQ 2015. LNCS, vol. 9013, pp. 300–317. Springer, Cham (2015). https://doi.org/10.1007/978-3-319-16101-3_22

23. Hutchins, E.: Cognition in the Wild. MIT Press, Cambridge (1995). (no. 1995)
24. Hutchins, E.: How a cockpit remembers its speeds. Cogn. Sci. **19**(3), 265–288 (1995)
25. Vaesen, K.: Giere's (in)appropriation of distributed cognition. Soc. Epistemol. **25**(4), 379–391 (2011)
26. Racheva, Z., Daneva, M., Herrmann, A., Wieringa, R.J.: A conceptual model and process for client-driven agile requirements prioritization. In: 2010 Fourth International Conference on Research Challenges in Information Science (RCIS), Nice, pp. 287–298 (2010). https://doi.org/10.1109/rcis.2010.5507388
27. Al-Ta'ani, R.H., Razali, R.: A framework for requirements prioritisation process in an agile software development environment: empirical study. Int. J. Adv. Sci. Eng. Inf. Technol. **6**(6), 846–856 (2016)
28. Hall, D.J., Davis, R.A.: Engaging multiple perspectives: a value-based decision-making model. Decis. Support Syst. **43**(4), 1588–1604 (2007)

Automatic Word Embeddings-Based Glossary Term Extraction from Large-Sized Software Requirements

Siba Mishra and Arpit Sharma[✉]

Department of Electrical Engineering and Computer Science,
Indian Institute of Science Education and Research, Bhopal, Madhya Pradesh, India
{sibam,arpit}@iiserb.ac.in

Abstract. [**Context and Motivation**] Requirements glossary defines specialized and technical terms used in a requirements document. A requirements glossary helps in improving the quality and understandability of requirements documents. [**Question/Problem**] Manual extraction of glossary terms from a large body of requirements is an expensive and time-consuming task. This paper proposes a fundamentally new approach for automated extraction of glossary terms from large-sized requirements documents. [**Principal Ideas/Result**] Firstly, our technique extracts the candidate glossary terms by applying text chunking. Next, we apply a novel word embeddings based semantic filter for reducing the number of candidate glossary terms. Since word embeddings are very effective in identifying terms that are semantically very similar, this filter ensures that only domain-specific terms are present in the final set of glossary terms. We create a domain-specific reference corpus for home automation by Wikipedia crawling and use it for computing the semantic similarity scores of candidate glossary terms. We apply our technique to a large-sized requirements document, i.e., a CrowdRE dataset with around 3000 crowd-generated requirements for smart home applications. Semantic filtering reduces the number of glossary terms by 92.7%. To evaluate the quality of our extracted glossary terms we manually create the ground truth data from CrowdRE dataset and use it for computing precision and recall. Additionally, we also compute the requirements coverage of these extracted glossary terms. [**Contributions**] Our detailed experiments show that word embeddings based semantic filtering can be very useful for extracting glossary terms from a large body of requirements.

Keywords: Requirements engineering · Natural language processing · Word embeddings · Term extraction · Semantic filter

1 Introduction

Requirements are the basis for every project, defining what the stakeholders in a potential new system need from it, and also what the system must do in order

© Springer Nature Switzerland AG 2020
N. Madhavji et al. (Eds.): REFSQ 2020, LNCS 12045, pp. 203–218, 2020.
https://doi.org/10.1007/978-3-030-44429-7_15

to satisfy that need [8,19]. All subsequent steps in software development are influenced by the requirements. Hence, improving the quality of requirements means improving the overall quality of the software product. A major cause of poor quality requirements is that the stakeholders involved in the development process have different interpretations of technical terms. In order to avoid these issues and to improve the understandability of requirements, it is necessary that all stakeholders of the development process share the same understanding of the terminology used. Specialized terms used in the requirements document should therefore be defined in a glossary. A glossary defines specialized or technical terms and abbreviations which are specific to an application domain. For example, if the system is concerned with health care, it would include terms like "hospitalization", "prescription drugs", "physician", "hospital outpatient care", "durable medical equipment", "emergency services", etc. Additionally, requirements glossaries are also useful for text summarization and term-based indexing.

In order to develop a glossary, the terms to be defined and added need to be first extracted from the requirements document. Glossary term extraction for the requirements document is an expensive and time-consuming task. This problem becomes even more challenging for large-sized requirements document, e.g., [16,17].

This paper focuses on automatic extraction of glossary terms from large-sized requirements documents. A first step in this direction is to extract the candidate glossary terms from a requirements document by applying text chunking. Text chunking consists of dividing a text in syntactically correlated parts of words. Since 99% of all the relevant terms are noun phrases [2,9], we only focus on extracting the noun phrases from a requirements document. Next, we apply a novel word embeddings based semantic filter to remove the noun phrases that are not domain-specific from the set of candidate glossary terms. Word embeddings are capable of capturing the context of a word and compute its semantic similarity relation with other words used in a document. It represents individual words as real-valued vectors in a predefined vector space. Each word is mapped to one vector and the vector values are learnt based on the usage of words. Words that are used in similar ways tend to have similar representations. This means that distance between two words which are semantically very similar is going to be smaller. More formally, the cosine of the angle between such vectors should be close to 1. To compute the similarity scores, we create a domain-specific reference corpus by crawling the home automation (HA) category on Wikipedia. The key idea is to use this corpus to check if the candidate glossary terms extracted by text chunking from a CrowdRE document are domain-specific or not. In other words, if a term in CrowdRE document has been used in a context which is different from the context in which it has been used in the domain-specific corpus for home automation then it needs to be removed from the final set of glossary terms.

We have applied our approach to the CrowdRE dataset [16,17], which contains about 3,000 crowd-generated requirements for smart home applications. Our detailed experiments show that advantages of this new approach for glossary extraction go in two directions. Firstly, our filter reduces the number of glossary terms significantly. Note that this reduction is crucial for large-sized requirements documents. Secondly, the semantic nature of our filter ensures that only terms that are domain or application-specific are present in the final set of glossary terms. Note that in the case of statistical filtering such terms would be removed from the final set of glossary terms if they have low frequency of occurrence. To the best of our knowledge, this is the first time that a word embeddings based semantic filter has been proposed for automatic glossary term extraction from large-sized requirements documents.

1.1 Contributions

We propose an automated solution for extracting glossary terms from large-sized requirements documents. Our solution uses state-of-the art neural word embeddings technique for detecting domain-specific technical terms. More specifically, our main contributions are as follows:

- We extract candidate glossary terms by applying text chunking. Next, we propose a semantic filtering technique based on word embeddings to ensure that only terms that are truly domain-specific are present in the final set of glossary terms. This semantic filter is based on the principle that words that are used in similar ways tend to have similar representations.
- We apply our technique to the CrowdRE dataset, which is a large-sized dataset with around 3000 crowd-generated requirements for smart home applications. Our semantic filter reduces the number of glossary terms significantly. More specifically, we reduce the number of glossary terms in CrowdRE dataset by 92.7%.
- To measure the effectiveness of our technique we manually extract the glossary terms from a subset of 100 CrowdRE requirements and use this ground truth data for computing the precision and recall. We obtain a recall of 73.2% and a precision of 83.94%. Additionally, we also compute the requirements coverage of these extracted glossary terms.
- Finally, we discuss the benefits and limitations of word embeddings based semantic filtering technique for glossary extraction.

The remainder of the paper is structured as follows. Section 2 discusses the related work. Section 3 provides the required background. Section 4 explains our approach. We present the results and findings in Sect. 5. Finally, Sect. 6 concludes the paper and provides pointers for future research.

2   Related Work

Word Embeddings for RE. In [4], an approach based on word embeddings and Wikipedia crawling has been proposed to detect domain specific ambiguities in natural language text. More specifically, in this paper authors investigate the ambiguity potential of typical computer science words using a Word2vec algorithm and perform some preliminary experiments. In [5], authors estimate the variation of meaning of dominant shared terms in different domains by comparing the list of most similar words in each domain specific model. This method was applied to some pilot scenarios which involved different products and stakeholders from different domains. Recently, in [15], we have measured the ambiguity potential of most frequently used computer science (CS) words when they are used in other application areas or subdomains of engineering, e.g., aerospace, civil, petroleum, biomedical and environmental, etc. For every ambiguous computer science word in an engineering subdomain, we have reported its most similar words and also provided some example sentences from the corpus highlighting its domain specific interpretation. All these applications of word embeddings to requirements engineering are very recent and only focus on detecting ambiguity in requirements documents.

Glossary Extraction for RE. In [1,7], authors have developed tools, e.g. findphrases and AbstFinder for finding repeated phrases in natural language requirements. These repeated phrases have been termed as *abstractions*. These tools can be used as the basis for an environment to help organize the sentences and phrases of a natural language problem description to aid the requirements analyst in the extraction of requirements. In [18], authors have described an approach for automatic domain specific glossary extraction from large document collections using text analysis. A tool named GlossEx has been used to build glossaries for applications in the automotive engineering and computer help desk domains. In [10], authors described a case study on application of natural language processing for extracting terms from the text written by domain experts, and build a domain ontology using them. In [21], a term extraction technique has been proposed using parsing and parse relations. In this paper, authors have built a prototype dowsing tool, called Dowser which is capable of achieving high precision and recall when detecting domain-specific terms in a UNIX manual page. A text mining technique using term ranking and term weighing measures for the automatic extraction of the most relevant terms used in Empirical Software Engineering (ESE) documents has been proposed in [22]. In [23], authors have developed a procedure for automatic extraction of single and double-word noun phrases from existing document collections. Dwarakanath et al. [3] presented a method for automatic extraction of glossary terms from unconstrained natural language requirements using linguistic and statistical techniques. Menard et al. [12] retrieved domain concepts from business documents using a text mining process. Their approach has been tested on French text corpora from public organizations and shown to be 2.7 times better than a statistical baseline for relevant concept discovery. Recently, Arora et al. [2] have proposed a solution for automatic extraction and clustering of candidate glossary terms from natural language requirements. This technique has been evaluated on three-small sized industrial case studies. Note that in [2] syntactic, e.g., Jaccard, Levenstein, Euclidean and knowledge-based similarity measures, e.g., WUP, LCH, PATH have been used for clustering of glossary terms. More recently, a hybrid approach which uses both linguistic processing and statistical filtering for extracting glossary terms has been proposed in [6]. This technique has been applied to the same CrowdRE dataset which we have used in our paper for experiments.

All the above mentioned approaches can be broadly classified into linguistic, statistical or hybrid approaches. Linguistic approaches detect glossary terms using syntactic properties. In contrast, statistical approaches select terms based on the frequency of their occurrence. A hybrid approach combines both linguistic and statistical approaches, e.g., [6].

Our work proposes a new approach for selecting glossary terms based on the use of state-of-the art neural word embeddings technique. We use word embeddings and similarity scores to create a semantic filter which selects only those candidate terms that are truly domain-specific. We believe that this paper is a first step forward in the direction of developing advanced semantic filters for glossary term extraction from large-sized requirements documents.

3   Preliminaries

This section introduces some preliminaries that are needed for the understanding of the rest of this paper.

3.1   Word Embeddings

Word embeddings are a powerful approach for analyzing language and have been widely used in information retrieval and text mining. They provide a dense representation of words in the form of numeric vectors which capture the natural semantic relationship of their meaning. Word embeddings are considered to be an improvement over the traditional bag-of-words model which results in very large and sparse word vectors. Out of various word embedding models, the model "Word2vec" developed by the researchers at Google [13] has been used in our work to learn and generate word embeddings from a natural language text corpus. We focus on the model named skip gram negative sampling (SGNS) implementation of Word2vec [14]. SGNS predicts a collection of words $w \in V_W$ and their contexts $c \in V_C$, where V_W and V_C are the vocabularies of input words and context words respectively. Context words of a word w_i is a set of words $w_{i-wind}, \ldots, w_{i-1}, w_{i+1}, \ldots, w_{i+wind}$ for some fixed window size $wind$. Let D be a multi-set of all word-context pairs observed in the corpus. Let $\vec{w}, \vec{c} \in \mathbb{R}^d$ be the d-dimensional word embeddings of a word w and context c. These vectors (both word and context) are created by the Word2vec model from a corpus and are analyzed to check the semantic similarity between them. The main objective of negative sampling (NS) is to learn high-quality word vector representations on a corpus. A logistic loss function is used in NS for minimizing the negative log-likelihood of words in the training set. For more details, we refer the interested reader to [11,13,14]. As the input corpus changes, word embeddings are also updated reflecting the semantic similarity between words w.r.t. new corpus.

Word Similarity Computation. The Word2vec model uses the *cosine similarity* to compute the semantic relationship of two different words in vector space. Let us assume two word embedding vectors $\overrightarrow{w'}$ and $\overrightarrow{w''}$, where $\overrightarrow{w'}$ is a word vector generated for CrowdRE and $\overrightarrow{w''}$ is a word vector for home automation. The cosine angle between these two word embedding vectors is calculated using Eq. (1).

$$cos(\overrightarrow{w'}, \overrightarrow{w''}) = \frac{\overrightarrow{w'} \bullet \overrightarrow{w''}}{\mid \overrightarrow{w'} \mid\mid \overrightarrow{w''} \mid} \tag{1}$$

The range of similarity score is between 0 to 1. A score closer to 1 means that the words are semantically more similar and used in almost the same context. On the other hand, a score closer to 0 means that the words are less related to each other.

3.2 Crowd-Generated Requirements

The CrowdRE dataset was created by acquiring requirements from members of the public, i.e., *crowd* [17]. This dataset contains about 3000 requirements for smart home applications. A study on Amazon Mechanical Turk was conducted with 600 workers. This study measured the personality traits and creative potential for all the workers. A two-phase sequential process was used to create requirements. In the first phase, user stories for smart home applications were collected from 300 workers. In the second phase, an additional 300 workers rated these requirements in terms of clarity and creativity and produced additional requirements.

Each entry in this dataset has 6 attributes, i.e., role, feature, benefit, domain, tags and date-time of creation. Since we are interested in extracting domain-specific terms from this dataset, we only focus on feature and benefit attributes of this dataset. An example requirement obtained from this dataset after merging feature and benefit attributes is as follows: "my smart home to be able to order delivery food by simple voice command, i can prepare dinner easily after a long day at work". For further details, we refer the interested reader to [16,17].

4   Approach

This section discusses the approach used to extract glossary terms from large-sized requirements documents. Figure 1 shows an overview of our approach. The first step includes the process of *data gathering*. In the second step we perform *data preprocessing*. The third step focuses on *extracting the candidate glossary terms* from preprocessed data. In the final step, *semantic filtering of candidate glossary terms* provides us the final set of domain-specific terms. The rest of this section elaborates each of these steps.

4.1   Data Gathering

CrowdRE. For each user story in the CrowdRE dataset, we merge the feature and benefit attributes to obtain a single textual requirement. This is done by using a comma (,) between the text present in two attributes and a full stop (.) to terminate the requirement. Let C_{CRE} denotes the CrowdRE corpus obtained after applying the above mentioned transformations.

Requirements-Specific Reference Corpus. We use some standard web scraping packages available in python[1] to crawl and build the corpus of home automation domain. Let C_{HA} denotes the home automation corpus obtained by Wikipedia crawling. C_{HA} has been built by retrieving the web pages from "Wikipedia home automation" (HA) category[2], which has a tree structure. Wikipedia categories group together pages on similar subjects. Categories are found at the bottom of an article page. They support auto linking and multi-directional navigation. For our case, the maximum depth used for subcategory traversal is 2. This is primarily because increasing the depth results in extraction of less relevant pages from Wikipedia. For the sake of completeness, we have crosschecked all the results (data extraction for the home automation Wikipedia category) with the help of a widely used Wikipedia category data extraction tool known as PetScan[3]. PetScan (previously CatScan) is an external tool which can be used to find all the pages that belong to a Wikipedia category for some specified criteria.

4.2   Data Preprocessing

This step involves transforming raw natural language text into an understandable format. All the steps of data preprocessing have been implemented using the Natural Language Toolkit (NLTK)[4] in Python. The NLP pipeline used in data preprocessing is shown in Fig. 2. The textual data (sentences) of each corpus are broken into tokens of words (*tokenization*) followed by the cleaning of all special symbols, i.e., alpha-numeric words. Note that tokenization preserves the syntactic structure of sentences. Next, we convert all the words to lowercase (*lowering of words*) followed by the removal of noisy words defined for the English language[5] (*stop word removal*). The tokens of each sentence are tagged according to their syntactical position in the text. The tagged tokens are encoded as 2-tuples, i.e., (PoS, word), where PoS denotes the part of speech. We have used the NLTK (pos_tag)[6] Tagger, which is a perceptron tagger for extracting PoS tags. A perceptron part-of-speech tagger implements part-of-speech tagging using the averaged, structured perceptron algorithm. It uses a pre-trained pickled model

---

[1] https://selenium-python.readthedocs.io/.
[2] https://en.wikipedia.org/wiki/Home_automation.
[3] https://petscan.wmflabs.org/.
[4] https://www.nltk.org/.
[5] https://www.ranks.nl/stopwords.
[6] https://www.nltk.org/_modules/nltk/tag.html.

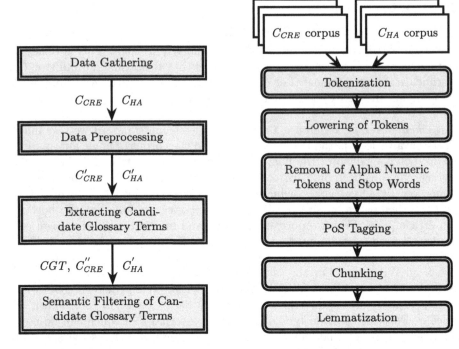

Fig. 1. Semantic approach for glossary term extraction.

Fig. 2. NLP pipeline.

by calling the default constructor of the PerceptronTagger class[7]. This tagger has been trained and tested on the Wall Street Journal corpus. After extracting the tags, we apply text *chunking* which consists of dividing a text in syntactically correlated parts of words. Finally, we lemmatize[8] the generated chunks (*lemmatization*) which removes the inflectional endings and returns the base or dictionary form of a word, i.e., *lemma*. For example, after the lemmatization step *books* becomes *book* and *cooking* becomes *cook*. Let C'_{CRE} and C'_{HA} be the new corpora obtained after applying these steps. Lemmatization is important because it allows for the aggregation of different forms of the same word to a common glossary term.

4.3   Extracting Candidate Glossary Terms

Since we are interested only in noun phrases (NPs), let GT be the set of all lemmatized NPs obtained from C'_{CRE}. Similarly, NPs have been extracted from the Wikipedia corpus, i.e., C'_{HA}. Let TW be the set of all lemmatized NPs obtained from C'_{HA}. Finally, we compute the set of NPs on which the semantic

---

[7] https://www.nltk.org/_modules/nltk/tag/perceptron.html#PerceptronTagger.

[8] https://www.nltk.org/_modules/nltk/stem/wordnet.html.

filtering needs to be applied. In other words, we identify those NPs which are common to both GT and TW. Let $CGT = GT \cap TW$.

4.4 Semantic Filtering of Candidate Glossary Terms

After computing the set CGT, C'_{CRE} is transformed into a novel corpus C''_{CRE} by replacing each occurrence of a NP that appears in the set CGT with a modified version of the NP. This modified version is obtained by prefixing and suffixing the NP by an underscore character. For example, the word *system* is replaced by *_system_*. This transformation helps us in distinguishing the context of a given noun phrase. Continuing the previous example, the word *system* denotes that it is being used in the context of home automation, and *_system_* denotes that it is being used in the context of CrowdRE.

Next, we use the Word2vec model to produce word embeddings and for computing semantic similarity scores of NPs present in CGT. The goal of this step is to check if each noun phrase of CGT has been used in a similar context in both C''_{CRE} and C'_{HA} or not. Learning of word embeddings is facilitated by joining the two corpora, i.e, $C''_{CRE} \cup C'_{HA}$ which is given as an input to the Word2vec model. We set the dimension ($d = 100$), the window size ($wind = 10$), and the minimum count ($c = 1$) for all the experiments. Note that several rounds of experiments have been performed to identify the most suitable Word2vec parameters for this case study. As mentioned earlier, the Word2vec model uses cosine similarity to compute the semantic relationship of two words in vector space. The final set of glossary terms includes only those candidate terms which have a similarity score greater than or equal to 0.5. This value has been selected based on our experiments with the corpora.

Table 1. Descriptive statistics of the corpora.

Data	Type	Total size	Total sentences	Total chunks (NPs)
C_{CRE}	Corpus	2,966 (R)	2,966	4,156
C_{HA}	Corpus	1,196 (P)	64,25,708	64,480

5 Results and Discussions

This section presents the results of our detailed experiments. The semantic approach for glossary term extraction has been implemented in Python 3.7 and executed on Windows 10 machine with Intel Core-i5-7500 CPU, 4 GB DDR3 primary memory and a processor frequency of 3.40 GHz. The first row of Table 1 reports the number of CrowdRE requirements used in our experiments and total number of unique chunks (NPs) extracted from these requirements. Here, R denotes the textual requirements. The second row of this table reports the number of Wikipedia pages crawled for (HA) category to build the domain-specific reference corpus and total number of unique chunks extracted from this corpus. Here, P denotes the Wikipedia pages. The detailed report of our experiments including modified CrowdRE dataset, ground truth, final set of extracted glossary terms and similarity scores can be found in this repository[9].

Table 2. Some examples of manually extracted glossary terms.

Req Id	Textual requirements	Glossary terms
R1	My smart home to be able to order delivery food by simple voice command, i can prepare dinner easily after a long day at work	Smart home, order delivery food, simple voice command, voice command, dinner, day at work
R2	My smart home to turn on certain lights at dusk, i can come home to a well-lit house	Smart home, home, certain lights, light, dusk, house
R3	My smart home to sync with my biorhythm app and turn on some music that might suit my mood when i arrive home from work, i can be relaxed	Smart home, biorhythm app, some music, music, mood, home, work
R4	My smart home to to ring when my favorite shows are about to start, i will never miss a minute of my favorite shows	Smart home, favorite show

5.1 Ground Truth Generation

Ground truth is used for checking the results of machine learning for accuracy against the real world. For glossary term extraction, ground truth generation involves manual creation of correct glossary terms by domain experts or by a team of experienced requirements engineers. Since CrowdRE dataset does not contain a reference list of correct glossary terms and it is not possible to create the correct glossary terms manually for a large body of requirements, i.e., 3000 requirements, we have manually created the ground truth for a subset of 100 requirements. This ground truth allows us to assess the performance of our approach by computing precision and recall. A total of 250 glossary terms have been manually extracted from a subset of 100 CrowdRE requirements. Note that this ground truth also includes the glossary terms (except role descriptions which do not appear in our subset of 100 requirements) that were manually selected by the authors in [6]. Some examples of manually extracted glossary terms have been shown in Table 2.

---

[9] https://github.com/SibaMishra/Automatic-Glossary-Terms-Extraction-Using-Word-Embeddings.

5.2   Precision and Recall

To evaluate the quality of our term extraction technique we compute precision and recall on this subset of 100 CrowdRE requirements. Precision gives us the fraction of relevant instances among the retrieved instances. On the other hand, recall gives us the fraction of relevant instances that have been retrieved over the total amount of relevant instances. As mentioned earlier, to compute the precision and recall we have manually extracted glossary terms from the subset of 100 requirements. We consider this set of manually extracted terms as ground truth. On applying our linguistic processing steps to these 100 requirements we extract 269 candidate glossary terms. Using our word embeddings based semantic filter, we reduce the number of glossary terms from 269 to 218. This set of final extracted glossary terms has 183 true positive terms. Note that we also count short terms that are included as parts of longer terms of the other set. These true positive terms lead to a recall of $\frac{183}{250} = 73.2\%$ and a precision of $\frac{183}{218} = 83.94\%$. These results indicate that our approach manages to strike a balance between the number of extracted glossary terms and recall rate.

5.3   Automated Glossary Term Extraction

Without applying our word embeddings based semantic filtering, the text chunking algorithm returns a total of 4156 candidate glossary terms when applied to the entire CrowdRE dataset, i.e., 2966 requirements. Since the number of glossary terms obtained is very large, we apply our semantic filter to reduce it by removing terms that are not domain-specific. Using our semantic filter we reduce the number of glossary terms significantly, i.e., from 4156 to 304. This means that the number of glossary terms gets reduced by 92.7%. Table 3 presents some

Table 3. Examples of final extracted glossary terms and their similarity scores.

Glossary terms	Similarity score
Automatic door	0.9161
Audio system	0.8517
Air conditioner	0.8042
Blood pressure monitor	0.8091
Comfortable temperature	0.9418
Entertainment system	0.8553
Electric blanket	0.9722
ipad	0.6262
Personal computer	0.6067
Smart light	0.9081
Smart alarm clock	0.9534
Smart card	0.5502

examples of glossary terms extracted by applying word embeddings based semantic filter. The second column of this table shows the similarity score, i.e., score obtained by computing the cosine similarity with the same word from the home automation Wikipedia corpus.

5.4 Coverage

In [6], requirements coverage has been advocated as another metric for a glossary's quality. Roughly speaking, the definition of coverage is the extent to which something is addressed, covered or included. In the context of glossary term extraction for software requirements, coverage gives us the percentage of requirements that are covered by the terms present in the glossary. It is important to note that high coverage rate does not necessarily means high quality glossary. For example, it is possible to achieve a very high coverage rate by including common words or terms that appear frequently in a requirements document even if they are not domain or application-specific terms. For CrowdRE dataset, without semantic filtering we obtain a total of 4156 glossary terms with a coverage rate of 99%, i.e., 2937 of 2966 requirements are covered by these glossary terms. On applying the semantic filter number of glossary terms reduces to 304 and the corresponding coverage rate is 51.88%, i.e., 1539 of 2966 requirements are covered by this new set of glossary terms. This reduction in coverage rate can be attributed to the following two reasons. Firstly, common nouns or noun phrases and terms which are not domain-specific but do appear frequently in requirements document would not be part of the final set of glossary terms obtained after applying semantic filter. Secondly, unlike [6] we do not include the content of role descriptions attribute of CrowdRE dataset as part of every requirement. Since the same role description can be part of many user stories it ensures a high coverage regardless of the specific content of the requirements. Some example role descriptions from CrowdRE dataset are as follows: student, cook, driver, parent, mother, wife, manager, adult, pet owner, nanny and husband. From these examples it is easy to see that role description does not give any useful information about the actual contents of a requirement. Semantic filtering reduces the number of glossary terms by 92.7% while coverage rate is reduced by 47.6%. In other words, the number of glossary terms gets reduced roughly by less than a factor of 14 whereas the coverage rate is reduced by less than a factor of 2. Since for a large-sized requirements document the glossary is required to be restricted to a manageable size, we believe that our approach is very effective in achieving a huge reduction in glossary size with a much smaller impact on coverage rate.

Some statistics related to coverage have been reported in Table 4. First row of this table presents the number of glossary terms that appear only once in the CrowdRE dataset. Similarly, i^{th} row of this table indicates the number of glossary terms that are present in i unique requirements from the CrowdRE dataset. As expected when i increases the number of glossary terms starts decreasing. The only exception to these findings is the 2nd row of this table where the number of glossary terms increases.

Table 4. Number of requirements covered by the extracted glossary terms.

Number of requirements	Glossary terms
1	48
2	98
3	46
4	23
5	18
6	10
7	8
8	5
9	6
10	4

To highlight the fact that our approach does not remove infrequent domain or application-specific terms, we have compiled a set of some example technical terms which have been extracted by our semantic filter (see Table 5). First column of this table reports some examples of extracted glossary terms that appear only once in the CrowdRE dataset. Similarly, second column of this table includes some examples of extracted glossary terms which appear only twice in the dataset.

Table 5. Examples of extracted glossary terms that appear only once or twice in CrowdRE.

Glossary terms (1)	Glossary terms (2)
Smart sensor	Motion sensor
Fingerprint scanner	Smart fridge
Smart tag	Smart tv
Amazon	Ideal temperature
Wireless speaker	Room thermostat
Rfid chip	Facial recognition
Carbon monoxide detector	iphone

5.5 Advantages of Our Approach

A major advantage of our approach is that only those technical terms are added to the final set of glossary terms which are truly domain-specific. This is primarily because we use word embeddings and similarity scores for detecting domain-specific terms. For example, terms that occur very frequently in the requirements document but are not domain or application-specific will not be part of the final set of glossary terms. In contrast, term extraction approaches which only use statistical filtering would include these terms in the final set of glossary terms. Additionally, our filtering technique can be used to significantly reduce the number of glossary terms for large-sized requirements documents.

Another advantage of this approach is that if the number of glossary terms needs to be reduced further, this can be done easily by selecting a higher similarity threshold used for labeling a term as relevant/domain-specific. Our semantic filtering technique can also be combined with other filtering techniques, e.g., statistical and hybrid. Finally, this technique can be used to detect multiple terms (NPs) with the same meaning, i.e., synonyms. This is helpful as we do not need to define synonyms as separate glossary terms in the requirements document. Similarly, terms having the same spelling but different meanings, i.e., homonyms can be detected. This would allow us to define these terms as separate candidate glossary terms.

5.6   Limitations of Our Approach

A major limitation of our approach is that for every application domain it requires a corresponding domain-specific reference corpus which is used by Word2vec model to filter the candidate glossary terms. This could be an issue for new application domains where a reference corpus cannot be built due to the unavailability of large-sized domain-specific documents. Moreover, even for application domains where it is possible to create a reference corpus, there are no specific guidelines for selecting the source from where the corpus should be generated. For example, it is possible that for a particular application domain multiple sources of relevant data are available, e.g., Wikipedia, existing requirements documents, product brochures, handbooks, etc. In this case, it is not clear which of these documents need to be mined or crawled to generate the reference corpus which gives us the most accurate results. For home automation domain, reference corpus created by Wikipedia crawling gives us good results but this may not be true for other application domains.

Another issue with semantic filters is that for very large-sized documents, generation of word embeddings and computation of similarity scores for thousands of NPs may take a long time to complete. For home automation domain, we were able to run the experiments on a laptop but this may not be true for other application domains.

6   Conclusions and Future Work

This paper proposes an automatic approach for glossary term extraction from large-sized requirements documents. The first step of our solution extracts candidate glossary terms by applying text chunking. In the second step, we use a semantic filter based on word embeddings to reduce the number of glossary terms. This semantic filter ensures that domain-specific terms are not removed from the set of candidate glossary terms. We apply our technique to a large-sized requirements documents with around 3000 crowd-generated requirements. Our experiments show that word embeddings based semantic filtering can be very useful for extracting glossary terms from a large body of existing requirements. This research work can be extended in several interesting directions which are as follows:

- Implement a tool that takes as input the large-sized requirements document and automatically mines the Web to build a requirements-specific reference corpus. In the next step, it should automatically extract the set of candidate glossary terms by applying our word embeddings based semantic filter.
- Extend this technique to automatically extract the glossary terms from a large body of natural language requirements for software product lines [20].
- Compare the effectiveness of Word2vec semantic filter with other word embedding techniques, e.g., GloVe and fastText.
- Come up with some guidelines to determine how to create the domain-specific reference corpus.

References

1. Aguilera, C., Berry, D.M.: The use of a repeated phrase finder in requirements extraction. J. Syst. Softw. **13**(3), 209–230 (1990)
2. Arora, C., Sabetzadeh, M., Briand, L.C., Zimmer, F.: Automated extraction and clustering of requirements glossary terms. IEEE Trans. Softw. Eng. **43**(10), 918–945 (2017)
3. Dwarakanath, A., Ramnani, R.R., Sengupta, S.: Automatic extraction of glossary terms from natural language requirements. In: 21st IEEE International Requirements Engineering Conference (RE), pp. 314–319, July 2013
4. Ferrari, A., Donati, B., Gnesi, S.: Detecting domain-specific ambiguities: an NLP approach based on Wikipedia crawling and word embeddings. In: 25th IEEE International Requirements Engineering Conference Workshops (REW), pp. 393–399, September 2017
5. Ferrari, A., Esuli, A., Gnesi, S.: Identification of cross-domain ambiguity with language models. In: 5th International Workshop on Artificial Intelligence for Requirements Engineering (AIRE), pp. 31–38, August 2018
6. Gemkow, T., Conzelmann, M., Hartig, K., Vogelsang, A.: Automatic glossary term extraction from large-scale requirements specifications. In: 26th IEEE International Requirements Engineering Conference, pp. 412–417. IEEE Computer Society (2018)
7. Goldin, L., Berry, D.M.: AbstFinder, a prototype natural language text abstraction finder for use in requirements elicitation. Autom. Softw. Eng. **4**(4), 375–412 (1997). https://doi.org/10.1023/A:1008617922496
8. Hull, M.E.C., Jackson, K., Dick, J.: Requirements Engineering, 2nd edn. Springer, Heidelberg (2005). https://doi.org/10.1007/b138335
9. Justeson, J.S., Katz, S.M.: Technical terminology: some linguistic properties and an algorithm for identification in text. Nat. Lang. Eng. **1**(1), 9–27 (1995)
10. Kof, L.: Natural language processing for requirements engineering: applicability to large requirements documents. In: Workshop on Automated Software Engineering (2004)

11. Levy, O., Goldberg, Y.: Neural word embedding as implicit matrix factorization. In: Proceedings of the 27th International Conference on Neural Information Processing Systems - Volume 2. NIPS 2014, pp. 2177–2185 (2014)
12. Ménard, P.A., Ratté, S.: Concept extraction from business documents for software engineering projects. Autom. Softw. Eng. **23**(4), 649–686 (2015). https://doi.org/10.1007/s10515-015-0184-4
13. Mikolov, T., Chen, K., Corrado, G., Dean, J.: Efficient estimation of word representations in vector space. arXiv preprint arXiv:1301.3781 (2013)
14. Mikolov, T., Sutskever, I., Chen, K., Corrado, G., Dean, J.: Distributed representations of words and phrases and their compositionality. In: Proceedings of the 26th International Conference on Neural Information Processing Systems - Volume 2. NIPS 2013, pp. 3111–3119 (2013)
15. Mishra, S., Sharma, A.: On the use of word embeddings for identifying domain specific ambiguities in requirements. In: 2019 IEEE 27th International Requirements Engineering Conference Workshops (REW), pp. 234–240 (2019)
16. Murukannaiah, P.K., Ajmeri, N., Singh, M.P.: Toward automating crowd RE. In: 25th IEEE International Requirements Engineering Conference (RE), pp. 512–515, September 2017
17. Murukannaiah, P.K., Ajmeri, N., Singh, M.P.: Acquiring creative requirements from the crowd: understanding the influences of individual personality and creative potential in crowd RE. In: 24th IEEE International Requirements Engineering Conference (RE), pp. 176–185, September 2016
18. Park, Y., Byrd, R.J., Boguraev, B.K.: Automatic glossary extraction: beyond terminology identification. In: COLING 2002: The 19th International Conference on Computational Linguistics (2002). https://www.aclweb.org/anthology/C02-1142
19. Pohl, K.: Requirements Engineering - Fundamentals, Principles, and Techniques, 1st edn. Springer, Heidelberg (2010)
20. Pohl, K., Böckle, G., van der Linden, F.J.: Software Product Line Engineering: Foundations. Principles and Techniques. Springer, Heidelberg (2005). https://doi.org/10.1007/3-540-28901-1
21. Popescu, D., Rugaber, S., Medvidovic, N., Berry, D.M.: Reducing ambiguities in requirements specifications via automatically created object-oriented models. In: Paech, B., Martell, C. (eds.) Monterey Workshop 2007. LNCS, vol. 5320, pp. 103–124. Springer, Heidelberg (2008). https://doi.org/10.1007/978-3-540-89778-1_10
22. Romero, F.P., Olivas, J.A., Genero, M., Piattini, M.: Automatic extraction of the main terminology used in empirical software engineering through text mining techniques. In: Proceedings of the Second ACM-IEEE International Symposium on Empirical Software Engineering and Measurement. ESEM 2008, pp. 357–358 (2008)
23. Zou, X., Settimi, R., Cleland-Huang, J.: Improving automated requirements trace retrieval: a study of term-based enhancement methods. Empir. Softw. Eng. **15**(2), 119–146 (2010). https://doi.org/10.1007/s10664-009-9114-z

Requirements Modelling

Conceptualizing Requirements Using User Stories and Use Cases: A Controlled Experiment

Fabiano Dalpiaz[1](✉) and Arnon Sturm[2]

[1] Utrecht University, Utrecht, The Netherlands
f.dalpiaz@uu.nl
[2] Ben-Gurion University of the Negev, Beer-Sheva, Israel
sturm@bgu.ac.il

Abstract. [**Context and motivation**] Notations for expressing requirements are often proposed without explicit consideration of their suitability for specific tasks. Consequently, practitioners may choose a sub-optimal notation, thereby affecting task performance. [**Question/problem**] We investigate the adequacy of two well-known notations: use cases and user stories, as a starting point for the manual derivation of a static conceptual model. In particular, we examine the completeness and correctness of the derived conceptual model. [**Principal ideas/results**] We conducted a two-factor, two-treatment controlled experiment with 118 subjects. The results indicate that for deriving conceptual models, user stories fit better than use cases. It seems that the repetitions in user stories and their conciseness contribute to these results. [**Contribution**] The paper calls for evaluating requirements notations in the context of various requirements engineering tasks and for providing evidence regarding the aspects that need to be taken into account when selecting a requirement notation.

Keywords: Requirements engineering · Conceptual modeling · Use cases · User stories · Controlled experiment

1 Introduction

Many notations exist for expressing requirements for software systems, ranging from natural language sentences [8], semi-formal models [22,32], to formal languages [3,13]. Among this landscape, requirements are most often expressed following some templates or controlled languages, like EARS [31], UML use cases, and user stories [6]. The adequacy of the notation depends on the type of system under design, the application domain, and the granularity of the requirements. Nevertheless, the research community overlooked the contextual adequacy of these notations, and thus evidence for practitioners on the selection of an effective notation that fits their needs is missing.

© Springer Nature Switzerland AG 2020
N. Madhavji et al. (Eds.): REFSQ 2020, LNCS 12045, pp. 221–238, 2020.
https://doi.org/10.1007/978-3-030-44429-7_16

Furthermore, the selection of a suitable requirements notation also depends on the expectations regarding the requirements. They can be used for communication among stakeholders (i.e., when they express high-level specifications), for analytical tasks such as finding inconsistency and detecting feasibility, or for serving the entire software development process. As a first step within the development process, an analyst refines an initial set of high-level requirements into lower-level specifications and may use conceptual models as an artifact that represents the major entities and relationships that are referred to in the high-level requirements [18,29,42]. In this work, we limit our attention to static/structural conceptual models that emphasize the domain entities and their relationships. Such conceptual models can be employed in requirements engineering in order to (i) provide a holistic overview for team members to understand the product domain [1,27]; (ii) identify quasi-synonyms that may lead to misunderstandings [9]; (iii) support model-driven engineering [24]; and (iv) analyze certain quality aspects such as security and privacy [28].

In this research, we study the process of deriving a conceptual model (like an entity-relationship diagram or an UML class diagram) that represents the main concepts in a collection of high-level requirements. This type of models has been shown to be a useful learning tool for new employees [27], for representing the domain in which the system is to operate [1], and for supporting the transition to later phases in object-oriented software development [15,44].

We investigate the relative suitability of two mainstream notations for expressing requirements regarding analysts' effectiveness in manually extracting conceptual models. Our main research question in this paper is as follows: *MRQ. How does the choice of a requirements notation affect the derivation of static conceptual models?*

The two natural language notations that we choose are use cases (UC) and user stories (US). The former are chosen because they are part of the UML and, despite some criticism on their suitability to express requirements [14], they are widely adopted in the software industry. The latter are chosen because of their popularity in projects that follow agile development methods like Scrum and Kanban [19,26].

We answer our MRQ via a controlled experiment in which senior undergrad students, taking a course on object-oriented analysis and design are briefed to individually derive conceptual models (UML class diagrams) starting from high-level requirements for two systems using either notation (US and UC). By defining a gold standard conceptual model, we are able to measure the precision and recall. Furthermore, we evaluate the preference of the students in extracting models from either notation.

The results show that, in a course where object orientation is explained in detail, user stories seem to be preferred for the task at hand. Besides such preference, the accuracy of the derived models tends to be higher with user stories. Although preliminary, we believe that these results may inspire other research on the effectiveness of alternative requirements notations for different requirements-related tasks.

The rest of the paper is organized as follows. In Sect. 2, we set the background for this study and review related studies. In Sect. 3, we present the design of the experiment we performed. In Sect. 4, we elaborate on the experiment results whereas in Sect. 5 we interpret and discuss those results. In Sect. 6, we indicate the threats to validity. We conclude and set plans for future research in Sect. 7.

2 Background and Related Work

Use cases are a popular notation, part of the UML [34], for expressing requirements that describe the interaction between a user and a system. Although typically used for expressing functional requirements, adaptations and extensions exist to make them suitable for representing quality aspects such as security and privacy [28, 35]. A use case defines a list of steps between an actor and the system; they are specified following a textual template and using a use case diagram. In the context of this work, we focus on a simple template notation adapted from Larman's book [23], illustrated in Listing 1, which is based on the widely used notations by Cockburn [4] and Kruchten [21].

Listing 1. A use case for the Planning Poker game website.

> **UC1. Set a Game**
> **Primary Actor**: Moderator
> **Main Success Scenario (or Basic Flow):**
> 1. Create a new game by entering a name and an optional description
> 2. The system records the game parameters
> 3. Set the estimation policy
> 4. The system stores the estimation policy
> 5. Invite up to 15 estimators to participate
> 6. The system sends invitations and add estimators to the game

User stories are another widespread notation [19, 26] that originates from the agile software development paradigm [6] and that consists of simple descriptions of a feature written from the perspective of the person who wants them. Multiple templates exist for representing user stories [39], among which the Connextra format is one of the predominant ones [26]: *As a <role>, I want <action>, so that <benefit>*. The "so that" part, despite its importance in providing the rationale for a user story [25], is often omitted in practice. In our study, we formulate user stories using the Connextra template and we group related user stories into epics. See Listing 2 for some examples.

Listing 2. Some user stories for the Planning Poker game website.

> **Epic. Set a Game**
> US1: As a moderator, I want to create a new game by entering a name and an optional description, so that I can start inviting estimators.
> US2: As a moderator, I want to invite estimators, so that we can start the game.
> US3: As a moderator, I want to have the "estimate" field filled in automatically if all estimators show the same card, so that I can accept it more quickly.
> US4: As a moderator, I want to enter the agreed-upon estimate, so that we can move on to the next item when we agree.

Conceptual models can help refine an initial set of high-level requirements into lower-level specifications, by representing the major entities and relationships that are referred to in the high-level requirements [18,29,42]. Several researchers have investigated the derivation of such models from use cases. Insfrán et al. [18] propose a process that assists in the refinement of high-level requirements, expressed as a mission statement, into lower-level models that can be automatically mapped to code. Part of their approach is the creation of use cases to facilitate the transition from natural language statements to executable models. Yue et al. [43] observe that informal use case specifications may contain vague and ambiguous terms that make it hard to derive precise UML models, including class and sequence diagrams. As a solution, they propose a restricted version of the use cases template for analysts to adopt. The approach was found easy to apply by practitioners and led to significant improvements in terms of class correctness and class diagram completeness.

Fewer methods exist that derive conceptual models from user stories. Lucassen et al. [27] propose an automated approach for extracting conceptual models from a collection of user stories by relying on and adapting natural language processing heuristics from the literature. The resulting models show good precision and recall, also thanks to the structure that is set by user stories, although perfect accuracy is not possible due to the large variety of linguistic patterns that natural language allows for. Wautelet et al. [38] introduce a process for transforming a collection of user stories into a use case diagram by using the granularity information obtained through tagging the user stories. Although this work is relevant, our goal is to study the independent use of UC and US. Trkman et al. [37] point out how user stories, being defined independently, do not clearly represent execution and integration dependencies. Their solution includes the use of a different type of conceptual model, i.e., business process models, to associate user stories with activities and, thus, to facilitate the discovery of dependencies by following the control flow in the business process model.

To the best of our knowledge, no experimental studies that compare the effectiveness of requirements notations (for certain tasks) exist. Therefore, practitioners have no concrete evidence regarding which notation suits best their needs. The closest works to ours regard the comparison of (graphical) notations used in information systems design. Ottensooser et al. [33] compare the Business Process Modeling Notation (BPMN) against textual user cases in interpreting business process descriptions. Their experiment shows that BPMN adds value only with trained readers. Cardoso et al. [2] conduct an experiment that shows how the adequacy of languages depends on how structured a business process is. Hoisl et al. [17] compare three notations (textual, semi-structured, diagrammatic) for expressing scenario-based model tests; their experimental results show a preference toward natural language based notations.

3   Experiment Design

We investigate how requirements can be *conceptualized* taking as input two different widely used requirements notations: use cases and user stories. By conceptualizing requirements, we refer to the manual derivation of a static conceptual model starting from a set of requirements specified in each of the notations.

3.1   Hypotheses

To compare the differences in the effectiveness of UC and US as a starting point for the manual derivation of a conceptual model, we measure *correctness* and *completeness* with respect to a gold standard solution. Furthermore, we collect and compare the preference of the subjects with respect to the use of the two notations for various tasks.

We observe that use case descriptions are organized in a transactional, process-oriented fashion, thus making it easier to comprehend the flow and the intended system. User stories, on the other hand, are short and refined statements that have a standard format, thus making it easier to understand each requirement separately. Nevertheless, even if organized into epics, it is difficult to understand the system and the way it operates as a whole. This difference leads us to have the following hypothesis:

> *H0: user stories and use cases are equally good for the derivation of a static conceptual model*

To measure the quality of a conceptual model, we use the recall and precision of the resulting model with respect to the gold standard one. Our hypotheses are formalized as follows:

$$H_0^{CM\text{-}Precision} : US^{CM\text{-}Precision} = UC^{CM\text{-}Precision}$$
$$H_0^{CM\text{-}Recall} : US^{CM\text{-}Recall} = UC^{CM\text{-}Recall}$$

3.2   Design

We describe the variables and their measurements, the subjects, and the tasks.

Independent Variables. The first variable is the notation according to which the requirements are specified. It has two possible values: User Stories (US) and Use Cases (UC). The second independent variable is the case study used. It has two possible values: Data Hub (DH) and Planning Poker (PP). These case studies are obtained from a publicly available dataset of user story requirements [7]. DH is the specification for the web interface of a platform for collecting, organizing, sharing and finding data sets. PP are the requirements for the first version of the *planningpoker.com* website, an online platform for estimating user stories using the Planning Poker technique.

Dependent Variables. There are two types of dependent variables that are specified by comparing the elements in the *subject solution* (the conceptual model derived by a subject) against the *gold standard solution*:

– *Recall*: the ratio between the number of elements in the subject solution that also exist in the gold standard (true positives) and the number of elements in the gold standard (true positives + false negatives).

$$Recall = \frac{|True\ Positives|}{|True\ Positives| + |False\ Negatives|}$$

– *Precision*: the ratio between the number of elements in the subject solution that also exist in the gold standard (true positives) and the true positives plus the number of elements in the subject's solution that do not exist within the gold standard solution (false positives).

$$Precision = \frac{|True\ Positives|}{|True\ Positives| + |False\ Positives|}$$

While measuring recall and precision, we refer to various ways of counting the elements of a conceptual model:

– Number of entities, i.e., classes
– Number of relationships between classes
– Total: number of entities + number of relationships

Furthermore, since relationships can be identified only when the connected entities are identified, we introduce an *adjusted* version of precision and recall for the relationships, which calculates precision and recall with respect to those relationships in the gold standard among the entities that the subject has identified. So, for example, if the gold standard has entities A, B, C with relationships R1(A, B), R2(B, C) and R3(A, C), but the subject has identified only A and C, then only relationship R3 is considered while computing precision and recall in the *adjusted* version.

Subjects. We involved third year students taking the course on Object-oriented Analysis and Design at Ben-Gurion University of the Negev. The course teaches how to analyze, design, and implement software based on the object-oriented paradigm. In the course, the students-subjects learned the notion of modeling and, in particular, class diagrams. They learned the use of user stories and use cases for specifying requirements as part of the development process. They also practiced class diagrams, use cases and user stories, through homework assignments. In those assignments, they achieved good results, indicating that they understood the notations well.

Recruiting the students was done on a volunteering basis. Nevertheless, they were encouraged to participate in the experiment by providing them with additional bonus points to the course grade based on their performance. Before recruiting the students, the research design was submitted to and approved by the department ethics committee.

Task. We designed the experiment so that each subject would experience the derivation of a conceptual model from both notations. For that purpose, we designed two forms (available online [10]), in which we alternate the treatment and the case study.

The form consists of 4 parts: (1) a pre-task questionnaire that checks the back-ground and knowledge of the subjects; (2) the first task, in which subjects receive the requirements of the Data Hub application, specified either in use cases or user stories, and were asked to derive a conceptual model; (3) the second task, in which subjects receive the requirements of the Planning Poker application, specified either in use cases or user stories, and were asked to derive a conceptual model; (4) questions that measure the subjects' perception of the two notations and their usefulness. We asked the subjects to derive a conceptual model that would serve as a domain model for the backbone of the system to be developed (as was taught in the course).

We prepared the requirements set used in the experiment through several stages. First, we collected the original requirements from [7]. Second, we filtered the requirements to fit the experiment settings and wrote corresponding use case specifications. Third, we double checked the specifications to align contents and granularity of the use cases and the user stories and verified that both can be used to derive the same conceptual model, which we then set as the gold standard solution. Finally, we translated the requirements to Hebrew, so the subjects can perform the task in their native language. The case studies had different complexity. Table 1 presents various metrics and indicates that the DH case introduces higher complexity than the PP case.

Table 1. Case studies metrics

	Data Hub	Planning Poker
Number of user stories	24	21
Number of use cases	4	3
Number of lines in use cases	38	36
Number of entities	10	6
Number of relationships	13	8

To create the gold standard, whose conceptual models are listed in Appendix A, the authors of this paper have first created independently a conceptual model that depicts the main entities and relationships from both the use cases and the user stories separately. We further verified the conceptual model by adopting the heuristics used by the Visual Narrator [27], which suggest to look for (compound) nouns to identify concepts and to detect relationships by searching for action verbs. Then, we compared our models and produced the reconciled versions in the Appendix A.

Execution. The experiment took place in a dedicated time slot and lasted approximately 1 h, although we did not set a time limit for the subjects to complete the tasks. The assignment of the groups (i.e., the forms) to the 118 subjects was done randomly. The distribution of groups was as followed:

- Form A: DH with user stories and PP with use cases: 57 subjects;
- Form B: DH with use cases and PP with user stories: 61 subjects.

Analysis. The paper forms delivered by the students were checked by the second author against the gold standard. We performed a lenient analysis of the solutions, in which we did not consider over-specification: if the student had identified an additional entity mentioned in the requirements, which we deemed as an attribute rather than an entity, we would not penalize the student. We also accepted solutions that deviated slightly from the gold standard, so we could cope with alternative solutions. The results were encoded into IBM's SPSS, which was used to calculate precision, recall, and the other statistics listed in Sect. 4. Both authors analyzed the data to cross-check the analyses and to identify the most relevant findings.

4   Experiment Results

We run a series of analyses over the results (all materials are available online [10]). We first compare the background of the two groups. Table 2 presents the comparison criteria among the groups, the mean ($\overline{x}$) and standard deviation (σ) for each, and the statistical analysis results in terms of statistical significance ($p < 0.05$), and effect size. For non-parametric tests, like Wilcoxon Signed-Rank test or Mann-Whitney U test, we follow Fritz *et al.*'s recommendation [12]: test statistics are approximated by normal distributions to report effect sizes. For parametric tests, like the T-Test, we employ Hedges' g value [16]. To facilitate

Table 2. Pre-questionnaire results: mean, standard deviation, significance, and effect size.

	Form A		Form B		p	Effect
	$\overline{x}$	σ	$\overline{x}$	σ		size
Class Diagram (CD) Familiarity	4.16	0.71	4.07	0.60	0.356	0.147
UC Familiarity	3.73	0.62	3.57	0.74	0.293	0.174
US Familiarity	3.92	0.76	3.70	0.69	0.111	0.298
UC Homework Delivered	4.45	0.80	4.34	0.66	0.153	0.237
US Homework Delivered	4.48	0.66	4.26	0.73	0.066	0.308
CD Homework Delivered	4.54	0.57	4.30	0.74	0.071	0.301
Participation in the UC Lecture	0.91	0.29	0.89	0.32	0.629	0.065
Participation in the US Lecture	0.95	0.23	0.90	0.30	0.349	0.186
Grade	85.54	5.87	81.49	14.58	0.048	0.360

the interpretation of the results, we transform effect sizes to Hedges' g. To do so, we employ an online calculator[1]. All criteria were indicated by the subjects except for the grade, which is the final grade of the course. The familiarity and the homework participation criteria were retrieved using a 5-point Likert-type scale (1 indicates low familiarity and participation and 5 indicates high familiarity and participation), lecture participation criteria take either true or false, while the grade is on a scale from 0 to 100.

Although the division into groups was done randomly, it appears that the background of the group of subjects assigned to Form A was superior than the group of subjects assigned to Form B. Applying a Mann-Whitney test [30] to the "subjective" criteria, we found no statistically significant differences, yet when applying a T-test [36] to the last three rows, we found that the difference for the *grade* was statistically significant and had a *small-to-medium* effect size ($g = 0.360$). These differences should be taken into account when analyzing the results.

In analyzing the results of the completeness and correctness of the conceptual models, we performed an Anova test [11] and found out that the interaction between the case study and the notation, concerning the adjusted total precision and recall, is statistically significant. This probably occurred due to the complexity differences between the two case studies as appears in Table 1. We thus analyze each case study separately.

Tables 3 and 4 present the results of the DH and PP case studies, respectively. For the user stories and the use cases columns, we report arithmetic mean and standard deviation for the related metric. Bold numbers indicate the best results, whereas gray rows indicate statistically significant differences (applying T-test).

In all metrics, the conceptual models derived from the set of user stories outperform the conceptual models derived from the set of use cases. For the DH

Table 3. Data Hub results.

| | User Stories | | Use Cases | | p | Effect size |
	$\overline{x}$	σ	$\overline{x}$	σ		
Entity Recall	**0.73**	**0.13**	0.70	0.14	0.258	0.222
Entity Precision	**0.66**	**0.14**	0.61	0.12	0.089	0.384
Relation Recall	**0.38**	**0.15**	0.34	0.12	0.047	0.296
Relation Precision	**0.34**	**0.14**	0.29	0.10	0.028	0.413
Total Recall	**0.54**	**0.11**	0.50	0.11	0.061	0.364
Total Precision	**0.48**	**0.11**	0.43	0.10	0.017	0.476
Adjusted Relation Recall	**0.66**	**0.19**	0.55	0.20	0.007	0.563
Adjusted Relation Precision	**0.52**	**0.19**	0.43	0.16	0.007	0.514
Adjusted Total Recall	**0.68**	**0.09**	0.63	0.10	0.004	0.525
Adjusted Total Precision	**0.58**	**0.11**	0.53	0.08	0.002	0.523

---

[1] https://www.psychometrica.de/effect_size.html.

Table 4. Planning Poker results.

	User stories		Use cases		p	Effect
	$\overline{x}$	σ	$\overline{x}$	σ		size
Entity Recall	**0.80**	**0.17**	0.78	0.17	0.520	0.118
Entity Precision	**0.75**	**0.18**	0.72	0.17	0.380	0.171
Relation Recall	**0.45**	**0.22**	0.42	0.28	0.623	0.120
Relation Precision	**0.37**	**0.21**	0.35	0.23	0.618	0.091
Total Recall	**0.62**	**0.17**	0.60	0.19	0.532	0.111
Total Precision	**0.54**	**0.17**	0.52	0.17	0.496	0.118
Adjusted Relation Recall	**0.63**	**0.25**	0.58	0.24	0.322	0.204
Adjusted Relation Precision	**0.48**	**0.23**	0.44	0.22	0.409	0.178
Adjusted Total Recall	**0.63**	**0.20**	0.60	0.20	0.440	0.150
Adjusted Total Precision	**0.53**	**0.17**	0.51	0.16	0.489	0.121

case study, the difference was statistically significant in the case of the relation, for all the adjusted metrics as well as for the total precision. Furthermore, the effect sizes for DH indicate an *intermediate effect* for many metrics, all those with $g > 0.5$ according to Cohen [5]. Analyzing the preferences of the students regarding the use of the two notations (Table 5)—using the Mann-Whitney test since our visual analysis of the distributions revealed non-normality for some statements—we found no statistically significant differences between the two groups. In the tasks related to deriving a conceptual model, identifying classes, identifying relationships, providing a system overview, and clearly presenting a single requirement, there was a consensus regarding the benefits of using user stories to describe the requirements. However, there was no consensus regarding their benefit over use cases with respect to comprehending the system structure. Furthermore, in both groups most subjects generally prefer to use user stories to use cases.

Gathering the preferences of both groups together, Table 6 indicates a clear preference towards user stories. These preferences are of statistical significance (applying Wilcoxon test [40]) in the case of developing a conceptual model, identifying classes, and clearly presenting a single requirement. The validity of these findings is confirmed by their *intermediate effect*, equal or above to 0.5.

Based on the results, we can conclude that for the Data Hub application we can reject both H_0 hypotheses on the equality of both notation in the effectiveness of deriving a conceptual model for the metrics defined above (the grey rows in Table 3). In that case, introducing user stories resulted in better conceptual models. For the other metrics, we accept H_0 hypotheses, and can infer that no difference exists in using both notations in deriving a conceptual model. Drilling down into the actual conceptual models and their alignment with the gold standard solution, we had additional observations.

Table 5. Preferences by group; effect size is omitted due to the high p values.

Statement	Form A	Form B	p
Use cases fit for developing a conceptual model	3.24	3.45	0.267
User stories fit for developing a conceptual model	**3.87**	**3.69**	0.324
Use cases help in identifying classes	3.48	3.46	0.966
User stories help in identifying classes	**3.74**	**3.86**	0.809
Use cases help in identifying relationships	3.63	3.46	0.531
User stories help in identifying relationships	**3.72**	**3.66**	0.534
Use cases help comprehend the system structure	3.50	**3.63**	0.402
User stories help comprehend the system structure	**3.57**	3.57	0.855
Use cases provide a system overview	3.28	3.36	0.563
User stories provide a system overview	**3.54**	**3.43**	0.648
A use case clearly presents a single requirement	3.41	3.32	0.730
A user story clearly presents a single requirement	**3.74**	**3.86**	0.583
Which method do you prefer?	**US = 31**	**US = 37**	0.413
	UC = 21	UC = 18	

Table 6. Preferences by notation.

Statement	User Stories		Use Cases		p	Effect size
	$\overline{x}$	σ	$\overline{x}$	σ		
Fit for developing a conceptual model	**3.78**	**0.91**	3.35	1.00	0.002	0.613
Help in identifying classes	**3.79**	**0.92**	3.46	0.87	0.010	0.500
Help in identifying relationships	**3.67**	**0.98**	3.53	0.96	0.336	0.183
Help comprehend the system structure	**3.59**	**0.89**	3.57	0.99	0.988	0.003
Provide a system overview	**3.49**	**1.09**	3.33	1.12	0.228	0.229
Clearly presents a single requirement	**3.81**	**0.99**	3.37	0.97	0.002	0.613
Which method do you prefer?	68		39			

For the Data Hub case study:

1. *Site Admin* was less recognized in the use cases (US-96%, UC-80%) – it appears only once in the use cases and 4 times in the user stories.
2. *Usage Metric* was less recognized in the user stories (US-31%, UC-69%) – it appears only once in the user stories and 4 times in the use cases.
3. *Billing System* was less recognized in the use cases (US-50%, UC-27%) – though in both techniques it appears only once.
4. *Account* was less recognized in the use cases (US-50%, UC-19%) – it appears twice in the use cases and 4 times in the user stories.
5. The *Publisher – Usage Metrics* relationship was less recognized in the user stories (US-5%, UC-44%)– it appears twice in the use cases and only implicitly in the user stories.

6. The *Publisher – User* relationship was less recognized in the use cases (US-59%, UC-18%) – this relationship is implicitly mentioned 3 time in the user stories and only once in the use cases.
7. *The Site Admin – User* relationship was less recognized in the use cases (US-59%, UC-18%) - it appears once in each of the descriptions.

For the Planning Poker case study, we had the following observations:

1. *Game Round* was less recognized in the user stories (US-37%, UC-61%) – it appears 9 time in the use cases and only twice in the user stories.
2. The *Moderator – Estimator* relationship was less recognized in the use cases (US- 37%, UC-14%) – an implicit relationship between the moderator and estimator appears 7 times in the user stories and only 2 times in the use cases.
3. The *Moderator – Estimation Item* relationship was less recognized in the use cases (US-50%, UC-14%) – an implicit relationship between the moderator and estimation item appears 6 times in the user stories and only 4 times in the use cases.

5   Discussion

As highlighted in Table 1, the *complexity of the case studies* affects the results. The Planning Poker case study was less complex than the Data Hub case study (14 versus 23 concepts). Even though Planning Poker was presented as the second case study in the experiment forms—one would expect the participants to be less effective because of being tired—, the conceptual models fit better the gold standard solution. For Data Hub, the complexity emerges due to various factors: the number of entities, the number of relationships, the introduction of an external system (the billing system) with which the system under design interacts, the multiple interactions among the roles/actors, and the existence of several related roles/actors with similar names. The results may also be affected by the *course context*: the focus was the design of a system, thus interactions among actors were of less importance, as well as those with external systems.

The results indicate the existence of *differences between the groups*. The best performing group had the Data Hub case specified with user stories and the Planning Poker specified with use cases. That group achieved better results in the case of the Data Hub (having user stories). The other group (inferior in the subjects' background and grading) also achieved better results when having user stories. The later results, related to Planning Poker, were not statistically significant; yet, this can be attributed to the fact that the group that had the user stories was inferior to the group that had the use cases. Another explanation can be related to the complexity of the case study: the Planning Poker case study was simpler and, therefore, differences were of low magnitude.

When referring to the qualitative inspection of the results, it seems that when related to actors, there are *multiple repetitions* of these concepts in the user stories and thus the subjects were able to better identify the actors as well as the relationships between them. In use cases, actors are usually mentioned only in the beginning of each use case (in the "actor" section), and the described actions are implicitly referring to the interaction between the actor and the system. In user stories, instead, actors are expressed in every user story in the "As a" part. Similar to actors, it seems that in the user stories there are entities that recur multiple times, as they are used in many operations. This also led to better identification of such entities when deriving the conceptual models.

Another explanation for the user stories supremacy may be the fact that these are focused on the specification of individual features that an actor needs, whereas use cases blur the identification of entities within a transaction flow. It would be interesting, therefore, to explore which of the two notations is the most adequate to re-construct a process model that describes how the actions are sequentially linked.

One major difficulty for the students was to understand the *difference between entities and relationships.* Several errors were made because the students did not mark the identified concepts correctly. This may be due to shallow reading, time pressure, or an actual difficulty in distinguishing them. However, it seems that the template structure of user stories made it easier for the students to distinguish entities from relationships.

The subjects also perceive the user stories notation as better fit for the tasks we ask them to perform. This is remarkable, since the course in which this experiment was embedded focuses on the use of the UML for system design. The students also acknowledge the benefits for other tasks, yet the difference was not significant.

6   Threats to Validity

Our results need to be considered in view of threats to validity. We follow Wohlin *et al.*'s classification [41]: construct, internal, conclusion, and external validity.

Construct validity threats concern the relationships between theory and observation and are mainly due to the method used to assess the outcomes of the tasks. We examined the use of two RE notations for the purpose of conceptual model derivation and we used two sets of requirements. The selection of the domains may affect the results; our choice is justified by our attempt to provide domains that would be easy to understand by the subjects. Moreover, it might be that the specification using the two notations were not aligned in the sense that they emphasize different aspects (process in the software vs. individual features). However, this is exactly one of the triggers of our research. To mitigate the risk of favoring one notation over the other, before the experiment, both authors created a conceptual model from either notation, independently, to minimize bias that could stem from the way the specifications were written.

Internal validity threats, which concern external factors that might affect the dependent variables, may be due to individual factors, such as familiarity with the domain, the degree of commitment by the subjects, and the training level the subjects underwent. These effects are mitigated by the experiment design that we chose. We believe that due to the domains characteristics, the students were not familiar with them, and thus they probably were not affected. The random assignment that was adopted should eliminate various kinds of external factors. Although the experiment was done on a voluntary basis, the subjects were told that they would earn bonus points based on their performance, and thus we increased the motivation and commitment of the subjects as they took advantage of entire time allocated for the experiment. The revealed differences among the groups may also affect the results, though the trend exist in both groups. In addition, it might be that acquiring reasoning abilities in extracting entities and their relationships affect the results. These indicate that the second task resulted in better conceptual model. Yet, we attribute this difference to the lower complexity of the second domain. This leads to another threat that the order of the domains within the experiment may also affect the results. Another threat could emerge from the multiple tasks and fatigue.

Conclusion validity concerns the relationship between the treatment (the notation) and the outcome. We followed the various assumptions of the statistical tests (such as normal distribution of the data and data independence) when analyzing the results. In addition, we used a predefined solution, which was established before the experiment, for grading the subjects' answers; thus, only limited human judgment was required.

External validity concerns the generalizability of the results. The main threat in this area stems from the choice of subjects and from using simple experimental tasks. The subjects were undergraduate students with little experience in software engineering, in general, and in modeling in particular. Kitchenham *et al.* argue that using students as subjects instead of software engineers is not a major issue as long as the research questions are not specifically focused on experts [20], as is the case in our study. In addition, it might be that the template selected for the two notations also affected the results. Yet, these are the most common ones in their categories. Generalizing the results should be taken with care as the case studies are small and might be different in the way user stories and use cases are written in industry settings.

7   Summary

We provided initial evidence on the benefit of using user stories over use cases for deriving static conceptual models. We performed a controlled experiment with 118 undergraduate students that we conducted as part of a system design course. The results indicate that, probably because of the conciseness and focus of user stories and the repetitions of entities in the user stories, the derived conceptual models are more complete and correct. This work is a first attempt in the direction of evaluating requirements notations side-by-side for a specific task. We started from the task of deriving a static conceptual model; this is a self-contained activity that can be performed in a relatively short time, especially for not-so-large specifications.

Our paper calls for further experimentation for this particular task, as well as for other tasks that are based on requirements notations. The research community needs to build a corpus of evidence to assist practitioners in the choice of a notation (and technique) for the RE tasks at hand. We plan to continue this research with larger case studies using qualitative methods to investigate the trade-offs among RE notations.

Appendix A

See Figs. 1 and 2.

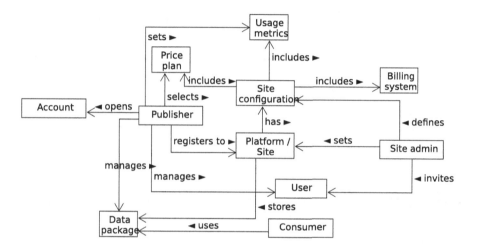

Fig. 1. The Data Hub gold standard solution

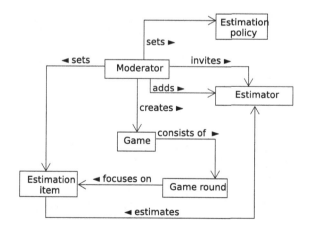

Fig. 2. The Planning Poker gold standard solution

References

1. Arora, C., Sabetzadeh, M., Nejati, S., Briand, L.: An active learning approach for improving the accuracy of automated domain model extraction. ACM Trans. Softw. Eng. Methodol. **28**(1), 1–34 (2019)

2. Cardoso, E., Labunets, K., Dalpiaz, F., Mylopoulos, J., Giorgini, P.: Modeling structured and unstructured processes: an empirical evaluation. In: Comyn-Wattiau, I., Tanaka, K., Song, I.-Y., Yamamoto, S., Saeki, M. (eds.) ER 2016. LNCS, vol. 9974, pp. 347–361. Springer, Cham (2016). https://doi.org/10.1007/978-3-319-46397-1_27

3. Ciancarini, P., Cimato, S., Mascolo, C.: Engineering formal requirements: an analysis and testing method for z documents. Ann. Softw. Eng. **3**(1), 189–219 (1997). https://doi.org/10.1023/A:1018965316985

4. Cockburn, A.: Writing Effective Use Cases. Addison-Wesley Professional, Boston (2000)

5. Cohen, J.: Statistical power analysis. Curr. Dir. Psychol. Sci. **1**(3), 98–101 (1992)

6. Cohn, M.: User Stories Applied: For Agile Software Development. Addison Wesley, Boston (2004)

7. Dalpiaz, F.: Requirements Data Sets (User Stories) (2018). http://dx.doi.org/10.17632/7zbk8zsd8y.1. Mendeley Data, v1

8. Dalpiaz, F., Ferrari, A., Franch, X., Palomares, C.: Natural language processing for requirements engineering: the best is yet to come. IEEE Softw. **35**(5), 115–119 (2018)

9. Dalpiaz, F., van der Schalk, I., Brinkkemper, S., Aydemir, F.B., Lucassen, G.: Detecting terminological ambiguity in user stories: tool and experimentation. Inf. Softw. Technol. **10**, 3–16 (2019)

10. Dalpiaz, F., Sturm, A.: Experiment User Stories vs. Use Cases (2020). https://doi.org/10.23644/uu.c.4815591.v1. Figshare

11. Fisher, R.A.: On the 'probable error' of a coefficient of correlation deduced from a small sample. Metron **1**, 1–32 (1921)

12. Fritz, C.O., Morris, P.E., Richler, J.J.: Effect size estimates: current use, calculations, and interpretation. J. Exp. Psychol.: Gen. **141**(1), 2 (2012)

13. Fuxman, A., Liu, L., Mylopoulos, J., Pistore, M., Roveri, M., Traverso, P.: Specifying and analyzing early requirements in tropos. Requirements Eng. **9**(2), 132–150 (2004). https://doi.org/10.1007/s00766-004-0191-7

14. Glinz, M.: Problems and deficiencies of UML as a requirements specification language. In: Proceedings of the International Workshop on Software Specifications & Design, pp. 11–22 (2000)

15. Harmain, H., Gaizauskas, R.: CM-Builder: a natural language-based CASE tool for object-oriented analysis. Autom. Softw. Eng. **10**(2), 157–181 (2003). https://doi.org/10.1023/A:1022916028950

16. Hedges, L.V.: Estimation of effect size from a series of independent experiments. Psychol. Bull. **92**(2), 490 (1982)

17. Hoisl, B., Sobernig, S., Strembeck, M.: Comparing three notations for defining scenario-based model tests: a controlled experiment. In: Proceedings of the International Conference on the Quality of Information and Communications Technology (2014)

18. Insfrán, E., Pastor, O., Wieringa, R.: Requirements Engineering-based Conceptual Modelling. Requirements Eng. **7**(2), 61–72 (2002). https://doi.org/10.1007/s007660200005

19. Kassab, M.: An empirical study on the requirements engineering practices for agile software development. In: Proceedings of the EUROMICRO International Conference on Software Engineering and Advanced Applications, pp. 254–261 (2014)
20. Kitchenham, B.A., et al.: Preliminary guidelines for empirical research in software engineering. IEEE Trans. Softw. Eng. **28**(8), 721–734 (2002)
21. Kruchten, P.: The Rational Unified Process: An Introduction. Addison-Wesley, Boston (2004)
22. van Lamsweerde, A.: Requirements Engineering: From System Goals to UML Models to Software Specifications. Wiley, Hoboken (2009)
23. Larman, C.: Applying UML and Patterns: An Introduction to Object-Oriented Analysis and Design and Iterative Development. Prentice Hall, Upper Saddle River (2004)
24. Loniewski, G., Insfran, E., Abrahão, S.: A systematic review of the use of requirements engineering techniques in model-driven development. In: Petriu, D.C., Rouquette, N., Haugen, Ø. (eds.) MODELS 2010. LNCS, vol. 6395, pp. 213–227. Springer, Heidelberg (2010). https://doi.org/10.1007/978-3-642-16129-2_16
25. Lucassen, G., Dalpiaz, F., van der Werf, J., Brinkkemper, S.: Improving agile requirements: the quality user story framework and tool. Requirements Eng. **21**(3), 383–403 (2016). https://doi.org/10.1007/s00766-016-0250-x
26. Lucassen, G., Dalpiaz, F., Werf, J.M.E.M., Brinkkemper, S.: The use and effectiveness of user stories in practice. In: Daneva, M., Pastor, O. (eds.) REFSQ 2016. LNCS, vol. 9619, pp. 205–222. Springer, Cham (2016). https://doi.org/10.1007/978-3-319-30282-9_14
27. Lucassen, G., Robeer, M., Dalpiaz, F., van der Werf, J.M.E.M., Brinkkemper, S.: Extracting conceptual models from user stories with Visual Narrator. Requirements Eng. **22**(3), 339–358 (2017). https://doi.org/10.1007/s00766-017-0270-1
28. Mai, P.X., Goknil, A., Shar, L.K., Pastore, F., Briand, L.C., Shaame, S.: Modeling security and privacy requirements: a use case-driven approach. Inf. Softw. Technol. **100**, 165–182 (2018)
29. Maiden, N.A.M., Jones, S.V., Manning, S., Greenwood, J., Renou, L.: Model-driven requirements engineering: synchronising models in an air traffic management case study. In: Persson, A., Stirna, J. (eds.) CAiSE 2004. LNCS, vol. 3084, pp. 368–383. Springer, Heidelberg (2004). https://doi.org/10.1007/978-3-540-25975-6_27
30. Mann, H.B., Whitney, D.R.: On a test of whether one of two random variables is stochastically larger than the other. Ann. Math. Stat. **18**, 50–60 (1947)
31. Mavin, A., Wilkinson, P., Harwood, A., Novak, M.: EARS (easy approach to requirements syntax). In: Proceedings of of the IEEE International Requirements Engineering Conference, pp. 317–322 (2009)
32. Mylopoulos, J., Chung, L., Yu, E.: From object-oriented to goal-oriented requirements analysis. Commun. ACM **42**(1), 31–37 (1999)
33. Ottensooser, A., Fekete, A., Reijers, H.A., Mendling, J., Menictas, C.: Making sense of business process descriptions: an experimental comparison of graphical and textual notations. J. Syst. Softw. **85**, 596–606 (2012)
34. Rumbaugh, J., Jacobson, I., Booch, G.: The Unified Modeling Language Reference Manual. Addison-Wesley Professional (2004)
35. Sindre, G., Opdahl, A.L.: Eliciting security requirements with misuse cases. Requirements Eng. **10**(1), 34–44 (2005). https://doi.org/10.1007/s00766-004-0194-4
36. Student: The probable error of a mean. Biometrika **6**(1), 1–25 (1908)

37. Trkman, M., Mendling, J., Krisper, M.: Using business process models to better understand the dependencies among user stories. Inf. Softw. Technol. **71**, 58–76 (2016)

38. Wautelet, Y., Heng, S., Hintea, D., Kolp, M., Poelmans, S.: Bridging user story sets with the use case model. In: Link, S., Trujillo, J.C. (eds.) ER 2016. LNCS, vol. 9975, pp. 127–138. Springer, Cham (2016). https://doi.org/10.1007/978-3-319-47717-6_11

39. Wautelet, Y., Heng, S., Kolp, M., Mirbel, I.: Unifying and extending user story models. In: Jarke, M., et al. (eds.) CAiSE 2014. LNCS, vol. 8484, pp. 211–225. Springer, Cham (2014). https://doi.org/10.1007/978-3-319-07881-6_15

40. Wilcoxon, F.: Individual comparisons by ranking methods. Biom. Bull. **1**(6), 80–83 (1945)

41. Wohlin, C., Runeson, P., Höst, M., Ohlsson, M.C., Regnell, B., Wesslén, A.: Experimentation in Software Engineering. Springer, Heidelberg (2012). https://doi.org/10.1007/978-3-642-29044-2

42. Yue, T., Briand, L.C., Labiche, Y.: A systematic review of transformation approaches between user requirements and analysis models. Requirements Eng. **16**(2), 75–99 (2011). https://doi.org/10.1007/s00766-010-0111-y

43. Yue, T., Briand, L.C., Labiche, Y.: Facilitating the transition from use case models to analysis models: approach and experiments. ACM Trans. Softw. Eng. Methodol. **22**(1), 1–38 (2013)

44. Yue, T., Briand, L.C., Labiche, Y.: aToucan: an automated framework to derive UML analysis models from use case models. ACM Trans. Softw. Eng. Methodol. **24**(3), 1–52 (2015)

A Semi-automated Approach to Generate an Adaptive Quality Attribute Relationship Matrix

Unnati Shah[1]([✉]), Sankita Patel[2], and Devesh Jinwala[3]

[1] C. K. Pithawala College of Engineering and Technology, Surat 395007, India
unnati.shah25@gmail.com
[2] National Institute of Technology, Surat 395007, India
[3] Indian Institute of Technology, Jammu, Jammu 181221, Jammu and Kashmir, India

Abstract. **[Context and Motivation]** A critical success factor in Requirements Engineering (RE) involves recognizing conflicts in Quality Requirements (QRs). Nowadays, Quality Attributes Relationship Matrix (QARM) is utilized to identify the conflicts in QRs. The static QARM represents how one Quality Attribute (QA) undermines or supports to achieve other QAs. **[Question/Problem]** However, emerging technology discovers new QAs. Requirements analysts need to invest significant time and non-trivial human effort to acquire knowledge for the newly discovered QAs and influence among them. This process involves searching and analyzing a large set of quality documents from literature and industries. In addition, the use of static QARMs, without knowing the purpose of the QRs in the system may lead to false conflict identification. Rather than taking all QAs, domain-specific QAs are of great concern for the system being developed. **[Principal ideas/results]** In this paper, we propose an approach which is aimed to build an adaptive QARM semi-automatically. We empirically evaluate the approach and report an analysis of the generated QARM. We achieve 85.67% recall, 59.07% precision and 69.14% F-measure to acquire knowledge for QAs. **[Contributions]** We provide an algorithm to acquire knowledge for domain-specific QAs and construct an adaptive QARM from available unconstrained natural language documents and web search engines.

Keywords: Requirements Engineering · Quality ontology · Quality Attribute Relationship Matrix

1 Introduction

In Requirements Engineering (RE), Quality Requirements (QRs or Non-Functional Requirements) describe the overall behavior of the system [1]. Requirements analysts have to acquire knowledge of Quality Attributes (QAs) and influences among them, when they specify QRs for the system. In literature, there exist various approaches to specify QRs [2–12]. We divide them into two categories such as the NFR Framework-based approach and QARM (Quality Attribute Relationship Matrix) based approach.

© Springer Nature Switzerland AG 2020
N. Madhavji et al. (Eds.): REFSQ 2020, LNCS 12045, pp. 239–256, 2020.
https://doi.org/10.1007/978-3-030-44429-7_17

The NFR Framework [4] is a systematic approach to define QRs for the system. It provides visibility to relevant QAs and their interdependencies[1]. The NFR Framework is based on the Soft-goal Interdependency Graph (SIG). It is a graph of interconnected soft-goals (means goals without clear cut criteria or hard to define) where each soft-goal represents a QR for the software under development. However, the NFR Framework approach suffers from limitations such as (i) It is mostly reliant upon drawing SIGs manually, which is time-consuming and error-prone; (ii) SIG provides an informal description of the goals. Even though graphical representation is suitable for interaction between requirements analysts and end-users, it does not support machine readability. Hence, for large scale software, it is impractical to use such graphical representations.

On the other hand, in the QARM based approach, requirements analysts specify QRs using QARM that represents a pair-wise relationship between QAs. Various QARM based work has been carried out in [5–8]. These QARMs are generic to any system. In addition, as discussed in [12], the advent of emerging technologies introduces new QAs such as *mobility* [13], *context-awareness* [14], *ubiquity* [15] and *invisibility* [16]. However, the limitations in [13–16] are as follows:

1. Usage of the manual process to define QAs and their relationship is tedious and their outcomes rely upon the participant's skills. Also, for each newly discovered QAs, the process needs repetition. Hence, it is difficult to reuse and refine.
2. Lack of information concerning the relationship among newly discovered QAs to the traditional ones such as *security*, *performance*, *usability* among others.

The goal of our research is to build an adaptive QARM semi-automatically, acquiring knowledge from available natural language quality standards, industry documents, and web search engines.

The paper is organized as follows: In Sect. 2, we review the related work. We present the proposed approach in Sect. 3. Then we describe our research methodology in Sect. 4. In Sect. 5, we present and discuss the results of our approach. In Sect. 6, we present threats to validity. Finally, we conclude the paper with the future directions in Sect. 7.

2   Related Work

A large number of quality models have been proposed to make the abstract concept of software quality more tangible [17]. The main purpose of the quality models [18–21] is to decompose quality concepts down to a level where one can measure and evaluates the quality. The quality model is *"the set of quality characteristics and the relationships between them (i.e. QARM) that provides the basis for specifying QRs and evaluation"* [19]. Various QARM based work has been carried out in [5–12]. We broadly classify them into two categories viz. *QA to QA relationship matrix* [5–8] and *QA to functionality relationship matrix* [9–12].

QA to QA relationship matrix represents how one QA undermines (−) or supports (+) achieving other types of QAs. From the literature, we observe four such matrices based

---

[1] In this work, the term "Interdependency" indicates the relationship among QAs (i.e. how QAs support or limit one or more QAs).

on: (i) Potential conflicts and cooperation relationship among QRs [5]; (ii) Standard quality model ISO/IEC9126 [6]; (iii) Positive and negative relationships among QRs [7]; and (iv) Relative, absolute and never conflicts relationship among QRs [8]. On the other hand, *QA to Functionality relationship matrix* represents how one technique to achieve QA undermines (−) or supports (+) achieving other types of QAs. This matrix was first proposed by the authors in [4]. The authors state that each QA should be specified by the level of operationalizing soft-goals. The soft-goals are the possible design techniques that will help to implement the QA. They can be operations, functions, data, and constraints which may affect other QAs. In Table 1, we provide a comparative study of the existing approaches to generate QARM.

Table 1. Comparative study of the existing approaches to generate QARM

QARM characteristics	[5]	[6]	[7]	[8]	[9]	[10]	[11]	[12]	Our approach
False conflict identification	Y	Y	N	Y	N	N	N	Y	N
Adaptive	N	N	N	N	N	N	N	N	Y
Domain-specific	N	N	N	N	Y	Y	Y	Y	Y
QARM generation process	M	M	M	M	M	M	M	M	SA
QA to QA relationship	Y	Y	Y	Y	N	N	N	Y	Y
QA to functionality relationship	N	N	N	N	Y	Y	Y	N	Y
QA level	H	H	H	H	L	L	H	H	L
QARM representation	Mx	Mx	Mx	Mx	Mx	Mx	Mx	SIG	Ontology

The table contains QARM characteristics such as false conflict identification (**Yes/No**), adaptive matrix (**Yes/No**), domain-specific (**Yes/No**), QARM generation process (**Manual/Semi-automated (SA)**), QA to QA relationship (**Yes/No**), QA to functionality relationship (**Yes/No**), QA level (**High/Low**), QARM representation (**SIG/Matrix (Mx)/Ontology**). Our comparative study shows that the relationship between QAs present in [6, 8] is inconsistent. In [6], security and usability have no relationship, while in [8], security and usability have a relative relationship (i.e. These QAs are sometimes in conflict and sometimes not, depending on the application domain and in which context they are used) that leads to the false conflict identification and analysis. In addition, more than 50% of QAs (such as autonomy, productivity, satisfaction) listed in the literature [8] do not have clear definitions and their relationship. Furthermore, non-adaptive QARMs are based on the past literature and industry experience. Hence, recently discovered QAs such as *recoverability, context awareness, mobility, transparency,* and their relationships need to be considered which are not available [12].

3 Proposed Approach

The objective of our proposed approach is to help the requirement analysts to semi-automatically acquire knowledge of the domain-specific QAs (from available quality standards, industry documents and web search engine) and generate QARM (Fig. 1). The approach consists of two modules viz. Acquiring knowledge and QARM generation. Here, we first provide a vector representation of the QAs and QA related documents: Let QA be the set of QAs $QA = \{QA1, QA2....QAn\}$. Let QAD be the set of QA documents $QAD = \{D1, D2...Dn\}$, where a document Dn contains information for the QAn. Let T be the set of terms extracted from the Dn represented by $\{t1, t2...tm\}$. We discuss these modules in the subsequent subsections.

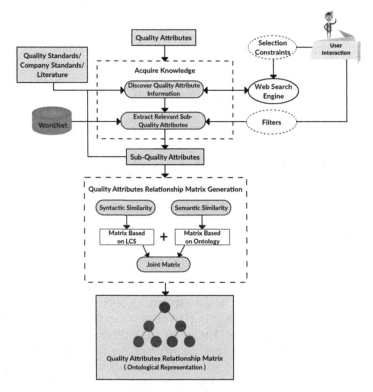

Fig. 1. Proposed approach

3.1 Acquire Knowledge

To acquire knowledge, the entire process is divided into two iterative steps. Firstly, we discover QA information from web search engines and available quality standards/documents for a given QAn and store it in the Dn. Secondly, we extract relevant sub-QAs from the Dn. We present the details of each step in the following sub-sections.

3.1.1 Discover QA Information

Definitions and/or descriptions of the QA are the basis that helps us to learn the relevant concepts of the QAs. We analyze a large number of quality documents and websites in order to find the relevant concepts for the QA by searching the QA's definitions. We notice that these definitions on the web differ from each other in some aspects and have similarities in others. Based on our study, we formulate the following questions and search queries in order to discover the information for a given QAn:

1. What are the *"Quality_Attribute"* definitions? This question aims to collect definitions available on the web/documents about a QAn;

Query 1: Define OR *definition* OR *about* OR *what is* + *Quality_Attribute* => *Dn*
Query 2: *Quality_Attribute* +*is/are* => *Dn*
Query 3: *Quality_Attribute* + *is/are* + *called* OR *defined as* OR *known as* OR *refer (s)* OR *described as* OR *formalized as* => *Dn*
Query 4: *is/are* + *called* OR *defined as* OR *known as formalized as* + *Quality_Attribute* => *Dn*

2. What are the *"Quality_Attribute"* definitions in *"Specific_Domain"*? This question aims to collect definitions available on web/documents about QAn in a specific domain;

Query 5: Define OR *definition* OR *about* OR *what is* + *Quality_Attribute* +*[in]* + *Domain_Name* => *Dn*
Query 6: *Quality_Attribute* +*[in]* + *Domain_Name* + *is/are* => *Dn*
Query 7: *Quality_Attribute* + *[in]* + *Domain_Name* + *is/are* + *called* OR *defined as* OR *known as* OR *refer (s)* OR *described as* OR *formalized as* => *Dn*
Query 8: *is/are* + *called* OR *defined as* OR *known as formalized as* + *Quality_Attribute* + *[in]* + *Domain_Name* => *Dn*

3. How is *"Quality_Attribute"* characterized? This question aims to collect existing sub-characteristics for QAn;

Query 9: *Feature* OR *Attributes* OR *Characteristics* OR *Matrix* + *[of]* + *Quality_Attribute* + *[in]* + *Domain_Name)* => *Dn*

4. What are the details available in *"Software Requirements Specification (SRS)"* to implement *"Quality_Attribute"*? This question aims to identify any kind of solution available in SRS to implement the QAn;

Query 10: *Implement* OR *Development [method/scheme]* OR *Execution [details]* OR *Technique* OR *Operationalization* OR *Achieve [of]* + *Quality_Attribute* => *Dn*
Query 11: *Function* OR *Procedure* OR *Algorithm* OR *Standard* + *[for]* + *Quality_Attribute* => *Dn*

5. How is the *"Quality_Attribute"* implemented in *"Specific_Domain"*? This question aims to identify any kind of solution used to implement the *QAn* in a specific domain;

Query 12: *Implement* OR *Development [method/scheme]* OR *Execution [details]* OR *Technique* OR *Operationalization* OR *Achieve [of]* + *Quality_Attribute* + *[in]* + *Domain_Name* => *Dn*

Query 13: *Function* OR *Procedure* OR *Algorithm* OR *Standard* + *[for]* + *Quality_Attribute* + *[in]* + *Domain_Name* => *Dn*

3.1.2 Extract Relevant sub-QAs

A detailed analysis of ambiguity in RE [22] shows that dealing with the ambiguity issue at an early stage makes the information accurate. To identify and resolve anaphora ambiguity in *Dn*, we follow the procedure present in [23]. After resolving ambiguity, we extract *Terms* such as adjectives, ending words with -bility, -bilities, -ness, -able, noun and verb phrases from *Dn*. We retain stop-words within noun and verb phrases as they are important for finding hierarchical relationships. To extract sub-QAs, we apply the following filters on *T*:

Filter1: Generic terms such as *data, system, computer, network, system, etc.* from *Dn*
Filter2: Terms that are present in 95% of the QA documents.
Filter3: Terms that violate the minimum size constraints.
Filter4: A stemming algorithm for the English language is used to reject plurals, verbal forms, etc.

For each sub-QA in *SubQAn*, we perform the following analysis to select the relevant sub-QAs for a *QAn*:

(i) Total number of appearances on all the web sites: this is the measure of the importance of the QA concept's to the domain and allows eliminating very specific ones;

(ii) A number of different websites that contain the QA concept at least once: this provides a measure of the generality of the terms for the domain (e.g. interface is quite common, but invisibility is not).

After analyzing the *SubQAn*, for each sub-QA, a new search string is constructed joining the sub-QA with the QA (e.g. *"Transparency (sub-QA) + Invisibility (QA)"*), and the entire procedure executes again. Quality experts will assess and confirm the final SubQAn. The experts can add/update/delete the relevant sub-QAs in *SubQAn*. Each relevant sub-QA is represented in a hierarchy by the searching pattern *"Noun Phrase 1 + [connector] + Noun Phrase 2"*; where the connector can be any combination of *verb phrase/preposition/adjective*. If *Noun Phrase 1 + connector + Noun Phrase 2* then *Noun Phrase 2* is likely to be the subclass of *Noun Phrase 1*. For example, *"Electronic signature (Noun Phrase 1) as (connector) authentication (Noun Phrase 2)"*, *"Biometrics (Noun Phrase 1) as (connector) authentication (Noun Phrase 2)"* indicates that *electronic signatures* and *biometrics* are the subclasses of the *authentication* and both are at the same level in the hierarchy. However, we observe that sometimes the order of the noun phrase may differ. For example, *"Authentication (Noun Phrase 1) via (connector) password (Noun Phrase 2)"*; *"Electronic signature (Noun Phrase 1) as (connector) authentication (Noun Phrase 2)"*. In this case, we check both noun phrases and if we find the exact match in any of the noun phrases, another is considered as sub-classes. We store the hierarchy with a standard representation language: Web Ontology Language (OWL) as follows:

<Declaration><Class IRI="#Security"/></Declaration>
<SubClassOf><ClassIRI="#Authentication"/><ClassIRI="#Security"/></SubClassOf>
<SubClassOf><ClassIRI="#Op_Biometric"/><ClassIRI="#Authentication"/></SubClassOf>
<SubClassOf><ClassIRI="#Op_Password"/><ClassIRI="#Authentication"/></SubClassOf>

The OWL is a semantic markup language for publishing and sharing ontologies on the World Wide Web. Moreover, OWL is supported by many ontology visualizers and editors, like Protégé 2.0, allowing the user to explore, understand, analyze or even modify the resulting ontology[2] easily. We present the algorithm to acquire knowledge for a QA as follows:

```
Algorithm 1: Acquire Knowledge
Input: QAn, Quality Standards/Documents, Selection Constraints
Output: SubQAn: Set of relevant Sub-QAs for a QAn
1. for all Qulaity_Doc do
2.    Dn: = Search_Concept (QAn, Quality_Doc)
3. end for
4. List_URLs : = Search_Engine(QAn)
5. for all URL in List_URLs do
6.    Page: = Download_Doc (URL)
7.    Dn: = Search_Concept(QAn, URL.Description)
8.    for all Link in Page do
9.    if Concept_match(QAn, Link.Description) then
10.    List_URLs: = Link
11.      end if
12.    end for
13. end for
14. for each statement (i) in Dn do
15. T: = Noun(Tagword(Dn[i]))UAdjective(Tagword(Dn[i]))U
          Verbs(Tagword(Dn[i])) U Adverb(Tagword(Dn[i])) U Wordsenwith (bility,
          -bilities, -ness) U NounPhrase(Dn[i]) U VerbPhrase(Dn[i])
16. end for
17. SubQAn = Filters(T)
18. Return SubQAn
```

---

[2] Ontology is a formal description of the concept of sharing, stressing the link between real entities [24]. The ontology helps domain users- to suggest their NFRs effectively and requirements analysts- to understand and model the NFRs accurately. Building ontology based on domain knowledge gives a formal and explicit specification of a shared conceptualization.

3.2 QARM Generation

In this module, we aim to define the relationship between sub-QAs. This procedure takes the input as a *SubQA* from the previous section and produces output as an ontological representation of QARM. The term-based weighting ignores the semantic relation between the SubQA. In order to overcome the weakness of the term-based weighting, in the proposed work we have combined two similarities- string similarity and ontology-based semantic similarity. For string similarity, we use the summation of normalized longest common subsequence (NLCS) measure, normalized maximum consecutive longest common subsequence starting at character 1 (NMCLCS1) and normalized maximum consecutive longest common subsequence starting at any character n (NMCLCSn) presented in [25].

$$v1 \leftarrow NLCS(SubQAi, \ SubQAj)$$
$$= len(LCS(SubQAi, SubQAj)) \ 2/len(SubQAi) \times len \ (SubQAj); \quad (1)$$

$$v2 \leftarrow NMCLCS1 \ (SubQAi, \ SubQAj)$$
$$= len(MCLCS1(SubQAi, SubQAj))2/len(SubQAi) \times len(SubQAj); \quad (2)$$

$$v3 \leftarrow NMCLCSn(SubQAi, SubQAj)$$
$$= len(MCLCSn(SubQAi, SubQAj))2/len(SubQAi) \times len(SubQA); \quad (3)$$

We take the weighted sum of these individual values *v1*, *v2*, and *v3* to determine string similarity weight: $wij = v1 + v2 + v3$. For ontology-based similarity, we use WordNet relatedness measure viz. Lesk [26] algorithm on our extracted knowledge for QAs. The Lesk algorithm [26] works on the concept of identifying relatedness of two terms based on the overlapping of the context of the two terms. The reason for using Lesk on our extracted knowledge is the unavailability of some of the sub-QAs in the existing ontology. For example, if we consider WordNet ontology, sub-QAs such as *login, operability, agility*, etc. are not defined and hence not able to find the similarity of such terms. We utilize the content of the *Dn* for the Lesk algorithm. The normalized QA relatedness:

$$w'ij = Nlesk(lesk(SubQAi, SubQAj)/100) \quad (4)$$

We present the algorithm as follows:

```
Algorithm 2: QARM Generation
Input   : SubQAn
Output: QARM Quality Attribute Relationship Matrix
1.Construct a string similarity matrix M1 = NLCS + NMCLCS1 +NMCLCSn
2.Construct an ontology-based relatedness (lesk) matrix M2
3.Construct a joint matrix QARM = M1 + M2
4.Return QARM
```

We represent the QARM in the form of triples such as *SubQA1, SubQA2, Relatedness/Relationship*. To determine how different QAs relate to each other, we compare every pair of QAs. By using such pairwise comparisons, it is possible to provide a matrix where the relation between QAs can be decided. To calculate relationship, we determine the percentage of similarity of each respective *SubQA:*

$$QAR = t + y/x \times 100\% \tag{5}$$

Where QAR = percentage of sub-QA similarity; t = QARM weight; $y = NSyno$ and $x = NAnto$. We find a number of synonyms and antonyms for each term using ontology WordNet as $NSyno = CountNum(Syno(Wi, Wj) \cup Hypo(Wi, Wj) \cup Poly(Wi, Wj))$ (Note that we use the hyponyms to identify the relationship between a generic term and a specific instance of it.) and $NAnto = CountAnto(Anto(Wi, Wj)$ respectively. Based on the percentage similarity of sub-QA, we define the relationship- (i) Positive (+): when one QA supports other QAs; (ii) Negative (−): when one QA adversely affects other QAs; (iii) Relative (*): when one QA, either supports or adversely affects other QAs.

4 Research Methodology

In order to assess the impact of our approach to construct an adaptive QARM semi-automatically, we conducted a controlled experiment on 18 QAs. We followed the guidelines provided in [27].

4.1 Research Questions

The following Research Questions (RQs) are established to evaluate our approach.

RQ1: *How can we semi-automatically extract the sub-QAs for a given QA?* The accuracy of our approach is partly driven by the sub-QAs extracted. With RQ1, we examine whether our approach can find the information for the QAs semi-automatically from available quality standards, industry documents and web search engines. Also, we analyze and compare the accuracy of the resulting sub-QAs.
RQ2: *To what extent the generated QARM can be useful to requirements analysts?* The overall goal of our experiment is to construct the QARM. In RQ2, we assess the accuracy of the generated QARM.

Viewing the RQs from an industry perspective, the questions would focus on how the requirements analysts semi-automatically discover the sub-QAs for newly discovered QA and perceive the relations among them. For example, the requirements analysts need to spend considerable time and non-trivial human effort to acquire knowledge for QAs and influence among them during the process of QRs conflict identification. This process involves the manual search and analysis of a large set of quality documents. Our approach parses these documents, extracts sub-QAs and constructs the QARM semi-automatically at requirements engineering phase. However, the requirements analysts should be aware of the QAs that are concerned with the system being developed. In addition, the approach needs an analyst to assess the correctness of the sub-QAs and QARM.

4.2 Experimental Setup

Our proposed approach has been developed in Java, due to the availability of a large number of libraries that facilitate the retrieval and parsing of web pages and the construction of ontologies. We use the following supporting tools/API:

1. Stanford-core NLP: It provides a wide range of algorithms for natural language processing, e.g. Stemming, PosTag, stop-word removal, etc.
2. Java API for WordNet Searching (JAWS): JAWS is a Java API for searching WordNet. It helps retrieve synonyms, hyponyms, etc. very easily.
3. jsoup: This HTML parser helps to fetch results from Google search and parse the html text.
4. Crawler4j: This is a web crawler API, that helps to crawl the websites retrieved from Google search.

To answer the RQs, we select 18 QAs viz. *Security, usability, performance, reliability, understandability, portability, maintainability, flexibility, supportability, testability, suitability, manageability, reusability, agility, mobility, ubiquity, invisibility,* and *enhanceability*. In our experiment, we classify these QAs into three categories:

(i) *Traditional QAs:* QAs that are well defined in the literature and their relationship details are available [5–8] such as *security, usability, performance, reliability, understandability,* and *portability*. With *traditional QAs*, we aim to validate the accuracy of the proposed approach with respect to the available literature.
(ii) *Traditional QAs but Lack of Relationship Details*: QAs that are well defined in the literature, but their relationship details are missing such as *maintainability, flexibility, supportability, testability, suitability, manageability,* and *reusability*. With this category of QAs, we aim to discover and analyze the relationship details that are missing in the literature [8];
(iii) *Emergent QAs*: QAs that are not yet systematically defined and their relationship details are missing [11, 12] such as *agility, mobility, ubiquity, invisibility,* and *enhanceability*. With *emergent QAs*, we aim to discover the sub-QAs for the recently discovered QAs and their relationships with the traditional QAs.

For experimental analysis, we use the following evaluation parameters:

(i)   Recall = TP/(TP + FN) *100;
(ii) Precision = TP/(TP + FP) *100;
(iii) F-measure = 2 *((precision * recall)/(precision + recall));

Where, TP = True Positive (Number of correctly identified sub-QAs), FP = False Positive (Number of incorrectly identified sub-QAs), and FN = False Negative (Number of sub-QAs incorrectly not identified).

4.3 Data Gathering and Analysis

To answer **RQ1**, we analyze quality standards and company documents that provide the definitions, characteristics, sub-QAs, and its implementation details. Moreover, we collect relevant concepts for the QAs, from the Google search. During our experimental study, we observed that some data are misleading, uninterpretable and required additional processing. We manually analyze the received data and define the following constraints:

(i)   According to our findings, the web search engine's initial pages are more comprehensive and important. Therefore, the maximum number of websites per search is limited to the first hundred results returned by the Google for our experimentation purpose.

(ii) We considered the maximum depth level (redirections) for finding the relevant terms.

(iii) We found from our experimental results that the minimum number of characters for a sub-QA should be at least four characters. Therefore, we have considered Sub-QAs with a minimum of four characters. The partial results of our experiments are available online[3]

(iv) In order to avoid processing irrelevant terms, the maximum number of results returned by the Google for each new sub-QA is set up to 1200 terms.

(v)   Different types of non-HTML document formats (.pdf and .doc) are processed by obtaining the HTML version from the Google's cache. Furthermore, through analyzing each sub-frame, we considered frame-based sites to obtain the complete set of texts.

We process the document in a text format. We extract adjective, noun, adverb, verb, noun phrase and verb phrase from the document. We retain stop-words within noun and verb phrases as they are important to find hierarchical relationships. From our experiment, we apply four filters as stated in Sect. 3.1. Our approach is based on the textual information available on the search engine and cannot deal with the information contained in the images and tables. To answer **RQ2**, we experimentally analyzed the semantic similarity of the collected sub-QAs. We define the range of positive, negative and relative relationships among QAs as shown in Table 2.

Table 2. Degree of relatedness based on semantic similarity

Percentage of similarity	Relationship
$45\% \leq QAR \leq 100\%$	Positive (+)
$31\% \leq QAR \leq 44\%$	Relative (*)
$QAR \leq 30\%$	Negative (−)

---

[3] https://github.com/UnnatiS/QARM-Generation/tesoutputfile1.txt.

5 Results and Discussion

In this section, we present and discuss the RQs based on the results of our approach.

5.1 Results

RQ1: In Table 3, we provide the results of the sub-QAs extracted semi-automatically for the 18 selected QAs. To validate the proposed approach, we first evaluate the accuracy of the sub-QAs collected (Table 3) for the *traditional QAs* by comparing them with the existing literature. We discover a total of 15 sub-QAs for the QA *performance*, where 12 sub-QAs viz. *Responsiveness, Latency, Throughput, Space, Capability, Execution rate, Delay, Loss, Consequence effect, Usage, Activeness, Resourcefulness* are matched with [8] and 3 sub-QAs viz. *Serviceability, Measurability* and *Reaction time* are new-found. We observed that in the literature [5–12], some sub-QAs are incorrect or redundant. For instance, in [8], the authors state 19 QAs viz. *Response time, Space, Capacity, Latency, Throughput, Computation, Execution speed, Transit delay, Workload, Resource utilization, Memory usage, Accuracy, Efficiency, Compliance, Modes, Delay, Miss rates, Data loss, Concurrent transaction Processing* for the QA *performance*.

However, QAs such as *"resource utilization and memory usage"*; *"transit delay and delay"*; *"computation, Execution speed and concurrent transaction processing"*;

Table 3. Experimental results of extracted sub-QAs

Category for Evaluation	QAs	Sub-Qas
Traditional QAs	Security (**S**)	Confidentiality, Integrity, Availability, Authentication, Access control, Privacy, Protection, Prevention, Reliability, Safety
	Performance (**P**)	Responsiveness, Latency, Throughput, Serviceability, Measurability, Capability, Resourcefulness, Space, Execution, rate, Reaction time, Scalability, Activeness
	Usability (**U**)	Simplicity, Understandability, Comfort, Informality, Operability, Ease of use, User service, Potentiality, Attractiveness, Likeliness, Accessibility, Familiarity
	Reliability (**R**)	Portability, Performance, Availability, Maturity, Accuracy, Precision, Recoverability, Operability, Maintainability, Consistency, Correctness, Satisfactorily, Dependability, Completeness, Robustness, Integrity
	Portability (**Po**)	Transferability, Changeability, Channelize, Transpose, Adjustability, Reusability, Interoperability, Extensibility, Dependability
	Understandability (**Un**)	Readability, Predictability, Organization of the document, Essential, Complexity, Verifiability, Visibility, Clarity, Controllability, Measurability, Reviewability

(continued)

Table 3. (*continued*)

Category for Evaluation	QAs	Sub-Qas
Traditional QAs but Lack of Relationship Details	Maintainability (**M**)	Operability, Upgrade, Performance, Evolution, Cost, Changeability, Analysability
	Suitability (**Su**)	Appropriateness, Usefulness, Readiness, Interrelate, Correctness
	Testability (**T**)	Ease, Validity, Examination
	Flexibility (**F**)	Ease, Interaction, Interface, Modifiability, Changeability, Maintainability, Adaptable, Simplicity
	Manageability (**Ma**)	Performance, Monitoring, Flexibility, Tractability
	Supportability (**Sp**)	Sustenance, Accompaniment, Reinforcement, Substantiate
	Reusability (**Ru**)	Probability, Changeability, Efficiency, Interchange, Evolution
Emergent QAs	Invisibility (**In**)	Transparency, Obviousness, Clearness, Diffusion, Interaction
	Enhancability (**En**)	Portability, Scalability, Flexibility, Evolution
	Ubiquity (**Ub**)	Attention, Safety, Privacy, Robust, Mobility, Efficiency, Inexpensive, Complexity, Context-aware, Transparency, Invisibility, Calmness, Availability
	Mobility (**Mo**)	Adaptability, Flexibility, Ubiquity, Portability, Multispace, support, Connectivity, Integrity, Availability, Motility, Movability, Manipulability
	Agility (**Ag**)	Changeability, Flexibility, Quickly, Operability, Easiness, Simplicity, Comfortness, Informality

"*Response time and processing*" are redundant. Furthermore, an attribute "*mode*" is not a valid sub-QA for the QA *performance*. To evaluate the extracted sub-QAs, we consider TP as sub-QAs that are matched with the literature (after removing redundant sub-QAs from literature); FN as sub-QAs that are newly discovered by our approach; FP as sub-QAs that are not identified by our approach. For instance, in [8], the authors stated a total of 19 sub-QAs for QA *performance*. From which 2 sub-QAs are redundant and 1 sub-QA is falsely considered. In our experiment, we identified a total of 15 sub-QAs for QA *performance*. From which 12 sub-QAs are matched with [8], 1 sub-QA is falsely considered and 3 sub-QAs are new-found. Based on these details, we calculate recall and precision for QA *performance* as **Recall** = Sub-QAs matched with the literature/(Sub-QAs matched with the literature + Sub-QAs newly discover by our approach) *100; Recall = $12/(12 + 3) = 80\%$; **Precision** = Sub-QAs matched with the literature)/(Sub-QAs matched with the literature + Sub-QAs our approach considered falsely))*100;

Precision $= 12/(12+4) = 75\%$. In Fig. 2, we provide a detailed analysis of the discovered sub-QAs with respect to the existing literature.

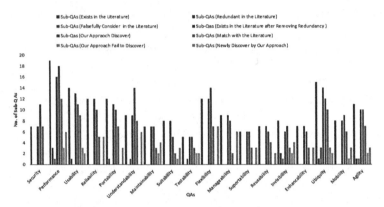

Fig. 2. Detailed analysis of the discovered sub-QAs

RQ2: In Table 4, we present the adaptive QARM generated semi-automatically after analyzing the QAs's taxonomy. The ontological representation of the constructed QARM is available online[4]. The constructed matrix (Table 4) extends and complements previously published QARM [8–11].

5.2 Discussion

The strength of the approach lies in its ability to quickly trawl through quality documents and web search engines to discover sub-QAs and to construct QARM. Even though the approach still requires an analyst to evaluate the correctness of the sub-QAs and QARM, it requires less manual effort than the approach discussed in [8–12].

An interesting observation of the results of our approach is how many sub-QAs we discovered semi-automatically compared to manual analysis. We discovered that the proposed approach achieves an average 85.67% recall, 59.07% precision and 69.14% F-measure to semi-automatically discover sub-QAs. We also observed that 38.88% (7/18) of the cases, the top 10–20 pages contain the relevant information and the top 20–50 pages contain the relevant information in 61.11% (11/18) of the cases. Furthermore, we found that 2.86% sub-QAs are falsely considered and 4.31% sub-QAs are redundant in the literature [5–8] on average. We discovered an average of 4% new sub-QAs for a given QA.

We constructed the QARM with positive, negative and relative relationships. According to existing literature [8–11], the resulting QARM is accurate. This QARM can be

---

[4] https://github.com/UnnatiS/QARM-Generation/.

Table 4. An adaptive quality attribute relationship matrix

QAs	S	P	U	R	Po	Un	M	Su	T	F	Ma	Sp	Ru	In	En	Web	Mo	Ag
S		*	*	+	−	*	−	*	*	−	+	*	−	−	*	*	−	−
P	*		*	−	+	+	−	+	−	−	−	−	*	−	*	−	−	−
U	*	*		*	+	+	*	+	*	+	−	−	+	*	−	+	*	*
R	+	−	*		−	*	−	+	+	+	*	*	−		+			
Po	−	+	+	−		*	−	*	+	+	−	+	+	−	+	+	+	−
Un	*	+	+	*	*		*	*	+	+	*	*	*	+	+	+	*	+
M	−	−	*	−	−	*		+	*	+	+	+	−	−	*		−	*
Su	*	+	+	+	*	*	+		+	−	*	*	*	+	+	+	*	−
T	*	−	*	+	+	+	*	+		−	−	*	*	−	*		−	−
F	−	−	+	+	+	+	+	−	−		−	*	−	+	−	+	+	+
Ma	+	−	−	*	−	*	+	*	−	−		*	*	−	+	*	−	−
Sp	*	−	−	*	+	*	+	*	*	*	*		*	+	+	*	+	+
Ru	−	*	+	−	+	*	−	*	*	−	*	*		−	+	−	+	+
In	−	−	*	*	−	+	−	+	−	+	−	+	−		*	+	+	*
En	*	*	−	+	+	+	*	+	*	−	+	+	+	*		*	+	+
Ub	*	−	+	−	+	+	−	+	−	+	*	*	−	+	+		+	*
Mo	−	−	*	−	+	*	−	*	−	+	−	+	+	+	+	+		+
Ag	−	−	*	−	−	+	*	−	−	+	−	+	+	*	+	*	+	

used to identify the conflicts among QRs in various software development phases. For instance, in the requirements engineering phase, during the elicitation process, system analysts would be able to identify the relationship among QRs. This analysis would allow developers to identify the conflicts among QRs early and to discuss this potential conflict with the system's stakeholders before specifying the software requirements. In addition, during the architecture design process, system designers would also be able to use the QARM to analyze the potential conflict among QRs in terms of the architecture decision. The relative relationship among QAs presented in the QARM would allow system designers to investigate the potential architecture strategies to get the best solution based on the type of conflicts among QRs. The proposed approach can be applied to the project management process when the project manager predicts QRs conflicts before implementing the system and then adjusts manpower, time, or cost-effectively and efficiently.

6   Threats to Validity

Even though we successfully construct QARM, we observe the following threats to the validity of our approach. A first possible threat is about the validity of the knowledge discovered from the search engine for the QAs, as the inaccuracy of the information leads to the false QARM generation. To mitigate this threat, we perform the experiments on 18 QAs. The experimental datasets and QARMs generated by the approach are manually analyzed by the authors. However, our evaluation might differ from an industry perspective because we use clear-cut definitions available on quality documents/search engine to identify QAs and influence among them, while industry relies on experience and implementation details. To mitigate this threat, the resultant sub-QAs and QARM are analyzed by three industry experts that are active in the field of software quality assurance. The industry experts observed that the approach identifies an average of 9.57% false relationships among QAs. For instance, we discovered a relative relationship between QAs *usability* and *manageability*. The industry experts argued that *"If the system is user-friendly then managing it will also be easy. Hence, QA usability has a positive relationship with QA manageability"*. In addition, our approach is based on textual information available on the search engine, for this reason, relevant information may be left undetected in several cases.

7   Conclusions

In this paper, we present an approach that semi-automatically constructs QARM, discovering knowledge from available quality standards/literature and search engines. This work helps the requirements analyst to visualize the relationship among QAs by means of the ontology. We evaluate the approach on 18 QAs and achieve 69.14% F-measure to extract sub-QAs. Also, we discover 4% of new sub-QAs that are not defined in the existing literature. Furthermore, we achieve 60% precision to identify the relationship between QAs. In the future, we aim to utilize the knowledge regarding operations through which QAs are to be achieved to enhance the QARM. The other direction of work we intend to pursue is to tackle the diverse meaning of the quality attributes such as *confidentiality* or *privacy*, *stability* or *robustness*, *fault-tolerance* or *resilience*, *flexibility* or *adaptability*, *evolution* or *adaptability*, *sustainability* or *durability*, *clarity* or *understandability*, *reasonability* or *predictability* that creates ambiguity using them in practice.

References

1. IEEE Computer Society, Software Engineering Standards Committee, and IEEE-SA Standards Board: IEEE recommended practice for software requirements specifications. Institute of Electrical and Electronics Engineers (1998)
2. Shah, U.S., Patel, S., Jinwala, D.: Specification of non-functional requirements: a hybrid approach. In: REFSQ Workshops (2016)
3. Guizzardi, R.S.S., Li, F.-L., Borgida, A., Guizzardi, G., Horkoff, J., Mylopoulos, J.: An ontological interpretation of non-functional requirements. In: FOIS, vol. 14, pp. 344–357 (2014)

4. Chung, L., Nixon, B.A., Yu, E., Mylopoulos, J.: Non-Functional Requirements in Software Engineering, 5th edn. Springer, Heidelberg (2012)
5. Egyed, A., Grunbacher, P.: Identifying requirements conflicts and cooperation: how quality attributes and automated traceability can help. IEEE Softw. **21**(6), 50–58 (2004)
6. ISO/IEC 9126-1:2001 Software engineering product quality-part 1: quality model. International Organization for Standardization (2001)
7. Duque-Ramos, A., Fernández-Breis, J.T., Stevens, R., Aussenac-Gilles, N.: SQuaRE: A SQuaRE-based approach for evaluating the quality of ontologies. J. Res. Pract. Inf. Technol. **43**(2), 159 (2011)
8. Mairiza, D., Zowghi, D., Nurmuliani, N.: Managing conflicts among non-functional requirements. In: Workshop on Requirements Engineering, pp. 11–19. University of Technology, Sydney (2009)
9. Sadana, V., Liu, XF.: Analysis of conflicts among non-functional requirements using integrated analysis of functional and non-functional requirements. In: 31st Annual International Computer Software and Applications Conference (COMPSAC 2007), vol. 1, pp. 215–218. IEEE (2007)
10. Abdul, H., Jamil, A., Imran, U.: Conflicts identification among non-functional requirements using matrix maps. World Acad. Sci. Eng. Technol. **44**, 1004–1009 (2010)
11. Mairiza, D., Zowghi, D., Gervasi, V.: Conflict characterization and analysis of non functional requirements: an experimental approach. In: 12th International Conference on Intelligent Software Methodologies, Tools and Techniques (SoMeT), September 2013, pp. 83–91. IEEE (2013)
12. Carvalho, R., Andrade, R., Oliveira, K., Kolski, C.: Catalogue of invisibility requirements for UbiComp and IoT applications. In: 26th International Requirements Engineering Conference (RE), pp. 88–99. IEEE (2018)
13. Maia, M.E., Rocha, L.S., Andrade, R.: Requirements and challenges for building service-oriented pervasive middleware. In: Proceedings of the 2009 International Conference on Pervasive Services, pp. 93–102. ACM (2009)
14. Carvalho, R.M., de Castro Andrade, R.M., de Oliveira, K.M.: AQUArIUM - a suite of software measures for HCI quality evaluation of ubiquitous mobile applications. J. Syst. Softw. **136**, 101–136 (2018)
15. Serrano, M.: Ubiquitous, pervasive and mobile computing: a reusable-models-based non-functional catalogue objectives of research. In: ER@ BR (2013)
16. Carvalho, R.M., de Castro Andrade, R.M., de Oliveira, K.M., de Sousa Santos, I., Bezerra, C.I.M.: Quality characteristics and measures for human-computer interaction evaluation in ubiquitous systems. Softw. Q. **25**(3), 743–795 (2017). https://doi.org/10.1007/s11219-016-9320-z
17. Miguel, J.P., Mauricio, D., Rodríguez, G.: A review of software quality models for the evaluation of software products. Int. J. Softw. Eng. Appl. **5**(6), 31–53 (2014)
18. Boehm, B.W., Brown, J.R., Kaspar, H.: Characteristics of Software Quality. North Holland, Amsterdam (1978)
19. McCall, J.A., Richards, P.K., Walters, G.F.: Factors in Software Quality. Volume I. Concepts and Definitions of Software Quality. General Electric Co., Sunnyvale (1977)
20. Grady, R.B., Caswell, D.L.: Software Metrics: Establishing a Company-Wide Program. Prentice Hall, Upper Saddle River (1987)
21. Dromey, R.G.: A model for software product quality. IEEE Trans. Softw. Eng. **21**(2), 146–162 (1995)
22. Shah, U.S., Jinwala, D.C.: Resolving ambiguities in natural language software requirements: a comprehensive survey. ACM SIGSOFT Softw. Eng. Notes **40**(5), 1–7 (2015)

23. Shah, U.S., Jinwala, D.C.: Resolving ambiguity in natural language specification to generate UML diagrams for requirements specification. Int. J. Softw. Eng. Technol. Appl. **1**(2–4), 308–334 (2015)
24. Gruber, T.R.: A translation approach to portable ontology specifications. Knowl. Acquis. **5**(2), 199–220 (1993)
25. Islam, A., Inkpen, D.: Semantic text similarity using corpus-based word similarity and string similarity. ACM Trans. Knowl. Discov. Data **2**(2), 1–25 (2008). Article No. 10
26. Banerjee, S., Pedersen, T.: An adapted Lesk algorithm for word sense disambiguation using WordNet. In: Gelbukh, A. (ed.) CICLing 2002. LNCS, vol. 2276, pp. 136–145. Springer, Heidelberg (2002). https://doi.org/10.1007/3-540-45715-1_11
27. Jedlitschka, A., Ciolkowski, M., Pfahl, D.: Reporting experiments in software engineering. In: Shull, F., Singer, J., Sjøberg, D.I.K. (eds.) Guide to Advanced Empirical Software Engineering, pp. 201–228. Springer, London (2008). https://doi.org/10.1007/978-1-84800-044-5_8

Evaluating the Effects of Different Requirements Representations on Writing Test Cases

Francisco Gomes de Oliveira Neto(✉), Jennifer Horkoff, Richard Svensson, David Mattos, and Alessia Knauss

Chalmers and the University of Gothenburg, Gothenburg, Sweden
{francisco.gomes,jennifer.horkoff,richard}@cse.gu.se,
{davidis,alessia.knauss}@chalmers.se

Abstract. [Context and Motivation] One must test a system to ensure that the requirements are met, thus, tests are often derived manually from requirements. However, requirements representations are diverse; from traditional IEEE-style text, to models, to agile user stories, the RE community of research and practice has explored various ways to capture requirements. [Question/problem] But, do these different representations influence the quality or coverage of test suites? The state-of-the-art does not provide insights on whether or not the representation of requirements has an impact on the coverage, quality, or size of the resulting test suite. [Results] In this paper, we report on a family of three experiment replications conducted with 148 students which examines the effect of different requirements representations on test creation. We find that, in general, the different requirements representations have no statistically significant impact on the number of derived tests, but specific affordances of the representation effect test quality, e.g., traditional textual requirements make it easier to derive less abstract tests, whereas goal models yield less inconsistent test purpose descriptions. [Contribution] Our findings give insights on the effects of requirements representation on test derivation for novice testers. Our work is limited in the use of students.

Keywords: Test design · Requirements representation · Experiment

1 Introduction

System testing is an essential activity for validation of a system before its release. Therefore, the set of test cases used to exercise the System Under Test (SUT) should achieve reasonable test coverage and be of good quality (i.e., be internally consistent, concrete, and independent). During test specification, a system tester can derive several test cases manually using the SUT requirements [7]. Similar to all complex manual activities, this kind of test case derivation is risky, as the resulting test suite can be biased by the tester's expertise and experience, and their comprehension of the SUT can be dependent on the type of specification [8].

© Springer Nature Switzerland AG 2020
N. Madhavji et al. (Eds.): REFSQ 2020, LNCS 12045, pp. 257–274, 2020.
https://doi.org/10.1007/978-3-030-44429-7_18

Providing test suites with good coverage and quality helps ensure, for example, that safety aspects and other non-functional requirements are fulfilled. However, the current state-of-the-art does not provide insights on whether or not the representation of requirements has an impact on the coverage, quality or size of the resulting test suite and test cases.

Hence, the objective of this study is to investigate how different requirements representations effect test case derivation. While requirements are traditionally specified in free text, recently two further types of requirements specifications have become popular in industry and/or academia: user stories and goal models. Goal models have a rich body of academic work [15], and have been advocated as a means to understand the motivations behind requirements. User stories are considered boundaries objects that facilitate sensemaking between different stakeholders and have proved popular in agile software development [3], which is becoming increasingly important in industry in different domains – even in safety critical domains [19]. Thus, in this initial study, we use textual requirements generally following the IEEE standard [17], user stories as per Cohn [3], and a simplified version of goal models as per the iStar 2.0 Standard [5]. Other representations may be equally valid, but we start with these selections due to their diversity and popularity.

Our general hypothesis is that by representing the same requirements in distinct formats (e.g. graphical models, text) we highlight different details that could facilitate or hinder the creation of sets of test cases. If our results showed that a particular requirements representation had a positive or negative impact on test case development, this would have an impact on the preferred format of requirements in practice, when requirements are used for test derivation.

The potential impact can be measured (i) on different attributes of a test case and (ii) on the challenges found when deriving tests for specific types of representation. Here, we focus on test suite size and quality attributes. Specifically, for size we measure the number of derived test cases (test suite size) [13], while for quality we measure errors in the derived tests and the coverage of the system's requirements. The measurement of errors is inspired by the taxonomy proposed by Felderer and Herrmann [8]. In turn, specific affordances of the different representation types can also affect practitioners in identifying relevant information, such as alternative scenarios or connection between requirements. Thus, we investigate the following research questions:

RQ1: Do the different requirements representations affect the derived tests?
    RQ1.1: Do they affect the number of tests created?
    RQ1.2: Do they affect the number of requirements covered by the tests?
    RQ1.3: Do they affect the number and nature of the test case errors?
RQ2: What are the challenges with deriving test cases from the different requirements representations?

In order to answer the research questions, we performed a family of experiments with three replications with 148 software engineering bachelor students. In three course instances (one for each replication), students were asked to derive system test cases based on different requirements representations, as described above. We analyse the artefacts created by participants (RQ1) and their answers to a questionnaires to identify obstacles during their derivation process (RQ2).

This paper is organized as follows: in Sect. 2 we provide background for the study and describe any related work, followed by the description of our methodology (Sect. 3). In Sect. 4 we describe our quantitative and qualitative results, and in Sect. 5 we use these results to answer our RQs, discussing threats to validity. We conclude and discuss future work in Sect. 6.

2   Related Work

Our experiment includes three different kinds of requirements representations (IEEE textual requirements, goal models, and user stories). Different requirements representations have their strengths and weaknesses in capturing and transferring different kinds of information [2]. For instance, goal models are an important requirements representations for self-adaptive systems due to the need of reasoning about requirements at runtime [1]; whereas, for agile software development, user stories are the method of choice [3].

This paper joins a large body of work experimentally evaluating requirements representations. Existing studies have looked at the effects of requirements formats on comprehensibility. For instance, in [12] authors compare Use Case and Tropos and show that Tropos models are more comprehensible, but more time consuming than Use Cases, such that their meta-analysis reveal that both languages yield similar productivity levels. Similarly, authors in [25] compare the comprehensibility of graphical and textual representations of requirements. The authors report no significant difference in participant's comprehensibility between both types, even though the subjects required more time and effort to work with the graphical representation. On the other hand, for specific purposes (e.g., security risk assessment), the difference between graphical and textual is more noticeable, particularly, tabular risk models are more effective [22]. Nonetheless, the studies suggest that the structure of the representation leads subjects to follow different strategies in understanding the system. But none of them evaluate requirements representations for their effect on test derivation.

In turn, manual test case derivations has been widely investigated in literature [8,9,13,18], given the benefits of having test cases properly aligned with system requirements [6]. For instance, researchers in [13] and [18] investigate the effects of derived tests in, respectively, test-driven (TDD) and behavioural-driven (BDD) development practices. Particularly, there is a statistically significant difference between the derived tests and the different levels of granularity used to describe development tasks [18]. Moreover, other empirical studies report that the difficulties of breaking down requirements into test cases hinders the alignment between requirements and tests, particularly, at large-scale companies [6].

The taxonomy in [8] is designed to measure errors based on elements of activity diagrams, used here as requirements input. The work examines elements such as missing conditions or very concrete input data. Authors analyse specific artefacts of the test case (e.g., scenario, expected result, condition), and their level of description (too concrete, abstract, or missing) from a single requirements representation. Since we have different representations, we reuse the idea of measuring errors in parts of test cases, but use fewer levels of description. For instance, we also detect abstract test cases and missing preconditions, but we do not measure the expected results of the derived tests. Instead, we measure the purpose of the test, density of scenarios described per test among other errors.

3   Research Method

We define our family of experiments in terms of the guidelines proposed in [26]. We analyse *different requirements representation* for the purpose of *comparison* with respect to *effectiveness* from the point of view of the *tester* in the context of *software engineering students*.

Subjects. The students participating as testers in the study are third-year Software Engineering and Management Bachelor's students at the University of Gothenburg (Sweden). Between 2017 and 2019, a total of 148 students (59, 54 and 35) participated in the experiments. We summarize the experience of the students in requirements and testing in Table 1. The students had a regular 2 month course in testing and verification, but did not have an explicit course in Requirements Engineering. Furthermore, several students had some industrial experience leading to a fairly heterogeneous sample, which can be seen in the high standard deviation (Table 1).

The experiments took place in a course on research methods, where participation in the experiment was optional, they could either attend the experiment or design a simple experiment themselves. Prior to the experiment, participants were made aware that participation is anonymous and their performance would not affect their course grade. In the last replication, students had the option to attend, but not submit their data for research use, thus the lower number of participants for 2019.

Table 1. Subjects experience (in months) in testing and with used requirements per treatment (Textual Requirements (TR), User Stories (US), Goal Models (GM))

	Experience with testing				Experience with requirements			
	All	TR	US	GM	All	TR	US	GM
Mean	7	7	6	9	11	11	19	3
Median	2	2	2.5	2	2.5	3	24	0
SD	10.9	12	7.8	12.5	13.9	14.8	12.9	8

Independent, Dependent, and Controlled Variables. Our experiment has one factor (requirements representation) with three levels: Goal Models (GM),

User Stories (US), and Textual Requirements (TR). In terms of controlled variables, all participants receive the same test case template (based on [16]) and worked with the same system under test (SUT). The SUT was a code editor tool similar to, e.g., Atom (https://atom.io/), which the main functional requirements were save files, syntax highlighting for supported languages (HTML, Java and Javascript), and live preview of webpages for HTML coding. In turn, non-functional requirements referred to compatibility with different Operating Systems (e.g. Windows 7, MacOS, etc.), browsers (Google Chrome, Firefox, Safari and Edge), and performance time of certain functions.

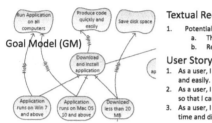

Textual Requirement (TR)
1.   Potential users must be able to download and install the application.
     a.   The application should run on Window 7 and above, and Mac OS 10 and above.
     b.   Release should have a size of no more than 20 MB.

User Story (US)
1.   As a user, I want to download and install the application so that I can produce code quickly and easily.
2.   As a user, I want the application to run on Window 7 and above, and Mac OS 10 and above so that I can run the application on all of my computers.
3.   As a user, I don't want to download an Application of more than 20 MB, so that I can save time and disk space.

Fig. 1. Excerpts of the equivalent requirements representations given to participants

The same requirements were specified in the three different representations. To ensure consistent and equivalent information as much as is afforded by the representations, we had a requirements engineering expert create and examine the different requirements documents used in our experiment. See Fig. 1 for an excerpt of the three requirements representations. The supplementary material can be found here: https://tinyurl.com/refsqexperiment.

The dependent variables are: (i) the size of the test suite measured as the number of derived test cases, (ii) the amount and types of errors in the derived test cases and (iii) the number of system requirements covered by the derived tests. In order to measure requirements coverage, we verify which of the following 18 requirements (functional or non-functional) are mentioned in the derived tests: (1) download the application, (2) install the application, (3) write/edit code, (4) save content in files, (5) save a file in less than 0.5 s, (6) syntax highlighting of code, working with (7) Java, (8) Javascript or (9) HTML, (10) have at least 20 MB of space for installing, running the application on (11) Windows or (12) MacOS, (13) see a live preview of HTML files, and usage of a (14) default browser, (15) Chrome, (16) Firefox, (17) Safari or (18) Edge. More details about the derived tests and the collected data is found in our supplementary material.

Hypotheses and Statistical Analysis. Each participant received a single requirements representation to derive tests. We use a balanced design [26] to randomly assign participants to treatments while keeping roughly the same amount of participants per treatment. Moreover, our null hypotheses is that there are no statistically significant differences between the different representation types, whereas our alternative hypotheses (two sided) checks for differences between the representation types (Table 2).

Table 2. Description of formal hypotheses and corresponding statistical tests for the variables size (S), coverage (C) and errors (E). Each row of hypothesis is connected to, respectively, RQ1.1, RQ1.2 and RQ1.3.

Null hypotheses	Alternative hypotheses	Statistical test
H_{01} : S(GM) = S(TR) = S(US)	H_{11} : S(GM) $\neq$ S(TR) $\neq$ S(US)	Kruskal-Wallis
H_{02} : C(GM) = C(TR) = C(US)	H_{12} : C(GM) $\neq$ C(TR) $\neq$ C(US)	Kruskal-Wallis
H_{03} : E(GM) = E(TR) = E(US)	H_{13} : E(GM) $\neq$ E(TR) $\neq$ E(US)	χ^2

We use a Kruskal-Wallis and a χ^2 test to compare statistically significant differences between all three levels, such that the alternative hypothesis is that the levels differ in *at least one*. Therefore, to identify specific differences between each pair of levels (e.g., GM vs. TR), we also do a posthoc analysis using a pairwise test with Bonferroni-Holm correction for the p-values to avoid validity threats related to alpha inflation [23]. For H_{01} and H_{02}, we use a pairwise Mann-Whitney test, whereas for H_{03} we use χ^2 between two levels. We choose non-parametric tests since they rely on fewer assumptions regarding the data distribution (e.g., normality) [23]. We choose χ^2 for H_{03} because we collect nominal data (error vs. no error). Conversely, we collect interval data for H_{01} and H_{02} (size and coverage) such that Kruskal-Wallis can be used.

Instruments and Execution. All groups were given the same lecture about system testing and test specification, along with paper instructions and examples for the specific requirements representation that they received. At the end of the experiment execution, we also gave them a questionnaire to capture qualitative data, such as background information (e.g., previous experience) and facilitators or inhibitors for generating test cases with that specific requirement.

The 90-min experiment execution session was divided in two parts of 45 min. During the first part, the participants were given a 30-min introductory lecture on system testing and a general description of the application that they needed to test (without pointing out specific requirements). Then, they spent 15 min reading through their assigned requirements representation. After a 15 min break, 45 min was focused only on deriving test cases for the application by filling in the provided template. Then participants had another 15 min to fill out the questionnaire, except for 2017, where we had online submissions, and participants could submit the questionnaire answers after the experiment ended. In 2017, test cases were written electronically, and a few participants submitted online after the experiment. The other years were executed on paper in class, to avoid risks with online submissions and availability of labs with computers for all students.

Data Analysis. After the experiments, the test cases and the questionnaires were anonymized and manually coded. The test cases were coded in a five-step

Table 3. Description of the test case error codes with corresponding inter-rater agreement (Krippendorff's alpha). The bold codes were used in the study.

Artefact	Error code	α_K	Code description
Test case	**Abstract**	**0.53**	The overall TC is not concrete enough, lacking important information to perform the test
	Many Scenarios	**0.64**	The TC covers too many scenarios
Purpose	**Inconsistent**	**0.44**	The purpose of the TC is inconsistent with the pre-conditions or the steps
	Unspecified	**0.51**	The purpose does not match any requirement
	Poor phrasing	0.15	The content written in the field is not phrased as a purpose
	Missing	1.00	Absence of the purpose field
Pre-condition	Dependent test	0.00	The test depends on another TC
	Poor phrasing	0.20	The pre-conditions are written either in terms of an action or are not a pre-condition
	Missing	**0.70**	When a precondtion is needed to execute the test, but it is not there
Step	Invalid	0.16	The step is not a system response
	Missing response	0.00	There is an action without a system response
	No steps	1.00	The whole step section is blank
Additional information	**Misplaced**	**0.56**	Information that should have been placed in other field of the same TC

process. In step 1, we reviewed the taxonomy in [8] and devised 13 codes to represent faults and errors in five different parts (artefacts) of the test cases as depicted in Table 3: test case (two error codes), the purpose of the test (four codes), the pre-conditions to execute the test (three codes), the test steps (three codes) and any additional information written by users (one code).

In step 2 and 3 of our coding process, we randomly selected 10% of the participants (stratified by year and representation), and had three authors code all of their derived test cases in order to test for inter-coder reliability. We measured agreement via the Krippendorff's α_K inter-rater reliability score. We chose α_K because it assesses the agreement between more than 2 independent raters and can be used on nominal data (error vs. no error). The result is a value between [-1,1], such that 1 means total agreement between raters, zero means a random agreement, and negative values indicate systematic disagreement between raters [14]. There are different thresholds to indicate strong, moderate or weak agreement based on the α_K value. Here, we use the thresholds defined in [11] previously used in other software engineering studies [21], where an α_K between 0.4 and 0.75 indicates fair to good agreement, whereas excellent agreement is seen on values above 0.75. After each step, we calculated α_K and discussed and refined the codes, removing those with low agreement (below 0.4).

Table 3 presents the α_K for each error (Krippendorff's α_K was calculated using the R package irr https://CRAN.R-project.org/package=irr, analysis scripts are provided in the supplementary material). In step 4, we reached agreement for eight codes. Even though the codes for *missing purpose* and *no steps* had excellent agreement ($\alpha_K = 1$), these codes occurred very infrequently. Therefore, we did not consider them in our analysis, focusing on six codes. In the fifth step, we split the remaining participants equally into three parts, and the three authors independently coded one part with the highlighted codes from Table 3. The same steps were used when coding the requirements coverage of each test. A requirement was considered "covered" if participants mentioned its particular characteristics in their test cases (e.g., test requires Windows or MacOS). For the sake of space, and since there was agreement on all coverage codes (i.e. all $\alpha_K \geq 0.4$), the specific α_K values are included in our supplementary material.

In order to answer RQ2, we use thematic analysis for qualitative analysis of the questionnaires in order to extract the different challenges reported by participants [4]. We coded the answers by dividing the questions among three of the authors. The coding was then later checked by a different author.

4   Results

4.1   RQ1: Do the Different Representations of Requirements Affect the Produced Tests?

First, we checked the data and found no severe outliers or inconsistencies between the results for each representation (Table 4) that could impact our statistical analysis. Then, we verify: (i) the size of the derived test suite (RQ1.1), (ii) the requirements coverage of each generated test suite (RQ1.2), and (iii) the number of errors found in the test cases (RQ1.3). For each, we first identify whether there is statistically significant difference between any of the levels ($p < 0.05$), then we do a pairwise test to identify which pair(s), specifically, is different, and lastly we analyse the effect size to detect the magnitude and direction of the difference.

Table 4. Summary of the data, aggregated by requirements representation.

Specification	Participants	Tests	Errors	Test suite size			Coverage		
				Mean	Median	SD	Mean	Median	SD
Goal model	48	209	277	4.2	4	1.8	8.9	9	3.5
Text requirement	49	214	280	4.3	4	1.8	10.7	10	3.9
User stories	51	232	267	4.9	4	2.8	9.0	8	3.6
Total	148	655	824	–	–	–	–	–	–

Table 5 shows the statistical test results for size and coverage. Regarding the size, there was no statistically significant difference between the number of tests generated by each participant. Both the Kruskal-Wallis tests ($p = 0.85$) and the post-hoc analysis ($p = 1$ for all pairwise comparisons) indicate that we cannot reject the null hypothesis (H_{01}) that there are no differences between requirements representations with respect to the size of the derived test suites.

Table 5. The p-values of all Kruskal-Wallis and Mann-Whitney (pairwise) tests. We highlight the values that are lower than our chosen level of significance $\alpha = 0.05$.

Dependent variable	GM = TR = US	GM = US	GM = TR	TR = US
Test suite size	0.85	1.00	1.00	1.00
Requirements coverage	**0.04**	0.95	0.07	0.07

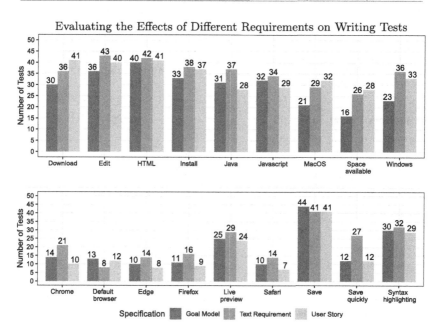

Fig. 2. Number of tests derived for each requirements and representation type.

Figure 2 shows the number of tests that cover each requirement. We asked the participants (Q8 in the questionnaire) to report reasons whenever they felt unable to cover all the requirements with test cases. Regardless of which type of requirement representations the participants used, all participants agreed that the two main reasons for not being able to cover all requirements with test cases were *Lack of time* (76% of all participants) and *Lack of experience* (20.3% of all participants), where the participants referred to lack of experience with requirements in general, testing in general, and with writing test cases. Nonetheless, text requirements have higher coverage in most cases (13 out of 18). In fact, our Kruskal-Wallis test revealed a difference in requirements coverage between the representations ($p = 0.04$). However, our post-hoc analysis (pairwise test) attributes this difference to TR ($p = 0.07$ in Table 5 when comparing TR with other representations). Looking closer at the data (Table 4), TR covers one or two more requirements compared to the other representations (both for mean and median), however, TR coverage has higher standard deviation.

For errors, the requirements representation yield a similar amount of errors when deriving test cases. However, looking at the significant differences in specific types of errors (Table 6) and the percentage of errors (Fig. 3), we notice differences between the requirements representations, particularly in three areas. First, participants using textual requirements derived fewer abstract test cases. Second, participants using user stories derived tests without many scenarios at once. Lastly, participants using goal models wrote fewer inconsistent purposes.

Table 6. The p-values of all χ^2 test. We highlight the values that are lower than our chosen level of significance $\alpha = 0.05$, and the corresponding variable.

Dependent variable	GM = TR = US	GM = US	GM = TR	TR = US
Inconsistent purpose	**0.02**	0.28	**0.03**	0.30
Unspecified purpose	0.60	1.00	1.00	1.00
Missing pre-condition	0.32	0.48	0.96	0.96
Misplaced information	0.40	0.98	1.00	0.98
Abstract tests	**0.01**	0.14	**0.01**	0.20
Too many scenarios	**0.01**	0.30	0.30	**0.01**

For effect size analysis of errors, we use the Odds Ratio to identify the ratio of the odds of making errors due to the requirements representation. Odds ration is recommended for data with binary categories and it does not assume specific data distributions (e.g., normality). A ratio value of 1 indicates that the odds

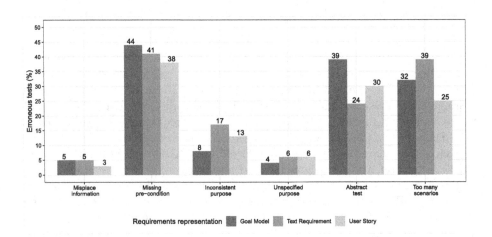

Fig. 3. Percentage of errors made when using GM, TR or US.

of deriving erroneous tests are the same for both requirements representations. When comparing the odds ratio between two requirements representations A and B, if the odds ratio is greater than 1, then compared to the requirements representation A, the opposing representation B *raises* the odds of making an error. Conversely, a value less than 1 indicates that B lowers the odds of making an error. The odds ratio for the statistically significant comparisons are presented in Table 7 and are summarised below:

- The odds are 2.05 greater that a participant wrote an inconsistent purpose when using text requirements instead of goal models.
- The odds are 1.93 greater that a participants writes an abstract test case using goal models, in comparison to text requirements.
- The odds are 0.54 less that a participant writes a test with too many scenarios using user stories, in comparison to text requirements.

Table 7. The odds ratio for each comparison with confidence intervals (CI).

Type of error	Comparison	Estimated odds	95% CI
Inconsistent purposes	GM vs TR	2.05	$[1.14, 3.71]$
Abstract test cases	TR vs GM	1.93	$[1.27, 2.92]$
Too many scenarios	TR vs US	0.54	$[0.36, 0.81]$

Note that the CI for both the inconsistent purposes and abstract test cases are wide, indicating high variance of the odds ratio. Nonetheless, results were significant at $\alpha = 0.05$ and it complies with the total differences seen in Fig. 3.

4.2   RQ2: What Are the Challenges with Deriving Test Cases from the Different Requirements Representations?

We found challenges using two perspectives: (i) deriving test cases from the requirement representations (Q3 in the questionnaire, see supplementary material) and (ii) writing test cases for requirements (Q5). Our goal was, respectively, to allow participants to report on difficulties related to thinking about test cases (e.g., extracting scenarios from the requirements) and documenting them (e.g., placing information in the test case template). Both questions were open-ended, thus the participants could write more than one challenge.

The results, including sub-challenges,are shown in Table 8. For the challenges *No challenge*, *Lack of experience*, and *Lack of time*, no sub-challenges were mentioned by the participants. Table 8 shows how many participants and the percentage of the participants that stated a certain challenge, e.g., for deriving test cases, 43 participants (referred to as *All* in Table 8) which is 31% of all participants, stated that there was no challenge (43/31 in column All under Deriving test cases). Note that the sum of the number of participants in the sub-categories

Table 8. Reported challenges with deriving/writing test cases. Each cell includes the number of participants that reported on the challenge (absolute/percentage).

Challenge	(i) Deriving test cases				(ii) Writing test cases			
	All	TR	US	GM	All	TR	US	GM
No challenge	43/31	17/37	12/24	14/33	56/41	18/39	21/42	17/40
Requirement representations	30/22	7/15	13/26	10/24	22/16	5/11	10/20	7/17
Too abstract requirements	5/4	1/2	1/2	3/7	0/0	0/0	0/0	0/0
Confusion with specific req.	4/3	2/4	2/4	0/0	2/1	1/2	1/2	0/0
Where to start/end	4/3	1/2	2/4	1/2	3/2	0/0	1/2	2/5
Unclear requirements	1/1	1/2	0/0	0/0	6/4	3/7	3/6	0/0
Req. not prioritised	3/2	2/4	0/0	1/2	2/1	0/0	1/2	1/2
Lack of details in req.	0/0	0/0	0/0	0/0	2/1	1/2	1/2	0/0
Completeness	0/0	0/0	0/0	0/0	2/1	0/0	1/2	1/2
Repetitive US	3/2	0/0	3/6	0/0	0/0	0/0	0/0	0/0
Vague US	3/2	0/0	3/6	0/0	0/0	0/0	0/0	0/0
US difficult	2/1	0/0	2/4	0/0	0/0	0/0	0/0	0/0
GM too complex	4/3	0/0	0/0	4/10	0/0	0/0	0/0	0/0
GM too hard to understand	1/1	0/0	0/0	1/2	3/2	0/0	0/0	3/7
Creating test cases	29/21	6/13	19/38	4/10	23/17	6/13	12/24	5/12
Level of abstraction	12/9	2/4	7/14	3/7	3/2	0/0	2/4	1/2
Decide what to test together	5/4	2/4	3/6	0/0	0/0	0/0	0/0	0/0
Completeness of TC	2/1	0/0	2/4	0/0	3/2	0/0	3/6	0/0
Hard to add details	2/1	0/0	2/4	0/0	2/1	0/0	2/4	0/0
Quality requirements	2/1	1/2	0/0	1/2	2/1	1/2	0/0	1/2
Too similar TC	2/1	1/2	1/2	0/0	0/0	0/0	0/0	0/0
Level of details in steps	1/1	0/0	1/2	0/0	3/2	0/0	2/4	1/2
TC template	0/0	0/0	0/0	0/0	6/4	2/4	2/4	2/5
Missing information	18/13	8/17	2/4	8/19	5/4	2/4	0/0	3/7
General information	12/9	4/9	1/2	7/17	1/1	1/2	0/0	0/0
Product information	8/6	6/13	1/2	1/2	2/1	0/0	0/0	2/5
Missing requirements	0/0	0/0	0/0	0/0	3/2	2/4	0/0	1/2
Lack of experience	11/8	4/9	6/12	1/2	9/7	5/11	3/6	1/2
Lack of time	6/4	1/2	3/6	2/5	7/5	4/9	2/4	1/2

may not be equal to the value of the main category in Table 8. There are two reasons for this. First, only sub-categories that were mentioned by at least two participants are shown in Table 8, but that participant is added to the value of the main category. Second, participants could write more than one challenge, e.g. one participant could write that one challenge was "vague US" and another one was "repetitive US", then the number for each of these sub-categories would increase by one, but the value of the main category would only be increased by one since we count number of unique participants. In total, 138 participants answered the questionnaire, of which 46 participants used TR, 50 used US, and 42 used GM.

Only 13 and 10% of all participants using TR and GM reported challenges related to creating test cases from the perspective of deriving test cases, whereas almost 40% (19 out of 50) of the participants using US reported difficulties. For challenges related to writing test cases, regardless of the representation, about 40% of the participants reported no challenges.

Looking into the challenge of *Requirement representations* when deriving test cases, for participants using TR, this challenge had a lower impact compared to participants using US and GM (Table 8). When looking into challenges related to *Requirement representations* when writing test cases, we see a similar pattern as for deriving test cases from the requirements, i.e., this challenge had a lower impact for participants using TR compared to US and GM.

When it comes to the different representations, our results show that US and GM led to slightly more challenges with deriving test cases from the requirements and for writing test cases compared to TR. One participant using GM explained that the goal models were too complex because *"the model seemed quite chaotic with lines crossing each other"*. One US participant explained that deriving test cases was challenging as the USes were very vague – we could write endless amounts of test cases for one US.

Looking into the challenge of *Creating test cases*, we see that this was considered to be a much bigger challenge for participants using US compared to participants using TR and GM, especially for deriving test cases (US: 38% of the participants, TR: 13%, GM: 10%), as illustrated in Table 8.

Regarding the challenge of "missing information" when deriving test cases, for TR, the main missing information was information about the product itself (6 out of 46 participants), while participants using GM was mainly missing general information (7 out of 42 participants). As an example, one participant using TR explained what kind of product information that was missing, *"with the lack of a GUI example of the system it became harder"*. One participant using GM explained, *"I found it hard to derive test cases from the goal models. Goals like 'Produce code' gives little to no help in regards to creating test cases."*.

Surprisingly, *Lack of experience* was reported as a bigger challenge for participants using TR and US than those using GM, despite their relative lack of experience with GM (Table 1).

5 Discussion

Here we discuss our results for each research question. Considering the effects of the representations on tests (RQ1), we found that the representations do not produce significantly or noticeably different number of tests per representation (RQ1.1). We also found weak evidence that TR produce better requirements coverage (RQ1.2); however, there was a lot of variance in this result. Furthermore, the representations do have some effect on the errors found in tests (RQ1.3).

Those with TR made more errors adding too many scenarios to one test case (e.g., installing and editing) compared to US. This may be due to the hierarchical nature of TR, e.g., sub-requirements (see TR in Fig. 1 for an example), leading participants to group these requirements into one test case. However, GMs also have an implicit hierarchy, and although they produced higher numbers of this type of errors than US, this difference was not significant.

Given the nature of GMs, it is not so surprising that they helped the participants create a purpose description which was consistent with the rest of the test when compared to TR. It is interesting that this positive effect could be observed even given that students had no experience with goal models (Table 1). This effect was not noticed in comparison with US, perhaps because they also have a build-in purpose, with the <so that> section. However, US did not perform better than TR in this regard. Thus, we see there is a positive effect of explicitly including purpose in the requirements, and this appears to be best served (amongst our three options) by GM.

However, GM had the disadvantage of producing more abstract test cases, not including specific technical information of the SUT (e.g., tests for specific browsers). This information was present in the model, but was superseded by a parent goal. Perhaps the participants focused on the parents and ignored the children. Thus, this hierarchical structure seemed to encourage abstraction, undesirable in testing [8]. However, TR also had a hierarchical structure via indenting requirements in sub-requirements, yet, this representation produced the least abstract test cases. It seems in TR, participants were more likely to notice these specific details.

In RQ2, we looked at reported challenges deriving test cases from the various representations. Here we see that many did not report challenges, either because there were none, or the students did not want to write them out. Many challenges reported were not directly related to the requirements format, e.g., missing product information, lack of experience and lack of time. We can conclude that writing test cases for students from requirements without seeing the SUT is difficult, regardless of the representation.

Further reported challenges related more directly to the different requirements formats. Quite a few participants reported that GMs were too abstract, too complex or hard to understand, and several participants also found US vague, difficult or repetitive, yet we do not see that either format performed significantly worse overall in terms of errors (Table 4). Overall, from the qualitative questionnaire results, we see issues with all requirements representations, GM and US both had specific complaints about their format, while TR were more often seen as unclear, but US had more complaints in terms of perceived completeness of tests, level of abstraction of test cases, and adding detail.

Comparing the two sets of results, it is interesting that participants particularly complained about abstraction when deriving tests from USes, yet the error results showed US performed better than GM in that respect (Abstract test in Table 3). Furthermore, it is interesting that only some participants perceived their US-derived tests to be relatively incomplete, when all representations performed similarly in terms of completeness.

To summarize, writing test cases without seeing the SUT is hard for novel testers, and one representation does not stand out as clearly better. This is in line with related work comparing graphical to textual requirements for other purposes, e.g., [25]. From the quantitative results, one may recommend US as a format which balances between errors. However, in our qualitative results, students struggle more with US, even though they have experience with this representation. As such, it may be desirable to provide more than one type of representation, if possible. Ideally, a goal model to emphasize the purpose and provide structure, but also a textual format which emphasizes technical details.

In the end, we can make recommendations over the desired properties of requirements representations, rather than recommend a specific (set of) representations. Our extracted desired properties (i.e. requirements over requirements representation for the purpose of system testing) can be summarized below. As with any realistic requirements, one can find conflicts.

- Requirements representations should contain the purpose, here a graphical form seems to work best.
- Hierarchical requirements lead to tests with too many scenarios, thus hierarchy should be avoided when using requirements to derive tests, or extra training is needed to emphasize individual testing of specific scenarios.
- Hierarchy can be good for noticing detail in requirements, thus either it should be used, or another way of emphasizing details is needed (e.g., font).

5.1   Threats to Validity

Construct Validity: One construct validity threat is the representativeness of our dependent variables to assess quality of derived tests. We mitigate this threat by choosing variables also used in software testing literature, such as test suite size, coverage [13] and comprehensibility [8,9].

We have described and provided the results of our qualitative coding process, including agreements scores (Table 3). Although we were able to reach sufficient agreement on several errors, we can observe that in general getting good agreement on test errors is challenging, there were several errors that either did not appear frequently enough to evaluate sufficiently, or over which we disagreed, and had to be dropped. It is our impression that if these further errors had been included, it would not have greatly changed our results, i.e., we did not notice significant differences in these errors with different requirements representations.

In order to ensure consistent information among different requirements representations [20], we asked a requirements engineering expert to write the requirements followed by reviews from all authors. However, the different representations provide different affordances, meaning that exact equivalence was not possible. Nonetheless, these differences in affordance are exactly what motivates our research, i.e., which representations better facilitate test derivation.-

Internal Validity: There were small design differences between 2017 and the following two years (electronic test cases, submission after the session). Although this is a potential threat, we see no statistically significant results across years. To mitigate internal validity threats, all students, regardless of the year, were given the same instruments, and their grade on the course was not affected by the performance in this experiment. Moreover, the introductory lecture on system testing helps to level participants' knowledge and skill in deriving test cases from a high-level specification, whereas the balanced design avoids grouping based on knowledge and disparate sample sizes.

External Validity: Here, we used students as subjects. However, existing work has shown similar results between students and professionals in experiments in some contexts [24] and we address the ethical and validity concerns related to using students in empirical studies [10]. Furthermore, our participants were third year bachelor students in software engineering with practical experience through project courses, sometimes carried out in industry. Nonetheless, we cannot generalize our results for the population of software testers. Additionally, this study was conducted only in one university in one country.

In this series of initial experiments we have used a simple application that would be understandable by our participants, and would better enable them to complete the task in time. More complex, detailed or unfamiliar applications may have had an effect on our results. Future work should repeat our experiment with applications from different domains with a variety of sizes and complexity closer to real-world problems in software development.

6   Conclusion

We have evaluated whether three types of requirements representations, common in the RE community, have an effect on the quality and coverage of produced test cases. Although we have found some qualitative and quantitative differences with the various representations, much of our findings points to the difficulty of creating test cases using only requirements for novice testers in general. We have used our findings which relate specifically to the representation types to provide some recommendations when using different requirements representations to derive tests. Our findings can help to understand the effects of different requirements formats on testing, can help us to improve our requirements representations for this purpose, and can help to guide better training for testers.

Future work should repeat this study with more experienced testers to investigate whether the different representations have more significant or different effects, and should look again at the types of errors that can be measured over the resulting tests, addressing the problem of consistently coding test errors.

References

1. Bencomo, N., Whittle, J., Sawyer, P., Finkelstein, A., Letier, E.: Requirements reflection: requirements as runtime entities. In: International Conference on Software Engineering, (ICSE), pp. 199–202. ACM/IEEE (2010)

2. Brill, O., Schneider, K., Knauss, E.: Videos vs. use cases: can videos capture more requirements under time pressure? In: Wieringa, R., Persson, A. (eds.) REFSQ 2010. LNCS, vol. 6182, pp. 30–44. Springer, Heidelberg (2010). https://doi.org/10.1007/978-3-642-14192-8_5

3. Cohn, M.: User Stories Applied: For Agile Software Development. Addison Wesley Longman Publishing Co., Inc., Redwood City (2004)

4. Cruzes, D.S., Dyba, T.: Recommended steps for thematic synthesis in software engineering In: International Symposium on Empirical Software Engineering and Measurement, pp. 275–284, September 2011

5. Dalpiaz, F., Franch, X., Horkoff, J.: istar 2.0 language guide (2016). https://arxiv.org/abs/1605.07767

6. de Oliveira Neto, F.G., Horkoff, J., Knauss, E., Kasauli, R., Liebel, G.: Challenges of aligning requirements engineering and system testing in large-scale agile: A multiple case study. In: 2017 IEEE 25th International Requirements Engineering Conference Workshops (REW), pp. 315–322, September 2017

7. Felderer, M., Beer, A., Peischl, B.: On the role of defect taxonomy types for testing requirements: Results of a controlled experiment. In: 2014 40th Euromicro Conference on Software Engineering and Advanced Applications (SEAA), pp. 377–384 (2014)

8. Felderer, M., Herrmann, A.: Manual test case derivation from uml activity diagrams and state machines: a controlled experiment. Inf. Soft. Technol. **61**, 1–15 (2015)

9. Felderer, M., Herrmann, A.: Comprehensibility of system models during test design: a controlled experiment comparing uml activity diagrams and state machines. Soft. Qual. J. **27**(1), 125–147 (2019)

10. Feldt, R., et al.: Four commentaries on the use of students and professionals in empirical software engineering experiments. Empir. Softw. Eng. **23**(6), 3801–3820 (2018). https://doi.org/10.1007/s10664-018-9655-0

11. Fleiss, J.L., Levin, B., Paik, M.C.: Statistical Methods for Rates and Proportions. Wiley Series in Probability and Statistics, 3rd edn. Wiley, Hoboken (2003)

12. Hadar, I., Reinhartz-Berger, I., Kuflik, T., Perini, A., Ricca, F., Susi, A.: Comparing the comprehensibility of requirements models expressed in use case and tropos: results from a family of experiments. Inf. Soft. Technol. **55**(10), 1823–1843 (2013)

13. Häser, F., Felderer, M., Breu, R.: Is business domain language support beneficial for creating test case specifications: a controlled experiment. Inf. Softw. Technol. **79**, 52–62 (2016)

14. Hayes, A.F., Krippendorff, K.: Answering the call for a standard reliability measure for coding data. Commun. Methods Meas. **1**(1), 77–89 (2007)

15. Horkoff, J., et al.: Goal-oriented requirements engineering: an extended systematic mapping study. Requir. Eng. **24**(2), 133–160 (2017). https://doi.org/10.1007/s00766-017-0280-z

16. ISO/IEC/IEEE: Software and Systems Engineering - Soft. testing - Part 3: Test documentation. ISO/IEC/IEEE standard 29119–3:2013 (2016)

17. ISO/IEC/IEEE: Systems and Software Engineering - Life cycle processes - Requirements Engineering. ISO/IEC/IEEE standard 29148:2018 (2018)

18. Karac, E.I., Turhan, B., Juristo, N.: A controlled experiment with novice developers on the impact of task description granularity on software quality in test-driven development. IEEE Trans. on Soft. Eng. 1 (2019). https://doi.org/10.1109/TSE.2019.2920377

19. Kasauli, R., Knauss, E., Kanagwa, B., Nilsson, A., Calikli, G.: Safety-critical systems and agile development: A mapping study. In: 2018 44th Euromicro Conference on Software Engineering and Advanced Applications (SEAA), pp. 470–477. IEEE (2018)
20. Larkin, J.H., Simon, H.A.: Why a diagram is (sometimes) worth ten thousand words. Cognit. Sci. **11**(1), 65–100 (1987)
21. Massey, A.K., Otto, P.N., Antón, A.I.: Evaluating legal implementation readiness decision-making. IEEE Trans. Soft. Eng. **41**(6), 545–564 (2015)
22. Matulevičius, R., Heymans, P.: Comparing goal modelling languages: an experiment. In: Sawyer, P., Paech, B., Heymans, P. (eds.) REFSQ 2007. LNCS, vol. 4542, pp. 18–32. Springer, Heidelberg (2007). https://doi.org/10.1007/978-3-540-73031-6_2
23. de Oliveira Neto, F.G., Torkar, R., Feldt, R., Gren, L., Furia, C.A., Huang, Z.: Evolution of statistical analysis in empirical software engineering research: current state and steps forward. J. Syst. Softw. **156**, 246–267 (2019)
24. Salman, I., Misirli, A.T., Juristo, N.: Are students representatives of professionals in software engineering experiments? In: 2015 IEEE/ACM 37th International Conference on Software Engineering, vol. 1, pp. 666–676. IEEE (2015)
25. Sharafi, Z., Marchetto, A., Susi, A., Antoniol, G., Guéhéneuc, Y.G.: An empirical study on the efficiency of graphical vs. textual representations in requirements comprehension. In: 2013 21st International Conference on Program Comprehension (ICPC), pp. 33–42. IEEE (2013)
26. Wohlin, C., Runeson, P., Höst, M., Ohlsson, M.C., Regnell, B., Wessln, A.: Experimentation in Software Engineering. Springer, Heidelberg (2012). https://doi.org/10.1007/978-3-642-29044-2

Requirements Visualization

Vision Meets Visualization: Are Animated Videos an Alternative?

Melanie Busch$^{(\boxtimes)}$, Oliver Karras, Kurt Schneider, and Maike Ahrens

Software Engineering Group, Leibniz Universität Hannover,
Welfengarten 1, 30167 Hannover, Germany
{melanie.busch,oliver.karras,kurt.schneider,
maike.ahrens}@inf.uni-hannover.de

Abstract. [**Context and motivation**] Creating a shared understanding of requirements between all parties involved about a future software system is difficult. Imprecise communication can lead to misunderstanding of requirements. Vision videos demonstrate and visualize the functionality, use and impact of a software system before the actual development process starts. They stimulate discussions about the software system and its associated requirements. [**Question/problem**] Vision videos should be produced with as little effort as possible, in terms of resources and time consumption, yet with sufficient quality. This raises the questions: Does the presentation of a vision video influence its perception by the audience? Do animated vision videos offer an alternative to real videos to communicate a vision? [**Principal ideas/results**] We conducted an experiment with 20 participants comparing animated and real videos showing the same content. The videos illustrate the population decrease in rural areas and envision a possible solution to counteract the consequences of grocery store closings. The participants suggested own solutions for the problem of grocery store closings, rated the videos and chose their preferred type of video representation. The results of the experiment show no difference in neither the amount of solutions proposed nor the rating of the videos. Likewise, the results show no difference in the preferred type of video representation. [**Contribution**] Our study indicates that animated vision videos offer an adequate alternative to real videos. Thus, vision video producers have another viable option to choose for achieving a shared understanding of a future software system.

Keywords: Requirements engineering · Animation · Vision · Video

1 Videos as a Vision Mediator

Whenever stakeholders discuss requirements, their shared understanding of requirements may differ. It is one of the most challenging tasks to build a shared understanding between stakeholders [9]. Various people have different mental models of their environments since different experiences lead to varying mental

© Springer Nature Switzerland AG 2020
N. Madhavji et al. (Eds.): REFSQ 2020, LNCS 12045, pp. 277–292, 2020.
https://doi.org/10.1007/978-3-030-44429-7_19

models [17, p. 17]. Creighton et al. [6] used videos to illustrate scenarios to avoid misunderstandings based on communication problems. Xu et al. [29] have also addressed the topic of videos in the context of scenarios. They focused on how scenario videos could be produced and updated in an easy and fast way by using virtual world technology [29].

Within the scope of our paper, we compare animated with real vision videos. Like Xu et al. [29] we strive for vision videos that are effective and take little effort. According to Karras et al. [14] vision videos visualize a vision or parts of a future system. Karras [12] stated that discussions between several stakeholders should be encouraged by using vision videos to support the exchange on deviating mental models of the future system. Based on this joint dialogue a shared understanding of the future system can arise [12]. Purposes of making and using vision videos are to create a shared understanding, to refine visions and to elicit feedback for a future system [14]. In our paper we want to investigate the question: *Do animated vision videos offer an adequate alternative to real videos to communicate a vision and to stimulate feedback?*

In the past we researched the field of real vision videos, because they are rather easy and affordable to produce [23, 24]. The aim of this paper is to investigate whether animated vision videos are an adequate alternative to real vision videos, not to replace them. An advantage of animated videos may be that they can show or create any environment. In contrast, real videos can be limited, because some environments may not be accessible or restricted of use, like in the airport scenario of Xu et al. [29]. When producing real videos, privacy issues must additionally be considered and taken into account. Furthermore, the organisation and coordination of required materials and parties involved impedes the production of real videos.

We conducted a study to compare animated with real vision videos. Short vision videos of two different types of video representation encouraged participants to develop new ideas and solutions for shopping in rural areas. Besides measuring how effectively videos stimulated feedback, we asked the participants about their preferred representation type of vision video.

The paper is structured as follows: Sect. 2 provides the background on the application context. Section 3 presents the representation types of videos considered. Section 4 discusses related work. Section 5 contains the experiment design. The results are presented in Sect. 6. In Sect. 7, we interpret and discuss the results of the experiment. Section 8 concludes the paper.

2   Application Context - Rural Areas

In Germany, the population of rural communities continues to decrease, albeit to a much lesser extent than in previous years [1]. It can be difficult to buy products of daily need without a grocery store nearby [2]. In the field of urban planning, Zibell et al. [31] focused on the local food supply in rural areas in the context of the demographic change. They looked at problems of rural locations and named various existing solutions, such as food delivery services [31]. Besides the use of widely used RE techniques, Schneider et al. [22] proposed to use vision videos in the context of public spatial planning. This domain deals with a large crowd of stakeholders who need to be part of the problem discussions and finding of a solution. Therefore, Schneider et al. [22] focused on the application example of food supply in rural areas. Schneider et al. [22] conclude that in the context of rural areas vision videos can be used to provide concrete context information, for example in town hall meetings.

In this paper we take a closer look at two different representation types of vision videos. We investigate (1) which type is more appealing to residents of smaller villages to communicate a vision and (2) which type stimulates them better to increase the amount of feedback. We have chosen the application context of shopping in rural areas since this problem could be supported by software systems [22]. With our experiment we wanted to find out, if animated vision videos offer an adequate alternative to real vision videos.

3   Type of Content Representation - Animated and Real Video

There are several ways to create videos. Vistisen and Poulsen [26] conducted a design workshop to use animation-based sketching within the design process of front-end-concepts. The workshop participants used i.a. stop motion technology in combination with LEGO figures or with real pictures containing drawn elements [26]. Additionally, paper prototypes were used to visualize the handling of the app interface [26].

In the past, we have already looked in more detail at the third and first person perspective in real vision videos, as in Schneider et al. [24]. In general, there is a large number of kinds of videos (workshop videos [8] or demonstration videos [25]), which can be represented in several ways due to the different application contexts and production options. In this paper, we focus on two specific representation types of vision videos: Animated and real vision videos. We compare the perception of the audience. We define the term *animated videos* as follows:

Definition: An **"animated video"** is a comic-like, 2D-representation with a strong simplification of people, environment and entities.

We use the term *real videos* as follows:

Definition: A **"real video"** is a video filmed with people as actors, real environment and materialized objects.

Figure 1 shows an excerpt of the animated and corresponding real vision videos in comparison. The screenshots stem from the videos used in the study (see Sect. 5 for details).

Fig. 1. Animated videos and respective real videos

4   Related Work

One key application context of videos in requirements engineering is the visualization of scenarios or interactions between humans and computers in sophisticated processes to envision different aspects of a future system: system context [10], product vision [4,5,18], or scenarios [15,20,30]. Vision videos often demonstrate a problem, one or more possible solutions in use, and sometimes the benefit they create [24]. While formal or textual descriptions are difficult to understand for some users and stakeholders, videos are easy to watch for all parties involved.

Creighton et al. [6] presented vision videos of sophisticated processes, e.g., in health care. UML diagrams were overlaid with the videos in order to establish shared understanding between stakeholders and developers. Thus, visible video elements could be mapped to underlying development objects in UML diagrams. In collaboration with Siemens, product visions were illustrated as high-end marketing videos. Brill et al. [4] contrasted this high-end with a low-effort approach of using vision videos. They compared the use of vision videos and use cases under time pressure. Darby et al. [7] followed a similar low-effort approach and showed how an envisioned software-based application in providing care to dementia patients could look like. Lay actors enact scenes and pretend to already use the future system. Schneider et al. [24] proposed showing one problem and three possible solutions in one vision video in order to create more feedback. In [23], Schneider and Bertolli described a process to create vision videos in both linear or interactive style at affordable effort.

Some researchers have used animated actors and videos for specific purposes. Xu et al. [29] emphasized the changes within an agile software development cycle as one of the major challenges in current software development. They proposed the so-called Evolutionary Scenario Based Design using an opensource virtual world platform called OpenSim. Animated persons replaced real human actors. Their behavior can evolve without a need to update a traditional video. Williams et al. [27] investigated how comic scenarios can be used in the context of requirements engineering. They found that pictorial representations help users in imagining revisions and in recognizing new or changed requirements. In ContraVision, Mancini et al. [16] provided two videos of a future system: One shows a positive vision of a system, while the other visualizes a negative usage scenario. Bennaceur et al. [3] used animated videos in their research in combination with ContraVision. They wanted to elicit user reactions to utopian (positive) and dystopian (negative) videos. Rodden et al. [21] used animated sketches to visualize future smart energy infrastructures to focus groups. The animated sketches were the basis to get feedback about concerns and thoughts of the participants about the not yet existing future energy systems.

All previously discussed related work used only one specific representation type for their videos (real or animated). Thus, it is not clear how the respective representation type affects the perception of the audience and the amount of solicited feedback. Within the scope of our paper we consider and compare these two video representation types for vision videos.

5   Experimental Design

The following section includes detailed information about our study. It starts with our research question, goal and hypotheses. The section proceeds with the used material, the selection of participants and the experiment design.

Research question:
Do animated vision videos offer an adequate alternative to real videos to communicate a vision and to stimulate feedback?

To formulate our research goal, we used the goal definition template according to Wohlin [28].

Goal definition:
We analyse two representation types of vision videos
for the purpose of evaluating their impact on perception of the audience
with respect to preference and performance (i.e. stimulated feedback from participants)
from the point of view of people who have lived in smaller villages for several months or currently do
in the context of an experimental setting with presence of an experimenter.

5.1   Hypotheses

We divided the hypotheses into two different thematic areas: preference and performance. The preference focuses on (1) which type of video is more appealing.

Performance considers (2) which type of video stimulates the participants better to create more ideas (see Sect. 2).

Preference

The preference was measured in two different parts of the experiment. On the one hand, the preference was measured after the participants watched videos of one type of representation. On the other hand, the preference was measured after both types of video representation were shown to the participants. The preference of the participants regarding the videos was measured partly through 6-point Likert-scales and partly through questions with predefined response options. Based on our research question and goal, we formulated the following hypotheses:

$H1_1$: There is a difference between the groups regarding the rating of the overall video quality being watched.

$H1_0$: There is no difference between the groups regarding the rating of the overall video quality being watched.

$H2_1$: There is a difference between the groups in terms of identification with the scene represented in the video.

$H2_0$: There is no difference between the groups in terms of identification with the scene represented in the video.

$H3_1$: There is a difference between the groups in terms of identification with the person represented in the video.

$H3_0$: There is no difference between the groups in terms of identification with the person represented in the video.

$H4_1$: There is a difference between the groups regarding the preferred presentation style of the videos.

$H4_0$: There is no difference between the groups regarding the preferred presentation style of the videos.

$H5_1$: There is a difference between the groups with regard to the assessment of the participants, which video provides more information.

$H5_0$: There is no difference between the groups with regard to the assessment of the participants, which video provides more information.

$H6_1$: There is a difference between the groups regarding the recommendation which type of video should be used in the future.

$H6_0$: There is no difference between the groups regarding the recommendation which type of video should be used in the future.

Performance

The performance was measured after three single videos of one representation type were viewed. The participants were asked to name solution ideas.

$H7_1$: There is a difference between the groups in the number of solution ideas triggered by the particular video being viewed.

$H7_0$: There is no difference between the groups in the number of solution ideas triggered by the particular video being viewed.

5.2   Material

Six videos were used in the experiment: three animated and three real videos. In both types of representation we used a thematic introductory video, a video that visualizes the product order via photo and a video that illustrates the product delivery via a drone. The introductory videos show the prevailing situation: village population decreases and (grocery) stores close. Solution ideas and suggestions for changing this problematic situation are being sought. The real video introduction is 66 s long, the animated one 68 s. The second videos show the ordering process by photographing a product and gets reordered automatically. Both video versions have a total length of 18 s. The third videos show the delivery process by a drone. An informing text message is sent to the recipient's mobile phone. The real video of the product delivery has a length of 28 s and the animated video has a length of 27 s, respectively. In the paper "Refining Vision Videos" of Schneider et al. [24] the real introductory video was already used. In terms of content, the videos visualize a subset of variants of the Refining Vision Video paper [24]. The real videos were made by simple means. The real and animated videos were produced and edited by one person. We used the software CrazyTalk Animator 3 of Reallusion[1] to record our animated vision videos. It took about one day to produce the real vision videos and one and a half days to produce the animated videos. The expertise of the video producer has a strong influence on the time span. In our study the video producer was unfamiliar with the animation software.

The following table (Fig. 2) shows an extract of the questionnaires. We have based the questionnaires used on our previous work (cf. Schneider et al. [24]). For more details on the setting and experiment design, see Sect. 5.4.

	Part of the questionnaires	Question / Statements	Type of answer
Segment 1	Q1	What innovative ideas or proposals have you come up with for shopping in rural areas throughout the video?	Free-text field
	Q1	Can you identify yourself with the depicted scene / the person portrayed within the video?	Likert scale (Range: 0 (Do not agree at all) to 5 (fully agree))
	Q2	I like the videos	Likert scale (Range: 0 (Do not agree at all) to 5 (fully agree))
	Q2	The videos offer me important information	Likert scale (Range: 0 (Do not agree at all) to 5 (fully agree))
Segment 2	Q3	Which of the videos shown do you like better according to the type of representation?	Selection of three predefined answer options: animated video, real video, both alike
	Q3	Which of the shown videos offers you more information?	Selection of three predefined answer options: animated video, real video, both alike

Fig. 2. Extract of the used questionnaire (not all questions and statements used in the context of our study are included)

---

[1] https://www.reallusion.com/de/crazytalk/default.html.

5.3   Selection of Participants

Living in smaller communities differs from living in the city in many ways. The connection to public transport and its availability can be limited. Local supply of daily need products is not guaranteed. Definitions and classifications of spatial areas often refer to larger settlements or include smaller villages in municipalities [19]. However, our study refers to smaller villages and their inhabitants. We define *smaller villages* as follows:

> **Definition:** A **"smaller village"** is a settlement with less than 5000 inhabitants.

We carefully invited only participants who currently live or have lived in smaller villages with less than 5000 inhabitants to take part in the study. We chose this group of participants because their experience of living in smaller villages might help them to identify better with the content than participants from larger cities. All participants took part voluntarily.

A total of 20 participants took part in the study. The participants were randomly assigned into two groups. Both groups had a final group size of ten participants. The participants were between 26 and 71 years old ($M = 45.3$, $SD = 16.7$). 16 participants currently live or have lived without a supermarket or discount store nearby. 18 participants use online shopping, but only seven of them ordered everyday products via online shopping at least once.

5.4   Setting and Experiment Design

The experiment was conducted with one participant at a time in a quiet room. At the beginning, participants received an overview of the experiment. Afterwards, the participants were asked to sign the declaration of consent.

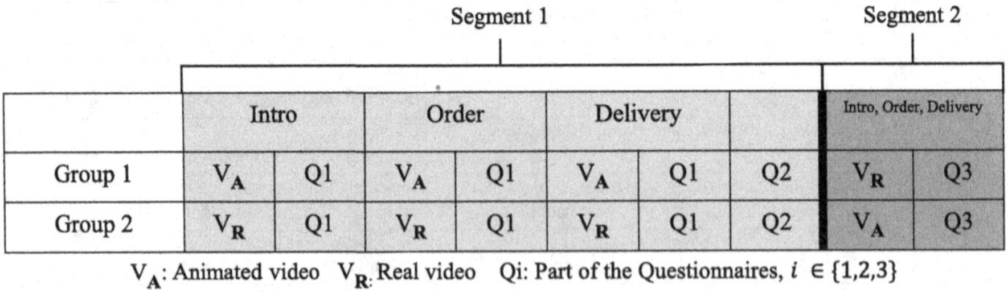

	Intro		Order		Delivery			Intro, Order, Delivery	
Group 1	V_A	Q1	V_A	Q1	V_A	Q1	Q2	V_R	Q3
Group 2	V_R	Q1	V_R	Q1	V_R	Q1	Q2	V_A	Q3

V_A: Animated video V_R: Real video   Qi: Part of the Questionnaires, $i \in \{1,2,3\}$

Fig. 3. Experiment design

Our selected study design is characterized by a subdivision into two large segments (colored light grey and dark grey), see Fig. 3. In each segment, the participants saw one type of video representation. Real and animated videos have the same content in introduction, order and delivery. The videos were shown on a 14-inch TN screen with a resolution of 1600×900 pixels, the laptop sound was turned on. The experimenter started the videos on the laptop and sat next to the participant during the experiment.

The first segment is divided into three parts in which three videos were shown to the participants: the introduction, ordering via photo and package delivery via drone. In the first segment Group 1 saw the animated videos and answered one page of the questionnaire after each video. Group 2 saw the real videos and answered the questionnaire respectively. At the end of segment 1, all participants rated several statements whether they agree or disagree. In segment 2, the other type of video representation was shown to each participant without pauses. Group 1 saw the three real videos and Group 2 the three animated videos. Afterwards, all participants were asked which type of vision video communicated more information and which one they prefer and recommend. In the end the participants filled out the background information sheet. We chose this experiment design for two main reasons (1) to keep the execution time for the participants as short as possible. (2) Both video types show the same content. Therefore, the participants already knew the content.

6   Results

Preference

$H1_0$: There is no difference between the groups regarding the rating of the overall video quality being watched.
Participants should rate on a Likert-scale from 0 (do not agree at all) to 5 (fully agree), whether the video quality is sufficient to convey the content. At that point in time the participants saw only one type of video representation. We performed a Mann-Whitney U test to investigate, whether the two groups differ from each other. The test indicated that there is no significant difference between Group 1 and Group 2, $Z = -0{,}265$, $p = .795$.
For this reason we cannot reject $H1_0$ and conclude: **There seems to be no difference between the groups regarding the rating of the overall video quality.**
$H2_0$: There is no difference between the groups in terms of identification with the scene represented in the video.
After the introduction video, the participants were asked whether they can identify themselves with the video scene. They were asked to give their answer on a six-point Likert-scale, 0 (do not agree at all) to 5 (fully agree). To assess whether there are differences between the groups of participants, we performed a Mann-Whitney U test. The test indicated that there is no significant difference between Group 1 and Group 2, $Z = -0{,}643$, $p = .522$.
Therefore, we cannot reject $H2_0$ and conclude: **There seems to be no difference between the groups in terms of identification with the represented scene.**

H3₀: There is no difference between the groups in terms of identification with the person represented in the video.

After seeing the order and the delivery video, the participants were asked in each case whether they can identify with the person depicted in the video. They were asked to give their answer on a six-point Likert scale, 0 (do not agree at all) to 5 (fully agree). We performed a Mann-Whitney U test to identify possible differences between the groups of participants. The test indicated that there is no significant difference between Group 1 and Group 2, $Z = -0,680$, p = .497.

Consequently we cannot reject H3₀ and conclude: **There seems to be no difference between the groups in terms of identification with the represented person.**

H4₀: There is no difference between the groups regarding the preferred presentation style of the videos.

At the end of the study, after the participants had seen both types of representation, they were asked which type of representation they preferred. To answer a single select question, the participants could choose between three different answers: real, animated or both. Because nominal data is given, we performed a chi-square goodness-of-fit test with a significance level $\alpha = .05$. In accordance with H4₀, a 0.5/0.5 distribution of the participant's preferred video representation type is expected. The result of the chi-square test is $\chi^2 = 2.13$, p = .144. The result is not significant so we cannot reject the null hypothesis. **It seems that there is no difference between the groups regarding the preferred type of video representation.**

H5₀: There is no difference between the groups with regard to the assessment of the participants, which video provides more information.

After seeing all animated and all real videos, the participants were asked which type of video representation provided more information. The participants could choose between three different answers again: real, animated or both. We performed a chi-square goodness of-fit-test, because of the nominal data with a significance level $\alpha = .05$. In accordance with H5₀, one would expect a 0.5/0.5 distribution. The result of the chi-square test is $\chi^2 = 0,471$, p = .493 and it is not significant. We cannot reject the null hypothesis and conclude that **there seems to be no difference between the groups regarding the assessment of the information content.**

H6₀: There is no difference between the groups regarding the recommendation which type of video should be used in the future.

At the end of the study, the participants were asked what type of representation they recommend to use in the future. Once again, the participants could choose between three different answers: real, animated or both. Because nominal data is given, we performed a chi-square goodness-of-fit test with a significance level $\alpha = .05$. In accordance with H6₀, one would expect a 0.5/0.5 distribution. The result of the chi-square test is $\chi^2 = 0,04$, p = .841 and is not significant. For this reason we cannot reject the null hypothesis and we draw the conclusion **that there seems to be no deviation between the groups with respect to the rating of video type presentation.**

Performance

H7₀: There is no difference between the groups in the number of solution ideas triggered by the particular video being viewed.

After each video part in the first segment of the experiment, the participants proposed solutions and ideas on the topic of shopping in rural areas. The solution ideas were counted. First, we have tested the data for normal distribution with the Shapiro-Wilk test. The result is $W = 0{,}952$, $p = .396$. The test result indicates that the results are normally distributed. Afterwards we performed the T-test, $t = -0{,}429$, $p = .673$. The result of the T-test is not significant, so we cannot reject the null hypothesis and conclude **that the visualization type of a video does not seem to have any influence on the number of solution ideas triggered by the video.**

Subjective Evaluation of the Video Types

Figure 4 illustrates the subjective rating of Group 1 and Group 2 ($N = 10$ for each) of different statements after one of the two video types has been shown. Overall,the majority of participants like the videos. When comparing the diagrams in Fig. 4, animated videos received better ratings in general. The variance is higher for real videos.

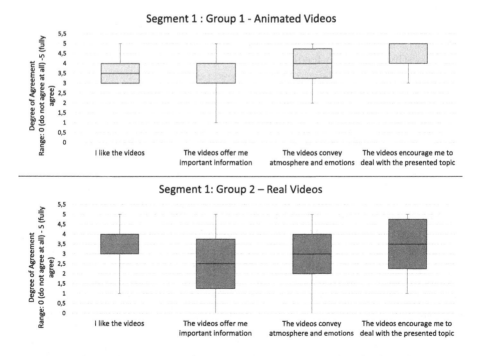

Fig. 4. Subjective evaluation of the animated and real videos

7   Interpretation and Discussion

7.1   Interpretation

Within the framework of our study, we examined if animated vision videos offer an adequate alternative to real vision videos to communicate a vision of a future system. The participants (all of them currently or formerly inhabitants of smaller villages) in our study have no significant preference regarding the type of video representation. The amount of feedback is the same for both type of video representation. Overall the statement *I liked the videos* was rated very positive for animated and real videos. In general the preference of both video representation types were mostly positive, although the evaluation of the animated videos were slightly better. Based on our results the answer to our research question is:

Answer to the Research Question:
Animated vision videos seem to offer an adequate alternative to real videos to communicate a vision and to stimulate feedback.

7.2   Discussion

Vision videos are one way to improve shared understanding in the early phases of a project: They visualize a complex envisioned product or process of use, and they stimulate feedback. In our research, we try to optimize the way affordable vision videos can be created and used [23]. In [24], we showed three alternative visions to stimulate more feedback. In the same study, we did not find a convincing advantage in first-person camera perspective over the usual third-party perspective. In this paper, we investigated whether animated vision videos are an adequate alternative to real videos, i.e., be accepted at a similar or better rate than real videos and whether they are able to stimulate feedback. If so, they can be a new tool in the toolbox of requirements engineers who use vision videos. Despite all our care in planning and designing the study, we have to mention that we focus on a single topic and chose a very specific group of participants. As of now, we can not make any statements about the transferability to other thematic areas nor can we formulate any general statements. One of the authors (Schneider) had expected less feedback in animated videos due to the fact that there are no unintended elements in an animated video. Even those accidental elements could have triggered feedback. However, our experiment showed no statistically significant differences between real and animated videos, neither in terms of performance (feedback solicited) nor in participants' preference. An important point to emphasize is the evaluation of the video quality. Participants rated the quality of both types of videos as sufficient to convey the content, i.e., the vision. It is encouraging to see that moderate effort is sufficient in the case of vision videos. Participants of our study do not seem to expect high-end movie quality in this domain. It should be noted that animated videos were neither clearly worse, nor much better than real videos. They should not replace real videos but be considered when privacy or economical aspects are weighed. The similarity of results for both types of videos indicates that the choice can be made on other criteria, e.g., based on effort and speed of video production. Producing an animated video requires animation software, such as CrazyTalk Animator 3 of Reallusion[2]. In our experiment, the production of the animated video took longer than filming the real video. Effort and speed of production may depend on the experience of the director and the target level of sophistication. Bishevsky[3] produced a short, affordable animation video for the RE Cares Track of the International Conference on Requirements Engineering (RE19), envisioning a software-based enhancement of the public transportation system at the venue of RE19. The animated video was produced in Israel while the RE Cares Track was running in South Korea. Filming with real actors and the real environment was impossible due to the distance. Since no human actors had to be filmed, privacy issues were avoided as a side-effect. The main conclusion of this paper is: Animated videos appeared as a viable option and an adequate alternative for the purpose of showing visions and soliciting feedback for requirements engineering.

7.3   Threats to Validity

We carefully chose our experiment design (see Sect. 5 for details). Several threats were taken into account for our experiment design.

Internal Validity

Real and animated videos of single scenes were made for the experiment. Despite similar content, length and spoken texts of the videos, it was not feasible to produce exactly identical scenes. This could be a confounding factor for the perception of the videos. In segment 2 of our experiment, the participants already knew the video content. This factor could have influenced the results, because the participants were no longer unbiased. The physical and mental state of participants, such as fatigue, boredom or decrease of concentration, could have affected the outcome of the experiment. We have tried to mitigate this factor by randomly distributing the participants to the two groups. We used only one video example in our study, this mono operation bias may have influenced the results. The specific content and the topic of the vision videos may have affected the results. Another threat to mention is that repeating the experiment might lead to different ratings.

External Validity

We selected inhabitants of smaller villages as study participants. Hence, participants had a similar background regarding their current or past place of residence. We chose this homogeneous group of participants to obtain a high conclusion validity. However, this limits the generalizability of our results to participants with a different background. Besides, the experiment requires replication with a larger sample size to improve generalizability.

---

[2] https://www.reallusion.com/de/crazytalk/default.html.
[3] https://drive.google.com/open?id=1Ta4hOIhVNf808CRsASTuNIyNcZwNfEfk.

Construct Validity

Some participants may have evaluated the videos better, because they are in a test situation. The experimenter was present throughout the entire experiment to start the videos and assist with questions. The experimenter's presence may have influenced the results. We have tried to keep this threat as small as possible by having the experimenter behave as quietly as possible. Responses to questions were kept to a minimum. In addition, this effect affected both participant groups equally.

Conclusion Validity

The participants have different experiences and mental models which could have influenced the evaluation and assessment of the videos. We tried to minimize this threat by inviting only participants who live or have lived in smaller villages. Due to the small sample size of 20 participants, there is a possibility that we have drawn false conclusions based on the results. Based on our small sample size and our focus on a single topic, we cannot derive an equality of the two approaches for visualizing a vision from our results. Our study did not aim to infer this equality, but to investigate whether animated videos are an adequate option to produce vision videos. Replications of our study in other contexts, other purposes and with a bigger sample size are needed to confirm our findings.

8 Conclusion

In the experiment we compared animated and real vision videos regarding preference and performance. Concerning the number of proposed solutions to the topic of shopping in rural areas, no difference was found between the two groups of participants. In addition, no significant difference with regard to preferred type of video representation were seen. Concerning our research question, animated videos do offer an adequate alternative to real vision videos to communicate a vision.

Future Work: There are many aspects to vision video production and perception that we want to research in the future. Among other things, we want to investigate how vision videos should be watched, for instance in a group with subsequent discussion or alone via video platforms with online questionnaires.

According to Karras [11] and Karras and Schneider [13] effort and simplicity are two major aspects that need to be addressed and researched in our future work. Nevertheless, we found evident leads that viewers like animated vision videos just as good as real vision videos and give a similar amount of feedback.

Acknowledgement. This work was supported by the Deutsche Forschungsgemeinschaft (DFG) under Grant No.: 289386339, project ViViReq. (2017–2019).

References

1. Informationen aus der Forschung des BBSR Nr. 3/2019. ISSN 1868-0089 (2019)

2. Hannoversche Allgemeine Zeitung: Federal mail will send bread. In rural areas, shopping gets increasing difficult - now, the postman could sell groceries on the doorstep (original in German), 15 September 2018

3. Bennaceur, A., et al.: Feed me, feed me: an exemplar for engineering adaptive software. In: 2016 IEEE/ACM 11th International Symposium on Software Engineering for Adaptive and Self-Managing Systems (SEAMS), pp. 89–95, May 2016. https://doi.org/10.1109/SEAMS.2016.018

4. Brill, O., Schneider, K., Knauss, E.: Videos vs. use cases: can videos capture more requirements under time pressure? In: Wieringa, R., Persson, A. (eds.) REFSQ 2010. LNCS, vol. 6182, pp. 30–44. Springer, Heidelberg (2010). https://doi.org/10.1007/978-3-642-14192-8_5

5. Broll, G., Hussmann, H., Rukzio, E., Wimmer, R.: Using video clips to support requirements elicitation in focus groups-an experience report. In: SE 2007 Workshop on Multimedia Requirements Engineering (2007)

6. Creighton, O., Ott, M., Bruegge, B.: Software cinema-video-based requirements engineering. In: 14th IEEE International Requirements Engineering Conference (RE 2006), pp. 109–118, September 2006. https://doi.org/10.1109/RE.2006.59

7. Darby, A., Tsekleves, E., Sawyer, P.: Speculative requirements: design fiction and RE. In: 2018 IEEE 26th International Requirements Engineering Conference (RE), pp. 388–393. IEEE (2018)

8. Fricker, S.A., Schneider, K., Fotrousi, F., Thuemmler, C.: Workshop videos for requirements communication. Requir. Eng. 21(4), 521–552 (2015). https://doi.org/10.1007/s00766-015-0231-5

9. Glinz, M., Fricker, S.A.: On shared understanding in software engineering: an essay. Comput. Sci. Res. Dev. 30(3), 363–376 (2015). https://doi.org/10.1007/s00450-014-0256-x

10. Jirotka, M., Luff, P.: Supporting requirements with video-based analysis. IEEE Softw. 23(3), 42–44 (2006). https://doi.org/10.1109/MS.2006.84

11. Karras, O.: Software professionals' attitudes towards video as a medium in requirements engineering. In: Kuhrmann, M., et al. (eds.) PROFES 2018. LNCS, vol. 11271, pp. 150–158. Springer, Cham (2018). https://doi.org/10.1007/978-3-030-03673-7_11

12. Karras, O.: Communicating stakeholders' needs - vision videos to disclose, discuss, and align mental models for shared understanding. IEEE Softw. Blog (2019). http://blog.ieeesoftware.org/2019/10/communicating-stakeholders-needs-with.html

13. Karras, O., Schneider, K.: Software professionals are not directors: what constitutes a good video? In: 2018 1st International Workshop on Learning from Other Disciplines for Requirements Engineering (D4RE), pp. 18–21. IEEE (2018)

14. Karras, O., Schneider, K., Fricker, S.A.: Representing software project vision by means of video: a quality model for vision videos. J. Syst. Softw. (2019). https://doi.org/10.1016/j.jss.2019.110479

15. Maiden, N., Seyff, N., Grunbacher, P., Otojare, O.O., Mitteregger, K.: Determining stakeholder needs in the workplace: how mobile technologies can help. IEEE Softw. 24(2), 46–52 (2007)

16. Mancini, C., et al.: Contravision: exploring users' reactions to futuristic technology. In: Proceedings of the SIGCHI Conference on Human Factors in Computing Systems, CHI 2010, pp. 153–162. ACM, New York (2010). https://doi.org/10.1145/1753326.1753350

17. Norman, D.A.: The Design of Everyday Things. Basic Books Inc., New York (2002)

18. Pham, R., Meyer, S., Kitzmann, I., Schneider, K.: Interactive multimedia storyboard for facilitating stakeholder interaction: supporting continuous improvement in IT-ecosystems. In: 2012 Eighth International Conference on the Quality of Information and Communications Technology, pp. 120–123. IEEE (2012)
19. Porsche, L., Milbert, A.: Kleinstädte in Deutschland - Ein Überblick (in English: Small Towns in Germany - An Overview). Informationen zur Raumentwicklung des BBSR Nr. 6/2018 (6) (2018)
20. Rabiser, R., Seyff, N., Grunbacher, P., Maiden, N.: Capturing multimedia requirements descriptions with mobile RE tools. In: 2006 First International Workshop on Multimedia Requirements Engineering, p. 2. IEEE (2006)
21. Rodden, T.A., Fischer, J.E., Pantidi, N., Bachour, K., Moran, S.: At home with agents: exploring attitudes towards future smart energy infrastructures. In: Proceedings of the SIGCHI Conference on Human Factors in Computing Systems, CHI 2013, pp. 1173–1182. ACM (2013)
22. Schneider, K., Karras, O., Finger, A., Zibell, B.: Reframing societal discourse as requirements negotiation: vision statement. In: 2017 IEEE 25th International Requirements Engineering Conference Workshops (REW), pp. 188–193, September 2017
23. Schneider, K., Bertolli, L.M.: Video variants for crowdRE: how to create linear videos, vision videos, and interactive videos. In: The 3rd International Workshop on Crowd-Based Requirements Engineering (CrowdRE 2019), International IEEE Conference on Requirements Engineering (RE 2019), Jeju Island, South Korea (2019)
24. Schneider, K., Busch, M., Karras, O., Schrapel, M., Rohs, M.: Refining vision videos. In: Knauss, E., Goedicke, M. (eds.) REFSQ 2019. LNCS, vol. 11412, pp. 135–150. Springer, Cham (2019). https://doi.org/10.1007/978-3-030-15538-4_10
25. Stangl, H., Creighton, O.: Continuous demonstration. In: 2011 Fourth International Workshop on Multimedia and Enjoyable Requirements Engineering (MERE 2011), pp. 38–41. IEEE (2011)
26. Vistisen, P., Poulsen, S.: Investigating user experiences through animation-based sketching. In: Murnieks, A., Rinnert, G., Stone, B., Tegtmeyer, R. (eds.) Motion Design Education Summit 2015 Edited Conference Proceedings, pp. 29–38. Routledge, Abingdon (2016)
27. Williams, A.M., Alspaugh, T.A.: Articulating software requirements comic book style. In: 2008 Third International Workshop on Multimedia and Enjoyable Requirements Engineering - Beyond Mere Descriptions and with More Fun and Games, pp. 4–8, September 2008. https://doi.org/10.1109/MERE.2008.3
28. Wohlin, C., Runeson, P., Höst, M., Ohlsson, M.C., Regnell, B., Wesslén, A.: Experimentation in Software Engineering. Springer, Heidelberg (2012). https://doi.org/10.1007/978-3-642-29044-2
29. Xu, H., Creighton, O., Boulila, N., Bruegge, B.: From pixels to bytes: evolutionary scenario based design with video. In: Proceedings of the ACM SIGSOFT 20th International Symposium on the Foundations of Software Engineering, FSE 2012, pp. 31:1–31:4. ACM, New York (2012)
30. Zachos, K., Maiden, N., Tosar, A.: Rich-media scenarios for discovering requirements. IEEE Softw. 22(5), 89–97 (2005)
31. Zibell, B., Diez, J.R., Heineking, I., Preuß, P., Bloem, H., Sohns, F.: Zukunft der Nahversorgung in ländlichen Räumen: Bedarfsgerecht und maßgeschneidert. In: Fachinger, U., Künemund, H. (eds.) Gerontologie und ländlicher Raum. VBG, pp. 141–165. Springer, Wiesbaden (2015). https://doi.org/10.1007/978-3-658-09005-0_8

Requirements Assessment in Smart City Districts: A Motivation Concept for Citizens

Svenja Polst$^{(\boxtimes)}$ and Frank Elberzhager

Fraunhofer IESE, Fraunhofer-Platz 1, 67633 Kaiserslautern, Germany
Svenja.polst@iese.fraunhofer.de

Abstract. **[Context and motivation]** Digitalization is increasingly influencing cities as they evolve into Smart Cities. However, involving citizens in order to develop digital solutions that address real needs of users is a challenging task. In the Smart City project "EnStadt:Pfaff", concepts are to be developed to encourage residents of a city district to participate in the development of a Smart City district by communicating their needs, wishes, and ideas. **[Question/problem]** In the context of Smart City districts, classic requirements engineering (RE) methods such as interviews can be used, but there is high potential for novel methods, as the residents are concentrated within a very limited physical space and can communicate their needs and wishes through a digital platform as well as through analog communication channels. Our research goal is to investigate such novel methods and their potential for improving Smart City districts with digital solutions. **[Principal ideas/results]** In this research preview, we describe an initial approach for encouraging a group of citizens (potentially without any software engineering background) to participate in requirements elicitation in the context of Smart Cities. **[Contribution]** The presented approach consists of nine steps providing guidance for the selection of motivational measures, the reduction of obstacles to participation, and communication of requirements elicitation activities. Furthermore, we present topics for future research.

Keywords: Smart City · Requirements engineering · Digital platform · Motivation

1 Introduction

Digital technologies are increasingly being used in city environments, and more and more cities are planning to develop and offer digital services to their citizens. Examples include digital platforms for supporting multimodal mobility or communication means linking citizens to municipalities and enabling them to report damaged infrastructure or other shortcomings.

Ideally, users of digital solutions, systems, and services (in this case the citizens) are involved in the development. As digitalization affects almost everyone, everybody should be empowered to contribute their requirements [1]. However, often not everyone is involved or even considered.

© Springer Nature Switzerland AG 2020
N. Madhavji et al. (Eds.): REFSQ 2020, LNCS 12045, pp. 293–299, 2020.
https://doi.org/10.1007/978-3-030-44429-7_20

Furthermore, Doerr et al. claim that there exists a huge potential to explore new ways of conducting RE activities in social contexts and provide two classifications (dimensions for end-users and RE methods) to support such derivation of new methods [2]. We follow this claim and believe that citizens can be involved better in the elicitation of requirements for digital solutions of real benefit for them. One main challenge in this context, however, is how to motivate the citizens to participate in this process. In this paper, we therefore present a structured nine-step process that describes how to gather feedback from citizens, and which explicitly considers motivational concepts for citizens. We attach examples from the "EnStadt:Pfaff" [1] research project where the goal is to build a climate-neutral Smart City district with the help of digital solutions.

Our basic idea for motivating citizens to participate in RE activities is to reduce obstacles regarding their participation and to integrate motivational elements already in the planning of the RE activities. We developed an initial approach consisting of nine steps that serve as guidance for planning RE activities. The approach is meant to address potential participants with low to medium intrinsic motivation of contributing to a requirements elicitation activity. The approach should be applied by requirements engineers. We believe that several steps could be conducted more efficiently with the support of tools, such as a set of classified methods. Therefore, we introduce our idea of what a toolbox could look like. In Sect. 2, we present related work and how we derived our assumptions and then introduce the 9-step approach in Sect. 3.

2   Related Work and Assumptions

The American Psychology Association (APA) defines "motivation" as: "the impetus that gives purpose or direction to behavior and operates in humans at a conscious or unconscious level. Motives are frequently divided into (a) physiological [motives] [...]; and (b) personal, social, or secondary motives, such as affiliation, competition, and individual interests and goals." [2]. Motives are also used in the area of gamification (e.g., [3]). In the area of gamification, concrete motivational measures are also applied, for example leaderboards, badges, and levels [4], which can be linked to motives.

Our approach is based on the assumption that motivational measures integrated into the method and into the execution of the method increase total motivation. Based on the above paragraph, we assume that the following aspects should be considered to increase the motivation of participants: interests, goals, and preferences. Interests refer to interests in topics, such as environmental protection and digitalization. Goals describe personal goals such as having a social network or prestige. Preferences refer to the participants' preferences regarding the design and execution of a method. In our opinion, unfulfilled preferences do not stop desired participants from participating, but their fulfilment might make participants feel more comfortable.

According to the literature, there is an interrelationship between motivation, obstacles, and resources. Rudolph et al. [5] developed an intention model that states that the motivation must be higher than any obstacles so that a person has the intention to

---

[1] https://pfaff-reallabor.de/.

[2] https://dictionary.apa.org/motivation.

behave in a certain way. Obstacles towards system usage arise if a person does not have the resources required by the system. For instance, an obstacle arises if a system was developed for software engineers and requires technical knowledge but the user does not have the required level of 'technical knowledge'. The level of technical knowledge is considered to be a resource.

We assume that obstacles arise when the characteristics of a method do not match the resources of the participants. We identified these resources based on the above as: intrinsic motivation, cognitive and physical capacities [5], time [2], and domain knowledge [2, 5]. We consider obstacles and motivation as a kind of equation. If the motivation to participate in an RE activity is greater than the obstacles, then a person is likely to participate in it. Higher motivation can be achieved in two ways. On the one hand, the obstacles can be lowered to such an extent that even someone with low motivation will engage in an activity. On the other hand, motivation can be increased so that someone will be willing to alter their resources (e.g., spend more time, gain knowledge) to overcome the obstacles. Our approach is based on the assumptions that obstacles can be reduced by matching the citizens' resources to the characteristics of an RE method and to the way a method is executed.

There is literature about RE methods in Smart Cities. The paper by Doerr et al. [2] presents a framework for a classification of RE methods and for social contexts in Smart Cities and Smart Rural Areas. The classification is intended to ease the creation of new ways of executing RE activities so that citizens are more likely to participate in them. This classification scheme for social contexts describes the characteristics of end-users, such as availability, domain experience, attitude towards IT, locality preference, degree of impact, and context of system usage. Some of these characteristics are similar to the characteristics in their scheme of RE methods, but others do not match, such as atmosphere and number of participants. We conclude that the characteristics of end-users and the methods could be refined. The authors point out that their work is at an early stage and that more research needs to be conducted in this field.

We assume that in Smart City districts, there are possibilities for executing a method in novel ways due to the fact that the desired participants time in the limited physical space of the district every day and, at least in the Pfaff district, a digital platform for communication is available. The creation of new methods could also be inspired by the fields of "Citizen Science" and "Co-Creation".

3 Approach

In this section, we describe the nine-step approach (see Fig. 1) and how some of the steps could be supported by a toolbox. Furthermore, we present an example describing the planning of an RE activity in the district studied in the context of the project "EnStadt:Pfaff", called Pfaff district. In the example, a service for elderly people in the district should be developed that facilitates contact with others in the district so that elderly people will feel less lonely. One RE activity is to analyze current and past ways of how these elderly people got in contact with others in their neighborhood. The example is currently fictive, since the district is under construction and therefore still uninhabited.

Fig. 1. 9-step approach for reducing obstacles and increasing participants' motivation

Before these activities can be carried out, the objectives (e.g., the elicitation of as-is scenarios) must be set.

(1) *Define desired participants:* The sub-group of stakeholders who are intended to participate in a specific RE activity has to be defined so that appropriate methods can be selected later on. In a Smart City district, the most relevant stakeholders are the direct users of the district and digital services offered there, i.e., the residents. We assume that requirement engineers do not need support in the form of a toolbox in this step, which is a common step in RE. *Example:* In our example, the desired participants are senior citizen who want to have more contact with others in the district.

(2) *Describe desired participants:* The characteristics of the desired participants have to be identified and documented so that they can be systematically considered when selecting a method. In the current phase of our research, we consider the following characteristics as relevant: resources, interests, goals, and preferences. The toolbox should describe a process guiding through the elicitation of these characteristics and a scheme for documenting the characteristics systematically. *Example*: The senior citizens have decreased cognitive capacities compared to younger persons; for instance, their ability to keep information in the working memory is reduced. They often have little experience with technical systems. Their physical capacities are reduced as well. Their goal is to have more contact with other people.

(3) *Compare resources to methods:* The properties of the methods have to be compared to the desired participants' resources and good matches have to be identified to avoid obstacles. In the Smart City context, classic RE methods such as interviews can be used, but there is much potential for novel methods such as text mining, as citizens are likely to use digital services a lot. The toolbox should provide a set of classical and novel methods already classified according to a scheme. In this classification scheme, the criteria are aligned to the resources, e.g., the required cognitive capacities (few, medium, high) so that it is easy to find a match between method and resources. *Example:* The methods "interview" and "6-3-5 brainwriting method" are compared to the senior citizens' resources. The 6-3-5 method requires at least medium cognitive resources since the participant has to keep the previously described answers in mind. An interview, on the other hand, requires only low cognitive capacities.

(4) *Search or create new methods:* If the method criteria do not match the resources, new methods should be searched or created. The toolbox should provide inspiration on where to find new methods and describe the procedure for classifying new methods according to the scheme mentioned in step 3.

(5) *Select method:* If two or more methods are identified, the quality of the expected results, the preferences, or the project constraints (e.g., budget) can be used as criteria for making the final decision about which method to use. If the project constraints and number of participants allows to apply several methods, several different methods could be applied.

(6) *Compare resources to execution options:* The options for executing the methods should be compared to the resources in order to avoid obstacles. The toolbox should provide a set of execution options and a scheme for matching the execution options to resources. *Example:* We decided to conduct interviews. Since elderly people's technical knowledge is often low, interviews should not be conducted via video telephony. Since their physical capabilities are often low (e.g., their mobility is restricted), interviews should be done at or close to their home or via telephone.

(7) *Select realization option:* If two or more execution options fit, the same selection criteria apply as for the methods (quality of expected results, pragmatic reasons, preferences). *Example:* Due to the senior citizens' preferences, interviews should be conducted face-to-face.

(8) *Add motivational measures:* The method and its execution should be enhanced through measures for increasing the motivation to participate. Motivational measures could address the participants' interests and goals, or be monetary benefits, such as vouchers that can be used within the district, or gamification elements such as leaderboards. The toolbox should provide a set of motivational measures and their relation to motives. *Example*: The senior citizens are motivated by a sense of connectedness. Therefore, the interviews could be conducted by other residents of the district so that the elderly people get directly in contact with others living in the district. The interviewers could be recruited via the platform and rewarded with vouchers for services on the digital platform.

(9) *Provide suggestions for invitation:* Since the requirements engineers cannot always contact the desired participants directly due to privacy regulations or because they do not host the appropriate communication channels, the requirements engineers should at least make suggestions to the responsible persons (e.g., the municipality) regarding what to communicate and via which channel. In addition to organizational information, such as date and time, the motivational measures should be communicated. In Smart City districts, a digital platform and its services could be used as communication channel, but so could information boards in public places such as bus stops, where people have time to read them. *Example:* In our example, letters are sent to the nursing home in the district and flyers are distributed by nursing care services. The letters stress the value of the interviews as a way of getting in touch with one's neighbors.

4 Summary and Future Work

We presented a first version of a 9-step approach that provides guidance for the planning of RE activities (e.g., elicitation of needs and ideas) with citizens of a Smart City district with a strong focus on motivational issues. The process is mainly based on our experience and identified gaps in our contexts. Of course, not all relevant aspects of involving citizens are currently considered in the approach, which is open to future work. Furthermore, we want to include several examples in the toolbox itself to better support requirements engineers during the different steps and to provide concrete motivational elements.

We have several further research questions that emerged during our initial work and will be considered in the future:

- Is it indeed possible to differentiate between methods and execution of the methods?
- The approach only describes how people can be motivated to engage in a single activity. Which factors have to be considered if people should be involved several times?
- The quality of the results might be negatively influenced by the execution of the method, which was aligned to the participants' resources and preferences.
- Is it possible to consider a very heterogeneous group? Does the type of execution determine the type of the actual participants?
- What else has to be considered when characterizing potential participant? Do aversions and concerns (e.g. regarding privacy) need to be considered?

Besides the general research questions, we will focus on the application of the approach in our research project and use feedback from the participants as well as from the organizers and moderators to improve our approach. Furthermore, the quality of the results might depend on different instantiations (e.g., selection of concrete methods) of our approach. If the parameters for adjusting the approach and the consequences are known, the approach might yield better results. Our goal is to identify these criteria in the future. Finally, trade-offs of the approach must be discussed. For example, are fast, but not so accurate results desired, or should more time be invested and a broader set of participants considered to obtain better requirements? Answering such questions might also influence our approach.

Acknowledgments. Parts of this work have been funded by the "EnStadt: Pfaff" project (grant no. 03SBE112D and 03SBE112G) of the German Federal Ministry for Economic Affairs and Energy (BMWi) and the German Federal Ministry of Education and Research (BMBF).

References

1. Villela, K., Groen, E., Doerr, J.: Ubiquitous requirements engineering: a paradigm shift that affects everyone. IEEE Softw. **36**(2), 8–12 (2019)
2. Doerr, J., Hess, A., Koch, M.: RE and society - a perspective on RE in times of smart cities and smart rural areas. In: IEEE 26th International Requirements Engineering Conference (RE), pp. 100–111. IEEE (2018). https://doi.org/10.1109/re.2018.00020

3. Marczewski, A.: User types. In: Even Ninja Monkeys Like to Play: Gamification, Game Thinking and Motivational Design, pp. 65–80. CreateSpace Independent Publishing Platform (2015)
4. Zichermann, G., Cunningham, C.: Gamification by Design: Implementing Game Mechanics in Web and Mobile Apps. O'Reilly Media Inc., Newton (2011)
5. Rudolph, M., Feth, D., Polst, S.: Why users ignore privacy policies – a survey and intention model for explaining user privacy behavior. In: Kurosu, M. (ed.) HCI 2018. LNCS, vol. 10901, pp. 587–598. Springer, Cham (2018). https://doi.org/10.1007/978-3-319-91238-7_45

Visualizing Feature-Level Evolution in Product Lines: A Research Preview

Daniel Hinterreiter[1], Paul Grünbacher[1(✉)], and Herbert Prähofer[2]

[1] Christian Doppler Laboratory MEVSS, Institute Software Systems Engineering,
Johannes Kepler University Linz, Linz, Austria
`paul.gruenbacher@jku.at`
[2] Institute System Software, Johannes Kepler University Linz, Linz, Austria

Abstract. [**Context and motivation**] Software product lines evolve
frequently to address customer requirements in different domains. This
leads to a distributed engineering process with frequent updates and
extensions. [**Question/problem**] However, such changes are typically
managed and tracked at the level of source code while feature-level awareness about software evolution is commonly lacking. In this research preview paper we thus present an approach visualizing the evolution in software product lines at the level of features. [**Principal ideas/results**]
Specifically, we extend feature models with feature evolution plots to
visualize changes at a higher level. Our approach uses static code analyses
and a variation control system to compute the evolution data for visuali-
sation. As a preliminary evaluation we report selected examples of applying our approach to a cyberphysical ecosystem from the field of industrial
automation. [**Contribution**] Integrating visualisations into state-of-the-
art feature models can contribute to better integrate requirements-level
and code-level perspectives during product line evolution.

Keywords: Product lines · Evolution · Visualization

1 Introduction

Software companies nowadays use product lines to provide highly individual
solutions for customers. Product lines need to evolve frequently to meet new customer requirements. Commonly, engineers customize and extend product lines
concurrently in different projects to quickly deliver solutions to customers, resulting in a distributed and feature-oriented development process [7]. Specifically,
engineers create new and modify existing features when developing customer-
specific solutions. Existing version control systems like Git provide code-level
tracking of changes in the solution space. This level of abstraction is, however,
insufficient for developers who first need to understand the impact [1] and magnitude of such changes at the level of features. In particular, product line engineers
need to assess the complexity of the updated features when integrating selected
features from existing customer projects into their product line to realize domain
requirements.

© Springer Nature Switzerland AG 2020
N. Madhavji et al. (Eds.): REFSQ 2020, LNCS 12045, pp. 300–306, 2020.
https://doi.org/10.1007/978-3-030-44429-7_21

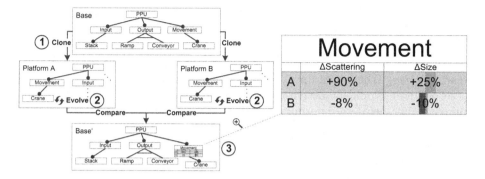

Fig. 1. A feature evolution plot for the feature *Movement* showing how developers modified this feature in products A and B compared to the base product line.

Feature models are widely used in industry to describe and manage complex systems [3]. Feature models, however, are often only weakly linked with code-level changes and they do not reflect ongoing development. Visualization techniques have been used widely and effectively to increase awareness [5,10] about software evolution [14]. For instance, Montalvillo et al. [13] presented 'peering bars', which extend version control systems to visualize how a product's features have been upgraded in other branches to support the merge process. Similarly, Lettner et al. [10] proposed a publish-subscribe approach to feature-evolution tracking in software ecosystems based on feature feeds and awareness models.

This research preview paper presents our ongoing research on extending feature models to visualize the impact of implementation-level changes at the level of features. We use change metrics based on data from a variation control systems (VCS) [12]. Our approach builds on our earlier work on feature modelling [15] and feature-to-artifact mappings [6]. Specifically, we rely on code analyses and feature-to-code mappings as presented in [6]. However, while this earlier work focused on computing the evolution of different types of feature interactions it did not address analyzing and visualizing the evolution of feature size or feature scattering. We further report results from a preliminary evaluation based on the evolution history of an industrial project and present a plan for further evaluating our approach.

2   Visualizing Feature Evolution Metrics

Feature-oriented engineering assumes that features are mapped to the artifacts realizing them [2]. For instance, many techniques exist for mapping features to code, models, or documentation [3]. Figure 1 shows a typical development scenario illustrating the purpose of our visualization extension for feature models. (1) A company maintains a *Base* product line of a Pick-and-Place Unit [16], which is shown as a feature model [8]. (2) Two products A and B are created to adapt and extend the base product line for two different customers. (3) When merging selected new features or feature revisions back to the product line the maintainer of *Base* needs to integrate the changes made in A and B, thereby creating *Base'*. The maintainer requires awareness, i.e., an understanding of these other development activities as a context for her own activity [5]. Our approach thus helps to determine *(purpose)* the complexity *(issue)* of evolved features *(object)* from the perspective of a product line engineer *(viewpoint)*. We are interested in two questions to assess the evolution of feature complexity: by how much did a feature change? Did the change(s) affect feature scattering?

In our approach features are mapped to arbitrary (parts of) artifacts such as statements in source code, model elements, or lines in documents. Our visualization technique relies on two metrics which can be calculated based on these detailed feature-to-artifact mappings:

Feature size evolution (FSiE). The size of a feature (FSi) is measured by the magnitude of artifacts mapped to a particular feature (e.g., the number of program elements in source code or the number of data elements in XML files). The FSiE is determined by the relative change of the artifact size between two different points in time t_1 and t_2:

$$FSiE = (FSi_{t_2} - FSi_{t_1})/FSi_{t_1}$$

Feature scattering evolution (FScE). Individual features are typically realized in multiple artifacts and locations. The number of contiguous locations of a feature's implementation determines its scattering (FSc). For example, if a feature is mapped to all source files within one directory, the directory represents the location of the implementation and the scattering is 1. However, scattering is 5 if the feature is mapped to five independent source files. FScE is then computed by the relative change of the FSc of a feature between two different points in time t_1 and t_2.

$$FScE = (FSc_{t_2} - FSc_{t_1})/FSc_{t_1}$$

As shown in Fig. 1 we extend feature models to visualize such feature evolution. Specifically, we add a stack of feature evolution plots to the basic feature block to visualize the changes of that feature in other customer products. Each feature evolution plot shows the name of the customer product variant the feature is attached to (1st column), the FScE (2nd column) and the FSiE (3rd column) for that product. The FSiE percentage is further detailed using two compartments. The left compartments represents the percentage of deleted artifacts while the right compartments shows the percentage of added artifacts for the feature in the system. In our example the feature *Movement* has been evolved in both products A and B: the developers of product A added code compared to the base product line, thereby also increasing the FScE. The developers of product B added but also deleted some code, overall only slightly affecting the FScE.

We have been implementing our approach to feature evolution awareness by integrating a feature modeling environment [7] with the VCS ECCO [12]

Ejector			NozzleHeating		
	ΔScattering	ΔSize		ΔScattering	ΔSize
A	+350%	+2%	A	0%	0%
B	0%	0%	B	+450%	+6%

Fig. 2. Feature evolution plots for the features *Ejector* and *NozzleHeating*.

as part of developing our feature-oriented platform. While existing VCS are mostly bound to specific artifact types [11], ECCO can be extended with plug-ins to support different domain-specific implementation languages and artifact types. ECCO creates and maintains feature-to-artifact mappings by computing differences in features and artifacts of products [12], i.e., our approach does not assume initial feature-to-artifact mappings, as they are created automatically when evolving the system (or replaying its evolution history). Our current research prototype extracts the required mappings from the VCS ECCO and performs all code-level analyses needed to compute the FSiE and FScE metrics.

3   Preliminary Evaluation

Our research is conducted in cooperation with KEBA AG, a company providing cyberphysical systems for industrial automation, such as their KePlast platform for developing injection molding machines. KePlast exists in specific platform variants, e.g., for the Chinese market or for an original equipment manufacturer. This makes it difficult to understand changes made to the different variants. For instance, extensions remain largely undocumented, making it difficult for engineers to understand changes at the level of features. For the purpose of our preliminary evaluation we analyzed the evolution history of a customer project conducted by an engineer of KEBA AG. The engineer used our tool FORCE [7] to track all changes in a feature-oriented manner, i.e., when committing a change the engineer clearly indicated the affected feature(s). Specifically, the engineer extended KePlast and committed 70 changes to address customer requirements. Based on this comprehensive data we (i) illustrate our visualization for selected features and (ii) show the usefulness of the FSiE and FScE metrics for this real-world engineering project.

Visualizing Selected Features. To demonstrate the visualization we replayed a development scenario, following the scenario shown in Fig. 1: we started with the *Base* version of KePlast and then created two new products *A* and *B*, evolving independently from each other to address customer needs. In both cases, new features were created and existing features were adapted by replaying commits from the project history. At some point in the evolution history of product *B* we assume the engineer wants to integrate changes made in product *A*. The visualization allows to quickly show how significant the changes are for selected features, thus estimating the resulting integration and maintenance effort.

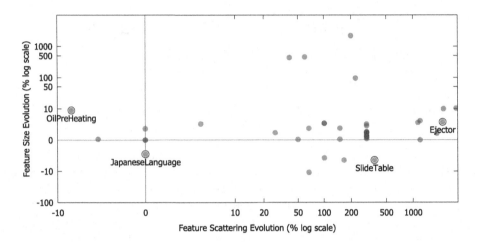

Fig. 3. Portofolio for 42 features of the industry project. We use a logarithmic scale for presentation after performing a log-modulus transformation. Darker color is used to indicate overlapping circles. (Color figure online)

Figure 2 shows the results of this feature-aware three-way diff for two features of the two evolved products. We can quickly see that both features were only changed in one of the products. The changes were also rather minor with a rather small increment in artifact size. However, the FScE is rather high showing that some changes increased the number of feature locations, thus likely increasing maintenance and integration effort.

FSiE and FScE Analysis. To give an overview of the usefulness of the defined metrics we compute their values by comparing the first und the last commit for all features modified in this industrial project. Figure 3 presents a portfolio showing the FSiE and FScE for 42 features. Typically these feature were involved in multiple commits. One can see that most features have rather small changes in artifact size, some of which are the result of the continuous refinement of feature-to-artifact mappings during evolution. However, in all cases the changes resulted in an increment of feature scattering. For example, the FScE of the *Ejector* (involved in 14 commits) increased by 2150% whereas the number of artifacts just increased by about 2.7%. A code inspection revealed that the high value was caused by user interface code added in many locations. A different example is the feature *JapaneseLanguage* (7 commits), which was added as a new feature in the project. After the feature was initially added, the feature was only slightly modified. In particular, the deletion of the translation for some features reduced the FSiE while leaving the FScE unchanged. A similar example is the newly added feature *OilPreHeating* (4 commits), which shows only a small increase in size during the project, but reduced FScE caused by the deletion of some no-longer-needed code fragments. The feature *SlideTable* (5 commits) is an example where artifacts were added and removed during the project, overall leading to a small reduction in size. Obviously, the newly added code significantly increased the scattering of this feature.

4 Evaluation Plan

We did not conduct a user study in our preliminary evaluation but analyzed data from an industrial project repository to validate our metrics. We also used selected examples from the results of our analyses to illustrate our visualization approach.

In future research, we will combine both a cognitive walkthrough and a user study to investigate the usefulness of our visualizations based on our current prototype. Our evaluation will follow the combined research method described in [9]. Specifically, we will evaluate feature evolution plots and feature portfolios as a requirements-level visualization of changes.

The walkthrough will be based on the Cognitive Dimensions of Notations Framework [4]. Based on the findings of this walkthrough we will improve the current prototype. The user study will then be based on an industrial scenario on integrating feature updates during product line evolution. In particular, we plan to evaluate the usefulness of our visualizations for estimating the complexity of feature updates. We will evaluate to what extent our requirements-level visualizations can guide engineers who are in charge of integrating new or updated features from related customer projects into a product line to realize domain requirements. We will further investigate how such visualizations can be combined with detailed feature interaction analyses presented in [6].

5 Conclusions

We presented a visualization approach to extend feature models with feature evolution plots as a means to increase awareness about feature-level changes in distributed development scenarios, which are common in software product line engineering. We also reported results of a preliminary evaluation based on an industrial product line. In the short term we will extend the Feature Editor of FORCE to visualize the FSiE and FScE as already computed in our evaluation. Our long-term plan is to evaluate our approach using large-scale product lines from our industry partner involving multiple industrial engineers. In particular, we will apply our tool and visualizations followed by the evaluation of their usefulness.

Acknowledgements. The financial support by the Austrian Federal Ministry for Digital and Economic Affairs, the National Foundation for Research, Technology and Development, and KEBA AG, Austria is gratefully acknowledged.

References

1. Angerer, F., Grimmer, A., Prähofer, H., Grünbacher, P.: Change impact analysis for maintenance and evolution of variable software systems. Autom. Softw. Eng. **26**(2), 417–461 (2019). https://doi.org/10.1007/s10515-019-00253-7

2. Apel, S., Batory, D., Kästner, C., Saake, G.: Feature-Oriented Software Product Lines: Concepts and Implementation. Springer, Heidelberg (2013). https://doi.org/10.1007/978-3-642-37521-7_1
3. Berger, T., et al.: What is a feature? A qualitative study of features in industrial software product lines. In: Proceedings of the 19th International Conference on Software Product Line, pp. 16–25 (2015)
4. Blackwell, A., Green, T.: Notational systems-the cognitive dimensions of notations framework. In: Carroll, J.M. (ed.) HCI Models, Theories, and Frameworks, Interactive Technologies, pp. 103–133. Morgan Kaufmann, San Francisco (2003)
5. Dourish, P., Bellotti, V.: Awareness and coordination in shared workspaces. In: Proceedings of the 1992 ACM Conference on Computer-Supported Cooperative Work, pp. 107–114 (1992)
6. Feichtinger, K., Hinterreiter, D., Linsbauer, L., Prähofer, H., Grünbacher, P.: Supporting feature model evolution by suggesting constraints from code-level dependency analyses. In: Proceedings of the 18th ACM SIGPLAN International Conference on Generative Programming: Concepts and Experiences, pp. 129–142 (2019)
7. Hinterreiter, D., Linsbauer, L., Reisinger, F., Prähofer, H., Grünbacher, P., Egyed, A.: Feature-oriented evolution of automation software systems in industrial software ecosystems. In: 2018 IEEE 23rd International Conference on Emerging Technologies and Factory Automation (ETFA), pp. 107–114 (2018)
8. Kang, K., Cohen, S., Hess, J., Nowak, W., Peterson, S.: Feature-Oriented Domain Analysis (FODA) Feasibility Study. Technical Report (1990)
9. Kritzinger, L.M., Krismayer, T., Rabiser, R., Grünbacher, P.: A user study on the usefulness of visualization support for requirements monitoring. In: Proceedings of 7th IEEE Working Conference on Software Visualization, pp. 56–66. IEEE, Cleveland (2019)
10. Lettner, D., Grünbacher, P.: Using feature feeds to improve developer awareness in software ecosystem evolution. In: Proceedings 9th International Workshop on Variability Modelling of Software-intensive Systems, pp. 11–18 (2015)
11. Linsbauer, L., Berger, T., Grünbacher, P.: A classification of variation control systems. In: Proceedings 16th International Conference on Generative Programming: Concepts & Experiences, pp. 49–62 (2017)
12. Linsbauer, L., Lopez-Herrejon, R.E., Egyed, A.: Variability extraction and modeling for product variants. Softw. Syst. Model. 16(4), 1179–1199 (2016). https://doi.org/10.1007/s10270-015-0512-y
13. Montalvillo, L., Díaz, O., Fogdal, T.: Reducing coordination overhead in SPLs: peering in on peers. In: Proceedings of 22nd International Systems and Software Product Line Conference, pp. 110–120 (2018)
14. Novais, R.L., Torres, A., Mendes, T.S., Mendonça, M.G., Zazworka, N.: Software evolution visualization: a systematic mapping study. Inf. Softw. Technol. 55(11), 1860–1883 (2013)
15. Rabiser, D., et al.: Multi-purpose, multi-level feature modeling of large-scale industrial software systems. Softw. Syst. Model. 17(3), 913–938 (2016). https://doi.org/10.1007/s10270-016-0564-7
16. Vogel-Heuser, B., Legat, C., Folmer, J., Feldmann, S.: Researching evolution in industrial plant automation: Scenarios and documentation of the Pick and Place Unit. Technische Universität München, Technical report (2014)

Correction to: Requirements Engineering: Foundation for Software Quality

Nazim Madhavji, Liliana Pasquale, Alessio Ferrari ⓘ,
and Stefania Gnesi ⓘ

Correction to:
N. Madhavji et al. (Eds.): *Requirements Engineering:*
Foundation for Software Quality, **LNCS 12045,**
https://doi.org/10.1007/978-3-030-44429-7

The book was inadvertently published with only two volume editors "Nazim Madhavji and Liliana Pasquale" whereas there should have been four "Nazim Madhavji, Liliana Pasquale, Alessio Ferrari and Stefania Gnesi". The missing two volume editors were added in the book and the source line was updated accordingly.

The updated version of the book can be found at
https://doi.org/10.1007/978-3-030-44429-7

Author Index

Printed in the United States
By Bookmasters